The Holocaust and its Contexts

Series Editors
Claus-Christian W. Szejnmann
Loughborough University
Loughborough, UK

Ben Barkow
The Wiener Library
London, UK

More than sixty years on, the Holocaust remains a subject of intense debate with ever-widening ramifications. This series aims to demonstrate the continuing relevance of the Holocaust and related issues in contemporary society, politics and culture; studying the Holocaust and its history broadens our understanding not only of the events themselves but also of their present-day significance. The series acknowledges and responds to the continuing gaps in our knowledge about the events that constituted the Holocaust, the various forms in which the Holocaust has been remembered, interpreted and discussed, and the increasing importance of the Holocaust today to many individuals and communities.

More information about this series at
http://www.palgrave.com/gp/series/14433

Nicholas Chare · Dominic Williams

The Auschwitz Sonderkommando

Testimonies, Histories, Representations

Nicholas Chare
Université de Montréal
Montreal, QC, Canada

Dominic Williams
University of Leeds
Leeds, UK

The Holocaust and its Contexts
ISBN 978-3-030-11490-9   ISBN 978-3-030-11491-6 (eBook)
https://doi.org/10.1007/978-3-030-11491-6

Library of Congress Control Number: 2018967212

© The Editor(s) (if applicable) and The Author(s), under exclusive license to Springer Nature Switzerland AG, part of Springer Nature 2019
This work is subject to copyright. All rights are solely and exclusively licensed by the Publisher, whether the whole or part of the material is concerned, specifically the rights of translation, reprinting, reuse of illustrations, recitation, broadcasting, reproduction on microfilms or in any other physical way, and transmission or information storage and retrieval, electronic adaptation, computer software, or by similar or dissimilar methodology now known or hereafter developed.
The use of general descriptive names, registered names, trademarks, service marks, etc. in this publication does not imply, even in the absence of a specific statement, that such names are exempt from the relevant protective laws and regulations and therefore free for general use.
The publisher, the authors and the editors are safe to assume that the advice and information in this book are believed to be true and accurate at the date of publication. Neither the publisher nor the authors or the editors give a warranty, express or implied, with respect to the material contained herein or for any errors or omissions that may have been made. The publisher remains neutral with regard to jurisdictional claims in published maps and institutional affiliations.

Cover illustration: Detail of the scale model of crematorium II at Auschwitz-Birkenau on display in the permanent exhibition of the U.S. Holocaust Memorial Museum. The model was sculpted by Mieczyslaw Stobierski based on contemporary documents and the trial testimonies of SS guards. © United States Holocaust Memorial Museum, courtesy of Arnold Kramer.

This Palgrave Macmillan imprint is published by the registered company Springer Nature Switzerland AG
The registered company address is: Gewerbestrasse 11, 6330 Cham, Switzerland

Acknowledgements

We wish to thank Doris Bergen, Valérie Bienvenue, Marta Boni, Ersy Contogouris, Patricia Correa-Romero, Michelle Gewurtz, Samantha Hinckley, Aurélia Kalisky, Anne Karpf, Andreas Kilian, Peter Kilroy, Michael Kraus, Peter Krausz, András Lénárt, Ben Lee, Sébastien Lévesque, Bruce Levy, Silvestra Mariniello, Walter Manoschek, Marie-Ève Ménard, Philippe Mesnard, Suzanne Paquet, Bernard Perron, Griselda Pollock, Helene Sinnreich, Dan Stone, Marcel Swiboda, Carl Therrien, Sue Vice, Louise Vigneault, Monika Vrzgulová, Emma Wilson, Carol Zemel, Esther Chare, Julie Chare, Peter Chare, Sara Chare, Milena Marinkova and Angela Mortimer for their intellectual and, sometimes, practical support during the preparation of this volume. For sharing her thoughts and memories related to her experiences working in the Kanada commando at Auschwitz-Birkenau, we are particularly grateful to Irene Weiss. We would also like to thank Serena Neumann and Lesley Weiss for furnishing us with further information on Kanada.

We received advice and help on language and translation from numerous sources. We are very grateful to the following for sharing their time and linguistic expertise: Ersy Contogouris (French and Greek), András Lénárt (Hungarian) and Zsombor Hunyadi (Hungarian and Yiddish), Krzysztof Majer, Jacek Nowakowski, Alicja Podbielska and Vincent Slatt (Polish), Liviu Carare (Romanian), Alina Bothe, Steven Feldman, Emil Kerenji, Monika Polit and Hannah Pollin-Galay (Yiddish).

We are also indebted to our students at Leeds and Montréal for their thought-provoking discussions related to many of the case studies treated in this book, particularly for the courses 'From Trauma to Cultural Memory' (Leeds) and 'L'art du témoignage' (Montréal).

For part of the writing of this book, Nicholas Chare was the Diane and Howard Wohl Fellow in the Jack, Joseph and Morton Mandel Center for Advanced Holocaust Studies at the United States Holocaust Memorial Museum and thanks are therefore due to the excellent staff at the Library and Archives Reference Desk there for their help in locating relevant references and sources. We are particularly beholden to Liviu Carare, Megan Lewis, Larissa Reed, Vincent Slatt and Elliott Wrenn. Additionally, we are indebted to Jeffrey Carter at the Institutional Archives of the United States Holocaust Memorial Museum. We are also grateful to Stephen Naron of the Fortunoff Video Archive for Holocaust Testimonies and the Visual Archive of the USC Shoah Foundation for granting access to specific video testimonies. Thanks to Stephanie Hirsch of the *Ludwigsburger Kreiszeitung* archive, and to Wojciech Płosa at the Auschwitz Museum, as well as staff at the National Archives in Kew, the Wiener Library and the British Library. Some of Dominic Williams's research was funded by the University of Leeds.

Finally, we are indebted to the anonymous reviewers of the manuscript for their helpful comments and criticisms and to the commissioning and production team at Palgrave, including Emily Russell, Sooryadeepth Jayakrishnan, Goutham Kamaraj and Oliver Dyer, who were a pleasure to work with throughout.

CONTENTS

1 Introduction: Figuring the Sonderkommando in History 1

2 Acts of Deposition: Gender and Testimony in the Scrolls of Auschwitz 25

3 Tragic Pictures: The Sonderkommando and Their Photographs 71

4 The Trials of Witnessing: Legal Testimony and the Sonderkommando 101

5 Figure Studies from the Grey Zone: David Olère 129

6 Matters of Video Testimony 171

7 The Voice of Bronze: Filip Müller and *Shoah* 219

Bibliography 249

Index 269

CHAPTER 1

Introduction: Figuring the Sonderkommando in History

Between March and April 1951, *Les Temps modernes* carried a report by the Auschwitz survivor Miklós Nyiszli.[1] Originally written and published in Hungarian, Nyiszli's account testified to his work performing autopsies in the crematoria of Auschwitz-Birkenau to support Josef Mengele's pseudo-scientific experiments. Along with this primary role, he also tended to the Sonderkommando (SK) or Special Squad who worked in the same buildings.[2] Through the SK, Nyiszli provided eyewitness descriptions of the workings of the gas chambers and the ovens of the crematoria: How squad members were tasked with pulling the dead out of gas chambers, removing anything of value left on or of their bodies (mainly hair and gold teeth), and then eliminating all trace of their existence. His testimony provided stories of how the SK were murdered and replaced in their entirety every three or four months, how members of the SK had at times played football with the SS guards, and how, on one occasion, a teenage girl had survived the gas chambers and they had made a desperate but unsuccessful attempt to save her. He told of the Sonderkommando's doomed uprising in October 1944 as well as his own survival.

Nyiszli's writing was certainly not the first to explain the role of the Sonderkommando. Post-war testimonies had been gathered in judicial procedures of investigation into Nazi crimes almost immediately after the liberation of the camps.[3] These investigations had also uncovered one manuscript written by a member of the Sonderkommando, dug up in the

© The Author(s) 2019
N. Chare and D. Williams, *The Auschwitz Sonderkommando*, The Holocaust and its Contexts,
https://doi.org/10.1007/978-3-030-11491-6_1

grounds of the crematoria. The SK's testimony was used as part of court cases against personnel of the Birkenau camp, most notably in a British military court in Lüneburg and in Polish trials in Warsaw and Kraków, and both had received some coverage in the press. Early post-war memoirs also referred to the SK. But Nyiszli provided the first sustained piece of writing from within the Sonderkommando that was published for a wide audience, and the translation into French made it available in the West.

The context of publication is significant. As Yannick Malgouzou documents, Nyiszli's memoir was published in a year when disputes among French intellectuals about the legacy of the camps were raging. In a flurry of books, libel cases and editorials, Jean-Paul Sartre, Albert Camus, Maurice Merleau-Ponty and David Rousset fought over whether concentration camps could be compared to gulags, and why the political crimes of Communism trumped those of colonialism or the other way round. In 1951, Sartre broke with Camus over his book *The Rebel*. David Rousset won a court case against Pierre Daix in January of that year.[4] What a camp was had come to be a central concern of French intellectuals. Nyiszli provided evidence that a 'concentration camp' had something that a gulag never had: a gas chamber, and so could be offered in support of the case that Sartre and Merleau-Ponty made against those trying to compare the two.[5] At the same time, the American Richard Seaver and the Scottish writer Alexander Trocchi were editing an avant-garde English-language magazine in Paris: *Merlin*. They negotiated with Sartre the right to use some material from his magazine. Nyiszli's writing, it turned out, was the only text that *Les Temps modernes* shared with them.[6]

Nyiszli's testimony was thus used and reused within different contexts in the early 1950s: judicial examination, political dispute and what might be called an 'aesthetic' environment (*Merlin* also published pieces by Samuel Beckett, Jean Genet, Eugene Ionesco and Italo Svevo). But it was also repurposed at other times. Ten years later, Bruno Bettelheim wrote a preface to Nyiszli's memoirs criticizing him and the Sonderkommando for their failure to resist. Nyiszli and the SK, were thus archetypal of the way he conceived Jews in general as simply allowing themselves to succumb to Nazi persecution. Bettelheim made this accusation in tandem with those of Raul Hilberg and Hannah Arendt, who also fitted the SK to their ideas of Jewish passivity. Two decades after that, Primo Levi made heavy use of Nyiszli in 'The Grey Zone'

(1986), which might be called an assay into moral philosophy. And fifteen years later, Tim Blake Nelson took Nyiszli's memoirs (albeit clearly mediated by Levi's own essay) as the main basis of his film *The Grey Zone* (2001).

What these constant returns to Nyiszli show is that there has always been an interest in the Sonderkommando of Auschwitz-Birkenau. They were crucial to conceptualizing key aspects of the Shoah. The SK provided some of the first evidence of the gas chambers, testimony that was central to several of the trials immediately post-war. They were vital for an understanding of the concentrationary universe, at least in the version of it that Sartre and Merleau-Ponty defended against the concept's originator, Rousset.[7] And they seemed to speak (in Seaver and Trocchi's judgement, at any rate) to something of the post-war condition, to say something on a par with the works being produced by Beckett and Ionesco. In later versions, they raised the central moral questions for Levi about what the Nazis had done to their victims. And at the turn of the millennium, the SK, in Nyiszli's version, provided a way for Blake Nelson to claim to be cutting through five decades of accreted representations and getting back to the reality of the Holocaust.

The fact that Nyiszli was the go-to informant on the condition of the SK was also indicative that the SK were surrounded by myths, that people were fascinated yet troubled by them. Testimony from actual members was neglected, and that of someone who had been associated with the squad but not part of it, became the guide to their existence. Many members of the SK lived longer than the four months Nyiszli attributed to them.[8] The incident of the girl surviving the gas chamber was not at all unique but happened so much that there was a routine of how to deal with it.[9] And other football matches than just those between SS and SK took place—indeed, any match between the latter two groups would at most have been a kick-about, as there were not enough members of the SS present at the crematorium to form a team.[10] These 'facts' that Nyiszli conveyed were all taken up by Primo Levi's essay 'The Grey Zone' (1985), one of the most formidable attempts to understand the SK. For Levi these pieces of information were key elements in his picture of the Sonderkommando and therefore of the grey zone that permeated the world of the camps: the SK submitted even though they knew how long they had allotted to them; their 'work' gave the SS a false sense of brotherhood with them, and they only returned to human normality when prompted by extraordinary events. The SK's own words, which

Levi quotes once, came from men who were too emotionally and psychologically damaged and tainted by their work and could not 'be taken literally'.[11] But it is worth examining the source of these words that Levi quotes, because they come, via a collection of testimony made by Hermann Langbein, from an early piece of survivor testimony, a memoir by Krystyna Żywulska.

A prisoner in Birkenau between 1943 and 1945, Żywulska gave an extraordinary account of her dialogue with a member of the SK in her memoir of 1946. Seeing a team of SK below her window, Żywulska feels contempt for these men who are prepared to 'burn human corpses', especially one 'who seemed quite intelligent'. When he challenges her gaze, argues that he has no choice and that he is waiting for his chance for revenge, she asks him why he does not rebel. 'Why don't you?' he replies. 'You think that the *Sonderkommando* are awful people. I assure you that they are like other people everywhere, only much more unhappy'.[12] These words were more or less replicated by Langbein and then Levi. But Żywulska's astonished reaction to this speech was not and is very different from that of Levi himself: 'those guys over there in the crematorium—they feel, they reflect, they are emotional?' Her fellow prisoners chastise her for judging the SK so harshly and seeing them as different from her: 'You are always afraid to evaluate yourself [...] And the most convenient way is always to put yourself in a better light at the expense of others'.[13]

Here, right at the beginning of a history of troubled thought over the SK, we see a different way of approaching them. Like Levi, Żywulska is horrified by the work carried out by the SK and considers them morally tainted. But unlike him, she is prepared to listen to their words, which shock her into reconsidering her repulsion. And her fellow prisoners blame that repulsion on a need to find someone more abject than herself.

The discourse of the grey zone, of anguished moral judgement mixed with unwillingness to judge, of failures of imagination and empathy and realizations that they still must be attempted, was, according to Żywulska, taking place in Birkenau itself. But we would argue further that its fixating on the SK was the result of the environment of Birkenau. Troubled moral discourse has been far more prevalent about this group than about their equivalents in camps such as Treblinka or Sobibór.[14] The Auschwitz Sonderkommando were forced to carry out their work not just isolated from other prisoners, but under their gaze, a gaze that often seems to have judged them. It is Auschwitz's hybrid nature, as extermination site and concentration camp, that caused it to contain enough of a society of prisoners for there to be a moral hierarchy, and for the SK to be placed at its bottom. The idea of the SK as denizens of the grey zone is therefore a product of the specific nature of Auschwitz-Birkenau, both in its operation as a camp and in the contingencies of its history that left many more survivors, from among the SK as well as from among those who had witnessed them.

But as shown by the process of restaging this encounter with the SK from Żywulska to Langbein to Levi, in which a dialogue was reworked into a monologue, this insight that they could be conceived as part of the society of prisoners and victims is often lost in attempts to think them through. There seems to be a difficulty in integrating the Sonderkommando into historical interpretations of the Holocaust.[15] It is telling, for example, that out of the single-volume general histories of the Holocaust, it is Martin Gilbert's that makes the most extensive use of the testimonies written by the SK. With his framework based on chronology rather than explanation or interpretation, and an emphasis on hearing victims' voices, Gilbert was able to quote extensively from some of their stories, particularly those of Leyb Langfus, without having to give them any meaning.[16] Saul Friedländer too found a place for Zalman Gradowski as one of the key witnesses whose voice comes into the historical text. But he functions mostly as a point where the horror reaches its worst, when it cannot be commented upon, but rather collaged with or cut to an entirely different strand of the narrative.[17]

Historians of the SK have frequently worked in isolation from the mainstream of Holocaust historiography, their projects often unpublished and incomplete. Erich Kulka and Ber Mark both died before their histories of the SK could be published. Gideon Greif still has an archive of interviews that have not been made public. Here, we see a fear of or difficulty in finding a wider audience for these men's stories. Perhaps this is not just the difficulty of finding people willing to listen to them, but the dangers of why they might be interested. Kulka had to threaten another Auschwitz survivor, Hermann Langbein, with a libel suit on behalf of the SK to make him withdraw some of the more lurid and implausible stories about them from his book *People in Auschwitz*.[18]

Gender in the Archive

Another of these survivor historians, alongside Kulka and Mark, was Tzipora Hager Halivni, a former classmate of Miklós Nyiszli's daughter Susanna.[19] Halivni makes reference to Susanna (who she refers to as Zsuzsi) as well as to Miklós Nyiszli in drafts for a book she was planning about the Sonderkommando revolt.[20] Halivni was deported to Auschwitz from Romania in May 1944. She was there for three months before being transferred to the slave labour camp at Fallersleben in Germany where she worked in an armaments factory. At the armaments factory, Halivni engaged in acts of sabotage, a covert resistance.[21] Her own engagement in rebellion may explain the deep sensibility with which she writes of the SK revolt. Halivni published an article about the revolt in 1979.[22] Her interest in the topic, however, clearly continued. The archive of her papers held at the United States Holocaust Memorial Museum includes drafts for this article but also much other material including computer printouts that describe a 'book [that is] in progress'.[23] She should be credited as one of the pioneer scholars of the SK alongside Kulka, Mark and Greif.[24]

The archive comprises hundreds of pages of handwritten and typed notes and drafts of articles and papers, many of which relate to the SK. These pages, clearly composed over a considerable period of time, are now in some disorder. The handwritten pages in the folders in the boxes of the Halivni archive are often organized backwards so that in multiple accounts of the revolt the researcher must read in reverse from the achievements and the aftermath of the revolt, to its unfolding and, finally, to methodological issues concerning how to approach the event as history. Even if they were carefully filed and ordered, the mess of thought that lies behind Halivni's published, more polished, academic writings would be apparent.[25] There are fragments from early drafts of articles and chapters that have been cut out and subsequently taped or stapled to newer versions. The taped fragments have occasionally become unmoored, free-floating. The loose fragments—scraps that initially formed part of a whole somewhere, were then deliberately detached and re-attached, and have now become detached again—reveal something about the process of Halivni's history writing, about what might be called its collagistic character. They also figure something of the nature of writing history more generally, of the task of imposing order upon, and finding sense in, past events which are often chaotic and of which the extant accounts are confused and contradictory.

1 INTRODUCTION: FIGURING THE SONDERKOMMANDO IN HISTORY   7

Some of the continual 'trying on for size' of phrases in varied contexts seems linked with Halivni reflecting upon the appropriate modes of expression for communicating the histories she wished to tell. There is considerable labour dedicated to finding the 'right words' in material about the SK and also about Halivni's personal experiences at Auschwitz. This labour is far less obvious in, for instance, her writings about the friar Maximilian Kolbe. The clear efforts she went to in order to find the right phrase to describe a specific person or a particular event linked with the Sonderkommando is, in itself, revealing. Repeatedly Halivni describes how the Sonderkommando have been wrongly labelled as collaborators or as all being callous and uncaring. Her attentiveness to her language (an attentiveness we will go on to provide some examples of), her assiduousness regarding words—which to choose and which to reject—bespeak a sense of responsibility towards her object of study. This is a theme to which we will return in several of the chapters to come. Halivni's crossings out, her reformulating, embody an ethical outlook. She does not want to commit an injustice by way of acts of misrepresentation (although, of course, gauging any representation requires the formulation of a benchmark).

Often Halivni's excisions and reformulations relate to language that is emotive. Her desire to reduce evidence of feeling is likely linked with her wish, as a historian, to appear as objective as possible. There are, however, multiple examples of her not disavowing emotion but rather striving to find a way of bringing the 'right' feelings to her account. She is not a positivist and views emotion in history as unavoidable, necessary even. She is often highly disparaging of the Polish resistance and makes scant effort to conceal her disdain for them. Halivni will sometimes tone down her prose, paring feeling but not entirely excising it. These feelings are usually related to the SK or to the Polish resistance or to herself. Halivni, like a number of survivors who would subsequently become historians, has an unusual relationship to the history that she studies. There is an occasional assertion that 'I' saw this, a reminder that Halivni lived within, was a part of, the past she now looks back upon and writes about. She differs, however, from a historian from within the SK such as Zalman Lewental, one of her major interlocutors, in that she can reflect on events sometime after they occurred. Lewental lived through the events that he relates in his history of the SK revolt but he did not survive to liberation.

When she writes of Auschwitz, Halivni looks back upon where she was, on her past. Occasionally, she writes of that past, of what she herself witnessed. These moments are unintentionally revealing about the practice of writing history:

> I recall being led into the barracks together with some 600 women. As we stood bewildered in a sun drenched room a [illegible] standing in the centre ordered 'Remove all clothes! Place them on the floor!' The SS guards were ubiquitous but silent.

This handwritten fragment was clearly intended to form part of an article or of the book that Halivni was working on. It is in a folder that mainly contains preparatory research and writing for an article on Kolbe but does not seem linked with that. The event Halivni recounts, which probably occurred upon her arrival at Auschwitz, was likely highly distressing. Something of the violence accompanying this undressing is disclosed by the words (now crossed out) she originally ascribed to what must be the blockova.[26] The words were 'Strip your clothes!' The change to 'remove all' may be because Halivni came to feel that she had initially misremembered the order she was given. It may also be linked to her efforts to faithfully translate a command such as '*alles ausziehen*'. Another factor is, however, likely a desire to soften the aggression of the event. The violence is mitigated in the second version. 'Remove all clothes!' places this forced stripping at more of a distance. Her rewording of the command, as a linguistic change, may index the humiliation of the forced undressing. Her desire to cover up the humiliation registers something of the violence and of her enduring shame at what happened. This is a shame which she does not wish to fully share with her putative reader here. Elsewhere, by contrast, she writes 'we undressed as we proceeded to the *Haarschneideraum*' but then crosses out 'undressed' and replaces it with 'stripped'.[27] It is possible that in this other moment she felt she was being too reticent, obviating the violence of the event.

In another fragment of text about a selection, Halivni writes '[...] when I was ordered to strip naked' but crosses it out.[28] She then rewrites 'ordered to strip naked' further down the page and leaves this in place. Later in her account of this forced undressing, she writes 'I desperately fight to maintain my inner balance' followed by 'It was a degrading moment'. She then crosses out this last sentence. Here, there is a strong sense of Halivni's feeling of mortification, a sense articulated through the struggle to write, through hesitancy coupled with determination. The degradation is here potentially affirmed through a wish to ultimately conceal it, to efface a direct reference to it. The effects of this event upon Halivni also register through her making multiple attempts to relate it. The violent disrobing hugely affected her, leaving her feeling '…as though I was losing ground [*sic*] under my feet, my world was crumbling…'.

1 INTRODUCTION: FIGURING THE SONDERKOMMANDO IN HISTORY

The trauma experienced by women at the hands of the SS impacted the Sonderkommando greatly. As we will explore frequently in the chapters that follow, the way the SS treated women and children caused the men of the SK intense distress. It is evident that gender influenced their experiences and has also subsequently informed representations of them. Women and girls appear repeatedly in stories of the SK. In later chapters, we will consider how depictions of men's and women's experiences at the extermination camp of Auschwitz-Birkenau have been structured by preconceived gender roles and how this has impacted the forms taken by testimony produced contemporaneously and retrospectively.

When Halivni studied the SK, she brought a first-hand knowledge of SS aggression and of their tactics of humiliation to her scholarship. She was attuned to gender issues as they intersected with violence at Birkenau. Halivni merits significant credit for her efforts to draw attention to the importance of women in the resistance movement at the camp.[29] She dedicated her article 'The Birkenau Revolt' to Róża Robota: 'Dedicated to Roza Robota (1921–1945) Died on the gallows on 6th January for procuring explosives'.[30] In an earlier, unpublished draft of the inscription she writes 'Dedicated to a Woman of Valor – Rosa [sic] Robota 1921–1944.'[31] This previous dedication places greater emphasis on the importance of gender. Róża Robota, a worker in Kanada, persuaded around twenty women detailed to the Union munitions factory, including Ella Gärtner, Ester Wajcblum, Hanka Wajcblum and Regina Safirsztajn, to smuggle out gunpowder.[32]

In drafts for the article, Halivni discusses in more detail how these women smuggled material to make explosives to the SK. She draws attention to how both racial and gender stereotypes influenced the way the Nazi men perceived Jewish women, informing their decision to employ women inmates in the factory. The Nazis hoped to exploit Jewish and feminine 'fragility' to their advantage. Halivni writes that: '[t]he SS assigned Jewish girls, the weaker sex of the weakest race, to work in the explosives pavilion of the Union munitions factory'. Drawing on the testimony of David Szmulewski, Halivni suggests that the young women 'carried explosives in the knots of their kerchiefs and in matchboxes betwixt their breasts'. The 'inferior' body was here used as a mode of smuggling, with key signifiers of sexual difference, breasts, consciously exploited. To some soldiers, although clearly not all, the hollow between the breasts may have been perceived as off-limits in a search.[33]

Although she possesses insider knowledge of some of the occurrences she refers to and was privy at the time to anecdotes and hearsay about others, Halivni seems well aware her perspective is partial rather than total, limited if not limiting. She openly views survivor testimony as suspect, writing: 'only too often eyewitnesses subject to human frailty have interspersed their testimony with fiction'.[34] For her, however, this tendency to embellish does not form an insurmountable obstacle because of 'the large volume of testimonies' and also 'the disinterred wartime manuscripts'.[35] Here, the Scrolls of Auschwitz are implicitly ascribed significant historical accuracy. Halivni makes use of all of the manuscripts of which she was aware (there is no mention of Nadjary or, seemingly, of Gradowski's *In the Heart of Hell*) but is particularly drawn to Lewental's history of the SK revolt and to Leib Langfus's *The Deportation*. For her, Lewental's history, in 'its authenticity and comprehensiveness make[s] it a yardstick for measuring the reliability of other available data'.[36]

It may be because of her faith in this document that Halivni's own accounts of the revolt so often echo Lewental's in terms of their condemnation of the Polish Resistance. Halivni makes no attempt to hide her contempt for most Poles who participated in resistance activities. Halivni's interest in Lewental's history of the SK revolt is complex. It seems he provided her with a means to articulate some of her own anger and frustration at the failure to prevent the Hungarian Aktion. The fate of Hungary's Jews is very much bound up with Halivni's personal history. Her childhood hometown of Vişeu de Sus was located in Northern Transylvania and was ceded by Romania to Hungary in 1940. After the autumn of 1940, the town became known by the Hungarian name of Felsővisó. Halivni's mother was able to flee to Romania from Felsővisó but the rest of the family were not. They were all deported to Auschwitz. Halivni recounts: '[my] youngest brother Menachem, two and a half years old, went with his fifty four year old grandmother to the crematorium. The time I saw in camp read 11am May 26, 1944'.[37] Halivni's father worked at Buna for a period of time. He died on a train journey from Poland to Slovakia in late 1944. The SK revolt was initially planned to prevent, or at least disrupt, the Hungarian Aktion. It is conceivable that in Halivni's mind had the uprising occurred earlier, in May 1944 for instance, it could have saved members of her own family.

Lewental's despair at the prevarication of the Poles provides a scaffold for Halivni to examine her own despair at the lack of resistance to the Nazis and their policy of extermination. Similarly, given the repeated drafts by Halivni that engage with Langfus's distress at the probable future loss of his son, it seems that 'The Deportation' also offered an indirect way for Halivni to explore her feelings regarding the murder of her younger brother. She uses the life histories of others both to write history and to process her life history. Her reception of the testimonies of Lewental and Langfus provides, if not a working through, at least a means of articulating her own traumatic experiences. In this context, her almost interminable drafting of her writing, her frequent repetitions, manifest not merely a desire for precision or clarity but can also be understood as a symptom of Halivni's reluctance to let go of what these events have become interwoven with: her own personal pain and loss. The scholarship is more than simply research. It does not solely offer an account or interpretation of events. There is a powerful performative dimension to Halivni's work. In this sense, her writing is on a continuum with the SK manuscripts which we discuss in Chapter 2.

Halivni is not, however, conscious of this aspect of her historiography, even though she writes in the context of a discussion of oral history that 'people [distort] facts to suit their political outlook, aesthetic taste, and personal needs', comments that could, partly, refer to her own practice as a historian. It would be unfair to describe Halivni's working methods as distortion, although her history does seem to be born, in part, of her own suffering and structured by that suffering. This makes her history writing also a powerful form of testimony. Additionally, there is a politics to her work, a pride in her Jewish identity, which emerges through her particular focus on resistance but also, unconsciously, through the rare moments when she doodles in her drafts. These doodles invariably represent the Star of David or Shield of David. The doodles in the margins of Halivni's work speak to how the events she studies and describes contribute to an ongoing process of shaping Jewish identity in the aftermath of the Shoah. This identity was, for Halivni, one bound up with acts of heroic resistance by Jews such as the men of the SK who revolted. Halivni felt that the revolt made sense only in the context of all the planning documented by Zalman Lewental. Lewental thus provided an answer to Arendt, Hilberg and Bettelheim, who criticized Jewish passivity and incarnated it in the SK.

Halivni's article on the SK revolt is threaded through with references in the first person, using her own experience to explain the difference in living conditions between Poles and Jews in Auschwitz, or expressing her own trust or admiration for other prisoners. Of Nyiszli himself she says: 'Indirectly, he saved my life'.[38] This method of seeking a connection with other prisoners, deciding whether or not they could be trusted, was a way of gaining information about the camp, both from within and from the outside afterwards.[39] Halivni uses the same method in her assessments of Langbein and Borowski. It is also a way of paying respect and tribute to them. She even writes herself into Lewental's narrative:

> I was in a transport which, I suspect, was placed as a human roadblock, on the thoroughfare in front of Sauna on the night that the SS preempted the revolt. On Saturday 26 August 1944, late in the afternoon, in an unusual move, the SS placed 1,000 Hungarian Jewish women on the thoroughfare 'in the zone' where we remained until about 11 A.M. the next day. That section of the road (see Plate) was precisely the projected theater of the battle. [...] 1,000 women on the thoroughfare, an unprecedented move to my knowledge, prevented these commandos from staging a united fight![40]

The Plate to which she refers places an X on the road outside the 'Sauna', between the two pairs of crematoria. This interpretation is certainly open to the criticism that Halivini's identification with Lewental and his narrative has gone too far. She blends together her own experience of Auschwitz and that which she sees recorded in Lewental's document. As with many survivor historians her research does not always adhere to commonly accepted academic historical standards.[41] As a survivor of the Shoah, she lived through a past that would subsequently become the subject of many histories. Perversely, however, her insider knowledge of historical events renders any account she provides suspect because she is not sufficiently detached from her object of study. She is too much *of* the past. Her life experiences render her categorically distinct from historians who have not lived through the events they study. In *History*, Siegfried Kracauer wrote of the historian as 'the son [*sic*] of at least two times – his own time and the time he is investigating' rendering the historian's mind unlocalizable, perambulating 'without a fixed abode'.[42] Halivni the historian demonstrates that this characterization does not readily apply to survivor historians. She is bound by the trauma of her experiences to the time she investigates, never able to fully detach herself from Auschwitz and its violence, to see it as in the past.

We want to suggest here that meaning is not exhausted by considering its plausibility or adherence to specific historical methodologies. Halivni's failure as a survivor historian to conform to common perceptions of what constitutes good historical practice is what permits her to provide important insights. In general, it is through this ability (or willingness) to bring Lewental's and her own experiences together that Halivni offers an account of the SK. She sees them not as separate from all the rest of camp life, but as a piece that can be laid alongside others to create a wider picture. The method is risky, but it shows an appreciation for what can be shared, what can be imagined and understood. Trying to understand them, one risks overwriting their story with one's own. Not to try to make sense of the SK is to abandon them.

Placing herself—placing a women's transport—into the middle of the picture is to assert that women too have a place in the story of the SK. Some practicalities make this obvious: the women's camp (BI) was right next to Crematoria 1 (II) and 2 (III). Kanada was staffed in part by women and right next to Crematoria 3 (IV) and 4 (V).[43] Women were witnesses to the daily life of the crematoria—and the extraordinary break from routine that was the revolt—in ways that men found much less easy to be (some skilled workers did enter the crematoria compounds, but they did not live next to them). Women bore witness to the SK. The SK bore witness to women: key accounts that they decided to record were about the last words and actions of women before they entered the gas chambers. Halivni also asserts that her experiences as a women are close enough to the SK for her to draw upon them. What we have previously called an implausible explanation of the revolt is therefore more than that. It is a misunderstanding that takes on some meaning, one that allows a different form of understanding.

The Uses of Testimony

What the examples of both Nyiszli and Halivni show is that the uses of testimony often take complex forms, beyond simply establishing or failing to establish facts, and also attempt to make meaning, to make ethical choices.[44] They show how people who were endeavouring to understand the SK were trying both to engage with them as a specific group and to see them as part of a greater whole. That is the aim of this book too. We will consider a range of testimony from the Sonderkommando, moving from that produced in Birkenau itself to that which was part of post-war projects, such as Holocaust trials, video archives and the films of Claude Lanzmann.

By considering the ways in which the Sonderkommando gave testimony and were represented over the post-war period, this book will give new insights into the history of the SK. But it will go beyond that, showing how the SK were central to many ideas of the Shoah and that examining their testimony in depth speaks to and revises some of these conceptions. We argued in *Matters of Testimony* that the conception of testimony provided by Dori Laub has no place for (and thus is challenged by) the writings of the Sonderkommando.[45] Even so, Dominic Williams has noted that Laub and Cathy Caruth's readings of testimony and trauma take forms for which the SK are archetypal examples, especially in Laub's referring to survivors as *Geheimnisträger* (bearers of secrets)—an epithet which, when used in English, is often applied specifically to the SK.[46] Here, we go further, to show how the SK play a key part in Laub's discussion of history and testimony.

As we discuss in Chapter 3, we can see something very much like Marianne Hirsch's concept of postmemory at work in the Sonderkommando's efforts to document and photograph what they were witnessing: a sense that they needed to find means to transmit what they witnessed, to allow others to assume the role of surrogates of memory that Hirsch (and Anne Karpf) have described.[47] This sense, we would contend, carries on into the post-war witnessing of the SK. Concepts that have been coined to theorize the relation to the past of non-witnesses have real bearing on the witnessing that the SK themselves provided. Ideas of 'travelling memory' (Astrid Erll) that consider memory not being constrained within national contexts but crossing boundaries are clearly applicable to the SK's testimony that takes place in different locations and different languages.[48] The court cases of the immediate post-war that we discuss in Chapter 4, even when carried out by national governments, were international affairs. What Alison Landsberg calls 'prosthetic memory',[49] memory that is mediated and supported by notes, documents or photographs, describes not simply the means used by surrogates to call up the past, but also the means used by members of the SK as witnesses in trials, in video testimony and even in *Shoah*, which purports to eliminate the difference between past and present.

The Sonderkommando were not simply witnessing for themselves, but witnessing on behalf of others, especially the victims of the gas chamber, including Jewish women from what were clearly a variety of backgrounds. The discussions of complicity and resistance, and of the difficulties of representing the Shoah, are ones that the SK have a central part in. And, as we show, those questions are also bound up inextricably with questions of gender: How could the SK relate to the women who were about to enter the gas chamber, how could they speak for, to and about them, how could they discuss the crimes that the SS carried out against them? As we will see in Chapters 2 and 5 especially, this was a task that they were considering contemporaneously and that survivors worked on long afterwards, with sometimes disturbing results, but ones that speak powerfully to recent work on gender and the Holocaust.

Joan Ringelheim, one of the pioneering researchers of gender issues in relation to Nazi genocide, titled an unpublished book manuscript on women and the Holocaust *Double Jeopardy*. The name *Double Jeopardy* is clearly intended to draw attention to how Jewish women during the Shoah were doubly imperilled because of their Jewishness and also their gender. Additionally, it is hard not to also hear echoes of Ringelheim's own trials as scholar, a tacit acknowledgement of the risks that accompany engaging with gender issues in this context. As she was laying the groundwork for what was to become the major event *Conference on Women Surviving the Holocaust* of 1983, Ringelheim was famously excoriated in a letter by Cynthia Ozick for appropriating the Holocaust for feminist ends to the detriment of Jewish victims.[50] This chastisement, however, would also have to be extended to the Sonderkommando working in the crematoria at Birkenau as they too sometimes clearly registered and reflected upon differences in the treatment of male and female victims. In this context, the importance accorded to women in their clandestine writings and photographs is deeply significant.

Our consideration of the SK writings through the prism of contemporary debates regarding gender and the Holocaust highlights ways in which the authors, Zalmen Gradowski and Leyb Langfus in particular, were already reflecting on some issues—such as the nature of sexual violence (as it is now usually referred to)—in the Holocaust that have assumed considerable importance in recent years. Gradowski's views on sadism and its relation to the male gaze and on how this relation came to intersect with the genocidal policies of the Nazis in Birkenau are especially relevant in this regard. It needs foregrounding that the reflections he offers are not only his but that he also shares the thoughts of specific victims. Through their own words, we are permitted a glimpse of how Jewish women experienced their final moments. The sexual dimension to Nazi sadism that Gradowski relates renders his understanding qualitatively different to that of Langfus, who also thinks about sadism but ultimately seems to find deliberate cruelty by the Nazis to be an end in itself rather than a means to sexually gratifying ends. Close readings of the SK manuscripts therefore provide crucial insights both into how men and women experienced violence in the death camp and into differing SK perspectives on that violence.

Ringelheim's decision to use a legal term for a book on the Holocaust and gender also implies some kind of shared terrain between the practice of history and of law. The judiciary and history as a discipline do operate with common frames of reference in terms of evidence, testimony and witnessing. These links, left implicit in Ringelheim, are alluded to more directly by Marc Bloch who writes of the artistry of the historian:

> The historian is not – indeed, he [*sic*] is less and less – that rather grumpy examining magistrate whose unflattering portrait is easily imposed upon the unwary by certain introductory manuals. To be sure, he has not turned credulous. He knows that his witnesses can lie or be mistaken. But he is primarily interested in making them speak so he may understand them.[51]

In this book, witnessing in the legal and historical senses of the term overlap in our consideration of the roles of the SK in post-war trials. The impact of trial testimony cannot be underestimated as it circulates beyond the courtroom through media reportage. It was not until he heard Adolf Eichmann's testimony at his trial, for instance, that Terrence des Pres came to a horrifying awareness of how victims died in the crematoria, reduced to 'a human pyramid of death'.[52] Including an analysis of trial testimonies enables us simultaneously to signal ways in which other modes of bearing witness permit different facets of the SK's experiences to register and emerge. Our analyses of video testimonies, for example, show how these enable more of the emotions that accompanied the horrors of labouring in the crematoria to be communicated. In a letter to Hadassah Rosensaft, Geoffrey Hartman emphasizes how the Yale approach to eliciting video testimony is one which employs questions that 'are meant not so much to elicit precise historical information as to draw out personal feelings, accounts of relationships, patterns of experience'.[53]

The following two chapters of *The Auschwitz Sonderkommando* consider the testimony that the SK produced from within the event: the writings known as the Scrolls of Auschwitz and the photographs taken by 'Alex' (possibly Alberto Errera). Our previous readings of these texts and images have tended to look at them in isolation, providing accounts of them that highlight their unique qualities. In these chapters, we take a different approach, considering them in comparison with other kinds of testimony, and with other ways of making sense of them. As previously noted, Chapter 2 reflects on gender roles in the Sonderkommando writings, more specifically on the ways in which the testimony from other survivors, including women, can be brought into dialogue with those writings. We argue that attending to the Scrolls provides important insights into sexual violence as it manifested in the extermination camp. This violence was one that members of the SK worked hard to bear witness to and understand.

Chapter 3 examines the SK photographs and how they have been considered alongside words describing them, from the message written by the Polish resistance that accompanied them to the claims of more recent scholars such as Dan Stone that they escape verbalization. We show that they demand a verbal, as well as a visceral, response. We also draw attention to the value photographs more broadly held for members of the SK. The significance they accorded photographs as forms of remembrance resonates in noteworthy ways with the idea of postmemory. Our consideration of the four images taken by 'Alex' builds on the readings of the Scrolls we offer in Chapter 2 to consider important ethical considerations linked to writing and to ways of seeing. In the Joan Ringelheim Papers at the United States Holocaust Memorial Museum, there are photocopies of photographs of women caught up in pogroms, some running, several of them still striving to hide their bodies.[54] It is clear that Ringelheim recognized how photography sometimes linked with persecution during the Holocaust and, potentially, the persecution of women in particular. The SK were also aware of photography's capacity for violence yet still chose to employ it as a means of bearing witness.

Chapter 4 offers a reading of the Sonderkommando's role in a number of post-war trials. We find that the account of a shift in the role given to witnesses between the immediate post-war period and the 1960s is an over-simplified one, which concentrates too much on the International Military Tribunal at Nuremberg and the trial of Adolf Eichmann in Jerusalem. Other trials of 'lesser' criminals—ones at which the SK were called to speak—show much more complex dynamics of witnessing taking place, with responsibility for producing testimony being shared between survivors of the SK and other members of the court and the court's structures being flexible enough to allow different kinds of witnessing. Viewing these forums as one stage in the process of the SK bearing witness rather than an overall attempt to conceptualize the Shoah allows us to listen to more of the nuances of what they say.

Chapter 5 considers the drawings and paintings of David Olère. Whereas most discussion of his work has tended to mine it for information, we pursue a line pioneered by Carol Zemel to consider the gender dynamics of his artworks. We see a troubled and at times troubling attempt to figure the crime to which Olère bore witness, an attempt which often employs depictions of women's bodies. Those bodies are represented both as objects of beauty and as testaments to something of the horror of the extermination process. We perceive continuity between the authors of the Scrolls of Auschwitz and the artist Olère's post-war corpus in that although employing different media, these members of the SK are each seeking to make some kind of sense of the horrific events they were forced to endure.

Chapter 6 looks at a range of video testimony from and about the SK. Revisiting Dori Laub's famous reading of a section of video testimony about the SK revolt, and the recent re-examination of his arguments and evidence by Thomas Trezise, we show that the Sonderkommando featured much more strongly in the testimony being discussed than either Laub or Trezise credit. The SK form a troubling presence connected to the testimony Laub receives and reflects on, with the women he interviews linked to the SK both by proximity and by familial relations. Having shown that these women, who all worked in the Kanada kommando, have more to say about the SK than had been previously acknowledged, we go on to demonstrate the importance of gender issues in relation to what members of the SK have to say in video testimony. We show that considering the gender dynamics of the interview process and the interviewees' self-image as men provides valuable insights into the nature and possibilities of testimony.

Chapter 7 concludes the volume by offering a close analysis of the place of Filip Müller in the film *Shoah*, building on our previous discussions of the testimony that the SK offered. We read Müller's place in the structure of *Shoah*, showing that he plays quite a different role from that of the equivalents to the SK in the other camps. His speech is much more heavily edited, and his voice is played over camerawork that is much more able to act out what he describes, because so much more of Auschwitz-Birkenau is extant. This produces a number of strange effects with his voice and its connection with his body, ones that trouble the straightforward sense of masculine embodied presence that some readings of the film have seen in it. This chapter therefore provides a new reading of *Shoah* as well as showing its place in a long history of the Auschwitz SK giving testimony.

Our working across different media—drawing, film, literature, painting, photography, trial testimony and video testimony—enables us to tease out similarities and variations in self-representations of the SK across different forms and modes of expression. As with *Matters of Testimony*, which combined textual and visual analyses, the kind of work we engage in here would be impossible without a transdisciplinary approach to the study of testimony. Analysing testimonies produced by members of the SK from within the death camp of Birkenau alongside retrospective testimonies enables us to trace both continuities and changes in terms of how the Sonderkommando narrated their experiences. We are able to tell a different story from the more common general accounts of the memory of the Shoah that speak of silence until the 1960s (or even work to challenge that account), or ones that show how different national memories of the Holocaust were constructed. With our tighter focus on this one group, we are able to trace the relationships between the testimonies produced in different forums, in different media, in different contexts. It also allows us to see the contingencies of how different testimonies have come into being and had unpredictable effects. In this way, we can show that an examination of the Sonderkommando's testimony, paradoxically central to the memory of the Shoah at the same time as often being excluded from it, brings important new insights to the broader study of Holocaust testimony.

Notes

1. Miklós Nyiszli, 'Journal d'un médecin déporté d'un crematorium d'Auschwitz,' trans. Tibère Kremer, *Les Temps modernes* 6.65 (March 1951): 1655–1672 and 6.66 (April 1951): 1855–1886. See Marius Turda, 'The Ambiguous Victim: Miklós Nyiszli's Narrative of Medical Experimentation in Auschwitz-Birkenau,' *Historein* 14.1 (2014): 43–58.
2. 'SK' was an abbreviation that does not seem to have been used in the camps for the Sonderkommando, but was certainly used by Nyiszli

himself. In using this abbreviation, we follow what is now common practice.
3. E.g. Seweryna Szmaglewska, Krystyna Zywulska, Olga Lengyel.
4. Emma Kuby, 'In the Shadow of the Concentration Camp: David Rousset and the Limits of Apoliticism in Postwar French Thought,' *Modern Intellectual History* 11.1 (2014): 148.
5. Yannick Malgouzou, *Les Camps nazis: Réflexions sur la réception littéraire française* (Paris: Classiques Garnier, 2012), pp. 263–268. Maurice Merleau-Ponty and Jean-Paul Sartre, Editorial, *Les Temps modernes* 6.60 (October 1950): 12–14.
6. Miklós Nyiszli, 'SS Obersturmführer Doktor Mengele,' *Merlin* 3 (1952–1953): 158–171 and Richard Seaver, *The Tender Hour of Twilight: Paris in the '50s, New York in the '60s—A Memoir of Publishing's Golden Age*, ed. Jeannette Seaver (New York: Farrar, Straus and Giroux, 2012), pp. 69–73.
7. See the series of books on the concentrationary produced by Griselda Pollock and Max Silverman, starting with *Concentrationary Cinema: Aesthetics as Political Resistance in Alain Resnais's Night and Fog (1955)* (New York: Berghahn, 2011).
8. This is most famously true of Filip Müller, who had two phases of working in the SK, from April to July 1942 in the so-called Fischl-Kommando in Auschwitz I and then from July 1943 until January 1945 in the SK in Birkenau. But it is also true of all of the writers of the Scrolls of Auschwitz. Three survived in the SK for a little under two years (1942–1944), one for about eighteen months (1943–1944), and one from April 1944 until after the end of the war. See Nicholas Chare and Dominic Williams, *Matters of Testimony: Interpreting the Scrolls of Auschwitz* (New York: Berghahn, 2016), pp. 5–7. Of the interviewees in Gideon Greif's *We Wept Without Tears*, four (Jews from Poland) were drafted into the SK in late 1942 and four (Jews from Greece) in spring 1944. Greif, *We Wept Without Tears: Testimonies from the Jewish Sonderkommando from Auschwitz*, trans. Naftali Greenwood (New Haven: Yale University Press, 2005).
9. At the Frankfurt Auschwitz trial, Dov Paisikovic and Filip Müller, both recalled that people survived the gassing, and that there was a routine for dealing with them: it was reported and the survivor was shot. 98. Verhandlungstag (8 October 1964). *Zeno.org: Der 1. Frankfurter Auschwitz-Prozess*, p. 20678 (cp. AP181.018) (Müller) and p. 20965 (cp. AP184.029) (Paiskovic).
10. See Andreas Kilian's note in Miklós Nyiszli, *Im Jenseits der Menschlichkeit: Ein Gerichtsmediziner in Auschwitz*, trans. Angelika Bihari, eds. Andreas Kilian and Friedrich Herber (Berlin: Karl Dietz, 2005), p. 171n.60 and Kevin E. Simpson, *Soccer Under the Swastika: Stories of Resistance and Survival* (Lanham, MD: Rowman & Littlefield, 2016), pp. 143–145.

11. Levi, 'The Grey Zone,' in *The Drowned and the Saved*, trans. Raymond Rosenthal (London: Abacus, 1988), p. 36.
12. Krystyna Żywulska, *I Survived Auschwitz*, trans. Krystyna Cenkalska (Warsaw: tCHu Publishing House, 2004), pp. 250–252.
13. Ibid., p. 253.
14. See, for example the handful of references to the Aktion Reinhard camps of Bełżec, Sobibór and Treblinka, *Gray Zones: Ambiguity and Compromise in the Holocaust and its Aftermath*, eds. Jonathan Petropoulos and John Roth (New York: Berghahn, 2005).
15. See Dan Stone, 'The Harmony of Barbarism: Locating the Scrolls of Auschwitz in Holocaust Historiography,' in *Representing Auschwitz: At the Margins of Testimony*, eds. Nicholas Chare and Dominic Williams (Basingstoke: Palgrave Macmillan, 2013), pp. 11–32 and Tom Lawson, 'The Sonderkommando and Cultural History,' *Telling, Describing, Representing Extermination: The Auschwitz Sonderkommando, Their Testimony and Their Legacy*, Centre Marc Bloch, Berlin, 12 April 2018 [Video of this paper available at https://www.dailymotion.com/video/x6nlbc1].
16. Martin Gilbert, *The Holocaust: The Jewish Tragedy* (London: Fontana, 1987), pp. 518, 633, 636–637, 649–653, 667–668, and 730. Although Dan Stone rightly points out that Gilbert often smuggles in some meaning to be wrung from the testimony, especially in his final paragraph (*Constructing the Holocaust: A Study in Historiography* [London: Vallentine Mitchell, 2003], pp. 153–157), at a micro-level the organization is often concerned solely with asserting the chronological relationship of the material. Thus, Gilbert stitches Leyb Langfus's story of the 3000 Naked Women together with other accounts from Madame Vaillant Couturier and Rudolf Vrba to create a continuous whole, but they could equally be read as a collage of different incidents. Gilbert, *The Holocaust*, pp. 648–649.
17. Saul Friedländer, *Nazi Germany and the Jews: Years of Extermination, 1939–1945* (New York: HarperCollins, 2007), pp. 577–584.
18. Katharina Stengel, *Hermann Langbein: Ein Auschwitz-Überlebender in den erinnerungspolitischen Konflikten der Nachkriegszeit* (Frankfurt: Campus Verlag, 2012), p. 558n.254.
19. Erich Kulka was interned at several concentration camps including Auschwitz where he spent 28 months. Ber Mark spent much of the war in exile in Moscow.
20. Halivni writes: 'On May 26 1944, Dr. Miklós Nyiszli arrived in A on a cattle train from the ghetto of Felsővisó, my [illegible] home town, together with his wife Margarita and his 15 year old daughter Zsuzsi, a former class mate of mine'. United States Holocaust Memorial Museum (henceforth USHMM), Tzipora Hager Weiss Halivni Papers. Accession

Number 2013.529.1. Box 18. File 3. Handwritten note paginated 53. Here, Halivni extrapolates wrongly that Nyiszli was deported from where he lived when she knew him. In reality, he was probably deported from a work camp in the village of Desze (Deseşti). See Turda, 'The Ambiguous Victim': Turda sources this information from the unpublished memoirs of Grigore Dăncuş. Oliver Lustig, however, suggests Nyiszli was deported from Oradea. See http://www.survivors-romania.org/text_doc/oliver_lusting_sr.htm. Accessed 4 May 2018. We are very grateful to Liviu Carare for bringing these references to our attention. In an unfiled notebook in Box 18, Halivni also refers to the Nyiszli family and to Miklós Nyiszli's efforts to have his wife and daughter transferred to a labour convoy. From an entry in the notebook, it is also evident that, at some point during her time at Auschwitz, Halivni received a message from the doctor. In her article 'The Birkenau Revolt,' Halivni credits Nyiszli in a footnote (fn. 97) with indirectly saving her life. In an earlier draft of the article, Halivni writes: 'On the strength of Nyiszli's advice, I opted for a labor transport. With this advice he saved my life'. Box 15. File 2.
21. For a short biography of Halivni, see Toby Axelrod, *In the Camps: Teens Who Survived the Nazi Concentration Camps* (New York: Rosen Publishing, 1999), pp. 26–27.
22. See Halivni, 'The Birkenau Revolt: Poles Prevent a Timely Insurrection,' *Jewish Social Studies* 41.2 (1979): 123–154.
23. Halivni Papers. Box 18. File 3. Printer paper paginated as p. 4.
24. The contribution of Esther Mark to Ber Mark's ground-breaking work on the Scrolls of Auschwitz is also unnoticed. As Mark Smith notes, qualified women historians often 'subsume[d] their careers to those of their husbands'. Mark Smith, *The Yiddish Historians and the Struggle for a Jewish History of the Holocaust*, PhD dissertation, University of California, Los Angeles, 2016, p. 50.
25. In relation to the Sonderkommando, these writings include the articles 'Preparation for Revolt in Auschwitz-Birkenau: Heroes and Martyrs' and 'The Birkenau Revolt: Poles Prevent a Timely Insurrection'.
26. This unpaginated, handwritten account can be found in Box 20, File 2 of the Halvini papers. There is another example of crossing out. Halivni originally wrote 'into a large hall'. This seems more likely as disinfection, of which the stripping of clothes was usually a precursor, was usually carried out prior to being assigned to a barracks. The 'large hall' could be a reference to the Sauna. In another fragment, Halivni refers to stripping at the Sauna before moving on to the *Haarschneideraum* (hair-cutting room).
27. Halivni Papers. Box 20. File 1. Unpaginated fragment in biro.
28. Ibid., Box 18. Unfiled, unpaginated notebook.

29. For a recent discussion of the role of women in the resistance movement, see Ronnen Harren, 'The Jewish Women at the Union Factory, Auschwitz 1944: Resistance, Courage and Tragedy,' *Dapim: Studies on the Holocaust* 31.1 (2017): 45–67.
30. Halivni, 'The Birkenau Revolt,' p. 123.
31. Halivni Papers. Box 15. File 1.
32. We discuss Kanada in more detail in Chapter 6.
33. Sexual violence was a feature of camp life for women and for some men and searches formed one means by which such violence was perpetrated.
34. Halivni Papers. Box 19. File 2.
35. Ibid.
36. Ibid., Box 19. File 1
37. Ibid., Box 15. File 2.
38. Halivni, 'The Birkenau Revolt,' pp. 127, 129 and 134, 152n.97.
39. Halivni, for example, was in contact with Erich Kulka during her research and spoke with several survivors of the SK including Filip Müller.
40. Halivni, 'The Birkenau Revolt,' p. 136.
41. See, for example our criticism of Halivni's explanation of the stymieing of the planned revolt in *Matters of Testimony*, p. 152n.36. For a general discussion of the suspicion with which survivor historians have been regarded, see Laura Jockusch, *Collect and Record!: Jewish Holocaust Documentation in Early Postwar Europe* (Oxford: Oxford University Press, 2012), pp. 193–202.
42. Siegried Kracauer, *History: The Last Things Before the Last* (New York: Oxford University Press, 1969), p. 93.
43. Our numbering of the crematoria follows that used by the majority of members of the SK in oral testimony. In their lived experience, there were only four crematoria. We have provided the Nazi numbering of the crematoria (which includes the crematorium at Auschwitz I) as roman numerals in brackets.
44. Nyiszli and Halivni, can also be seen to be using testimony as all historians do, subjecting it to what are often unconscious processes of identification and projection. In their writings, however, this process is amplified.
45. Chare and Williams, *Matters of Testimony*, pp. 14–16, 70 and 104. Laub's conception of the concentration camp victim as having experienced an event without witnessing it is still influential. See, for example, Petra Schweitzer's *Gendered Testimonies of the Holocaust* which embraces Laub's conception of the Holocaust survivor as witness. Schweitzer, *Gendered Testimonies of the Holocaust: Writing Life* (Lanham: Lexington Books, 2016).
46. Dominic Williams, 'Figuring the Grey Zone: The Auschwitz Sonderkommando in Contemporary Culture,' *Holocaust Studies* (2018): 3.

47. Marianne Hirsch, 'Family Pictures: *Maus*, Mourning and Post-memory,' *Discourse: Journal for Theoretical Sudies in Media and Culture* 15.2 (Winter 1992–1993): 3–29, idem., *The Generation of Postmemory: Writing and Visual Culture After the Holocaust* (New York: Columbia University Press, 2012), and Anne Karpf, 'Chain of Testimony: The Holocaust Researcher as Surrogate Witness,' in *Representing Auschwitz: At the Margins of Testimony*, eds. Nicholas Chare and Dominic Williams (Houndmills: Palgrave Macmillan, 2013), pp. 85–103.
48. Astrid Erll, 'Travelling Memory,' *Parallax* 17.4 (2011): 4–18.
49. Alison Landsberg, *Prosthetic Memory: The Transformation of American Remembrance in the Age of Mass Culture* (New York: Columbia University Press, 2004).
50. For a discussion of this letter, see Zoë Waxman, *Women in the Holocaust: A Feminist History*, p. 1. The letter now forms part of the Joan Ringelheim papers held at the USHMM, Accession number 2007.416.16.
51. Marc Bloch, *The Historian's Craft*, trans. Peter Putnam (New York: Alfred Knopf, 1953), p. 90. For further discussion of the historian figured as judicious, see Sande Cohen, *History Out of Joint: Essays on the Use and Abuse of History* (Baltimore: Johns Hopkins Press, 2006), p. 113.
52. Terrence des Pres Papers, USHMM Accession Number 2016.528.1. Box 44. File 1.
53. 'Letter from Geoffrey Hartman to Hadassah Rosensaft,' 18 May 1981. Terrence des Pres Papers, Box 12. File 7.
54. Joan Ringelheim papers, Box 4.

CHAPTER 2

Acts of Deposition: Gender and Testimony in the Scrolls of Auschwitz

THE DEATHS OF SCHILLINGER

As part of his description of the liquidation of the Czech family camp in March 1944 in his composition *In the Heart of Hell*, Zalman Gradowski makes brief reference to the killing of *Unterscharführer* Joseph Schillinger. *In the Heart of Hell* is one of the Scrolls of Auschwitz, one of the manuscripts written clandestinely by members of the SK during their time engaged in forced labour in the death factory. Gradowski recounts that a young dancer from Warsaw, who is left nameless, stole *Oberscharführer* Walter Quackernack's revolver and then shot Schillinger with it.[1] This act of defiance inspired other women from the transport to fight as well. They began to hit the SS men and throw bottles and other projectiles at them. Gradowski contrasts these acts of physical resistance with the mute compliance of other transports, who went to their deaths like 'sheep to the slaughter'.[2] The killing of Schillinger features in many survivor accounts of Auschwitz.[3] Haya Bar-Itzhak has examined how the story functioned as part of concentration camp folklore and likely had a therapeutic role for inmates.[4] Kirsty Chatwood reads the varied narratives that exist of this event as demonstrating complex relationships between 'resistance, agency, and sexual violence'.[5] She compares and contrasts numerous versions of the death of Schillinger including those produced by members of the Sonderkommando and by other inmates. Chatwood examines four versions of the event by survivors of

© The Author(s) 2019
N. Chare and D. Williams, *The Auschwitz Sonderkommando*, The Holocaust and its Contexts,
https://doi.org/10.1007/978-3-030-11491-6_2

the SK, those of Filip Müller, Shlomo Dragon, Ya'akov Silberberg and Stanislaw Jankowski (Alter Feinsilber). Gradowski's brief rendering does not feature although his telling of the story can also be seen to link with the themes of agency, resistance and sexual violence. In addition to Gradowski's account and the other SK versions mentioned by Chatwood, Zalman Lewental also refers to the woman's defiance in his 'Addendum to the Łódź Manuscript' and David Nencel provides a first-hand account in film footage for a documentary.[6]

There is no definitive account of the killing of Schillinger but it is sometimes claimed that his attacker was the professional ballerina Franceska Mann.[7] The woman also injured another member of the SS, *Unterscharführer* Wilhelm Emmerich. She is said to have distracted Schillinger by performing something like a striptease. Some such as Hermann Langbein (who favoured the account of Rudolf Höss, Commandant of Auschwitz at the time, in which the role of a woman in this act of resistance is suppressed) dismiss the woman's purported actions as the stuff of legend.[8] It is certain that the act, like the later SK revolt at Auschwitz, prompted exaggerated retellings and also confused mistellings. In George Wellers's 1949 account, for example, the death of Schillinger is referenced alongside two other events of women attacking SS men. Wellers describes a young Belgian Jewish mother seizing an SS man's revolver and killing him and also an Italian Jewish woman doing the same. This is in addition to the attack on Schillinger (in which a group of women are claimed to have also scalped one SS man and torn the nose off another).[9] Here Wellers seems to be interpreting differing versions of the killing of Schillinger as distinct events.

Efforts by men even in such opposed roles as a perpetrator (Höss) and a resistance member (Langbein) to downplay the reality of the woman's act of revolt may well reflect fears of emasculation. In the draft manuscript for her unpublished book *Double Jeopardy: Women and the Holocaust*, for instance, Joan Ringelheim explores how Bruno Bettelheim interprets the woman's act of resistance as an expression of masculinity.[10] In *The Informed Heart*, Bettelheim describes the dancer as regaining her autonomy through practising her profession once again. He writes: 'No longer was she a number, a nameless, depersonalized prisoner, but the dancer she used to be'.[11] Of Mann's willingness to die to regain her autonomy he observes: 'If we do that, then if we cannot live, at least we die as men'.[12] These remarks about the woman are similar to those Bettelheim makes in his preface to Miklós Nyiszli's *Auschwitz: A Doctor's*

Eyewitness Account where he suggests that (what he described as) the twelfth SK had 'rediscovered freedom in the last days of its existence, and on the very last day regained it; therefore they died as men not as living corpses'.[13]

Ringelheim's gloss on the psychologist's discussion of the killing of Schillinger is that Bettelheim 'not only compliments this woman for acting like a man, but absorbs her into "manhood"'.[14] Chatwood provides a comparable example of incorporation: the website 'Women and the Holocaust: A Cyberspace of Their Own'. This site offers a version in which 'using her sexuality to commit (male) violence allows Mann to transgress her gendered identities, but the competing contexts of sexual violence and agency subsume the transgression under the rubric of male resistance'.[15] For Ringelheim, being forced to dance for the SS is 'certainly a scene of *sexual* exploitation that would be uncommon in stories about men'.[16] She states: 'The equation is startling: becoming a person entails acting like a man; in this instance dying like one'.[17] Ringelheim understands the event as a whole as defined not by masculinity but femininity with the dancer's act of defiance clearly related to her sexuality. She situates the event within a history of 'various forms of sexual exploitation and humiliation' expected and often experienced by women.[18] For her, the strict binary that some seek to impose on the event in which the woman switches from (sexual) object in the striptease to (defiant) subject through the shooting, from 'femininity' to 'masculinity', is untenable. The show the woman puts on is precisely that, a performance of a particular vision of femininity. Her agency is already at work within her act of dissimulation, within her seeming conformity to images of women as sexually available, as passive and as powerless. As Chatwood observes, 'because she utilized her female sexuality to challenge her abusers, that which made her vulnerable also became a source of power, the power to enact violent resistance'.[19] For Chatwood, however, the story of Schillinger remains a 'straightforward signifier of resistance, a "masculine" violent resistance'.[20]

Ringelheim goes on to discuss sex as functioning as a commodity in the ghettos with sexuality sometimes 'a woman's most valuable bargaining tool'.[21] Here she may be drawing on stories of the kind told by Gertrude Schneider at the *Women Surviving the Holocaust* conference, an event that Ringelheim herself convened. She explained that the commandant of the Riga ghetto, Kurt Krause, had a 'breathtakingly beautiful' Jewish girlfriend, Olly Adler.[22] Schneider stated that because Krause made the law in the ghetto he was 'above and beyond *Rassenschande* which means the racial sin that a German and a Jew could not have intercourse'.[23] Ringelheim does not discuss precisely how the woman's actions against Schillinger link with the actions of women in the ghetto but she seems to be implying that the dancer's attractiveness, what might now be called her 'erotic capital', is what permits her to distract the SS officer.[24] Later in the same chapter, Ringelheim refers to women using their sexuality to manipulate men.[25] For Ringelheim, contra Bettelheim, Schillinger is disarmed by the woman's physical charms, her feminine wiles, before the ballerina employs her agility and strength to literally dispossess him of his revolver. There is a continuum between the superficial seduction and the physical attack. In this effort to reclaim the woman's female agency, Ringelheim treads a difficult path. There is a risk she too sees Mann through cultural stereotypes, implicitly framing her as akin to a femme fatale. Ringelheim's critique of Bettelheim and her own understanding of the killing of Schillinger nevertheless demonstrate that the *way* that the story is told is crucial to understanding its significance. For Ringelheim, and later for Chatwood, the event assumes considerable importance in efforts to think through the complexities of defining (female) resistance and of understanding aspects of women's experiences during the Holocaust. Gradowski's account of the event is enlightening in this context, revealing important information about Sonderkommando attitudes towards women and resistance, about how the men of the SK saw women and about their expansive outlook on what constituted defiance against the Nazis.

As we discuss in *Matters of Testimony*, Gradowski's account of Schillinger's death features in his lengthy description of the liquidation of the Czech family camp on the night of the 8 March 1944. It is included as a means to introduce the theme of resistance, a theme that recurs several times in the account that follows.[26] Gradowski does not dwell on the sexuality of the woman; he rather restricts himself to affirmations of her bravery and courage. The woman's actions provide the material for a brief meditation on resistance and its perceived absence in the transports. Lewental's mention of the event is even shorter: 'a young Jewish [w]oman succeeded in grabbing the gun from the Oberscharführer and shooting several people'.[27] Both Gradowski and Lewental note her youth. Lewental additionally foregrounds the woman's Jewishness. His discussion of the defiant act, like Gradowski's, is part of a broader consideration of resistance, one in which he also praises the Warsaw ghetto uprising.

Post-liberation accounts by survivors of the SK tend to dwell more on what might be viewed as salacious details of the event. Filip Müller recalls:

> Quackernack and Schillinger were strutting back and forth in front of the humiliated crowd with a self-important swagger. Suddenly they stopped in their tracks, a strikingly attractive woman with blue-black hair had stirred their curiosity. As she removed a shoe, Schillinger almost mechanically again ordered the people to take off their clothes. When the woman realized that she had attracted the attention of two SS men, she glanced at them coquettishly, pretending to find them desirable. Her face, full-lipped, looked seductive. With a knowing smile, she raised her skirt so high that you could see her suspenders, then she gracefully undid a stocking and peeled it off her leg. From out of the corner of her eye she carefully observed what was going on around her. The striptease she performed in front of the two SS men so captivated them that they became clearly sexually aroused and paid no attention to anything else. Hands on hips, they stood there staring at the woman, their truncheons dangling from their wrists.
>
> She proceeded to take off her blouse and stood in front of the lecherous onlookers in her brassiere. Then she steadied herself against a concrete pillar with her left arm, bent down and lifted her left foot to take off her shoe. What happened next occurred with lightning speed: quick as a flash she struck Quackernack with the heel of one of her stilettos. He winced with pain and covered his face with both hands. In the blink of an eye, the young woman flung herself at him and made a quick grab for his pistol. Then there was a shot. Schillinger cried out and fell to the ground. Seconds later there was a second shot aimed at Quackernack which, despite his proximity, narrowly missed him.[28]

Müller's memory of events is presented as remarkably detailed, written up to provide an intricate choreography of the woman's movements.[29] The account appears intended to stimulate elements of the book's foreseen readership (seemingly implied to be heterosexual men), the glimpse of suspenders potentially conjuring images of Liza Minnelli singing *Mein Herr* in *Cabaret* (Dir. Bob Fosse, USA, 1972) or of one of the promotional posters for that film, a film very much in European public consciousness in the 1970s. The description encourages readers to share in the contemplation of the unfolding performance, to take vicarious pleasure in it. The highly visual text has designs on (some of) its readers, luring them into the position of voyeur. They are encouraged to visualize the erotic spectacle that the tarrying description of the first paragraph nurtures, to lose themselves in the unfolding process of corporeal revelation, before being jolted out of their voyeuristic reveries by the 'bolt from the blue' midway through the second paragraph that is the attack on Quackernack.

These carefully crafted passages clearly invite readers to imaginatively identify with the SS men viewing the woman's 'performance' and then figuratively punish the readers for their act of projection. They also engineer a series of contrasts between the men and the woman that are designed to showcase the complex gender dynamics and power relations of what is unfurling. The gaze of the men becomes transfixed on the woman. They are visually bewitched by her, their eyes coming under her control. The woman, by contrast, maintains a broad field of vision, retaining a capacity for careful observation. The men are rendered inert, their hands on their hips, while the woman is portrayed as in continual, careful motion. She is figured as active, they as stalled in passive contemplation. The truncheons—symbols of the men's power—hang limp. The woman strikes Quackernack with her high heel and steals his revolver—another symbol of his status—which she uses to fell Schillinger.[30] In this sense, the woman's guile and agency are affirmed. She contests stereotypes regarding female comportment by way of her flesh, embodying actions that it is possible to understand as expressions of what is now called 'physical feminism'.[31]

There is, however, still something disconcerting about how the (nameless) woman in Müller's account is presented to readers. She is highly fetishized, reduced to desirable body parts. Her hair, her legs and her feet are directly referenced. The brassiere forms a metonym for her breasts and the stockings and high heels for her legs. The woman is figured very much as body. A potential motivation for her heightened fetishization may be because of her emasculating potential. In some accounts, it seemingly becomes necessary to disavow her sex, her femininity, through incorporating phallic substitutes into the retelling by way of fetish objects such as the brassiere and the high heels. Instead of attacking Quackernack with a high heel, the woman is described in different SK versions of this event as attacking Schillinger with her knickers (Nencel) or with her bra (Shlomo Dragon).[32] Both Dragon and Nencel claim to have been standing very close to the woman as events unfolded yet their accounts differ.[33] It is therefore possible that individual desires intersect with retrospective testimony here, overlaying and governing the kind of account that emerges.

None of this detail about what the woman wore or about the performance she put on is present in Gradowski's and Lewental's accounts. In part, this may be because they were not present at the event and their telling of the tale is based on second-hand information. They may also not wish to detract attention from other aspects of their accounts which they feel are more important. Gradowski was certainly not wary of describing events in detail or of focussing on the physical appearance of women yet here he restricts himself to mentioning this woman's youth and the fact she was a dancer. Different emphases are placed on aspects of the killing of Schillinger depending on the needs and desires of each witness. Taken together, however, the accounts, the varied deaths of Schillinger, attest to the major status accorded to this event by the men of the SK, to how inspirational it was for them. The multiple versions also cumulatively reveal complex ways in which figures of femininity contributed to efforts by the Sonderkommando to affirm their identity and their masculinity.

THE SCROLLS OF AUSCHWITZ

Inspired by Tadeusz Borowski's writings, Sarah Cushman suggests that 'unable to protect, help, or even raise a hand in defense of women calling for their aid, men [at Auschwitz] were limited to mute witnessing, which emphasized to men their own loss of gender as well as that of their female counterparts'.[34] Doris Bergen makes a similar observation, noting that during the Holocaust men may potentially have felt the secondary effects of sexual violence through loss of dignity and feelings of emasculation.[35] Members of the SK saw horrendous violence perpetrated against women on a daily basis. In *Matters of Testimony*, we discuss how they felt impotent because of their inability to help women and children who had been sent to their deaths. For us, however, bearing witness through writing formed an important way to counteract those feelings of powerlessness. Many members of the SK wrote during their time working in the crematoria although perhaps only a tenth of their manuscripts have survived.[36]

The writings we do possess were composed in the period 1943–1944 and buried in the grounds of the crematoria by members of the Sonderkommando in 1944. They were subsequently retrieved over a period spanning 1945–1980.[37] In addition to the writings, hair and teeth, photographs, religious artefacts and other objects were also concealed in the ground. These were meant to be understood in tandem with the writings.[38] The SK manuscripts were predominantly composed in Yiddish although letters in French and Greek, and a list in Polish, were also found. The list was written after the 7 October revolt staged by the Sonderkommando and makes reference to those who were killed in the right-hand margin.[39] It also shows that killings continued in the immediate aftermath of the revolt. From the list, it is clear that Crematorium 3 (IV) was no longer in use but that the other crematoria still received transports and groups of prisoners from the concentration camp. As well as the point of origin of each group of people, the list details their numbers, and whether they comprised men, women, children or families. In her paper 'Women and the Holocaust: Taking Numbers into Account', Joan Ringelheim notes that there is a tendency for scholars working with records of deportations and killings to round off numbers which she likens to 'losing people again'.[40] The member of the SK who wrote the list is, however, not rounding off but estimating. Far from losing people, this list seeks to hold onto them in some form, to carry them forward to the future. The list of figures is qualitatively different from the typed or handwritten documents prepared by the Nazis to record the transport of inmates, documents that often also included names, documents which might be deemed more comprehensive. The list was an expression of compassion and a form of resistance rather than an exercise in dispassionate bureaucracy.[41] It was not intended to act as a standalone document. It formed part of a far larger, concerted effort to bear witness to genocide, as it would later come to be named.

At one point, the list makes reference to the ages of a group of children, they are identified as between 12 and 18 years old. This more precise information indicates that the list was not meant to be read independently of the other documents it was concealed with. It was found on the 17 October 1962 buried alongside an exercise book signed by Zalman Lewental which details the preparations for, and the unfolding of, the Sonderkommando revolt, and also some loose sheets of paper. These sheets of paper feature two compositions—unsigned, but written by Leyb Langfus—entitled 'The 600 Boys' and 'The 3000 Naked Women'.[42] The list forms the hinge between the loose sheets and the notebook because it includes references both to the revolt and to the two episodes described by Langfus. In the list, horizontal writing in the right margin refers to the murder of 460 members of the Sonderkommando (these killings occurred during and immediately after the insurrection). 'The 3000 Naked Women' refers to the women sent to Crematorium 1 (II) on the 12 October. 'The 600 Boys', as Ber Mark noted in his book *The Scrolls of Auschwitz*, describes the fate of the 600 boys out of the 1000 men and boys sent to Crematorium 2 (III) on 20 October. The two episodes described by Langfus and the history of the revolt by Lewental flesh out three of the rows of numbers in the list. Ringelheim describes 'the resounding way' in which numbers can begin to speak when they are studied closely and from within a broad knowledge of Holocaust testimony. Here the numbers assume a similar rhetorical power when they are read in combination with the other texts buried with them. Langfus's two case studies in tragedy make the reader reflect on the other columns in the list to which there is no matching text. These three manuscripts were prepared by men conversing with each other, planning together, writing as a team. Reading the documents together rather than separately gives greater insight. Studied in tandem, the writings give a sense of the kinds of debates that were taking place between members of the SK, as well as recording friendships or alliances within the group.

Yet despite collaborative dimensions to their writings, as we explore in *Matters of Testimony*, each of the men in the SK likely wrote for different reasons and conceived of their authorial practice and presumed readership in their own way. For Gradowski, for example, being able to bear witness to the horrors of the Holocaust was a masculine prerogative. As he prepares his readers for the account he will provide of the transport from the Kiełbasin camp to Auschwitz, he urges them: 'gird up your loins like a man'.[43] He asks the putative witness to prepare for physical hardships that will be akin to a battle. The reception of testimony is here figured in terms of a combat, the account as something that must be physically endured, fought through. As he has survived the horrors his narrator will go on to recount, Gradowski is, in a sense, simultaneously affirming his own masculinity.[44] That the reader is clearly conceived as male is reaffirmed by some of the instructions the narrator gives him as he prepares him for the journey that will be the testimony itself, he calls upon him to forget his wife and children. The horrors he will strive to *show* his readers—he consciously strives to be imagistic—are composed with a male gaze in mind. This gendering of his readership (and, by extension, of their gaze) shapes the form and content of his writings as is also the case for, for instance, in the letter in French to a wife and daughter that has long been attributed to Chaim Herman.[45]

Considerations of gender issues as they manifest in the Scrolls of Auschwitz are not extensive. In his often thoughtful reflections on the Scrolls, Nathan Cohen devotes little attention to gender.[46] Susan Pentlin makes only passing reference to how the SK were forced to watch 'young girls raped and children thrown into fire pits'.[47] In their sustained and sophisticated analyses of Gradowski's writings, Ana Firoiu and Fleur Kuhn perceive Gradowski's corpus as comprising an affirmation of hope, an assertion of individuality, a means of preserving the voices of individual victims and a mausoleum to house the dead.[48] They do not, however, address how Gradowski's status as a man intersects with these aims and potentially influences how and what he writes.

The most focussed engagement with gender in relation to the Scrolls is provided by Zoë Waxman in her self-proclaimed 'feminist history', *Women in the Holocaust*. The readings she provides of the SK writings, which feature at the beginning of her chapter on 'Concentration Camps', build on her earlier engagement with the manuscripts in *Writing the Holocaust*. There (like Ber Mark, who clearly inspires her), Waxman emphasizes the role of the writings as expressions of resistance.[49] In *Women in the Holocaust* she also addresses resistance, foregrounding Gradowski's disenchantment that the women in the Czech transport did not revolt and physically attack the SS who were guarding them: 'he was disappointed at their apathy'.[50] Waxman treats Gradowski's account of the Czech transport uncritically. She does not outwardly embrace the conception of resistance he operates with—one in which the women fail to defy the Nazis and are interpreted as essentially listless—yet also fails to contest it, seemingly unwilling to attend to the ideological complexity of his writing. It is, however, possible to read Gradowski's account as strongly influenced by his preconceptions about gender. A reading of the kind we offer here, which is sensitive to the influence of Gradowski's religious beliefs and his sociocultural moment upon his ideas about masculinity and femininity and, by extension, his writing, enables his prejudices to be unpacked and also his sensitivity and the admiration he holds for the women to be acknowledged.

As we argued in *Matters of Testimony*, *In the Heart of Hell* should not be read as a straightforward, factual account of events at Birkenau. One of the three sections that form the manuscript, for instance, consists of a lengthy address to the moon. The section that recounts the murder of the Czech transport discusses real events but does so through a carefully crafted framework that is designed to do more than merely communicate information. The writings of Gradowski (and also of other authors, particularly Langfus) possess a performative dimension which it is unwise to overlook. They do not simply recall occurrences. The writings need to be regarded as events in themselves. The unfolding process of writing provided a means for Gradowski to try and get a handle on his situation. What we now read as finished product was, like all writing, also process. Composing texts offered a possibility within the historical situation that was the death factory to carve a space for invention and reflection. Here we want to focus primarily on how the writings reflect upon femininity, masculinity and sexuality and the creative strategies and decisions employed by Gradowski and other writers to broach these themes.

The writings need to be understood within the broader context of gender and sexuality as it was experienced at Auschwitz if their insights and also their limitations are to be appreciated. Waxman begins her chapter with a consideration of literature from the death camp at Auschwitz to illustrate what befell those women who were not selected for work upon arrival. The chapter then moves on to a consideration of women's experiences in the concentration camp. Waxman is, however, aware that the Czech transport provides an example of prisoners who were interned in the concentration camp prior to their extermination. This is one of the reasons why Gradowski is disappointed by their failure to resist: they knew they were going to their deaths whereas many arriving on the transports only suspected this. The Czech women were under no illusion about the ruthlessness of the Nazis. They had already had ample experience of it in the camp, experience that shaped how they perceived the SS. As the example of the Czech transport demonstrates, those sent to their deaths in the gas chambers had varied understandings of the fate that awaited them depending upon their individual histories and also reacted in different ways to that fate.

SEX AND GENDER IN AUSCHWITZ-BIRKENAU

The women of the Czech family camp also had a different experience of Birkenau the concentration camp than other women interned there.[51] Women (and men) experienced the camp dissimilarly dependent on factors such as their class, nationality and religious background. Their life in the camp was also shaped by the kind of work they performed and the length of their incarceration.[52] Pascale Bos stresses the need to think beyond generalizations about women's experiences and recognize their diversity and the sometimes exceptionality.[53] Any consideration of women's and of gender issues more broadly in relation to Auschwitz (as with other camps) must therefore acknowledge the heterogeneity of both men's and women's experiences. As Henry Friedlander noted, it must also be remembered that everyday ideas about sex and sexuality cannot be transposed to concentration camps where sexual behaviour was conducted under duress with limited options.[54] Despite the fraught nature of the subject, there is a rapidly expanding literature analysing gender and sexuality, with much scholarship focussing on hitherto overlooked or marginalized experiences of men and women in Auschwitz (and elsewhere) considering themes such as prostitution, sexual violence and gay or lesbian relations.

Writers in the field of gender and the Holocaust such as Ringelheim initially focussed on the specificities of women's experiences, seeking to foreground the voices and knowledge of female survivors.[55] The emphasis on differentiation of Holocaust experience by gender led to criticism that such an approach fostered victim blame.[56] Additionally, as Sara Horowitz has noted, viewing 'women as a more or less unified group with similar behavioural characteristics ignores important differences in cultural background, social class, age, economic standing, level of education, religious observance and political orientation – differences that, like gender, contribute to the way victims responded to their circumstances'.[57] The need for a more nuanced consideration of women's experience which acknowledged its heterogeneity was recognized. There were growing efforts to move beyond the early approaches as they 'relied on falsely neutral or essentialist treatments of gender and sexual differences'.[58] Issues related to gender continue to inform contemporary research in Holocaust studies. In the past decade increasing attention has been given, for example, to sexual violence against Jewish women during the Shoah.[59] The recent publication of Maddy Carey's monograph *Jewish Masculinity in the Holocaust* also demonstrates that masculinity is becoming a topic of considerable interest.[60]

We are interested in how an attention to differing feminities and masculinities as they manifested at Auschwitz can enhance our understanding of the Sonderkommando and their testimonies. Men and women at Auschwitz often viewed members of their own sex differently depending on their country of origin, with these views sometimes clearly shaped by ethnic stereotypes but also likely embodying real cultural and linguistic differences. In *Matters of Testimony*, we examined how Ashkenazi and

Sephardic men in the SK regarded each other and interacted, identifying differences as well as common interests between these religious groups.[61] That research showed us that in studying the men of the SK we are studying Jewish masculinities rather than a singular form of Jewish masculinity, with Ashkenazi and Sephardic men sometimes viewing and experiencing their situation differently based on their conceptions of maleness. Daniel Boyarin, who focusses primarily on Ashkenazi conceptions of gender in his crucial research on Jewish masculinities, emphasizes that Sephardic Jews possess their own specificity and differences from Jews of Northern Europe.[62] Maddy Carey's analysis of Jewish masculinity in the Holocaust focusses on Jewish men from Poland, Belgium, France and Holland, ignoring the distinctiveness of Jewish masculinities of Southern Europe. Carey also does not examine masculinities in the concentration and death camps, arguing that their nature caused them to display 'their own very particular form of gendered practice'.[63] We are less inclined to see a radical break in terms of masculine behaviour in the camps compared to the experiences of men (and women) pre-internment.[64]

Like the SK men, women recognized disparities in outlook and appearance that were shaped by factors such as religion and geography. They were subject to intra-group differences, a reality for which Kimberlé Crenshaw's idea of intersectionality provides a useful explanatory framework.[65] Crenshaw initially used the term to draw attention to how racism and sexism intersect in Black women's lives in ways that mean considering either form of oppression separately cannot adequately account for. She focussed on the implications of intersectionality for delivering social justice. In the context of Holocaust historiography and testimony, intersectionality enables a more encompassing recognition of the heterogeneity of women's experiences. In Auschwitz, alongside racism and sexism, ageism, class, nationalism and religion, for instance, also sometimes intersected in different ways as elements of identity of women inmates and impacted upon how they experienced the camp.

The survivor Claudette Bloch, for example, notes of French female inmates in her essay 'Les femmes à Auschwitz', 'we were so different from the women from Eastern Europe. Not only in our language but also our manners, our reactions and our emotions'.[66] Vera Laska suggests that 'the Poles were the sturdiest, perhaps because they were on home grounds and so numerous'.[67] Austrian survivor Ella Lingens-Reiner described the Slovaks as 'robust' in contrast to the Greek Jewish women who were 'delicately made, like deer, with tiny feet and enormous dark eyes' that gave them a 'fairy-tale beauty'.[68] Slovak women, in turn, contrasted their femininity with that of women from other parts of Europe. Mrs. R. G. distinguishes Eastern Slovak women such as herself from Dutch women: 'we weren't the kind of girls that had painted nails on our toes and fingers, and those faces, everything made up, elegant'.[69] Many of these differences relate to physical appearance and were clearly registered visually.

Physical appearances were sometimes a matter of life or death at Auschwitz, a reality condensed in the *Selektion*, the selection process carried out upon arrival and then routinely thereafter which was used to decide who was fit for work and who was unfit and therefore to be sent to the gas chambers. There are various accounts of techniques employed by women to give themselves seemingly healthy complexions before being subject to a selection. The criteria employed in selections were not consistent and sometimes capricious. Looking too beautiful, for example, could provide grounds for a woman to be sent to her death. Olga Lengyel remembers of selections directed by Irma Grese that it was 'those who, despite hunger and torture, still showed a glimmer of their former physical beauty [who] were the first to be taken'.[70] Usually, however it was signs of ill health that were thought to represent the criteria for being chosen. Looking hale could therefore make the difference between life and death. Lingens-Reiner has remarked how Slovakian Jewish women at Auschwitz used their experience, their knowledge of 'camp-technique', to good effect, managing to look 'healthy and spruce, some even elegant'.[71] This technique was acquired with time and length of incarceration was therefore a valuable commodity.

Having a healthy physical appearance was also exploited by some women who traded their bodies for food or other materials. Prostitution was common at Auschwitz. The SK member Alter Feinsilber recounts in his trial deposition that sex could be bought for a few cigarettes in the Gypsy camp, 'where would take place relations with Gypsy women'. He does not state that he engaged in such a transaction but it cannot be discounted. To visit the Gypsy camp, Feinsilber explains, it was first necessary to bribe the guard on duty with a packet of cigarettes. This was likely a considerable sum but one that men working in the Sonderkommando could certainly afford. Gisella Perl also describes the latrines as serving as a 'love-nest' where 'men and women met for a furtive moment of joyless sexual intercourse in which the body was used as a commodity with which to pay for the badly needed items the men were able to steal from the warehouses'.[72] Susan Cernyak-Spatz, who worked for a time in Kanada, names the Sonderkommando as one group who might help women inmates by bringing them food.[73] She does not mention if anything was expected in return for the food but sex may have been involved. Leon Welbel, one of the SK kapos, recalled that 'many many many boys not only from Sonderkommando, say [i.e. for example] my brother, got a girl you know over there in the Frauenlager'.[74] Sexual activity at Auschwitz was more commonplace than is sometimes realized. David (Dario) Pardo describes seeing men and women having intercourse either at Birkenau or Sachsenhausen.[75] Suzanna Eisdorfer remarks of sex that 'it was the ones who were there longer and were better fed who had interest in [it]'.[76] Anna Pawełczyńska makes a similar observation, suggesting that 'it was a better physical condition, which depended on standing higher in the camp structure or having the privilege of receiving food packages, that defined the particular socioeconomic category of people for whom erotic needs existed'.[77] This might be true of those buying sex but the sellers were often forced into such transactions through desperation. Sex interested them but only as a means to barter. Their bodies, if they were lucky, had exchange value. Their needs were not erotic but their 'erotic capital' (in a limited sense of the term) helped them satisfy other requirements linked with, for example, food or clothing.

Sexual desirability for women (and, likely, men) in Auschwitz the concentration camp was linked to beauty ideals which differed from mainstream norms of beauty of the period. These ideals had emerged within the specific conditions of the camp. The kinds of bodies which were esteemed and desired in the camp can be deduced from survivor testimony. In her interview with Henry Levy, Shelly Roberts asks him if he found a particular woman (a prisoner who was a bookkeeper at Block 10) attractive to which he responds 'Yes, I can say she was attractive, yeah. And well fed. And well fed, yes'.[78] Here Roberts' question may be prompted by Levy describing the woman as tall and blonde (a description that resonates with contemporary ideals of beauty). His response, although it seemingly details attractiveness and being well fed as distinct qualities, may reveal a link between pulchritude and body fat, the camp ideal of beauty being more closely associated with corpulence rather than leanness. Lengyel remarks on this stating 'women – few enough – who miraculously retained some flesh were envied by others who a year earlier, would have endured tortuous diets to reduce their weight'.[79]

Homosexual as well as heterosexual sex occurred in the camp. Ringelheim, for instance, cites a survivor called Susan who described lesbian relationships occurring at Auschwitz.[80] Kitty Hart also discusses occasional sexual liaisons, instances in which mutual delousing developed into 'stroking, caressing, and murmuring'.[81] Pawełczyńska attests that 'spatial segregation of the sexes [...] led to the spread of homosexuality among the healthier and better nourished prisoners in the camp'.[82] Ringelheim deduces that 'it is probable that there were more homosexual relationships than most survivors are willing to admit'.[83] Male homosexuality took many forms including prisoners pursuing a relationship as equals or adolescent boys acting as *pipels* [small boys], as sexual partners, to prisoner functionaries in return for privileges.[84] In the Scrolls of Auschwitz and in post-war testimonies that have so far been disseminated there is no mention of gay relations of any form within the special squads. Although no evidence can therefore be presented for the existence of such relations, it is entirely possible they existed.

There are also accounts of sexual relations between prisoners and members of the SS. Often sexual relations between camp guards and Jewish women are described as unusual because of *Rassenschande*.[85] As Doris Bergen observes, 'Nazi leaders and propagandists worked to discourage German killers and their henchmen from considering women from groups marked for destruction as objects of sexual desire'.[86] There are also accounts of members of the SS being punished for forming sexual liaisons with Jewish women. Dissuasion, however, if it was ever effective, only seems to have functioned if contact between Nazi men and Jewish women was short term. When in close proximity for extended periods of time, sexual taboos clearly broke down. Kitty Hart states of her time in Kanada that she only knew of one relationship between an SS man, [Franz] Wunsch, and a Jewish woman who 'had managed in spite of everything to stay attractive'. Hart recalls that 'several of us stood guard while the two of them made love behind heaps of goods'.[87] Perhaps referring to the same relationship, Erna Low (who also worked in Kanada) described a 20-year-old Jewish girl being the 'sweetheart' of an SS commander. They had formed an illicit liaison which was 'only whispered about' as 'it was Rassenschande'.[88] This situation may not have been unique. Irene Weiss describes her Slovak Jewish blockova as regularly being coerced into sex by an SS guard.[89] Judy F. also says of the SS in Kanada, 'They weren't allowed to have Jewish girlfriends yet some of them did. Some of the poor girls were forced to it'.[90]

Additionally, Ringelheim cites a survivor from Kanada called Susan who was approached by an SS officer who wanted sex.[91] The relative isolation of Kanada made such relations easier and it is also likely the women who worked there, who had access to better food and clothing, looked more physically appealing. These relationships should all be viewed as, to varying degrees, coerced.

These experiences all relate to life in the concentration camp of Auschwitz-Birkenau. The death camp at Birkenau usually provided, we would suggest, a qualitatively different set of experiences for both the inmates and the guards who worked there and the victims sent to die there. There was some crossover in that there was contact between those working in the death factory and those in the main camp. Men who were part of the special squad over a long period of time will have had experience of living in the main camp of Birkenau before being barracked in the crematoria. Some very few, most notably Filip Müller, had also worked at the crematorium at Auschwitz I, as well as spending some time away from the SK. The squad at Birkenau were initially housed in Block 2 of BIb before being moved to Block 13 of BIId. Block 13 (along with Block 11 which housed the penal group) was supposedly isolated from the main camp but it is clear that members of the SK were still able to move around the camp even if in sporadic and restricted ways. Feinsilber's testimony about prostitution in the Gypsy camp, for example, points to this. Even when the SK were predominantly billeted in the crematoria, some may have continued to have occasional access to Kanada. SS guards, like those in Kanada, also seem occasionally to have formed relations with Jewish women inmates. In his 1945 trial deposition which we discuss in more detail in Chapter 4, Shlomo Dragon (Szlama Dragan) states of an SS guard working in the crematoria, that 'he took services from a girl from Slovakia'.[92] The reference to services is ambiguous but as Dragon felt it worthy of mention it is possible to speculate that he is being euphemistic and these services are sexual.

The death factory, however, was also where people were sent to be murdered, a kind of non-place for most that was characterized by fleeting, terrifying encounters. This rendered it a highly different environment from the concentration camp and it seems to have generated habitual extremes of behaviour including sexual violence which were less common elsewhere. In this context, the testimony of the SK is crucial as none of the victims sent to the gas chambers survived to attest to their experience. Explorations of sex and gender at Auschwitz-Birkenau that ignore witness accounts by the Sonderkommando necessarily contain lacunae. Aspects of sexual violence that were perpetrated in the death factory may have helped to make the work more psychologically bearable for SS guards. Doris Bergen reads sexual violence as it occurred in the extermination process as a means to 'dehumanize the victims and thereby maximize the distance between killers and their prey'.[93] She rightly observes that Nazi ideology 'did not constitute a barrier to violence of a sexual nature'.[94] Sexual violence may, in fact, have been experienced as a means of expressing belief in Nazi racist ideology. Helene Sinnreich, who has explored the rape of Jewish women by German men during the Holocaust, cautions against relying 'on German sexual purity laws and the notions of Jews as subhuman as a way to preclude the [...] possibility of sexual violence' against Jewish women by Germans.[95] For Sinnreich, rape is possible precisely because it is not sex but rather an expression of violence against the women involved. In the crematoria, sexual violence was not restricted to rape. As the SK recorded, it took many forms.

THE PLAY OF GAZES

One form of sexual violence that receives repeated mention in the Scrolls is that of naked humiliation. This humiliation is one that characterizes both the concentration and death camps. Nakedness was felt as degrading and embarrassing by both men and women. David (Dario) Pardo tells of being ashamed at seeing his father naked (nude, as he puts it) for the first time upon arriving at the concentration camp of Auschwitz.[96] The spectacle of nakedness was one from which the SS are described as deriving considerable pleasure, in both the concentration and the death camp. Something of the violent spectacle that was undressing registers in narratives of the killing of Schillinger. Abe Korn, for example, writes of Schillinger's killer (who he identifies as an Italian woman), that 'when the German SS men saw her, sexual fever rose in their eyes'. One guard 'watched with unholy glee as the prisoners undressed'. Korn here draws attention to the scopic violence in the undressing room and its sexual dimension. Tellingly, in the account of the killing, the woman also assaults the guard's vision: 'when she was left wearing only her panties and bra, with the SS man [...] pawing at her body, she tore off her own bra and swung it into the eyes of her attacker, momentarily blinding him'. Korn states that the version he has given was transmitted to him by members of the SK.[97]

Gradowski's account of the murder of the Czech transport, the Czech family camp, also explores the violence that inhered in the viewing dynamics between the guards and their victims.[98] The gaze of the SS is described as 'barbaric' and 'savage'. It forms an extremely violent mode of perception that works to objectify the victims. Gradowski, however, does not restrict himself to a discussion of how the SS see their victims. He also describes the gaze of the SK. It is qualitatively different from that of the Nazis in that it is not actively violent, violating. The women are, nevertheless, described in a way that affirms the patriarchal ideology underpinning Gradowski's way of envisioning them. Ringelheim has written of how sometimes in the Shoah 'the sexism of Nazi ideology and the sexism of the Jewish community met in a tragic and involuntary alliance'.[99] This alliance was in part forged through common ways in which men saw women. We want to suggest, however, that while there is a shared mode of looking operating here there is also evidence that Gradowski has an awareness of this issue and is striving to see beyond it.

In his description of the Czech women in the undressing room, he contrasts the SK, 'we the men, still in our clothes, stand now opposite them [the women], and watch, frozen', with the naked women, asking if he is in a museum or a painter's studio.[100] The victims are described as if alabaster, a group of statues inviting admiration. Here the dynamics of viewing, ones that—crucially—Gradowski will not quite commit to, are those of the male artist or spectator consuming a pleasing vision of sexualized femininity. Griselda Pollock has examined the sexual hierarchy of the male artist and his female model as it figures in twentieth-century modernist painting. For Pollock, this juxtaposition of two bodies in space instantiates the painter's body as 'art' and the feminine body as its other, 'nature'. The painter is described as 'upright', as standing.[101] For Pollock, 'the representation of the female body in art in effect signifies its positivized antithesis: the masculine artist as the possessor of both an aestheticizing and an erotic gaze, who invests the pathways of sight and its objects of visual representation with the scopic terms of his sexuality (voyeurism, fetishism, scopophilia) and its sublimation into a creative practice'.[102] There seem to be elements present in the description of the women in the undressing room that conform to this creative dynamic. The women are, after all, the material from out of which Gradowski's crafts his account. His questioning, however, means the account resists such a straightforward reading. Gradowski asks not only if he is looking at artist's models but also if he is confronting some kind of satanic ritual.

The description, with its questioning, its doubt in what the SK are seeing, renders the scene somewhere between dream and reality.

This dimension foregrounds the need not to read Gradowski's description of the fate of the Czech transport as a simple, factual account of events. The description of what happened is supplemented by performative and self-reflective dimensions. There is a complex interplay of historical account and psychological investigation at work in the prose. Müller's account of the same event in *Shoah* brings to the fore the brutal treatment meted out to the Czech inmates from the onset. The SS foresaw trouble and were extremely brutal towards the inmates in an effort to discourage any thoughts of resistance. In Müller's testimony, the victims are repeatedly assailed as they are driven forcibly to the gas chamber. Gradowski's account operates in a different temporality, one that slows down events, enabling the author to focus on details and attend to individual voices. This deceleration is coupled with a minimization of violence. Gradowski's prose shields most of the women and children he describes from SS brutality. This is not to say that he sidesteps the violence perpetrated by the Nazis but this violence becomes mostly condensed in the repeated image of the nakedness of the victims. The bodily humiliation is initially established by way of the contrast just discussed but Gradowski will go on to repeatedly return to their state of undress. The women's nakedness is emphasized not solely through direct references to it but also indirectly by way of discussion of their hair, which is often referenced in terms of its physical appearance, its colour or its curliness.[103] For some observant Jewish women, as Zoë Waxman explains, 'hair is akin to physical nudity and expresses a woman's sexuality'.[104] Gradowski's continuous references to hair parallel his recurring mentions of nakedness, serving to reinforce the shame and degradation experienced by the women and also to signal the shocking sights men of the SK had to confront, aspects of which were particularly troubling to those from orthodox backgrounds.

The relative absence of direct physical violence in the account forms a way by which Gradowski can retrospectively provide protection that he was unable to literally offer to the victims. He metaphorically proffers succour by way of his writing. In this sense, the telling may seem to provide a means by which Gradowski can assume his manly responsibilities, safeguarding the victims. Additionally, as Henry Krystal suggests, helping people enabled concentration camp internees to retain a sense of humanity.[105] In the death camp, Gradowski cannot give direct aid to victims but writing offers him the means to provide imagined relief. These may be unconscious motivations but it seems the mode of retelling of the event is also carefully crafted to enable the author to address specific themes in substantial depth rather than rapidly and superficially. This account is not simply about what happened, it is also a lengthy meditation on violence and how to resist it, and, towards the end, on loss. Approaches such as Waxman's, which treats Gradowski's testimony uncritically and uses it as illustration, fail to bring out some of the complexities of the writing. Waxman does, nonetheless, at least acknowledge the existence of the composition. Some historians of a positivist bent would likely refuse to engage with the account because of its subjective dimensions.[106]

Perhaps motivated by an awareness of issues of objectivity, Gradowski states that he remains at a distance from the two groups he is describing, positioning himself as a kind of neutral observer. Despite his calling the women his sisters, the author does not forcefully locate himself as victim. He exists somewhere outside the binary opposites he bears witness to. He looks on rather than participating in the play of gazes that develops between oppressors and oppressed. From within this massively unequal power dynamic, the women are still able to craft what we identify as resistance at the level of the gaze. The women as a group, for example, adopt a way of looking askance that, in its cultivated indirectness, denies the SS the ability to view them as filth, as inhuman, to expose them to a desubjectifying gaze: 'All cast contemptuous looks at the line of officers, not wishing to accord them the slightest direct look'. There is clearly a recognition among the women that Nazi violence, which is bound up with ways of seeing, requires an Other to enact itself upon: 'They do not want to provide [the SS] with the great pleasure of seeing them in despair, begging'.[107] Humiliation only functions if the effects of violence are rendered visible through the frightened or imploring look of the victim.[108]

This studied cockeye, a resistance by way of a refusal to see, to look directly, is not the only way resistance is manifested. One woman, the mother of a nine-year-old girl, confronts the guards and tells them the Russians are coming and that vengeance will be enacted upon the soldiers. The guards are left speechless by this tirade. They are also rendered unable to look at each other, deprived of their gaze: 'They stayed silent, shocked. They didn't have the courage to look at each other'.[109] The woman is subsequently described as having laid bare the reality of their situation.[110] In this sense, she has forced a figurative undressing on them. Shortly after this act of defiance, another woman 'a beautiful, young blonde' addresses the SS. Her speech merits quoting in full:

> You shady criminals! You devour me with your thirsty, bestial eyes [*durshtige, khayishe oygn*], you have your fill of the nakedness of my enticing body [*reytsenden kerper*]. Yes, it is currently your time. In your everyday life, you could never have dreamed of this. You, gangsters and criminals, you have found here the right spot to give your sadistic eye [*sadistish oyg*] its fill. But you will not enjoy this for much longer. Your game is coming to an end, you cannot kill all the Jews. You will pay for everything.[111]

Here the violence of the Nazi gaze as it is embodied in the eyes of the SS is explicitly described as sadistic. Sadism is a term which recurs in Gradowski's writings in relation to the Germans. It is linked not just with an objectifying way of seeing but also with duplicitousness. Dissembling of the kind perpetrated by the SS against the family camp—giving the appearance they were to be transported elsewhere to work—also links with how events are seen. The Nazis cultivate dishonest appearances that do not conform to reality.

In his earlier composition, Gradowski describes the Nazis as demons displaying 'cruel sadism' [*sadistishe akhzoryes*], he also already links sadism with dissimulation, discussing the 'refined sadistic means' [*rafinirte sadistishe metodn*] by which the Jews of Europe have been murdered.[112] Gradowski's narrator also refers to the 'diabolical, sadistic and cruel law' which has led the Jews to be expelled from their homes.[113] Upon arrival at Auschwitz, the narrator notes the heartlessness of the senior inmates: 'How can they be such sadists as to make fun of lonely broken people'.[114] Sadism therefore contaminates some of those interned in the camp, rendering them akin to the Nazis. In the context of the objectifying gaze as it is experienced by the woman Gradowski quotes, sadism is not solely associated with callousness but also accorded a sexual dimension. Cruelty as it is enacted in the field of vision by the SS possesses an erotic element.

For the woman, racism was clearly no barrier to sexual objectification. The SS men regard some of the female inmates as titillating, as pleasurable to look at. Nazi pseudo-science fostered fear in the Jewish body as inferior and unhealthy, as abject and disgusting. Here, however, anxiety towards Jewish women's bodies seems sidelined by fascination, even desire. This is not to argue that the Jewishness of the women was forgotten but rather that in the complex entanglement of racial and sexual violence which was played out in the camps, sexualized oppression sometimes overshadowed (rather than simply intersected with) racist brutality. Lisa Tickner describes how the 'image of woman as fetishized object' acts as a 'repository for male sexual fantasies and fears'.[115] In the camp, these fantasies and fears were always bound up with race and sex yet sometimes privileged one over the other.

The sadistic gaze in the specific circumstances Gradowski details was primarily felt by the woman as sexual in nature: she perceived her nude body as enticing, as tempting to the men. In this instance, it seems it is not solely the spectacle of naked humiliation that arouses the guards, it is seeing beautiful bodies humiliated that adds to the titillation. As with Müller's account of the death of Schillinger, the sadistic pleasure of the SS that the woman draws attention to would seem to be reliant upon looking at a Jewish woman's body as other than abject. It is a sexually appealing body rather than a racially abject body that is eroticized. Even if this is the case, for the SS there is a reassuring level of detachment at work: women remain the object of the gaze, appreciated for their physical appearance. The crematoria usually offered spaces where cruel pleasures derived from the contemplation of naked humiliation could occur uninterrupted. In this context, through denouncing the sadistic eye of her oppressors the woman in Gradowski's account refuses to be cowed and seeks to disrupt their voyeurism and to contest her objectification, affirming her individual subjectivity.

The woman's excoriating attack provided Gradowski with insight into how women experience the male gaze, a gaze that, in some respects, he shared with the SS men. Her understanding of sadism, with its erotic component, differs from someone such as Jean Améry. Améry thought the Nazis were not sadists 'in the narrow sexual-pathological sense', stating of his own experiences (including as an inmate in Auschwitz): 'I don't believe that I encountered a single genuine sadist of this sort during my two years of imprisonment by the Gestapo and in concentration camps'.[116] As a man, his experience of sadism, it seems, was qualitatively different from that of women. The woman's understanding of SS violence as possessing a sexual component is one that resonates with many survivor accounts of the concentration camp, something that is unsurprising given the Czech women had been interned in Auschwitz for six months.[117] This account, however, differs from survivor accounts in that it is not that of a named individual and is only one of several voices, each of which is folded into a broader literary work that seeks not only to archive these voices but also simultaneously to use them as a means by which to think through the psychology of the SS and of their victims.

In *In the Heart of Hell*, Gradowski was mulling the ethics of representation. His writing should be read as forming an effort to open a space where the violent gaze the woman identifies (and that he had already referenced earlier in the composition) could be resisted. The testimony embodies a sensitive response to sexual violence; it is saturated by a desire to look differently, to see beyond the framing effects of the SS's perception of Jewish women and outside the objectifying force of the male gaze as it is nurtured by patriarchy. As we have previously discussed, Gradowski's florid descriptions of the naked women, his noting of their desirability, provide a means to humanize them. He rejects a sadistic gaze but, despite his best efforts, he cannot entirely overcome the objectifying tendencies of patriarchal viewing dynamics. This is because his own way of seeing, his 'period eye', to borrow Michael Baxandall's term for the cognitive style of a given historical period, forms part of the problem.[118] He is trying to see a way through an ideology that structures his own mode of perception, subtending his gaze. This ideology is likely not solely linked to traditional Jewish articulations of sexual difference but also to broader cultural influences (as his repeated use of cinematic metaphors indirectly indicates). Gradowski's patriarchal outlook is, perhaps, clearest in his conception of resistance. The account of the Czech transport includes many examples of what we would name 'defiance' but which Gradowski, despite his best efforts, does not seem able to see as such.

The songs the women sing as they are being forced to their deaths are described by Gradowski in terms that render them a kind of acoustic attack on the SS, one with violent effects. He here imagines a particular reception (one he can have no direct knowledge of) in which the chorus hurts the SS. Through singing *The Internationale*, the women exploit German fears of Soviet military success. The sounds of this song pierce the guards like daggers, 'like barbs that stick in their hearts'. They force the SS to 'see the tragic and terrible reality' of their situation.[119] The women then go on to sing the Hatikva, the Czech national anthem and, even after the gas chamber is sealed, ballads of the partisans. It is clear that this singing, as well as potentially unnerving the Nazis, also deeply impacted the SK. It prompted Filip Müller, for example, to attempt suicide.[120] For Gradowski, nonetheless, it clearly does not constitute resistance. When he turns his attention to the murder of the men from the family camp, he says of the murder of the women that it went off without a hitch, 'with no struggle, no resistance'.[121] Gradowski seemingly only equates resistance with inflicting physical injury on the enemy. Tellingly he relates that there was no loss of life among the guards. For him, an incident such as the killing of Schillinger would have counted as real opposition to the SS. The passive resistance embodied in the singing, despite the mental turmoil Gradowski believes it causes the guards, does not. Nor, clearly, do the three slaps (delivered by the woman who gives the speech about the 'sadistic eye') visited on *Oberscharführer* Voss register as adequate defiance. The young girl who retrieves a scarf from the abandoned clothes and takes it into the gas chamber, who disobeys instructions, also does not resist.[122]

Gradowski is clearly struck by all these actions, he faithfully records them, appreciates them, but his too restrictive notion of resistance means he fails to fully recognize their power.[123] The women did not live up to the ideals of heroic masculinity that are central to Gradowski's conception of resistance. Eric Sundquist notes the deep admiration Gradowski expresses for the woman who killed Schillinger.[124] What differentiates this woman from the one who slaps Voss or the mother who earlier spits at the guards is that she takes a life.[125] Gradowski sees the actions of the Czech women—he recognizes, for example, their conscious cultivation of a way of seeing that is designed to refuse the sadistic gaze—yet his understanding of what he is witnessing is restricted by the limiting vision of resistance that he operates with. In his extended and nuanced consideration of resistance in peasant communities in Malaysia, James Scott suggests that because many acts of resistance fail it is wise to focus on intentions rather than consequences. Scott's discussion of the problems that inhere in distinguishing *real*, organized, consequential collective resistance from *token*, haphazard, inconsequential individual resistance is also pertinent here.[126] These distinctions—which can to some extent be mapped onto Gradowski's outlook regarding resistance—are too polarized. A more nuanced approach is necessary that recognizes physical resistance is not the only resistance worthy of the name. In fact, it is possible to admire the women's rejection of violent resistance, their refusal to conform to particular male ideas of what forms commendable defiance: the infliction of physical injury and death. Gradowski bears witness to this courageous resistance but his terms of reference leave him unable to name it or quite see it for what it is.

We believe that Langfus was in dialogue with this work by Gradowski when he composed 'The 3000 Naked Women'. By the time Langfus finished this text, Gradowski was already dead. He was one of the 460 Sonderkommando members whose deaths were recorded on the list that was deposited alongside Langfus's two compositions and Lewental's history of the revolt. As we discuss in *Matters of Testimony*, it is in 'The 3000 Naked Women' that Langfus writes of not wishing to observe the women (a group from Birkenau who had been confined in Block 25 without food for three weeks prior to being sent to the crematorium). The Yiddish word Langfus uses for 'observe' is *beobakhtet*, akin to the German word *beobachten* which can be used to refer to surveillance. Observing, for Langfus, is therefore potentially linked with a way of looking bound up with control. As we note, Langfus appears to be 'refusing certain ways of witnessing, *observing*, that might themselves be part of that system of crimes'.[127] Like Gradowski, he clearly recognizes that bearing witness requires attending carefully to how one sees. Langfus, however, does not seem to conceive observation as a mode of looking as expressing sexual violence. It is bound up with mastery, with enacting visual sovereignty over another, but not with lasciviousness. This is likely because, as a man, there are limits to his comprehension, he cannot know objectification as readily as a woman, only recognizing observation.[128]

'The 3000 Naked Women' also parallels the account of the murder of the Czech transport in *In the Heart of Hell* in that it examines an exchange of gazes. In Gradowski's account, the women refused to look the guards directly in the eye as a means to defend against their own objectification. Here, an expression of sympathy by a member of the SK, a recognition of the humanity of the women, prompts a lengthy speech by a young girl. In the speech—clearly perceived as important by Langfus—she bemoans how 'the sight of the worst horrors' no longer generates a reaction in most inmates. She also seems to find a modicum of solace in the sight of 'a man who feels'.[129] Langfus draws our attention to different ways of seeing in the crematorium, to the violence of observation and the succour of a look of compassion. The gaze that affirms subjectivity derives from a member of the SK but is described by a woman. As with Gradowski, it is a woman who thinks through the significance of a particular kind of looking, one that is here the opposite of sadistic.

Na'ama Shik has argued that 'in the reality of the camps, Jewish female inmates, like their male counterparts, inevitably internalized whatever conceptions the Nazi guards and other prisoners formed about them'.[130] The woman who berates the guards for their lascivious gaze in Gradowski's account, however, demonstrates that these conceptions did not always go unchallenged and were not uniformly embraced. The Czech woman in *In the Heart of Hell* vehemently opposes how the men see her. The woman, it bears repeating, was not a new arrival, she had been in the camp for many months. Her behaviour—and also the broader conduct of the Czech women as a group who collectively refuse to be objectified—demonstrates the need for a more granular approach to the experience of Jewish women at Auschwitz-Birkenau. Similarly, in Langfus's 'The 3000 Naked Women', a woman shows considerable awareness of viewing dynamics, here of how inmates commonly looked at each other: unfeelingly. She views this uncaring way of seeing negatively. We are able to achieve granularity, in part, through engaging critically with accounts such as Gradowski's and Langfus's, accounts the very limitations of which are in themselves revealing and of considerable historical interest.

Sadism

Our discovery that the archives of Yad Vashem hold the manuscript by Langfus which was found in 1952 (a document which we had previously thought lost) has enabled us to extend our engagement with this particular composition, exploring the importance not just of what Langfus has written but of decisions he made about content during the process of writing.[131] As Ika Willis notes, 'for some readers and in some acts of reading, the material properties of a text are framed as meaningless or as obstacles to meaning'.[132] We, however, believe that these material properties enrich our understanding of Langfus's text. There are visible additions and excisions in the original Langfus manuscript which are not reproduced in transcription yet which provide a valuable guide to some of the author's decision-making and which allow us to pinpoint passages he was particularly concerned about. The decisions we can now *see* in the original manuscript reinforce some of the readings of Langfus we advanced in *Matters of Testimony* and also enable us to refine them.

The manuscript consists of three distinct yet interrelated sections. The lengthiest section, titled 'Particulars', provides brief anecdotes about events in the crematoria. Our initial reading focussed in significant part on this section, which we interpreted as crafted to foster an emotional response in the reader rather than simply to convey information. In *Matters* we also detected a shift in tone in 'Particulars' that is at odds with the author's other writings, with Langfus now sometimes employing irony. Additionally, we also briefly examined the section 'Notes', which was written by Langfus shortly before he was killed. We read 'Notes' as foregrounding how important writing was to Langfus's sense of self. Our reading did not attend to the section entitled 'Sadism' which discusses not Auschwitz but events at Bełżec and Majdanek. Langfus had heard about these events second-hand from other members of the SK. Here, however, we want to consider all three sections and how they relate to each other.

In 'Particulars', we discerned a carefully crafted composition that drew parallels between distinct events, weaving patterns between occurrences rather than imposing a chronology. These patterns, we would suggest, are designed so Langfus can explore specific psychological themes through the details he has chosen, themes that include delusion, denial, resistance and sadism. The details from out of which Langfus composes this section are all examples of distinct human behaviours in the camps manifested by perpetrators and by victims. The account of 100 young men from Hungary brought to the crematorium to be shot, for instance, seems intended to foreground their naked humiliation. Studying the original manuscript it becomes clear the nakedness of the men was something Langfus wished to emphasize as strongly as possible. He describes how the men are made to undress and stand naked in the courtyard of Crematorium 1 (II). Langfus notes that each man's head was shaved but they had been left with 'only a stripe of hair running down the middle of their heads'.[133] The SS decide to move the men to Crematorium 2 (III). Oberscharführer Muhsfeldt is concerned the group may seek to escape to the nearby public road so he orders members of the Sonderkommando to form columns on either side of the path they must traverse. The men must 'guard the naked Jews', preventing them from fleeing: 'Thus, totally naked, they were rushed all the way like sheep with clubs waving over their heads'. This third and final reference to their nakedness was added to the account later. It is in smaller script. Clearly on rereading his description Langfus felt more emphasis needed to be placed on their being completely naked.

The theme of nakedness also recurs later in the account of a young woman from the Polish resistance, described as 'totally naked', who makes an impassioned speech prior to being gassed. In this account,

Langfus revisits the words of the speech that she directs specifically at the SK, subsequently adding the words we bracket here: 'Remember your sacred purpose is to avenge our innocent blood! [Tell the brothers of our people that] we are going to our death with pride and deep dedication'.[134] The addition seems to have been made in the interests of precision. She asks the Jewish men to tell her story and those of her companions to her Polish brethren. Langfus is here fulfilling her wish. He also makes a correction in the next line deleting the words '[the Poles] sang in unison'. This change, by contrast, seems informed by stylistic concerns. Langfus had recognized that a description of the Poles kneeling, praying and singing had become too convoluted. He later crosses out another phrase, 'well developed conscience' in a discussion of a rabbi whose naivete is exposed too late.[135] At the beginning of this story there is another addition made for reasons of accuracy. Langfus adds the word 'before' to 'end of summer 1943'.[136] Later he again seemingly corrects the words he attributes to a boy of seven or eight.[137] Cumulatively these subsequent changes to the text demonstrate the complexity of Langfus's approach to his writing, his multiple concerns. He recognizes the need to be precise, the responsibility he holds as a witness to get things right. He also finds it important to write well. These demands he places on his writing obviously sometimes intersect.

Langfus's changes register his forward-thinking, his effort to foresee how his compositions might be read and what details might be of importance for a future reader. This includes forthright testimony to sexual violence. In an unsparing but succinct account of sexual abuse perpetrated by Oberscharführer Voss (referred to as Forst by Langfus) he reworks a single sentence. His revision to the sentence, to the account, is included in square brackets:

> Oberscharführer Forst would stand [at the doorway of the undressing room] and feel the private parts of young women entering the gas bunker. There were also instances of SS men of all ranks pushing their fingers into the sexual organs of pretty young women.

Here Langfus keeps the account short; he knows what he needs to say and also that to say any more than that would be prurient. There is therefore, as so often in his writing, a remarkable ethical sensibility in operation here: a refusal to inflict textual violence on the women, to violate them a second time. In our discussion of Dario Gabbai's testimony in Chapter 6, we will examine how this kind of caution with words carries into some Sonderkommando survivor accounts of the crematoria. The words that Langfus does subsequently add to the account serve to situate Voss, to detail precisely where he carried out his crimes. There are several possible reasons for this addition. One is that Langfus is thinking ahead to how the account might be used (in a court of law, for instance) and therefore wants to be more specific. Another is that he feels including the exact location where this violation took place, not just in the undressing room (horrible enough) but on the very threshold of the gas chamber, at the portal to death, amplifies the callousness of the SS officer. The addition makes a horrific event even more atrocious. The women entered the gas chamber with feelings of violation, feelings very shortly replaced by the terror of impending and agonizing death.[138] The addition is minimal yet its effects are substantial. Langfus recognized the power of economy in use of language in a way that Gradowski, for instance, did not.

Although we detected a change in Langfus, a kind of growing cynicism in these final writings, a cynicism that manifests itself through the use of irony, there are also potentially continuities. Langfus retains his sense of ethical responsibility towards those he is writing about. In 'The Deportation', on a loose leaf of paper that forms a draft for the final section of that composition, Langfus crosses out a word because, we think, he came to view it as dehumanizing and therefore ethically negligent. In the section titled 'Sadism' of the later work, there is an account of Jews being dumped in pits and shot to death in a forest. Langfus initially writes 'they came with the trucks opened the tarpaulin and threw out packed full into [the pits]'.[139] He crosses out 'packed full' [*fiel gepakt*], however, and substitutes 'Jews'. 'Packed full' does not make grammatical sense and could be a transcription error linked with the preceding text but it also seems possible—as with 'The Deportation'—that Langfus feels his initial choice of language was too objectifying, reducing people to mere cargo, a simple load.[140] The change reinforces that these are people being dumped into the pits, Jewish people. Here upon rereading his initial account he may have recognized not just his grammatical error but also that he risks dehumanizing the people in the trucks and he therefore acts to avoid that. In a section exploring sadism, Langfus strives to avoid writing in a way that might be conceived of as sadistic.

The section 'Sadism' as it does not deal explicitly with Auschwitz might appear tangential, a curiosity. We think there is evidence, however, that Langfus viewed it as very important. The significance he accorded it is obscured by how the notebook is reproduced in transcription. Published versions impose a coherence on the manuscript which is lacking in the original. There are gaps of several pages between descriptions of events. This is a series of fragments even if there are continuities across the sections. Most notably, Langfus's instructions about what to do with his writings occur at the very end of the notebook yet in the Marks' version they are positioned just prior to the author's last words. In reality, Langfus's last words are towards the middle of the notebook, written adjacent to 'Sadism'. We would suggest this positioning was not haphazard but deliberate. The description of what to do with the writings was written the day before the final entry and occurs on what is now labelled page 64, the last page of the notebook. This entry was also carefully crafted, with Langfus initially writing that he has hidden 'The Deportation' in 'the pit of Crematorium 1' before then adding 'bone' to 'pit'.

It is clear from choosing to write these instructions at the end of the notebook that Langfus wanted to signal a kind of finality here. He knew his time was short and added this considered conclusion to the fragmented writings the notebook contains, deliberately skipping blank pages in order to write at the back. He wants his ending to be at the end. He probably does not think his own end will come for some days if not weeks as Crematorium 2 remains to be dismantled. Yet the next day he finds that he has been selected, that he is about to die. In this moment, he finds himself again wanting to write, to describe what is going on, to record the date that he will die in a few short, heartrendingly simple words. The lack of 'finish' to these final words powerfully brings home the condition of urgency in which they were composed. Langfus is nonetheless still collected. Something of the measure of this extraordinary man, a man soon to die, is held in the sharpness and neatness of the script, the continued control. Possibly it is the very act of writing that accords him this control, permitting him to keep his composure. Yet this final entry, made by tilting the notebook so the script is written horizontally, so it stands out, is not designed to affirm anything about writing's sustaining power.[141] Is it not by chance that Langfus appends this last textual trace of himself to the text titled 'Sadism'. 'Sadism' is the most abject of the writings in the notebook. It provides an account of events at Bełżec 'where the horrors and cruelty were even greater than those of Auschwitz'.

In 'Sadism' we think Langfus was engaging in a broader reflection on the psychology of the Nazis, one that looked beyond the confines of Birkenau. He is seeking to provide a psychological history. In *The Historian's Craft*, Marc Bloch notes the difficulty of his writing as a historian when the reading and research necessary for the practice of his profession are denied him in wartime. Bloch's book, which explores the nature of historiography, is marked by his historical circumstances, by the German occupation of French and his joining the French Resistance. In Langfus's 'Sadism' reflections on history are also combined with a living out of history. Bloch suggests that the historian is 'in the predicament of a police magistrate who strives to reconstruct a crime he has not seen'.[142] Langfus, however, writes from amid the horrors of the murders he describes. In 'Sadism', it seems he feels a need to draw back from that unmediated understanding of Nazi crimes, the better to gain insight into them. He therefore turns to events perpetrated elsewhere to think through his own situation.

Sadism is a word which features in many survivor accounts of the Shoah in relation to perpetrators. It is, however, usually employed without reflection. As with Gradowski's account of the Czech transport, that is not the case here. Langfus clearly feels that in order to understand sadism, a quality he sees as central to the Nazi worldview, he must look to a larger historical context than Birkenau. He consequently draws on testimonies of fellow SK members with experience of other camps who have witnessed what he plainly identifies as sadistic behaviour. Their accounts enable him to step outside his present and offer an indirect knowledge of past events, one that supplements his first-hand experience of atrocity. 'Sadism' provides condensed barbarism, short description of tremendous violence including shootings, electrocutions and excremental assaults.[143] In relation to the latter, Jewish inmates are described as being forced to shit on one of their own until he chokes to death. Langfus does not gloss his account, the events he describes are meant to show what sadism is.

Designed to act cumulatively, the descriptions 'think' through the nature of sadism. It seems that for Langfus, who is striving to understand Nazi psychology and to reflect on his situation, sadism came to mean something like it would subsequently for Elie Cohen. Sadism, for Cohen, meant the SS viewing the Jews as 'the scum of humanity'.[144] It meant the kind of seeing that the woman in 'The 3000 Naked Women' rails against, seeing without any trace of humanity. Sadism was seeing human beings as worthless shit, as utterly expendable. It was an aggression without limits that was enacted upon others who were perceived as abject.

This sadism seems qualitatively different to the 'sadistic eye' identified and experienced by the woman from the Czech family camp. It lacks the erotic dimension. Elsewhere, Gradowski does detail a conversation in which sadism is described in a way that seems closer to Langfus's conception: 'Oh, how terrible, how dreadful; can it be possible, can such brutality come to power? Can such sadism of --- to kill thousands, thousands of innocent people and to still have a place in the world?'.[145] Despite its fragmentary nature, the conversation seems to refer to sadism as a kind of baffling destructivity, one unchecked by moral qualms.

The two authors reveal that sadism as it was endured by victims was heterogeneous in nature. Sadism as it manifested through the Nazi gaze sometimes seems to have involved an erotic component linked with bodies seen as sexually desirable. The woman whose words are recorded by Gradowski calls the guards to account for their sadistic eye. She clearly feels theirs was a lecherous gaze. Langfus's description of the sexual violence perpetrated by Voss, by contrast, seems devoid of this kind of sexual motivation. The sadistic assaults Voss enacted upon women entering the gas chamber focussed on their genitalia only as a means to maximize cruelty. His treatment of the victims confirms he perceived them as abject. He found nothing about the women enticing (although he may have found pleasure in aggressing them). Their gender was simply something to capitalize on to enhance their humiliation.

Langfus's work titled 'Sadism' enables him to group together various events to demonstrate a pattern of behaviour that illustrates Nazi sadism. Through turning to past occurrences, he is simultaneously able to show something of the history of that sadism's emergence. Writing in 1944, he makes reference to incidents from 1940 to 1941. The sadism he discusses seems cultural, overarching. It is not linked with individual pathology. Sadism for Langfus (and, frequently, for Gradowski) is not a personality disorder. He therefore provides an early effort to reflect on the nature of Nazi sadism. Langfus consciously links his last words with 'Sadism' as he too is about to fall victim to this destructive behaviour. It is a behaviour characterized by the refusal to recognize Jewish lives as human lives, one that regularly draws upon practices of defilement for its symbolic expression.[146] He carefully positions his final entry so it becomes a coda to 'Sadism', a last instance of deliberate cruelty to be related. Langfus becomes his own example here, writing himself into the history and exploration of sadism he has been providing, offering himself as testament to its horrors.

Notes

1. This conforms to the post-war trial testimony of Alter Feinsilber.
2. Gradowski, *In Harts Fun Gehenem* (Tel Aviv: Wolnerman, n.d. [1977]), p. 55. A recent edition published by the Auschwitz museum finally brings both this manuscript and that published by Ber Mark together in a (nearly) complete English translation. Zalmen Gradowski, *From Heart of Hell: Manuscripts of a Sonderkommando Prisoner, Found in Auschwitz*, trans. Barry Smerin and Janina Wurbs (Oświęcim: Auschwitz-Birkenau State Museum, 2017). One short chapter from *In the Heart of Hell*, which was not published in the 1977 Yiddish edition, has so far only been published in the Hebrew translation of Gradowski's writings. It will also appear in Salmen Gradowski, *Die Zertrennung: Aufzeichnungen eines Mitglieds des Sonderkommandos*, trans. Almut Seiffert and Miriam Trinh, ed. Aurélia Kalisky (Frankfurt: Suhrkamp, 2020), forthcoming. See Aurélia Kalisky's introduction to that edition for a discussion of this chapter, which describes the clouds of smoke from the chimneys of Birkenau as bringing together the remains of the dead of the family camp. Thanks to Avichai Zur and Aurélia Kalisky for discussing this missing chapter with us.
3. The way that certain events recur in survivor accounts, events survivors often did not directly witness, demonstrates their importance as sustaining narratives for the inmates. As well as the killing of Schillinger, the SK revolt and the hangings of Auschwitz escapee Mala Zimetbaum and the women smugglers from the Union Factory often feature. All these events include acts of resistance and can be understood as nurturing thoughts of defiance in the prisoner population.
4. Haya Bar-Itzhak, 'Women in the Holocaust: The Story of a Jewish Woman Who Killed a Nazi in a Concentration Camp: A Folkloristic Perspective,' *Fabula* 50.1–2 (2009): 75.
5. Kirsty Chatwood, 'Schillinger and the Dancer: Representing Agency and Sexual Violence in Holocaust Testimonies,' in *Sexual Violence Against Jewish Women During the Holocaust*, eds. Sonja Hedgepeth and Rochelle Saidel (Waltham: Brandeis University Press, 2010), p. 62.
6. Zalman Lewental, 'Addendum to the Łódź Manuscript,' in *The Scrolls of Auschwitz*, trans. Sharon Neemani, ed. Ber Mark (Tel Aviv: Am Oved, 1985), pp. 236–240 and 238. Ber Mark, *Megiles Oyshvits* (Tel Aviv: Yisroel Bukh, 1977), p. 432.
7. Katerina Horovitz, Lola Lipmann, Regina Cukier and Nora Ney have also been suggested as being the woman in question. See Bar-Itzhak, 'Women in the Holocaust,' p. 71.

8. Hermann Langbein, *Against All Hope: Resistance in the Nazi Concentration Camps 1938–1945*, trans. Harry Zohn (New York: Paragon, 1994), p. 280.
9. Georges Wellers, 'Révolte du sonderkommando à Auschwitz,' *Le Monde juif* 18 (1949): 18.
10. Joan Ringelheim, *Double Jeopardy: Women and the Holocaust* [Draft for unpublished monograph], Joan Ringelheim Papers, USHMM Accession Number 2007.416.16. Box 3.
11. Bruno Bettelheim, *The Informed Heart* (London: Penguin, 1986), p. 265. Bettelheim is wrong to think of the woman as numbered. She was sent to the gas chamber directly from a transport and would not have received a tattooed number.
12. Ibid.
13. Bruno Bettelheim in Nyiszli, *Auschwitz: A Doctor's Eyewitness Account*, p. vi. It is notable too that Bettelheim places the story of the dancer immediately after that of the SK revolt in *The Informed Heart* (pp. 264–265).
14. Ringelheim, *Double Jeopardy*, p. 45.
15. Chatwood, 'Schillinger and the Dancer,' p. 63.
16. Ringelheim's emphasis. Ringelheim, *Double Jeopardy*, p. 45.
17. Ibid. In the margin, Irene Eber who read and commented on the manuscript has added a remark about social practices derived from stereotypes. She appears to imply that Bettelheim's understanding of active resistance is informed by stereotypes about masculine action and feminine passivity.
18. Ibid., 46.
19. Chatwood, 'Schillinger and the Dancer,' p. 72.
20. Ibid. Chatwood does not countenance that the woman's act might be understood as an example of counter-violence, as women's violence against violence against women. As Dianne Chisholm explains in her measured analysis of strategies of counter-violence, 'direct attack on male bodies has become a legitimate strategy of self-defense and survival for desperately battered women'. Chisholm, 'Violence Against Violence Against Women: An Avant-Garde for the Times,' in *The Last Sex: Feminism and Outlaw Bodies*, eds. Arthur Kroker and Marilouise Kroker (New York: St. Martin's Press, 1993), p. 35.
21. Ringelheim, *Double Jeopardy*, p. 46.
22. *Proceedings of the Conference on Women Surviving the Holocaust*, eds. Esther Katz and Joan Ringelheim (New York: Institute for Research in History, 1983), p. 48.
23. Ibid.

24. Catherine Hakim defines erotic capital as comprising various attributes including beauty, sexual attractiveness, social skills, liveliness, social presentation and sexual competence. Mann's performance manifests the attributes of liveliness and sexual attractiveness. Hakim links the latter with styles of physical comportment. For Hakim, erotic capital is an asset that can be developed and the possession of which can alter how a person is perceived and enhance how they are treated within a given society. See Catherine Hakim, *Erotic Capital: The Power of Attraction in the Boardroom and the Bedroom* (New York: Basic Books, 2011).
25. Ibid., 48. Vladka Meed, who spoke at the *Women Surviving the Holocaust* conference that Ringelheim organized, suggests that 'if a woman was young and good-looking, it would be easier for her to face the danger of coming across a Gestapo person; she would be able to get out of it'. *Proceedings of the Conference on Women Surviving the Holocaust*, p. 81.
26. David Roskies contrasts the extensive description of the murder of the Czech family camp with the two brief discussions of resistance which prefigure it yet these earlier accounts of resistance need to be read as performing a vital layering-in of the theme of defiance and as forming part of a compositional continuum. Roskies, 'Wartime Victim Writing in Eastern Europe,' in *Literature of the Holocaust*, ed. Alan Rosen (Cambridge: Cambridge University Press, 2013), p. 30.
27. Mark, *Megiles Oyshvits*, p. 432. The Yiddish reads: 'a yudishe yunge [f]roy'. Here the contingent smudge that renders the word 'woman' only partially legible works to visually figure the kind of gender related complexity the woman's attack on Schillinger provokes. She at once affirms and calls her 'femininity' into question through the confrontation.
28. Filip Müller, *Eyewitness Auschwitz: Three Years in the Gas Chambers*, trans. Susanne Flatauer (Chicago: Ivan R. Dee, 1999), pp. 87–88. Translation amended with ref to: Filip Müller, *Sonderbehandlung: Drei Jahre in den Krematorien und Gaskammern von Auschwitz*, literary collaboration with Helmut Freitag (Munich: Steinhausen, 1979), pp. 137–138.
29. It is possible, although by no means certain, that writing in this way resulted from the influence of Helmut Freitag, who was Müller's 'literary collaborator'. Müller's version is the one adopted by Halivni who writes that a 'beautiful and agile' woman attracted the attention of Quackernack and Schillinger. While they were 'ogling her she launched a titillating seductive strip-tease act'. Tziporah Hager Weiss Halivni Papers. USHMM. Accession Number 2013.529.1. Unpublished manuscript, p. 53.

30. A similar mode of attack features in the comedy horror film *Elvira: Mistress of the Dark* (Dir. James Signorelli, USA, 1988) in which Elvira (Cassandra Peterson) impales the warlock Vincent Talbot (W. Morgan Sheppard) in the forehead with one of her high heels. *Elvira* as parody amplifies anxieties about female sexuality and empowerment that are played out in more straight horror films. Given the long-standing phallic connotations of high heels, similar kinds of anxiety may potentially be at work in Müller's account. That the woman wears high heels in Müller's account is, of course, also revealing. She is figured as embodying a particular kind of femininity, framed already as liberal in outlook, as a different vision of womanhood from that of many of the young women sent to their deaths at Auschwitz. High heels have traditionally been interpreted as signifying both eroticism and female empowerment. See Claudia Wobovnik, 'These Shoes Aren't Made for Walking: Rethinking High-Heeled Shoes as Cultural Artefacts,' *Visual Culture and Gender* 8 (2013): 82–92.
31. Martha McCaughey explicitly uses the term 'physical feminism' in *Real Knockouts* to describe how women's self-defence can be conceived as a feminist practice. Leslie Heywood's conception of women's bodybuilding as a third wave feminist practice played out through the flesh also merits mention in this context as does Elizabeth Grosz's idea of corporeal feminism, with its emphasis on the plasticity of bodies and on the body's sometimes capacity to live in excess of cultural expectations about it. See Elizabeth Grosz, *Volatile Bodies: Toward a Corporeal Feminism* (Bloomington: Indiana University Press, 1994), Leslie Heywood, *Bodymakers: A Cultural Anatomy of Women's Bodybuilding* (New Brunswick: Rutgers University Press, 1998), and Martha McCuaghey, *Real Knockouts: The Physical Feminism of Women's Self-Defense* (New York: New York University Press, 1997).
32. Ya'akov Silberberg only observes that the woman overpowered an SS man and does not go into specifics. He does mention that she was 'a dancer, a beautiful woman'. Gideon Greif, *We Wept Without Tears*, p. 325. Whether the woman used her stiletto, her bra or her knickers, it is clear that she improvised a weapon. For a discussion of improvisation in relation to women's self-defence, see Paxton Quigley, *Stayin' Alive: Armed and Female in an Unsafe World* (Bellevue: Merrill Press, 2005), pp. 22–23.
33. Nencel, however, does not claim to have witnessed the actual shooting, only the woman striking the unnamed SS man in the face 'with her panties', an act to which the Nazi did not react. When questioned as to why the Nazi didn't retaliate, Nencel says: 'He didn't react it. He didn't react it. Or he enjoyed looking on her, on a

beautiful woman body. He didn't react it'. David Nencel interviewed by Joe Russin in 1996. USHMM Accession Number 2003.76. RG-50.560.001. Tape 9. 16:30–21:00. In his account, Dragon claims that Schillinger died in the undressing room whereas it is accepted that he died on the way to hospital (as Müller recollects).

34. Sarah Cushman, *The Women of Birkenau*, PhD thesis, Worcester, MA: Clark University, 2010, p. 257.
35. Doris Bergen, 'Sexual Violence in the Holocaust: Unique and Typical?' in *Lessons and Legacies VII: The Holocaust in International Perspective*, ed. Dagmar Herzog (Evanston: Northwestern University Press, 2006), p. 182.
36. Ya'akov Gabbai, for instance, writes of keeping a diary from the day he started in the SK (15 May 1944) until the evacuation of Auschwitz. It ran to roughly 500 pages. He abandoned it when he left the camp. Greif, *We Wept Without Tears*, pp. 193–194. Dov Paisikovic told Hermann Langbein of a notebook he buried in the grounds of the crematoria which included details about his experiences in the SK including the names of SS members who oversaw the gassings. Langbein felt that if the notebook could be found it provides valuable evidence of Nazi crimes at the impending Frankfurt trial (or he used the trial as a pretext to encourage a search for the artefact). Letter from Hermann Langbein to the Auschwitz Museum dated 8 November 1962. See our discussion of how Paisikovic's diary was mentioned in the Frankfurt Auschwitz Trial in Chapter 4.
37. Chare and Williams, *Matters of Testimony*, pp. 1–5.
38. See, for instance, our discussion in the next chapter of photographs buried by the SK.
39. The author of the list is unknown. In *Matters of Testimony* we speculate that because of the idiosyncratic Polish it may be by Lewental. According to Halivni in testimony given shortly after liberation by Lemke (called 'Leite' by Halivni) Pliszko and Avraham Beril Tokol, others who kept lists were Zalman Gradowski, David Nencel (referred to as 'David Gensil from Ripin'), Leyb Langfus, a man referred to only by his surname of Warszawski, and a man referred to only by his forename of Leon (who is described as a Polish Jew deported from France and therefore was likely Leon the cook). Of these people, Gradowski was dead by the time the list in question was written. Langfus and Nencel were definitely alive. Tziporah Hager Weiss Halivni Papers. Box 18. File 1, sheet of printer paper numbered 2.
40. Joan Ringelheim, 'Women and the Holocaust: Taking Numbers into Account' [Unpublished Paper delivered at the Women and Society Seminar, Columbia University, 16 January 1986] USHMM Joan Ringelheim Papers Accession Number 2007.416.16. Box 3. File 3, p. 5.

41. As part of his thoughtful exploration of the observance of memory, Marquard Smith describes lists of the names of the dead from the Shoah as serving both referential and symbolic functions. The SK list includes no names but is similarly simultaneously informational and commemorative. See Smith, 'Observance, Notes Towards Decipherability,' *Journal of Visual Culture* 17.1 (2018): 90.
42. For a discussion of the authorship of these two compositions, see Chare and Williams, *Matters of Testimony*, p. 96. In her discussion of the Scrolls in *Women in the Holocaust*, Zoe Waxman, following Gideon Greif's lead, attributes 'The 600 Boys' to Zalman Lewental. Waxman, *Women in the Holocaust: A Feminist History* (Oxford: Oxford University Press, 2017), p. 85.
43. Zalman Gradowski, 'Writings,' in *The Scrolls of Auschwitz*, ed. Ber Mark, p. 175.
44. The narrator is phantom-like, a ghostly presence summoned by the author to guide his readers. This narrator is shaped by Gradowski's perspectives but should not be read as equivalent to him.
45. The attribution of this letter to Chaim Herman by the Auschwitz museum has recently been challenged by Andreas Kilian, who provides evidence that it was written by Herman Strasfogel. Andreas Kilian, 'Abschiedsbrief aus dem Krematorium: das verschollene Original und sein anonymer Verfasser,' *Mitteilungsblatt der Lagergemeinschaft Auschwitz / Freundeskreis der Auschwitzer* 38.1 (2018): 5–21. For further discussion of the letter by Strasfogel and also that of Marcel Nadjary, see Nicholas Chare, Ersy Contogouris and Dominic Williams, 'Disinterred Words: The Letters of Marcel Nadjary and Herman Strasfogel,' in *Testimonies of Resistance: Representations of the Auschwitz-Birkenau Sonderkommando*, eds. Nicholas Chare and Dominic Williams (New York: Berghahn, 2019), in press.
46. Nathan Cohen, 'Diaries of the Sonderkommandos,' in *Anatomy of the Auschwitz Death Camp*, eds. Yisrael Gutman and Michael Berenbaum (Bloomington: Indiana University Press, 1994), pp. 522–534.
47. Susan Pentlin, 'Testimony from the Ashes: Final Words from the Auschwitz-Birkenau Sonderkommando,' in *The Genocidal Mind*, eds. Dennis Klein et al. (St. Paul: Paragon, 2005), p. 260.
48. Ana Firoiu and Fleur Kuhn, '*Au coeur de l'enfer* de Zalman Gradowski: expérience collective et subjectivité dans le témoignage immédiat,' in *La psychologie de masse, aujourd'hui*, eds. Michel Gad Wolkowitz et al. (Paris: Des Rosiers, 2012), pp. 81–104. See also Fleur Kuhn-Kennedy, '"Écoute, mon ami, ce qui se passe ici": Autour de Zalmen Gradowski et du témoignage comme espace d'interlocution,' *Plurielles* 20 (2017): 63–70.

49. Zoë Waxman, *Writing the Holocaust: Identity, Testimony, Representation* (Oxford: Oxford University Press, 2006), pp. 81–85.
50. Waxman mistakenly believes Gradowski wrote in Russian, Polish, German and French. Although Gradowski prefaced one of his manuscripts with messages in those languages, his accounts are in Yiddish. Waxman also asserts that Gradowski's manuscript *In the Heart of Hell*, which she quotes from using a translation by David Roskies, was discovered in 1962 when it was actually discovered in 1945. Waxman, *Women in the Holocaust*, p. 81.
51. Women in the Family Camp were not subject to a selection on their arrival and did not have their hair shaved. See Ruth Bondy, 'Women in Theresienstadt and Birkenau,' in *Women in the Holocaust*, eds. Dalia Ofer and Lenore J. Weitzman (New Haven: Yale University Press, 1998), p. 324.
52. See, for example, Anna Pawełczyńska, *Values and Violence in Auschwitz: A Sociological Analysis*, trans. Catherine S. Leach (Berkeley: University of California Press, 1979).
53. Pascale Rachel Bos, 'Women and the Holocaust: Analyzing Gender Difference,' in *Experience and Expression: Women, Nazis, and the Holocaust*, eds. Elizabeth R. Baer and Myrna Goldenberg (Detroit: Wayne State University Press, 2003), p. 27.
54. *Proceedings of the Conference on Women Surviving the Holocaust*, p. 127.
55. For a summary of the development of research into women's experiences of the Holocaust, see Waxman, *Women in the Holocaust*, pp. 2–19.
56. Margaret-Anne Hutton, *Testimony from the Nazi Camps: French Women's Voices* (Abingdon: Routledge, 2005), p. 103.
57. Sara R. Horowitz, 'Women in Holocaust Literature,' in *Women in the Holocaust*, eds. Dalia Ofer and Lenore J. Weitzman (New Haven: Yale University Press, 1998), p. 370.
58. Karyn Ball, 'Unspeakable Differences, Obscene Pleasures: The Holocaust as an Object of Desire,' *Women in German Yearbook* 19 (2003): 20.
59. See, for example, Sonja M. Hedgepeth's and Rochelle G. Saidel's ground-breaking collection of essays, *Sexual Violence Against Jewish Women During the Holocaust* (Lebanon: Brandeis University Press, 2010).
60. Maddy Carey, *Jewish Masculinity in the Holocaust* (London: Bloomsbury, 2017). Earlier treatments of the constructions of masculinity of concentration camp prisoners can be found in Kim Wünschmann, 'Männlichkeitskonstruktionen jüdischer Häftlinge in NS-Konzentrationslagern,' in *Männlichkeitskonstruktionen im Nationalsozialismus: Formen, Funktionen und Wirkungsmacht von Geschlechterkonstruktionen im Nationalsozialismus und ihre Reflexion*

in pädagogischen Praxis, eds. Anette Dietrich and Ljiljana Heise (Frankfurt: Peter Lang, 2013), pp. 201–219 and Maja Suderland, 'Männliche Ehre und menschliche Würde. Über die Bedeutung der Männlichkeitskonstruktionen in der sozialen Welt der nationalsozialistische Konzentrationslager,' in *Prekäre Transformationen: Pierre Bourdieus Soziologie der Praxis und ihre Herausforderungen für die Frauen- und Geschlechterforschung*, eds. Ulla Bock, Irene Dölling, and Beate Krais (Göttingen: Wallstein, 2007), pp. 118–140.

61. What Raewyn Connell has noted of masculinity in general, that it is pluriform and thereby that it is necessary to speak of masculinities, is also true of the SK at Birkenau. Their experience of masculinity was not homogenous. See R. W. Connell, *Masculinities*, 2nd ed. (Cambridge: Polity, 2005).
62. Daniel Boyarin, *Unheroic Masculinity: The Rise of Heterosexuality and the Invention of Jewish Man* (Berkeley: University of California Press, 1997), p. 23n71.
63. Carey, *Jewish Masculinity in the Holocaust*, p. 8.
64. It is also clear that the ghettoes were conceived by many living within them as forming an experience without precedent. The ghettoes therefore potentially had a major impact on traditional social units and practices, one distinct from the camps yet no less significant in its effects. As part of his current research project 'The Genealogy of the Ghetto', for example, Daniel Schwartz has found Jewish communities in the ghetto struggled to find historical precedents which they could draw upon to articulate their experiences and use to make sense of their environment.
65. Kimberlé Williams Crenshaw, 'Mapping the Margins: Intersectionality, Identity, Politics, and Violence Against Women of Colour,' *Stanford Law Review* 43.6 (1991): 1241–1299.
66. Claudette Bloch, 'Les femmes à Auschwitz,' in *Témoignages sur Auschwitz* (Paris: Éditions de l'amicale des déportés d'Auschwitz, 1946), p. 22.
67. Vera Laska, 'Auschwitz: A Factual Deposition,' in *Women in the Resistance and in the Holocaust: The Voices of Eyewitnesses*, ed. Laska (Westport: Greenwood Press, 1983), p. 174.
68. Ella Lingens-Reiner, *Prisoners of Fear* (London: Victor Gollancz, 1948), p. 122.
69. Cited in Peter Kozman, 'I Could Hold onto That Camera…,' in *We Saw the Holocaust*, ed. Monika Vrzgulová (Bratislava: Milan Šimečka Foundation, 2005), p. 34.
70. Olga Lengyel, *Five Chimneys: A Woman Survivor's True Story of Auschwitz* (Chicago: Academy Chicago Publishers, 1995), pp. 103–104
71. Lingens-Reiner, *Prisoners of Fear*, p. 122.

72. Given the reference to warehouses, these men may well have worked in Kanada. Gisella Perl, *I Was a Doctor in Auschwitz* (New York: Arno Press, 1979), p. 78.
73. *Proceedings of the Conference on Women Surviving the Holocaust*, p. 142.
74. Leon Welbel interviewed by Phyllis Dreazen on 30 March 1995. USC Shoah Foundation. Interview Code 1770. Segment 98.
75. The memory of this occurrence is triggered when Pardo recounts being part of a mixed work detail at Sachsenhausen after having left Birkenau but there is some ambiguity as to where the sexual acts he witnessed took place. USHMM Accession Number 1995.A.1261.201. RG Number RG-50.431.0781. David Pardo interviewed by Nancy Solomon on 12 May 1998. 1:39.03.
76. Susan Eisdorfer interviewed by Randy Goldman on 16 May 1995. USHMM RG-50.030.0326. Tape 7. 7:31:58.
77. Pawełczyńska, *Values and Violence in Auschwitz*, p. 98.
78. Henry Levy interviewed by Shelly Roberts on 10 February 1997. USC Shoah Foundation. Interview Code 26580. Tape 4. Segment 22, 24:30.
79. Lengyel, *Five Chimneys*, p. 197.
80. Ringelheim, *Double Jeopardy*, p. 65. See also Ringelheim, 'Women and the Holocaust: A Reconsideration of Research,' *Signs* 10.4 (1985): 745.
81. Kitty Hart, *Return to Auschwitz* (Frogmore: Granada Publishing, 1983), p. 78.
82. Pawełczyńska, *Values and Violence in Auschwitz*, p. 98.
83. Ringelheim, *Double Jeopardy*, p. 65.
84. See Robert Sommer, '*Pipels:* Situational Homosexual Slavery of Young Adolescent Boys in Nazi Concentration Camps,' pp. 86–101. Sommer provides specific examples of testimony relating to *pipels* in Auschwitz.
85. Bos, 'Women and the Holocaust,' p. 33.
86. Doris Bergen, 'Sexual Violence in the Holocaust: Unique and Typical?' p. 189.
87. Kitty Hart-Moxon, *Return to Auschwitz*, p. 163.
88. Erna Low, 'I Was in Oswiecim,' Unpublished manuscript, circa 1952. USHMM Accession number 2017.466.1, p. 7.
89. Irene Weiss interviewed by Ileane Kenney on 26 July 1996. USC Shoah Foundation. Interview Code 17212. Tape 5, 26:15.
90. Judy F. interviewed by Robert Prince and Susanna Neumann on 31st October 1982. Fortunoff Video Archive for Holocaust Testimonies. HVT-211. Tape 2. Segment 25, 7:22.
91. Ringelheim, *Double Jeopardy*, p. 48.
92. 'Protokół [Official Record]—Shlomo Dragan,' Proces Rudolfa Hoessa, Sygn. GK 196/93, NTN 93, Volume 11, 1946–1947. USHMM Accession Number 1998.A.0243. RG Number RG-15.167M, p. 10 (p. 111).

93. Bergen, 'Sexual Violence in the Holocaust,' p. 187.
94. Ibid., p. 180.
95. Helene Sinnreich, '"And It Was Something We Didn't Talk About": Rape of Jewish Women During the Holocaust,' *Holocaust Studies* 14.2 (2008): 2.
96. David Pardo interviewed by Nancy Salomon on 12 May 1998, USHMM Accession Number 1995.A.1261.201. RG-50.431.0781 1:08:22
97. Abe Korn, 'Fate,' Unpublished manuscript, c1969. USHMM Collection Number RG-02.191, pp. 96–98.
98. Zalman Gradowski, *In Harts Fun Gehenem* (Tel Aviv: Wolnerman, n.d.), pp. 68–81.
99. Joan Ringelheim, 'The Split Between Gender and the Holocaust,' in *Women in the Holocaust*, eds. Ofer and Weitzman, p. 345.
100. Gradowski, *In Harts Fun Gehenem*, p. 73.
101. Pollock, 'Killing Men and Dying Women,' in *Avant-Gardes and Partisans Reviewed*, eds. Fred Orton and Griselda Pollock (Manchester: Manchester University Press, 1996), p. 241.
102. Griselda Pollock, *Encounters in the Virtual Feminist Museum: Time, Space and the Archive* (Abingdon: Routledge, 2007), p. 109.
103. Gradowski, *In Harts Fun Gehenem*, pp. 70, 101–102.
104. Waxman, *Women in the Holocaust*, p. 88. In Poland, observant women often wore wigs or, when these were prohibited, kerchiefs, hats and berets. See Shimon Huberband, *Kiddush Hashem: Jewish Religious and Cultural Life in Poland During the Holocaust*, trans. David E. Fishman (New York: Yeshiva University Press, 1987), p. 213.
105. Henry Krystal, 'Resilience: Accommodation and Recovery,' in *Living with Terror, Working with Trauma: A Clinician's Handbook*, ed. Danielle Knafo (Lanham: Jason Aronson, 2004), p. 77. Krystal's essay also emphasizes the importance of forming temporary alliances to survive in the camps, using the community formed by the Auschwitz-Birkenau SK as a prime example. The Scrolls of Auschwitz are a continual point of reference for Krystal in his efforts to theorize how some inmates in concentration camps (he does not differentiate between the concentration camps and death camps in terms of their psychological impact) developed resilience. Krystal also makes reference to the Scrolls in his essay 'What Cannot Be Remembered or Forgotten,' in *Loss of the Assumptive World: A Theory of Traumatic Loss*, ed. Jeffrey Kauffman (New York: Brunner-Routledge, 2002), p. 215.
106. For a discussion of this issue, see Hutton, *Testimony from the Nazi Camps*, pp. 28–30.
107. Gradowski, *In Harts Fun Gehenem*, p. 78.
108. Rosa Joseph's description of her grandmother's behaviour when forced to strip and shower at Bergen Belsen is revealing in this context. Joseph

recalls that her grandmother 'who was an older lady [...] was walking around completely naked right in front of the German soldier as if nothing was happening'. Here, the grandmother refuses to be intimidated, to register humiliation, resisting the violent dynamic encouraged by the situation. Rosa Joseph interviewed by Milene Modiano on 20 February 1998. USC Shoah Foundation. Interview Code 38714. Tape 3. Segment 87, 26:39. It is possible these moments of resistance to the sadistic gaze of the Nazis are sometimes overlooked in artistic survivor testimonies of the camps. In a discussion of sexual humiliation in Naomi Judkowski's 'Cugangi' (The New Inmates), Mor Presiado reads the impassive facial expressions of naked women confronted by an SS guard as they wait to be shaved at Auschwitz as symptomatic of the artist's dissociation, as embodying a traumatic defence mechanism. It is possible, however, that this group of women refused to display signs of their distress, resisting Nazi efforts at intimidation.

109. Gradowski, *In Harts Fun Gehenem*, p. 79.
110. Ibid.
111. Ibid., p. 80.
112. Mark, *Megiles Oyshvits*, p. 289.
113. Ibid., p. 304.
114. *Megiles Oyshvits*, p. 333.
115. Lisa Tickner, 'The Body Politic: Female Sexuality and Women Artists Since 1970,' in *Framing Feminism: Art and the Women's Movement, 1970–1985*, eds. Rozsika Parker and Griselda Pollock (London: Pandora, 1987), p. 269.
116. Jean Améry, *At the Mind's Limits*, trans. Sidney Rosenfeld and Stella P. Rosenfeld (London: Granta, 1999), p. 34.
117. Ruth Elias, for example, reported to Claude Lanzmann that SS men made young women stay in Block 6 of the Family Camp and frequently came in and raped them. https://collections.ushmm.org/film_findingaids/RG-60.5003_01_trs_en.pdf, pp. 33–34. This testimony was also included in *The Hippocratic Oath*, the first film of the *Four Sisters* series (2017).
118. Michael Baxandall, *Painting and Experience in Fifteenth-Century Italy*, 2nd ed. (Oxford: Oxford University Press, 1988), pp. 29–108.
119. Gradowski, *In Harts Fun Gehenem*, p. 82.
120. See our discussion of Müller's account of this moment in *Shoah* in Chapter 7.
121. Gradowski, *In Harts Fun Gehenem*, p. 94.
122. Ibid., p. 76.
123. Ana Firoiu and Fleur Kuhn suggest ('Au cœur de l'enfer,' pp. 84 and 93–94) that in Gradowski's writings there are echoes of the story of

Esther, the Jewish heroine who saved the Persian Jewish population from annihilation. Esther's heroism, however, was rhetorical in nature. She argued on behalf of the Jewish people rather than taking up arms. If Esther was a template for Gradowski, a precursor he had in mind, he would have been better able to appreciate the acts of resistance of the Czech women.

124. Eric Sundquist, 'The Historian's Anvil, the Novelist's Crucible,' in *Literature of the Holocaust*, ed. Alan Rosen (Cambridge: Cambridge University Press, 2013), p. 262.
125. Gradowski, *In harts fun Gehenem*, p. 79.
126. James C. Scott, *Weapons of the Weak: Everyday Forms of Peasant Resistance* (New Haven: Yale University Press, 1985), pp. 290–292.
127. Chare and Williams, *Matters of Testimony*, p. 110.
128. This effort to refuse to engage in oppressive ways of seeing raises interesting questions about the nature of Langfus's masculinity. As part of his exploration of Jewish masculinities, Daniel Boyarin contrasts what he identifies as *mentsh* masculinity with the dominant strain of masculinity in European culture which he associates with activity, domination and aggressiveness. *Mentsh* as a Jewish male ideal is associated with delicacy and gentleness. Boyarin traces the genealogy of the *mentsh* to meditations on the ideal male in the Talmud. He links this ideal with masochism as passivity. Masochism is read positively by Boyarin as 'a politically significant form of resistance to phallic imaginations of maleness and imperial power' (p. 82). Maddy Carey has criticized Boyarin for offering a vision of a religious, feminized masculinity for which there is a paucity of evidence for its practical existence. For Carey, independent Jewish normative masculinity of the period involved a love of family and a pride in ancestry but not a radical passivity. Langfus, however, potentially provides an example of a consciously cultivated passivity manifested through his reflections on the (male) gaze that conforms in some ways to Jewish masochism as Boyarin outlines it. For Boyarin's discussion of Jewish masochism, see *Unheroic Conduct*, pp. 81–126.
129. Langfus, 'Di 3000 nakete,' *Megiles Oyshvits*, p. 367.
130. Na'ama Shik, 'Sexual Abuse of Jewish Women in Auschwitz-Birkenau,' in *Brutality and Desire: War and Sexuality in Europe's Twentieth-Century*, ed. Dagmar Herzog (Basingstoke: Palgrave Macmillan, 2009), p. 241.
131. Yad Vashem, Item ID 3728415, File No: 2674. Yad Vashem advised us that the manuscript was donated to them by Esther Mark in 1990. Our understanding of the significance of the materiality of the manuscript as a register of the historical moment of its production is indebted to Gabrielle Spiegel's foregrounding of literary texts as material

embodiments of situated language. See Gabrielle M. Spiegel, 'History, Historicism and the Social Logic of the Text in the Middle Ages,' *Speculum* 65 (1990): 84–85.
132. Ika Willis, *Reception* (London: Routledge, 2018), p. 146.
133. *Megiles Oyshvits*, pp. 352–353.
134. Translation amended.
135. We discuss some of the changes to this anecdote in *Matters of Testimony*, p. 113.
136. This 'before', used to qualify a temporal moment, is included in the 1977 Hebrew edition but not the English translation.
137. Adds 'among', p. 208.
138. Shlomo Venezia describes how even once inside the gas chamber victims were subjected to further mental torment prior to their murder: 'The German whose job it was to control the whole process often enjoyed making these people, who were about to die, suffer a bit more. While waiting for the arrival of the SS man who was going to release the gas, he amused himself by switching the light on and off to frighten them a little more'. Venezia, *Inside the Gas Chambers*, p. 67.
139. Translation amended.
140. We are grateful to Emil Kerenji for suggesting the potential ethical motivation for this change.
141. Amos Goldberg has argued that autobiographical writing 'is, in its most extreme moments, an attempt to recount symbolic death and thereby overcome it, if only very partially' (p. 79). He reads such writing as offering a kind of resurrection. In this moment of extreme, however, Langfus seems to be striving to symbolize his soon to be literal death and to link that death with his reflections on Nazi cruelty. Langfus's text therefore reveals the dangers of generalizing about writing during the Holocaust. See Goldberg, *Trauma in First Person* (Bloomington: Indiana University Press, 2017), p. 79.
142. Marc Bloch, *The Historian's Craft*, trans. Peter Putnam (New York: Vintage, 1953), p. 48.
143. Terrence Des Pres explores the phenomenon of 'excremental assault' in *The Survivor*. He makes mention of Auschwitz as part of his analysis. Des Pres, *The Survivor: An Anatomy of Life in the Death Camps* (Oxford: Oxford University Press, 1976), p. 61.
144. Elie A. Cohen, *Human Behaviour in the Concentration Camp* (London: Free Association Books, 1988), p. 251.
145. *Megiles Oyshvits*, p. 336.
146. For a discussion of abjection as it intersects with Nazism's genocidal policies, see Chare, *Auschwitz and Afterimages*.

CHAPTER 3

Tragic Pictures: The Sonderkommando and Their Photographs

INTRODUCTION: ON ATTRIBUTION

Sometime in August 1944, a member of the Auschwitz-Birkenau Sonderkommando, a Greek Jew usually referred to simply as Alex, aided by Abraham Dragon (also Dragan), Shlomo Dragon (also Szlama Dragan), Alter Feinsilber (also Fajnzylberg) and David Szmulewski, took at least four photographs of Crematorium 4 (V) and its environs.[1] These photographs have prompted important critical responses from, among others, Georges Didi-Huberman and Dan Stone.[2] The images are crucial as they were taken as an act of resistance, intended to secure evidence of Nazi crimes, rather than by perpetrators as mementoes of mass death.[3] The photographs have circulated in a variety of contexts since their production, a history explored by Andreas Kilian.[4] As early as 1946–1947, two of the images (albeit after having been cropped) featured as evidence in the trial of Rudolf Höss.[5] More recently, the four photographs are integral to Gerhard Richter's series of artworks known collectively as *Birkenau* (2014) which, although abstract in appearance, developed from out of the images and are exhibited alongside reproductions of them.[6] A scene in the film *Son of Saul* (Dir. László Nemes, Hungary, 2015), in which members of the SK clandestinely photograph the burning of corpses, is also inspired by the pictures.

Drawing on a letter written by Feinsilber in 1978, Alban Perrin suggests that the photographs were taken by the Greek Sonderkommando member Alberto Errera, who was heavily involved in the resistance movement at Auschwitz-Birkenau.[7] In the letter, Feinsilber claimed not to know the identity of the photographer other than that his name was Alex and that he was Greek but he does mention an escape attempt Alex made which conforms in some details to one made by Errera. Errera had adopted the assumed name Alekos (Alex) Michaelides prior to his capture and deportation to Auschwitz.[8] He was well known by members of the Sonderkommando for overpowering two guards while on a work party and then attempting to escape by swimming the Vistula. Errera was likely shot and injured while in the river and was apprehended shortly afterwards. His body, severely mutilated, was put on display so other members of the SK would know what awaited them if they tried to flee. In notebooks written shortly after the war, Feinsilber discusses Errera's escape although he does not attribute the photographs to him. He also insisted that the images were a group project: 'even though the Greek Jew, Alex, was the person who pressed the shutter, one can say that the pictures were taken by all of us'.[9]

Given the vagaries of memory, particularly the issue of suggestibility, the later testimony pointing towards Errera as the photographer cannot be viewed as definitive (although Perrin regards it as such) but it is credible.[10] Perrin is firm in his belief that he has returned the photographs to their rightful author, correcting a historical error: the images were taken not by an anonymous Greek but by a hero of the resistance, forming a deed that adds to Errera's already celebrated exploits. Here, however, we will continue to refer to the photographs as by Alex.[11] This is in part because if they are by Errera he still took them while known as Alex—while living under a pseudonym—a reality that is significant and speaks of their context of production. Another motivation is the possibility that Perrin is mistaken and that Alex was the photographer's real name, he was indeed an anonymous member of the SK, and the four images remain the only traces of him.[12]

Rarely have images been burdened with representing so much, even if provisos and qualifiers about their limits as visual testimony are usually provided by those who analyse them.[13] The photographs are often discussed as efforts to attest to genocide, considered in terms of their success or failure as evidence and/or memorial.[14] In this chapter, we also examine the images as forms of remembrance, particularly in relation to the idea of postmemory as it is understood by Marianne Hirsch. To do this, we situate the photographs in relation to broader ideas about testimony and remembrance articulated by members of the SK in the Scrolls of Auschwitz. These ideas are revealing concerning the relationship between writing and photography in efforts to bear witness to destruction and loss. As we will discuss, one of the SK authors, Zalman Gradowski, possessed a particularly nuanced understanding of the role of photographs as a means of attesting to the Shoah.

Limits of Seeing

The four photographs form a deliberate series. Their ordering is open to debate but it is usually accepted that the two images of bodies being burned in the grounds of Crematorium 4 (V) were taken first, followed shortly thereafter by the two images of a wooded area close to the crematorium, an area where a transport of women are being forced to undress. The first photograph of the series, of the incineration pits, is blurred. It features several members of the SK standing within the pile of corpses, some bending over the dead, two central figures appearing to be dragging the same corpse, sharing the burden. It seems likely the second crisper picture was taken very soon after this one. The man visible in the first photograph standing farthest right, at the edge of the frame, semi-visible, seems to be in the same pose in the second, yet is now more central and in full view, with those he is talking to revealed to our right. Georges Didi-Huberman notes of the second sharper image that it is more 'posed', 'clearer'.[15] The composition is more measured, considered. Alex exercises greater agency before this scene, focussing on what he wants the image to 'mean', interpreting the seen. He 'selects' this scene in a way he does not in his earlier effort.

In Vilém Flusser's terms, the second photograph is more 'set up'.[16] The setting up of an image 'implies that photographs are not "objective" descriptions'.[17] They are the product of choices, manifesting an individual's specific feelings and views about what is being photographed. Didi-Huberman clearly recognizes this but believes Alex undergoes a change between the taking of the first and second image. In the later one, he has become a photographer. The images, separated by seconds, belong to different registers of representation: the improvised and the pre-planned. Spontaneity (a spontaneity bound up with a measure of forethought in that Alex already knows he will take a picture and why he will take it) is replaced by formulation. He thinks about how best to take the picture: with greater pause, better framing. Alex does not know the first image is blurred but he senses that his initial effort may be lacking, that he must have another go.

In the second effort, a trace of aesthetic sensibility can be detected. Alex reflects on how things *should* appear, on how he should tell the story, the history, he is tasked with providing. This image, more so than the first, evinces the relative calm that Didi-Huberman suggests enabled Alex to 'establish an iconography' of the 'nerve centre' of the death factory.[18] There is more forethought here about how best to illustrate the process of mass murder for a future audience. The difference between the two images, the two perspectives, is minimal but substantial. When Didi-Huberman calls the second image *posed*, he is referencing the additional effort made to set up the seen. The Sonderkommando members who are at work, immersed in their tasks, clearly do not strike a pose. The posing, the interrelated artistic and testimonial purpose, comes from behind the camera not in front of it. Alex, through his framing of the scene, adopts the pose of 'photographer', displaying a changed attitude, becoming attentive to issues such as framing, clarity, perhaps even concerns about light source, about being too in the shadows. In the first photograph Alex witnesses, in the second, adopting a perilous composure, he witnesses again but this time with a discernible measure of artistry.

From his description, it seems this artistry disappoints Didi-Huberman. There is no sense the increased clarity that accompanies this posing is a positive attribute. Alex's move forwards seems a testimonial step back. The greater prescriptiveness that manifests in the second photograph appears to unnerve Didi-Huberman. He prefers the quality of qualified naivety that is manifest in the first.[19] The same dynamic, the same move from the spontaneous to the reflective, manifests in the third and fourth photographs. The third photograph shows a group of women, some undressing, some already naked, being forced to run. The camera points upwards in the fourth photograph, capturing tree boughs and treetops, showing sunlight streaming through the upper branches and twigs of silver birches.

Superficially, the third and fourth images may seem to shift from the considered to the haphazard, changing from a clear subject to being bereft of subject. The context of the taking of the photographs, however, potentially suggests otherwise. As we argue in our reading of the images in *Matters of Testimony*, it seems possible that Alex's fumble is prompted by his embarrassment and discomfort when confronted by the scene of the women, some of whom are striving to shield their nakedness.[20] The fumble may index his encountering a moral limit. In this reading, the few moments between the taking of the third and fourth photograph, like those between first and second, also involve a change in Alex's attitude, chronicling the emergence of a nascent ethical awareness about photography as a medium of witnessing. This awareness, like that of Alex becoming a photographer, is not something we consider he registered consciously. The shift in demeanour is, however, discernible in the differences between the photographs.

Our reading was informed, in part, by writings of two of the SK authors, by Gradowski's complex response to comparable subject-matter in *In the Heart of Hell*, in which, as we discussed in the previous chapter, he attests to the gassing of a group of women, and also by Leyb Langfus's clear reluctance to engage in certain forms of witnessing when faced by naked women, namely witnessing bound up with emotional detachment and objectification.[21] It is a reading that refuses to reduce the photograph to a mere fumble, a clumsy gesture, a simple mistake. Whether the slip, the tilting the camera upwards, is a 'straightforward' accident or error, nothing more than a botched action, meaningless, or is, in fact, an index of Alex's moral distaste for his task hinges upon several factors including how the causes of physical lapses are understood.[22] For Sigmund Freud, 'bungled' actions carry out unconscious intentions. In *The Psychopathology of Everyday Life* (1901), he discusses how 'bodged' motor activities manifest unconscious trains of thought.[23] Such actions seem like errors but actually ably fulfil a concealed purpose. The conditions under which Alex took his photographs at Birkenau clearly do not qualify as everyday life yet it does not seem unlikely that psychopathology also applies to extreme circumstances, that 'bungles' at Birkenau could also represent unconscious ideas and impulses. Even if a Freudian paradigm is refused, 'slips' are still attributed to causes, to the influence of particular conditions upon actions.[24] It therefore seems reasonable to offer a possible motivation for Alex's 'bodge', one attentive to the specific circumstances in which it occurs.[25]

We nonetheless qualified our assertion, accepting that the situation is not a simple one but deciding that conjecture was merited. To deprive Alex of motivation for his slip is potentially to divest him of a manifestation of his humanity, a humanity clearly on display in writings by some of the Sonderkommando authors. Their moral pain is worded. If we accept Alex experienced comparable pain, it emerged through a medium, a visual technology, associated with distanced vision, a medium often implicated in acts of violent objectification. Alex's looking away, however, conceivably demonstrates that photography can also register a moral questioning.[26] This places it on a continuum with the SK writings rather than at a remove from them.[27] Like the writings, the photographs express the feelings of their author, the emotions he expresses and must cope with.

This is not to say that the photographs show us what Alex saw. It is a mistake to view the mechanically captured image as equivalent to human perception. We have a restricted sense of what was the focus of Alex's attention, of what his eyes sought out and drew near and of what was rendered peripheral in his field of vision. In photographs, framing can give a sense of what is central to a photographer's interest but often it presents everything within the frame with equal resolution. This kind of simultaneous overview of a scene is not similar to human perception in which only certain things are pulled into focus. Human seeing is guided by varying thoughts and emotions. These influence what is seen and how it is perceived. Although the naked women in the third photograph are restricted to one corner of the image—with the birch woods occupying much more pictorial space—they were highly likely the foci of his attention. Despite being some distance away, they were what Alex's perception was fixed upon. The psychological dimensions to Alex's seeing and how these intersected with his act of perception render his vision qualitatively different to that of the camera 'eye'. We argue, however, that Alex's feelings as they inflected his perception influence how he handles the camera. In *Images malgré tout*, Didi-Huberman powerfully demonstrates the insights provided by an attentiveness to these feelings, to the emotional tenor they bring to the photographs. Dan Stone's reading of the images, which hinges on an analysis of the fourth one, also attends to feelings but more at the point of reception than production. His engagement with the pictures demonstrates how difficult Alex's images are to work with and think through.

Wanting Immediacy

From his early works such as *Constructing the Holocaust* (2003) through to very recent interventions in debates regarding the philosophy of history, Stone has sought to foster what he regards as more innovative approaches to Holocaust historiography, bemoaning the positivist bent undergirding the historical method that predominates in the field.[28] Positivism, rooted in empirical enquiry, renders ethics and politics surplus to scholarly requirements. Through endeavouring to void the subjective, it risks embodying a dehumanizing tendency. Stone's essay, 'The Sonderkommando Photographs', in keeping with his views on historiography, cannot be characterized as positivist. It lays the groundwork for an ethics of viewing in relation to visual testimony to the Holocaust, an ethics that centres on both acknowledging and seeing beyond the representational: '[t]here is an urgency, an immediacy about these photographs that appears to render the whole discussion of representation problematic'.[29] Stone draws on a variety of theories of photography, most notably those of Roland Barthes and Walter Benjamin, to articulate his idea of how historians may best approach materials such as the SK photographs.

'The Sonderkommando Photographs' begins by examining the sensory impact of the photographs upon those who view them before going on to argue that the idea the photographs might bring us closer to the reality of historical events is a false one. For Stone, there is not anything to observe in the images (or very little) but much to feel: 'there is nothing that can be examined in a moment of quiet reflection, because everything is always and all at once bursting out of the photograph, carving a path of terror through our senses'.[30] He therefore does not *see* the photographs. Seeing requires meaning making, it necessitates at least minimal contemplation, reflection of some kind, studied attentiveness, a process of interpretation, a hermeneutics.[31] Stone is rather overwhelmed by them. This makes his reception of the images categorically different to that of someone such as Didi-Huberman or, indeed, of us. He divorces sensation from sense. Stone's language, his reference to terror, and later to the photographs being 'truly frightening', connotes the sublime.[32] The sublime, as distinct from the beautiful, is an aesthetic experience that causes dread and horror. For Immanuel Kant, a sublime experience, at least initially, exceeds the mind's grasp, is beyond comprehension, causing fear.[33] If an object we perceive nullifies our capacity to conceptualize it, it becomes 'monstrous'.[34] Stone seems to view the horror of the SK photographs as embodying a magnitude of horror that causes such an experience of nullification. They cannot be interpreted because the horrors they portray surpass our understanding.

For Stone, the 'visceral impact' of the images is their meaning.[35] His ideology of the sublime postulates a capacity for the images to index horror in an unmediated way, one requiring no contextualization. This sublime aspect operates alongside the representational content of the photographs yet cannot be reduced to it. The images have an 'intrinsic power' to shock that exceeds the grasp of those who employ the photographs as Holocaust memory.[36] Stone appears to view the shock the photographs cause as akin to some conceptualizations of trauma, in which trauma functions like an unclaimed experience, one that has overloaded the senses.[37] Efforts to discuss the photographs as forms of representation overwrite this trauma, refuse it. In this reading, what Alex ultimately achieves through his effort to bear witness is an affirmation of the impossibility of bearing witness. The horrors he captures are of too great a magnitude to be made into sense. Anyone who reads the images otherwise, claiming they do successfully attest to horror, by implication, fails to do justice to them.

Stone's repeated references to the photographs using the metaphor of ossification, his view of them as bones, intimates he regards them as relics.[38] Treating the photographs as relics, as human remains, accords them a status superior to images.[39] Relics incarnate what they commemorate. The sacred nature of the photographs to Stone, their status as secular icons, is also emphasized by his referring to them as epiphanic.[40] Carol Zemel, as part of her discussion of pictures of Nazi concentration camps, describes the Christological framework which is often used to frame responses to photographs of the Holocaust. She cites Susan Sontag as an example of someone who adopts such a framework. Like Sontag, Stone invokes 'a language of Christian revelation'.[41] It may be for this reason that among the few minor changes made to Stone's essay when it was republished as a chapter in *History, Memory and Mass Atrocity* were alterations to the references to ossification. In the later version of the essay, the photographs no longer depict a moment in time that is ossified but one that is 'statically preserved'.[42] The images demonstrate that a photograph 'captures' rather than 'ossifies' a moment in time.[43]

Alex's failure to attest, as Stone sees it, becomes clear through the discussion of the fourth photograph. It is the photograph Stone judges as aesthetically superior to any other photograph to emerge from the camps: 'ultimately, what "better" image to come out of the concentration camps than absence, impossibility, black, a space informed not by human consciousness but by the unconscious'.[44] This unconscious, Stone explains in a footnote, is the unconscious optics formulated by

Walter Benjamin. He cites Benjamin's 'A Small History of Photography' but the philosopher's remarks on the movie camera in 'The Work of Art in the Age of Mechanical Reproduction' are equally apposite. There he explains that 'a different nature opens itself to the camera than opens to the naked eye – if only because an unconsciously penetrated space is substituted for a space consciously explored by man [*sic*]'.[45] Benjamin also observes that 'the camera introduces us to unconscious optics as does psychoanalysis to unconscious impulses'.[46] For Stone then, the fourth photograph is unintended. It must be. Alex can only successfully bear witness through happenstance when he fails to bear witness. Efforts to deny Alex his accident, to accord him agency, compromise the insight this blinding final image can provide.

Stone is not negating the value of the archive. He is, however, asserting, by way of his aesthetic ideology, through his claims for immediacy, that there is a dimension to the images which cannot be *seen* by the historian or, by extension, the art historian. This dimension is the horror of Birkenau. To read the images without acknowledging their traumatic kernel is to behave as if the photographs can attest to this horror. Stone concludes by observing that 'with the Sonderkommando photographs, just when we think we are closest to the actuality of genocide, standing on the edge of a mass grave, we are farther away than ever'.[47] Here the historian studying the photographs is prevented from understanding what they are seeing, from seeing, by sublime experience.

Texts and Images

Stone justifies his reading of the photographs as images which simultaneously proffer and withhold insight into the Holocaust by quoting from a translation of a note in Polish despatched by the political prisoners Józef Cyrankiewicz and Stanisław Kłodziński on 4 September 1944:

> Urgent. Send two iron reels of film (2 ½ x 3 ½ in.) as soon as possible. It is possible to take pictures. We send you photographs from Birkenau – people who have been gassed. The photograph shows a heap of bodies piled outdoors. Bodies were burned outdoors when the crematorium could not keep pace with the number of bodies to be burned. In the foreground are bodies ready to be thrown on the heap. Another photograph shows one of the places in the forest where people were told to undress, allegedly for a bath, but in fact before being driven to the gas chambers. Send a reel as soon as possible. Send the enclosed photographs to Tell.[48]

Stone's gloss is that the 'instructive' note bespeaks a 'desire to bring the reader closer while [making] plain the inability to do so'.[49] The note 'forbids as well as beckons us to approach the reality of genocide'.[50] It is difficult to discern how a prohibition on witnessing manifests in this entreaty. Stone may, perhaps, be reading the call for more film as evidence that no one set of photographs will ever be enough to adequately attest to the horrors of Birkenau. Such a sensible refusal of a totalizing vision of the photographs is, however, different from claiming that the reality of genocide is inaccessible or, more specifically, unattainable by way of photographs. It is also noteworthy that Stone omits the last few words of this paragraph of the note: 'we think that an enlarged photo can be sent further'. The two are advising Tell, identified as Teresa Łasocka-Estreicker by Janina Struk, that at least one of the images held on the film—a film smuggled out of Birkenau by Helena Dantón—merited broad dissemination.[51] The role of these two women resistance members in the history of the photographs is not always remarked on.

We want to suggest that what actually renders Cyrankiewicz's and Kłodziński's note invaluable for thinking about the SK photographs is the way it draws attention to the need to send words along with the seen, to explain what is 'in' the photographs. The two men are well aware that the images cannot function as standalone testimony. They realize that, once developed, the series of images will require context and description. Pictures need words to do some of their work. Susan Sontag recognized this in *Regarding the Pain of Others*, suggesting: 'all photographs wait to be explained or falsified by their captions'.[52] It may be that this fear of falsification is what prompts Stone to reject offering detailed accounts of the content of the SK photographs.[53] He recognizes the mediating effects of description. Language, as Michael Baxandall observed, is tendentious, putting 'pressure on us to discriminate in its way'.[54] Cyrankiewicz and Kłodziński,[55] however, worked hard to find the right words to describe the content of the images. Several words in the section describing that content are scribbled out.

Cyrankiewicz and Kłodziński are clearly striving for precision, recognizant of the import of their choice of language. They seem to struggle, for instance, over how to describe the pile of bodies, crossing out a first attempt before settling on 'jeden ze stosów' [one of the heaps]. They also hesitate when referring to the dead being incinerated, scribbling out a word and then opting for 'na których palono' [on which were burned]. We would argue that it is not coincidental that the moments where the prose temporarily fails, requires correcting, is in relation to the picturing of the burning of bodies. The destruction of corpses, rather than the gassings, was conceived by the SK as the 'heart of [the] hell' of Birkenau.[56] The faltering description provided by the Polish envoys for this visual testimony from the Sonderkommando seem to have taken on board how troubling the content of the pictures is. Their note would be introduced as evidence alongside two of the SK photographs at Rudolf Höss's trial. It therefore has a history of functioning to anchor the interpretation of the images.

It is also possible Zalman Lewental makes reference to the photographs in his account of the SK uprising of 7 October 1944. As part of a discussion of how badly let down by the Polish resistance the Sonderkommando felt they were, Lewental writes of: 'tragic pictures [*tragishe bilder*] which [...] among us here [...] made and sent away with [...] further furnished and [...] attributed to them'.[57] From the fragmentary nature of the text, it is impossible to be certain what Lewental is referring to but a few pages afterwards he describes how the squad will 'hide everything in the ground' from now on. This suggests that they have given up on efforts to smuggle testimony (written and, perhaps, visual) to the outside world by way of the camp resistance. If Lewental is indeed referring to the photographs taken by Alex, the allusion with its mention of attribution may refer to tensions over the ownership of the photographs. He is fearful the Polish resistance is taking credit for acts of testimony when it should not. The adjective used to describe the pictures, 'tragic' [*tragish*], is also revealing. It is a reference to their content but may also indicate how Lewental expects them to be received and understood as testimony, as distressing or harrowing depictions of atrocity. His choice of adjective, like the more expansive description of Cyrankiewicz and Kłodziński, also frames how the photographs should be understood.

Lewental clearly viewed himself as a historian.[58] If he is discussing the SK photographs, he obviously recognized their value as historical documents of atrocity. This, even though he is referring to images he has never seem. He knows their content because he sees it first-hand every day. He easily imagines what is there to be seen in the pictures. Looking at the photographs, we now see what he could not. Yet we are only afforded the slightest glimpse of what, for him, was encompassing. It is near to impossible to imagine what took place, what he endured. Didi-Huberman, however, insists on the historian's responsibility to strive to envision the circumstances in which the pictures were produced. His own efforts at imagining are intimately bound up with the passages of description he provides in *Images malgré tout*. He endeavours to aid the reader in the task of imagining through reconstructing Alex's actions and emotions. This imagining is necessary, for Didi-Huberman, as it demonstrates claims the Holocaust is unsayable or unimaginable are untenable.[59] Often, however, historians are fearful of language in relation to images.

Stefan Hördler, Christoph Kreutzmüller and Tal Bruttman, for instance, dedicate very little of their lengthy critical analysis of the Auschwitz Album (a series of photographs taken by a member of the SS that show the arrival of transports of Hungarian Jews at Birkenau towards the end of May 1944) to interpreting what is to be seen in the photographs, several of which are reproduced in the essay.[60] Details in the images are put to work to establish times of day and locations, to contribute to the production of a historical context for the images, but there is something unnerving about the minimal prose. It seems too emotionless given the unfolding tragedy it particularizes. The idea may be to allow the images to 'speak' for themselves but, in that case, they should have no prose accompaniment. There may also be a reluctance to engage too closely with perpetrator images but, as Ulrich Baer has demonstrated, it is possible to read such images against the grain.[61]

Hördler et al. call for the photographs in the Auschwitz Album and in the Karl Höcker Album to cease to be treated as iconic.[62] They call for a more critical engagement with such images as a means to bridge [*überbrücken*] or overcome expressive and perceptual limits regarding the subject-matter.[63] In a sense, their attitude towards the images is the inverse of Stone's, this because they are attentive to the dangers of sacralizing such imagery. Their mode of analysis, however, shares some similarities with Stone's in that they are reluctant to expand upon what they observe. They say very little about content. Hördler et al. do not usually interpret what they see beyond converting specific details into data: a shadow indexes a particular time of day, the physical gestures of inmates indicate a rain shower. The specific is employed to build a general picture. There are, nevertheless, rare occasions when they point to individual personalities, most notably in their brief discussion of a young woman, an 'unknown girl', who sticks out her tongue.[64]

The woman's gesture is interpreted as one that repudiates the bullyboy tactics of the photographer, a man who presses upon his unwilling subjects, invading their personal space. The insubordinate tongue, mentioned in passing, may be read as standing for the thousands of other physical instances of resistance enacted by inmates, the foot dawdling, the surreptitious pushback, the deliberate 'misstep', which went unrecorded: the many minimal non-verbal utterances that bespoke agency and defiance. The woman who sticks out her tongue also looks at the photographer, visually confronts him, as do at least two other women in the group. The index finger of her right hand trails over the rope that separates her space from his, the rope which demarcates her place, dictating limits to her movements (it is rope that cuts into the jacket of the woman behind). Her finger casts a shadow across the rope and her coat, a shadow that gives full measure to her pluck. Yet it is the tongue which stands out, iconoclastic, challenging the mastery of the photographer over the scene. The woman, refusing to hold her tongue in the face of an effort to violently objectify her, merits more than a few words. Description can guide the eye, hold the attention and impress the importance of something upon us.[65]

Stone believes the SK photographs raise issues about the role of photography as a medium of representation that bears witness and also about representation as a whole in the context of the Holocaust. There is, however, another kind of representation which Stone neglects to discuss, one that is intimately connected with these other forms, that of writing. Verbal description itself is a kind of representation, 'a representation of thinking about a picture more than a representation of a picture'.[66] In *Patterns of Intention*, Michael Baxandall draws attention to the fact 'language is not very well equipped to offer a notation of a particular picture', constituting 'a generalizing tool'.[67] Its 'repertory of concepts' in the face of the subtle differentiations of form and colour that can characterize an image, are 'rather crude and remote'.[68] For Baxandall, this crudeness and detachment denote a difficulty to be confronted rather than a reason to abandon description altogether.

Despite ostensibly privileging unmediated sensation in his response to the SK photograph, Stone must also employ verbal language to communicate his experience of the images. The fourth photograph, for example, is 'absence, impossibility, black, a space informed not by human consciousness but by the unconscious'.[69] This experience, as worded, does not resemble something immediate. Stone *sees* that something is not present, that something cannot come into being. He also *sees* black, a colour that absorbs all light. He is conscious of perceiving these attributes. In *Images malgré tout*, Didi-Huberman *sees* different attributes. He describes the photograph as showing the impossibility of aiming the camera, the risk Alex was taking, the urgency he felt, perhaps his running, his clumsiness, his being dazzled by the sun in front of him, possibly his breathlessness.[70] Didi-Huberman's measured, powerful—even occasionally poetic—prose describing the actions and emotions of the photographer as they can be revived from a close reading of the photograph, contrasts markedly with Stone's nominal description of the photograph's content (his description of the emotional impact of the photographs is effusive by comparison). Stone's use of language, we would suggest, betrays the historian's mistrust of words in relation to images. It is a mistrust which can also be detected in the response of Hördler et al. to the Auschwitz Album. Words seemingly threaten the integrity of visual evidence. They are to be avoided as much as possible.

Ideally, for Stone, images are capable of functioning independently of the verbal. He writes of the SK photographs, 'what we have before us here is a sequence, a basic narrative of the genocide of the Jews that exists even without textual help'.[71] The ordering of the images that Stone adopts is, however, based on their numbering in the archive in the Auschwitz Museum, referring back to a kind of textuality. He also ignores the recognition of the resistance movement at Auschwitz-Birkenau that words were central to the success of the images as testimony. The Sonderkommando themselves also display a complex recognition of the need for words and images to work together to attest to their appalling circumstances. This reality is most evident in Gradowski's reflections on writing and witnessing.

Postmemory *Avant La Lettre*

Zalman Gradowski refers to the capacity of material objects to bear 'witness to a life', possessing a kind of physical memory of their owners.[72] As part of his account of the liquidation of the Czech family camp, he writes of the discarded clothes of women in terms of a kind of material memory: '[The women] feel still attached to them, with these things which still hold the warmth of their bodies'.[73] Shortly afterwards, he refers to the clothes as like orphans. In the section titled 'The Separation', he writes of some belongings abandoned by a member of the SK sent to the gas chamber: 'Not long ago this was held by your friend and brother. You can still feel the heat of the hand that the object was in. And on it still lingers the last look he gave it before he threw it to the ground in despair'.[74] Something of these now dead SK men survives through these objects. Gradowski describes how accidentally treading on one of the discarded objects is highly upsetting because of what the objects recall to mind. In these passages, a complex understanding of personal possessions emerges, one in which the objects are accorded a kind of vitality.[75]

In both these examples, Gradowski is discussing objects owned by camp inmates rather than those of new arrivals. This is important for understanding the kinds of investment prisoners made in seemingly mundane items. For inmates—who had been deprived of most of their possessions—small items and articles of clothing came to assume immense importance. Henry Krystal linked the confiscation of possessions with the process of the 'deprivation of conscious individuality' of inmates.[76] Taking away belongings formed part of what Krystal identified as a sadistic assault on the ego. In this context, any possession an inmate was able to retain or procure potentially became a means to resist their deindividualization. In *Matters of Testimony*, we explored how writing provided a way to safeguard selfhood. Gradowski, however, points to the most mundane of items performing a similar role.

Once their owners have been sent to their deaths, the things he refers to seem to embody what could be described as a kind of postmemory. The concept of postmemory is commonly associated with the work of Marianne Hirsch. Hirsch initially used the term in relation to second-generation children of Holocaust survivors but now employs it more broadly to describe the relationship 'that the "generation after" bears to the personal, collective, and cultural trauma of those who came before – to experiences they "remember" only by means of the stories, images, and behaviors among which they grew up'.[77] Hirsch calls postmemory 'retrospective memory by adoption'.[78] Anne Karpf, who prefers the term surrogate, explains that the role of such witnesses involves a 'heavy burden of responsibility' positioning them as it does 'in a relay of memory – a chain of testimony in which they act as a medium for the transmission of first-hand accounts to future generations for whom the Holocaust will be nothing but history'.[79] In a post-survivor world, adopters or surrogates will stand in the stead of those who lived through the Holocaust. They will be a link in a crucial chain of remembrance.

Postmemory, however, is not a carbon copy of memory; it is a mediated experience of the past, albeit a profound and intense one. It 'approximates memory in its affective force and its psychic effects'.[80]

Hirsch's understands postmemory as a belated coming to terms with trauma, stating that it is possible that 'it is *only* in subsequent generations that trauma can be witnessed and worked through, by those who were not there to live it but received its effects'.[81] Postmemory accompanies the 'return of traumatic knowledge'.[82] The experience of trauma is, however, heterogeneous. It is certain that some who did not survive produced powerful testimonies that did bear witness to trauma and its effects, people we might refer to as pre-survivor witnesses. The majority of the authors of the Scrolls of Auschwitz form witnesses of this kind. Additionally there are survivors of the SK whose post-liberation testimony indicates that traumatic experiences were being processed during the event. Didi-Huberman refers to Alex's photographs as 'survivors' [*survivantes*].[83] Hirsch views photographs more as ghosts, as residual traces of the dead. She describes them as revenants.[84]

Hirsch's preferred medium to facilitate postmemory's emergence is the photograph. She writes of photography's 'privileged status' as an instrument of postmemory.[85] Photographs are able to structure the shape and content of postmemory.[86] Oral and written testimony are found wanting as, for Hirsch, they lack the indexical power of photographs. James Young similarly emphasizes the perceived power of photographs, which he refers to as illusory surrogates, to 'establish the event's factual authority'.[87] Photographic images point to 'the having-been-there' of the past, underscoring a 'material connection between past and present'.[88] This connection enables the breach caused by genocidal destruction that separates first- and second-generation witnesses to be bridged.

In this context, it is striking that members of the Sonderkommando also recognized the vital role photographs belonging to the victims of genocide could provide as forms of testimony. The survivor David Nencel, a former inhabitant of Maków Mazowiecki, recounts in filmed testimony:

> We took photographs from every transport that came. And always was written a little history from where it came. And pictures included that they should see that these are people that came here. They're not alive. So this [*sic*] type of things were taken and buried in quite a few places.[89]

Here photographs were tasked with 'remembering' those who were murdered, with archiving communities that were reduced to ashes. The SK *adopted* these orphan images, 'cared' for them, carefully preserving the abandoned likenesses, making sure a written explanation of their origin accompanied them in burial. The photographs, in Nencel's interpretation of this activity, granted a posthumous existence to those who were murdered. Like the quantities of teeth buried by members of the SK, the images were clearly intended to serve as a means of resistance to Nazi efforts to efface their crimes. Given Gradowski's description of the value accorded possessions, it is also likely the act of retrieving the photographs and preserving them in improvised archives had an even more complex significance than this for the SK. Laurent Olivier therefore rightly remarks of the SK burying artefacts that their hope was that we would heed 'the slightest remains from their past which, for them, are all imbued with meaning'.[90] He draws attention to how materials other than the writings were equally tasked by the SK with bearing witness to the destruction wrought at Birkenau.

The Sonderkommando made the abandoned photographs their own, taking responsibility for the fate of the images. As Didi-Huberman invites us to do, we need to picture the SK in 1944 and try to imagine what it meant to bury photographs alongside an explanation of their source, and then to continue the work forced upon you, knowing that beneath your feet were archived the faces of those who had been murdered and of their relatives. In this context, photographs perform functions far more complex than the mere recording of what someone looked like and, crucially, it is clear the SK were well aware of this complexity. They recognized the power of images as forms of remembrance, as a means to assert their own agency and individuality, and as a way to defy Nazis efforts at effacing their crimes. They also recognized the agency of the photographs themselves.

For Gradowski, the power of artefacts as forms of remembrance manifested at moments when men from the SK intentionally or accidentally interacted with them. During such interactions, materials engendered sensations and emotions in the men, acted upon their sensibilities and sensitivities. If Gradowski's descriptions are reflective of a general attitude towards specific kinds of objects among the SK, it is likely the group thought that the materials they were concealing possessed agency. In burying groups of photographs, the SK were consciously also burying an agential potential, one they hoped would be realized sometime in the future. This potential, which was of a mnemonic kind, was reliant upon the images and also the text that accompanied them in order to be realized. For the SK, the photographs possessed the capacity to act upon a future finder, to prompt remembrance and also a recognition of loss. This potential was not fulfilled as the caches of images were never found.

Aside from the photographs they interred, it is also certain that many of the Sonderkommando men possessed pictures which they retained on their person or in their sleeping quarters. It is possible a photograph of the woman who killed Schillinger was retrieved and circulated among members of the SK.[91] The image presumably served as an aide-memoire to a heroic act of resistance. In the aftermath of the SK revolt, Marcel Nadjary was one of those tasked with burning the bodies of the men from Crematorium 1 (II). He recalls that although 'the SS had searched the bodies, there were many photographs that I collected, but later lost'.[92] These photographs were presumably of the men's loved ones. Our knowledge of these different acts of pictorial preservation clearly demonstrates that the SK thought about photographs and their contemporary and potential future value. Equally, it is clear from Nencel that there was the recognition the images could not adequately speak for themselves: 'always was written a little history'. Here the SK members as writers of histories worked in tandem with images rather than expressing suspicion towards them.

The Sonderkommando, in their efforts to bear witness, held differing views over how to attest to the horrors that surrounded them. Gradowski appears to display mistrust of photography as an appropriate medium to record atrocity.[93] He would therefore not necessarily have condoned the actions of Alex. Gradowski, however, did appreciate the power of photographs, their agency, in a way Hirsch would recognize. In *In the Heart of Hell*'s three prefaces, he states each time that he wishes his writings to be published and calls for specific photographs to be included in the publication. These are a family portrait and a photograph of him and his wife, Sonia (Sarah).[94] The pictures will situate his writings, give a face to them and to the names he has listed, family members who were killed at Auschwitz in December 1942. Gradowski recognizes the pictures already perform a memory function but he also wants these pictures included to generate an emotional reaction: 'you unknown "free" citizen of the world, I implore you to shed a tear for [my family] once you have their image before your eyes'.[95] Here a combination of text and image form the catalyst for the work of mourning to begin. It is a work of mourning Gradowski has not been permitted to undertake while in the living hell of the crematoria: 'I [...] "can" not, don't have the chance to, utter a sigh or shed a tear for them'.[96] It thus falls to the reader, to someone who is not related to Gradowski, to react to the text and the images, remembering the author and his family and mourning for them. Gradowski therefore calls for the kind of 'imaginative investment, projection and creation' that Hirsch associates with postmemory.[97]

WORDS FOR PICTURES

Gradowski's request to publish photographs alongside his writings demonstrates his recognition of their ability to gainfully supplement his words. The images *survive*, and through them so does something of their owners. Without Gradowski's accompanying text, however, the photographs would not rise above generality. It is through his writing, that they are able to achieve their capacity to 'remember'. Gradowski referred to the objects left behind by his murdered friends as 'abandoned orphans'.[98] The photograph of him and his wife and the one of his family would risk similar abandonment without his words. Each of Gradowski's prefaces explains the significance of the photographs and also works to situate them in a caring environment.

The photographs taken by Alex, images of mass murder, are very different. These too, however, need words if they are to attest successfully as the resistance movement at Birkenau clearly recognized. In a fragment of text from an archive of her papers now held at the United States Holocaust Memorial Museum, Tzipora Hager Halivni writes of the photographs:

> These photographs of the 'Hungarian Action', the extermination of the Hungarian Jews in June [*sic*] 1944 show naked women, one tall, slender, beautiful, on their way to the gas chambers, and corpses being lugged to smoke laden pyres by wretched men of the *Sonderkommando* – they are the only photographs of the Birkenau extermination.[99]

The majority of the text is typed but in her discussion of the woman who Halivni has identified as beautiful, the author has added the words 'tall' and 'slender' in pencil when revising the text. Ultimately, in the article she published for which this appears to be a draft, Halivni wrote simply that the photographs: 'show naked women on their way to the gas chambers and corpses being lugged to smoke-laden pyres by men of the SK'.[100] The likelihood is that she was working from a retouched version of the photograph in which clearer faces and breasts have been constructed for two of the women. It is probably one of these retouched figures that Halivni is referring to, conceivably the woman who is noticeably taller than another woman standing beside her (whose head is bowed).

Halivni's initial decision to single out one of the women and foreground her beauty was clearly intended to emphasize the ugly brutality of her murder. A similar strategy may be present in Zalman Gradowski's florid depiction of a group of women on their way to the gas chamber in *In the Heart of Hell*.[101] Halivni, however, has second thoughts and opts not to involve beauty aesthetics and, by extension, ideas of visual pleasure in her description. Such a way of seeing should not be bolstered in this context. She also excises the reference to the wretchedness of the SK which was likely intended to suggest their misery but also risked carrying negative moral connotations. These slight changes encompass significant decisions. Halivni does not let the images 'speak' for themselves but she does reflect carefully on how her voicing of them will inflect their reception. She recognizes a duty of care towards them.

As we discuss in the introduction, Halivni had herself experienced the humiliation of stripping naked in front of SS guards upon her arrival at Auschwitz. Her viewing therefore possesses a level of empathy non-survivors cannot readily emulate. There are many accounts by women survivors which detail the humiliation of undressing. Gisella Perl, for example, makes reference to the sexual excitement exhibited by SS men towards naked newly arrived female inmates at Auschwitz. She writes of the SS men having eyes shining with expectation and shortly afterwards of their 'curious, hungry eyes'.[102] Violence was enacted, in part, by way of the male gaze. In the context of the crematoria, Marcel Nadjary recalls how in the undressing room 'the young girls felt shy and found it difficult to undress, and would cry from embarrassment'.[103] It is probable the women forced to strip in the woods were faced with a similarly brutal and humiliating experience. As these women are near the burning pits, it is quite possible they already know what fate awaited them. Nazi efforts at deception were not as effective at crematoria 3 (IV) and 4 (V) because of the close proximity of the burning pits. In a state of terror, the women were surreptitiously photographed by Alex, burdened with standing for mass murder.

Griselda Pollock has linked looking that involves mastering, knowing and dominating with sadism.[104] She aligns this form of looking with Michel Foucault's eye of power, with technologies of discipline and surveillance. Alex's photographs of the women are not of this kind. He is motivated by the need to record rather than a desire to control. The pictures he takes are not, however, consensual. We can never look without knowing this. He knew this. His dilemma was that he needed to bear witness, he knew the power of visual evidence, yet he also recognized the inherent violence of his mode of witnessing. Alex burdened a group of terrified women—headed by specific individuals with now not quite discernible faces—to be the proof of mass murder. They were instruments for him, a reality we think he was tragically aware of, an awareness his final image attests to. In that image, he wishes (consciously or unconsciously) to look away. It is therefore possible that in the photographs, like some of the SK writings, there is reflection going on regarding the nature of the gaze in its varied dynamics and its potential for violence.

Discussion of images such as the Sonderkommando photographs must seek not to master them, not to impose on them, not to force them to fit unfamiliar frames of reference.[105] Nor, however, must they embrace a radical masochism, an entirely passive reception, one devoid of comment or critical reflection. Didi-Huberman's analysis of Alex's photographs in *Images malgré tout*, with its thoughtful hesitancy, provides an important example of an appropriate mode of writing. It is a mode which is clearly connected with close reading. Didi-Huberman has studied the images rather than glancing at them. He has then sought words to 'remember' Alex's actions and emotions—words he feels are appropriate to those actions and emotions—and also to describe what he sees. Didi-Huberman is not afraid to register uncertainty. He writes of the fourth photograph that it attests to: 'the impossibility of aiming, the risk involved, the urgency, perhaps the running, the clumsiness, the frontal glare of the sun, perhaps breathlessness'.[106] He says of this image that it is 'very blurred'.[107] There is also a blurriness to his description of the conditions of Alex's taking of it, conditions extrapolated from the image. Didi-Huberman's account reads like a train of thought, registering ideas not yet settled upon but emergent, readings in development.

In this context, Didi-Huberman's seeming preference for the first of the two photographs taken from inside the gas chamber may explain his favoured approach for writing about the images. Alex's first image does not master its subject. It refuses to possess it. This refusal to master makes the testimony ethically preferable to that of the second photograph. The initial effort, in its looseness, runs less risk of being viewed in iconic terms as giving the 'whole' picture, and refuses to wholly possess this seen.[108] The difference between the two photographs in terms of their composition demonstrates that while photography may be impersonal and mechanical, its dehumanizing effects can be moderated in some circumstances. The first image, in its hesitancy, carries none of the conscious burdening with meaning that John Tagg, for example, famously associates with documentary photography.[109] For Tagg photography (usually accompanied by writing) can be complicit in processes of control and domination. The prisoner photographs taken by the Nazis of inmates at Auschwitz would form clear examples of photography of this type. Alex's second photograph risks falling prey to a comparable process of objectification and subjection. The dead and the living are deftly framed to represent extermination. Like the first, the third image, however, is non-mastering. Didi-Huberman and Halivni have worked hard to emulate the looseness, the accidental openness, of such images through their writings. They consciously strive to find the right words, words that provide context and commentary but that do not oppress or injure the seen in the way Stone's reduction of the fourth photograph to an allegory of unrepresentability risks doing. This need to find the right words also features in some of the post-war trial testimony provided by members of the SK which we will discuss in the next chapter.

Notes

1. Andreas Kilian cites the testimony of Henryk Swiebocki who suggests that there are actually seven photographs in total, three photographs of incineration pits, two of naked women ('undressing photographs' or *Entkleidungsfotos*) and two of trees ('failed tree photographs' or *misslungenen Baumfotos*). See Kilian, 'Zur Autorenschaft der Sonderkommando-Fotografien,' *Mitteilungsblatt der Lagergemeinschaft Auschwitz – Freundeskreis der Auschwitzer* 35 (2016): 9–19, 9. Swiebocki appears to be referring here to the fact multiple copies of the same image were handed over to the archive at the same time. On a research trip to Auschwitz relating, in part, to the photographs, we asked to see the photographs that were donated to the museum archive and were only presented with four images. The negative numbers of the four photographs reproduced regularly do, however, imply that three other copies of images exist (277; 278; 282; 283). Additionally, it is possible the camera was subsequently used to take more photographs once further film was secured. Henryk Mandelbaum mentions that the SK buried a camera in the grounds of the crematoria. It is unlikely they would have taken the trouble to do this unless it contained film. Jan Południak, *Sonder: An Interview with Sonderkommando Member Henryk Mandelbaum*, trans. Witold Zbirohowski-Kościa (Oświęcim: Frap, 2008), p. 94.

2. Georges Didi-Huberman, *Images malgré tout* (Paris: Éditions de Minuit, 2003) and Dan Stone, 'The Sonderkommando Photographs', *Jewish Social Studies* 7.3 (2001): 132–148. For a measured summary of the controversy generated in France by Didi-Huberman's take on the photographs, see Sven-Erik Rose, 'Auschwitz as Hermeneutic Rupture, Differend, and *Image malgré tout*: Jameson, Lyotard, Didi-Huberman', in *Visualizing the Holocaust*, eds. David Bathrick, Brad Praeger, and Michael Richardson (Rochester: Camden House Press, 2008), pp. 127–129.
3. In this context, the photographs of the construction of Auschwitz-Birkenau that were buried in a flask by Ludwik Lawin have a complex status. The pictures are taken from a perpetrator perspective (by Dietrich Kamann or those working for him) but Lawin transforms them through his act of resistance, rendering them contemporary evidence of a crime.
4. Kilian, 'Zur Autorenschaft der Sonderkommando-Fotografien'.
5. See Proces Rudolfa Hoessa, United States Holocaust Memorial Museum RG-15.167M Volume 11 (NTN93), pp. 48–50.
6. For a discussion of this series of artworks, see Georges Didi-Huberman's 'Sortir du Plan.' An English translation of the fourth letter in this series of letters to Gerhard Richter is forthcoming in *Testimonies of Resistance: Representations of the Auschwitz-Birkenau Sonderkommando*, eds. Chare and Williams (Berghahn, 2019).
7. Kilian describes Perrin's findings, which were delivered at the conference *Écrits au coeur de la catastrophe* as part of Perrin's paper, '"Ce que j'ai vu à Auschwitz" d'Alter Fajnzylberg,' in *Zur Autorenschaft der Sonderkommando-Fotografien*, p. 19.
8. Katherine E. Fleming, *Greece: A Jewish History* (Princeton: Princeton University Press, 2008), p. 160.
9. Teresa Świebocka and Renata Bogusławska-Świebocka, 'Auschwitz in Documentary Photographs,' in *Auschwitz: A History in Photographs*, ed. Teresa Świebocka (Bloomington: Indiana University Press, 1993), p. 43.
10. It should be noted that Feinsilber's testimony regarding the camera used (which he suggested was a Leica) has been found to be inaccurate. See Clément Chéroux, 'Photographies de la résistance polonaise à Auschwitz,' in *Mémoire des camps: Photographies des camps de concentration et d'extermination nazis (1933–1999)*, ed. Clément Chéroux (Paris: Éditions Marval, 2001), p. 86n.3.
11. In *Sortir du noir*, written subsequent to Perrin's discovery, Georges Didi-Huberman also chooses to continue to refer to the photographer as Alex although he is clearly aware of the attribution to Errera. See Georges Didi-Huberman, *Sortir du noir* (Paris: Les Éditions de Minuit, 2015).

12. The names of many Greek members of the Sonderkommando are unknown to us. See Photini Tomai, *Greeks in Auschwitz-Birkenau* (Athens: Papazisis Publishers, 2009), p. 159.
13. For a discussion of some of these provisos, see Chare and Williams, *Matters of Testimony*, pp. 205–206.
14. For a recent exploration of the photographs as testimony, one which engages primarily with Georges Didi-Huberman's analysis of them, arguing for their agency of absence as a facilitator of remembrance, see Silke Helmerdig's, *Fragments, Futures, Absence and the Past: A New Approach to Photography* (Bielefeld: Transcript Verlag, 2016), pp. 149–159. Helmerdig over simplifies Didi-Huberman's position, suggesting that he reads the SK photographs primarily as historical proof of events at Birkenau (150).
15. Didi-Huberman, *Images malgré tout*, p. 20.
16. Vilém Flusser, *Gestures*, trans. Nancy Ann Roth (Minneapolis: University of Minnesota Press, 2014), p. 74.
17. Ibid.
18. Didi-Huberman, *Images malgré tout*, p. 56.
19. For Flusser, there is no such thing as 'naïve photography'. The act, the gesture, of taking a picture is always knowing. Didi-Huberman's analysis, however, points towards the presence of degrees of knowingness.
20. The gesture of one of the women, her arms crossed across her upper torso shielding her breasts, is the same as a gesture the Sonderkommando member David Nencel recreates to illustrate the embarrassment experienced by women in the undressing room, an embarrassment the SK clearly recognized and shared. See David Nencel interviewed by Joe Russin in 1996. Jeff and Toby Herr Oral History Archive, USHMM, Accession Number 2003.76. RG-50. 560. 0001.
21. Despite these literary parallels, our interpretation has met with scepticism. In a round-table discussion concerning *Matters of Testimony* held at the Wiener Library in London in June 2016, Stone, for instance, affirmed of the fourth photograph: 'It was a photograph that went wrong. No more than that'.
22. Another factor is how you understand photography. To us, the four photographs—like the writings—comprise consciously conceived textual narratives and embody processes of reflection on their maker's part. Some, by contrast, may view photography as a more basic medium of representation incapable of arriving at the level of ethical contemplation that writings can attain.
23. Sigmund Freud, *The Psychopathology of Everyday Life: Penguin Freud Library*, Vol. 5, trans. Alan Tyson (London: Penguin, 1991), p. 227.
24. J. T. Reason, 'The Psychopathology of Everyday Slips: Accidents Happen When Habit Goes Haywire,' *The Sciences* 24.5 (1984): 45–49.

25. To use a formulation by Adrian Rifkin produced in a different context: 'The object of attention is to hear the archive, not to call on it as a body of evidence, as if it were incontrovertible in its eventually discoverable truth'. See Rifkin, *Ingres Then, and Now* (London: Routledge, 2000), p. 19. Here Rifkin formulates a way of seeing that is akin to listening in psychoanalysis.
26. This is, of course, not a new claim to make for the medium. Vivian Uriah notes that not long after photography's invention, photographic images became understood as 'not merely a record of reality as it is, but also of reality as interpreted by the photographer himself [*sic*], whose worldview, values and moral perception influence the choice of the object and how it is presented'. See Uriah, 'Photography During the Holocaust,' in *Flashes of Memory: Photography During the Holocaust* (Jerusalem: Yad Vashem, 2018), p. 12.
27. Ana Firoiu and Fleur Kuhn also see the photographs as comparable to some of the writings. They understand Zalman Gradowski's texts to be akin to the photographs in that they transmit something of what the SK saw at Birkenau to the outside world. See 'Au cœur de l'enfer de Zalmen Gradowski – Expérience collective et subjectivité dans le témoignage immédiat de la Shoah,' in *La Psychologie de masse, aujourd'hui*, eds. Michel Gad Wolkowicz, Thibault Moreau, Alexis Nouss, and Gérard Rabinovitch (Paris: Des Rosiers, 2012), p. 95.
28. Dan Stone, *Constructing the Holocaust: A Study in Historiography* (London: Vallentine Mitchell, 2003) and Stone, 'Excommunicating the Past? Narrativism and Rational Constructivism in the Historiography of the Holocaust,' *Rethinking History* 21.4 (2017): 549–566.
29. Stone, 'The Sonderkommando Photographs,' p. 131.
30. Ibid., p. 138.
31. David Patterson draws attention to the need to 'ease into the [SK] photographs'. Through this easing in, Patterson feels able to explore spiritual dimensions he perceives in the pictures. Although our reading of the photographs differs, we share his commitment to meditating on the images rather than viewing them as artefacts that bestow their significance immediately. Patterson, *The Holocaust and the Nonrepresentable* (New York: SUNY, 2018), p. 250.
32. Ibid., p. 140.
33. For a nuanced discussion of the sublime in relation to Holocaust photography, see Carol Zemel, 'Emblems of Atrocity: Holocaust Liberation Photographs,' in *Image and Remembrance: Representation and the Holocaust*, eds. Shelley Hornstein and Florence Jacobowitz (Bloomington: Indiana University Press, 2003), pp. 201–219.
34. Immanuel Kant, *Critique of Judgement*, trans. Werner S. Pluhar (Indianapolis: Hackett, 1987), p. 109 (253), § 26.

35. Stone, 'The Sonderkommando Photographs,' p. 141.
36. Ibid.
37. See, for example, Cathy Caruth, *Unclaimed Experience: Trauma, Narrative, and History* (Baltimore: Johns Hopkins University Press, 1996).
38. Stone, 'The Sonderkommando Photographs,' pp. 135, 139.
39. Helen Hills, *The Matter of Miracles: Neapolitan Baroque Architecture and Sanctity* (Manchester: Manchester University Press, 2016), p. 47.
40. The idea of photographs as secular icons was first advanced by Vicki Goldberg. See Goldberg, *The Power of Photography: How Photographs Changes Our Lives* (New York: Abbeville Press, 1991). The idea has subsequently been taken up by Cornelia Brink who cautions against the myth of immediacy that underlies views of photographs regarded as icons. Brink describes how the perceived inviolability of such images 'seems to preclude a detailed pictorial analysis'. Brink, 'Secular Icons: Looking at Photographs from the Nazi Concentration Camps,' *History & Memory* 12.1 (2000): 144.
41. Zemel, 'Emblems of Atrocity,' p. 203.
42. Dan Stone, *History, Memory and Mass Atrocity: Essays on the Holocaust and Genocide* (Elstree: Vallentine Mitchell, 2006), p. 20.
43. Ibid., p. 23.
44. Stone, 'The Sonderkommando Photographs,' p. 138.
45. Walter Benjamin, 'The Work of Art in the Age of Mechanical Reproduction,' in *Illuminations*, trans. Harry Zorn, ed. Hannah Arendt (London: Pimlico, 1999), p. 230.
46. Ibid.
47. Stone, 'The Sonderkommando Photographs,' p. 143.
48. Świebocka and Bogusławska-Świebocka, 'Auschwitz in Documentary Photographs,' p. 172.
49. Stone, 'The Sonderkommando Photographs,' p. 142.
50. Ibid.
51. Janina Struk, *Photographing the Holocaust: Interpretations of the Evidence* (London: I.B. Tauris, 2004), p. 114. See also Struk, 'Images of Women in Holocaust Photography,' *Feminist Review* 88 (2008): 118.
52. Susan Sontag, *Regarding the Pain of Others* (London: Hamish Hamilton, 2003), p. 9.
53. This is despite Stone affirming elsewhere that a photograph clearly acts 'as a substitute for the missing object', thereby tacitly emphasizing the importance of content. Stone's reading of the SK photographs treats them as images without object, as presenting nothing to be mindful of or to study. See Stone, 'Chaos and Continuity: Representations of Auschwitz,' in *Representation of Auschwitz*, ed. Yasmin Doosvy (Oświęcim: Auschwitz-Birkenau State Museum, 1995), p. 29.

54. Michael Baxandall, *Giotto and the Orators: Humanist Observers of Painting in Italy and the Discovery of Pictorial Composition 1350–1450* (Oxford: Clarendon Press, 1986), p. 9.
55. The photographs, including one of the note, are to be found in Proces Rudolfa Hoessa, pp. 49–50.
56. See Chare and Williams, *Matters of Testimony*, pp. 198–199. See also Griselda Pollock, 'Knowing Cruelty: The Negation of Death and Burial in SS Violence,' in *Testimonies of Resistance*, eds. Nicholas Chare and Dominic Williams (New York: Berghahn, 2019), in press.
57. Zalman Lewental MS, Auschwitz archive 26b (right-hand side).
58. See Dan Stone's essay, 'The Harmony of Barbarism: Locating the Scrolls of Auschwitz in Holocaust Historiography,' in *Representing Auschwitz: At the Margins of Testimony*, eds. Nicholas Chare and Dominic Williams (Houndmills: Palgrave Macmillan, 2013), pp. 11–32. See also our discussion of Lewental in *Matters of Testimony*, pp. 125–153.
59. For a discussion of Didi-Huberman's conception of unsayability, see Dorota Glowacka, *Disappearing Traces: Holocaust Testimonials, Ethics, and Aesthetics* (Washington: University of Washington Press, 2012), pp. 12–13.
60. Stefan Hördler, Christoph Kreutzmüller, and Tal Bruttman, 'Auschwitz im Bild: Zur kritischen Analyse der Auschwitz-Alben,' *Zeitschrift für Geschichtswissenschaft* 63.7/8 (2015): 609–632. We are indebted to Dan Stone for bringing this essay to our attention.
61. The Auschwitz Album (referred to in the essay as the Lili Jacob Album) is described as 'rassistisch verbrämten', as embellished by racism. Hördler, Kreutzmüller, and Bruttman, 'Auschwitz im Bild: Zur kritischen Analyse der Auschwitz-Alben,' p. 630. Ulrich Baer suggests in *Spectral Evidence* that through formal analysis some (not *all*) photographs taken by Nazis and their sympathizers can be made to break with their original uses and something in them saved from the Nazi gaze. See Baer, *Spectral Evidence: The Photography of Trauma* (Cambridge, MA: MIT Press, 2002), pp. 174, 177.
62. Hördler, Kreutzmüller, and Bruttman, 'Auschwitz im Bild: Zur kritischen Analyse der Auschwitz-Alben,' p. 631.
63. Ibid.
64. Ibid.
65. Nicholas Chare discusses the relationship between words and photographs in more depth in his essay 'Puncture/Punctum'. Nicholas Chare, 'Puncture/Punctum: Out of Shot,' in *Conceptual Odysseys: Passages to Cultural Analysis*, ed. Griselda Pollock (London: I.B. Tauris, 2007), pp. 95–97.
66. Michael Baxandall, *Patterns of Intention: On the Historical Explanation of Pictures* (New Haven: Yale University Press, 1985), p. 5.
67. Ibid., p. 3.

68. Ibid.
69. Stone, 'The Sonderkommando Photographs,' p. 138.
70. Didi-Huberman, *Images malgré tout*, p. 54.
71. Stone, 'The Sonderkommando Photographs,' p. 141.
72. Zalman Gradowski, *In Harts Fun Gehenem* (Tel Aviv: Wolnerman, n.d.), p. 127.
73. Ibid., p. 76.
74. Ibid., p. 128. Translation adapted from Gradowski, *From the Heart of Hell*, pp. 89–90.
75. Gradowski's understanding of how materials behave, his notion of materiality, is a complex one in which substance is perceived not as a thing but as a doing. Locally determined materials such as clothes and teeth are seen by Gradowski as possessing agency. In this, his understanding of matter bears some similarities to that of Karen Barad. Barad, however, sees agency as matter, manifesting in matter's intra-acting, rather than as a quality possessed by pre-given entities. For Gradowski, agency is an *attribute* of pre-existing things. See Barad, 'Posthumanist Performativity: Toward an Understanding of How Matter Comes to Matter,' *Signs* 28.3 (2003): 801–831.
76. Henry Krystal, 'Studies of Concentration Camp Survivors,' in *Massive Psychic Trauma*, ed. Henry Krystal (New York: International Universities Press, 1968), p. 32.
77. Marianne Hirsch, *The Generation of Postmemory: Writing and Visual Culture After the Holocaust* (New York: Columbia University Press, 2012), p. 5.
78. Marianne Hirsch, 'Surviving Images: Holocaust Photographs and the Work of Postmemory,' *The Yale Journal of Criticism* 14.1 (2001): 10.
79. Anne Karpf, 'Chain of Testimony: The Holocaust Researcher as Surrogate Witness,' in *Representing Auschwitz: At the Margins of Testimony*, eds. Nicholas Chare and Dominic Williams (Houndmills: Palgrave Macmillan, 2013), p. 87.
80. Hirsch, *The Generation of Postmemory*, p. 31.
81. Hirsch, 'Surviving Images,' p. 12.
82. Ibid.
83. Didi-Huberman, *Images malgré tout*, pp. 63, 226.
84. Hirsch, *Family Frames*, p. 22 and Hirsch, *The Generation of Postmemory*, pp. 36, 134.
85. Hirsch, 'Surviving Images,' p. 13.
86. Hirsch, *Family Frames*, p. 127.
87. James Young, Writing and Re-writing the Holocaust, PhD thesis, Santa Cruz: University of California, 1983, p. 267.
88. Hirsch, 'Surviving Images,' p. 14.

89. David Nencel interviewed by Joe Russin in 1996.
90. Laurent Olivier, *Le sombre abîme du temps* (Paris: Éditions du Seuil, 2008), p. 162.
91. Abraham Berski, who was not a member of the SK, recounts that her photograph was retrieved from a suitcase and 'passed on as a sacred relic from hand to hand'. Cited in Haya Bar-Itzhak, 'Women in the Holocaust: The Story of a Jewish Woman Who Killed a Nazi in a Concentration Camp: A Folkloristic Perspective,' *Fabula* 50.1/2 (2009): 74.
92. Berry Nahmia, *A Cry for Tomorrow 76859...*, trans. David R. Weinberg (Jacksonville: Bloch Publishing, 2011), p. 87
93. See Chare and Williams, *Matters of Testimony*, pp. 203–204.
94. The writings have been published alongside the photograph of Gradowski and his wife but not the family photograph.
95. Gradowski, *In Harts Fun Gehenem*, p. 36. Translation adapted from Zalmen Gradowski, *From Heart of Hell: Manuscripts of a Sonderkommando Prisoner, Found in Auschwitz*, trans. Barry Smerin and Janina Wurbs (Oświęcim: Auschwitz-Birkenau State Museum, 2017), p. 110.
96. Gradowski, *In Harts Fun Gehenem*, p. 110.
97. Hirsh, 'The Generation of Postmemory,' p. 205.
98. Gradowski, *In Harts Fun Gehenem*, p. 127.
99. Unpaginated fragment, Tziporah Hager Weiss Halivni Archive, United States Holocaust Memorial Museum, Accession Number 2013.529.1. Box 20.
100. Tziporah Hager Halivni, 'The Birkenau Revolt: Poles Prevent a Timely Insurrection,' *Jewish Social Studies* 41.20: 123–154, 130.
101. See Chare's discussion of Gradowski's, *In the Heart of Hell* in 'On the Problem of Empathy: Attending to Gaps in the Scrolls of Auschwitz,' in *Representing Auschwitz: At the Margins of Testimony*, eds. Nicholas Chare and Dominic Williams (Houndmills: Palgrave Macmillan, 2013), pp. 11–32. See also Chare and Williams, *Matters of Testimony*, pp. 75–82.
102. Gisella Perl, *I Was a Doctor in Auschwitz* (New York: Arno Press, 1979), pp. 43–44.
103. Cited in Nahmia, *A Cry for Tomorrow 76859...*, p. 82.
104. Griselda Pollock, *Art in the Time-Space of Memory and Migration: Sigmund Freud, Anna Freud, and Bracha L. Ettinger in the Freud Museum* (Leeds: Wild Pansy Press, 2013), p. 106.
105. Our thinking here is informed by Griselda Pollock's approach to writing about the paintings of Charlotte Salomon. Pollock seeks to respect their singularity. See Griselda Pollock, 'To Play Many Parts: Reading Between

the Lines of Charlotte Salomon's/CS's *Leben? Oder Theater?* *RACAR* 43 (2018): 64–66.
106. Didi-Huberman, *Images malgré tout*, p. 54.
107. Ibid., p. 23.
108. For a discussion of Didi-Huberman's notion of the iconic see Griselda Pollock's essay 'Photographing Atrocity: Becoming Iconic?' in *Picturing Atrocity: Photography in Crisis*, eds. Geoffrey Batchen et al. (London: Reaktion Books, 2012), pp. 67–68.
109. See John Tagg, *The Burden of Representation: Essays on Photographies and Histories* (Minneapolis: University of Minnesota Press, 1993).

CHAPTER 4

The Trials of Witnessing: Legal Testimony and the Sonderkommando

An Interested Audience

Two of the images produced by Alex were submitted in cropped form as documentary evidence in the 1947 trial of Rudolph Höss. Numbered 33 and 34, they featured among many photographs presented as part of the prosecution's case.[1] Photograph Number 1, for instance, is of a plan of Auschwitz-Birkenau as seen from above, an overview of two of the camps for which Höss was responsible during his time as commandant. The crematoria are clearly marked on the plan. That they are central to the trial is clear from this first image. Other photographs that are included portray the ruins of the crematoria at Birkenau as seen from distance and, in one instance (Number 7), from a viewpoint seemingly designed to look down the stairs into the ruins of the undressing room, conceived to take the viewer inside the (ruins of the) building. There are also architectural plans for the crematoria. All these documents as evidence are supplemented by explanatory text to aid in their interpretation. The photographs and plans formed only a small, if important, part of the judicial evidence used in the case against Höss.

In some sense, then, we could say that the witnessing of the Sonderkommando had found an audience, one finally interested in hearing and acting upon the testimony that they were trying to bring to the outside world. But it was not under the circumstances that they had anticipated or chosen. Rather than the photographs being evidence which helped to stop the genocide, they were now part of a case after the event. They were also placed into a context in which, paradoxically perhaps, the SK might be said to have had far less control, surrounded by explanations, and other forms of testimony, oral as well as written, retrospective as well as contemporaneous, some of it produced by survivors of the SK themselves.

In Auschwitz, testimony was supposed to be impossible. Members of the SK had to invent, improvise and create everything: the materials used to write or take photographs, an imagined interlocutor, a space in which to bear witness (both a place to write and a psychic space), ways to convey what they saw and means to bring the testimony to the outside (whether by burying them or smuggling them out in some form). This inventiveness was of course a response to overwhelming restrictions, but it might also be said to have permitted a kind of freedom. Within the bounds in which they were working, whatever possibility the SK found was what they had to use, but also what they were able to use. The responsibility that the SK left to the rest of the world was a legacy, a gamble on the future but also a duty that they could imagine they would impose on their readers from beyond the grave.

Courts, on the other hand, precisely because they were set up to hear testimony, had an idea of what kind of testimony they wanted to hear. Responsibility for the testimony was not passed on from witnesses to whomever their testimony reached, but shared and co-created: the rules of the court, the strategies and arguments pursued by the prosecutor, and the judgements of the judges also went into shaping the testimony produced. A court also bore more than one responsibility. Added to the duty to hear victims and survivors was the duty to treat defendants fairly, to observe the rule of law, even a responsibility to the well-being of witnesses themselves. The courts therefore marked one of the major points of transition from the SK representing themselves and what they witnessed to their being represented. This was not a point at which they were utterly powerless, but it did involve a different relationship of power from what they had worked with (or against) before that.

Of course, the courts themselves were improvised affairs, ones that were often created specifically, and specially, to prosecute crimes for which it was hard to find precedent.[2] New names for these crimes were invented, or referenced (genocide [*ludobójstwo*], crimes against the peace). Evidence was allowed that would not have been accepted in British or American criminal proceedings for reasons of admissibility and reliability. Different legal systems were combined. The courts also had more than one function, sometimes in ways that did not sit easily together. There was the need to prosecute and punish individual criminals. There was also the need to establish some kind of historical record.

Historians and theorists have criticized trials for failing to carry these functions out. Most famously, Hannah Arendt excoriated Gideon Hausner's direction of the Eichmann trial and use of hundreds of witnesses who had nothing to say about Eichmann's guilt.[3] Devin Pendas and Rebecca Wittman both see the German legal system especially as failing to adequately conceptualize the guilt of the perpetrators.[4] Donald Bloxham argues that an overly coherent and centre-led version of the Holocaust came out of the IMT's desire to prosecute the crime as a conspiracy, and especially as one that stemmed from the waging of aggressive war.[5]

The role of witnesses (especially survivors) is also often seen as limited and sometimes stymied by the rules of the court.[6] Arendt embraced this restriction, complaining about and verging on mocking the prosecution strategy in the Eichmann trial and even some of his witnesses.[7] Shoshana Felman follows on from Arendt to say that the restriction of the trial setting brings out a kind of silence that can be listened to. Her focus in particular is on the encounter of 'trauma, art and law' in Yehiel Dinoor (KaZetnik)'s testimony, or rather failure to give it: Dinoor collapsed and was unable to answer the judge and prosecutor's questions.[8] Devin Pendas contrasts the state of 'bearing witness' with that of 'being a witness', and claims that the former, with its experiential element, was not the concern of the Frankfurt trial (and, by implication, of most trials), which was concerned primarily with evidence.[9] Both Felman and Pendas focus on one kind of witness who fails to testify (at least in the court's own terms): Dinoor who fainted in the middle of his testimony, or (in the case of Pendas) someone who cannot be understood, because of problems with translation.[10]

But this is to overly simplify the purposes of both the trial and the witnesses. The collection documents prepared for the Höss trial, for example, go beyond even the two goals of amassing evidence and establishing historical fact, by including survivor memoirs and, remarkably, poetry written by prisoners in Auschwitz. Rather than seeing the multiple goals of human rights trials as simply contradictory or a form of mission creep, many theorists have seen this multiplicity as part of their strength.[11] Trials lend themselves to being used in more ways than one, both by actors within the court itself, and by those outside it. Devin Pendas provides examples of how testimony at the Auschwitz trial was taken and repurposed in Hermann Langbein's thematic collection of witness testimony, and Peter Weiss's play *The Investigation*, claiming that these kinds of approaches fail to acknowledge the place of the testimony within a particular legal framework.[12] But the very fact that they were able to extract testimony from its context suggests that the testimony signified outside that context. Indeed, one factor that is often lamented about the trials, that attention waxed and waned over them, that people attending them often became bored, or that the press presence varied greatly from day to day, also suggests that the structure was not readily discernible during the proceedings. Daniela Accatino and Cath Collins discuss the different kinds of 'transitional truths' that come out in human rights trials between different processes, but these come out in different points of a trial too.[13] In many trials, key moments from witnesses make it directly into the press long before a case is fully made or a verdict pronounced. We will think of the trials, therefore, more as relay stations or nodes in memory: points where testimony is collected and redistributed, and where the significance of that testimony is disputed and discussed, rather than a procedure to produce some overall picture that we judge on how it 'matches' the actual event.

Acknowledging the fractured nature of a trial also allows us to see different roles for the victim-witnesses. Of course, different witnesses had different purposes and different competences and confidence in achieving them, and that needs to be recognized. It is also important to acknowledge that testifying was a painful and difficult process. But witnesses do not need to be seen simply as passive, constrained by the court's procedures, and unable to give voice to a private pain which has little evidentiary value.[14] Examination of trial testimony shows first of all that there often was room for survivors to tell of their suffering.[15] Beyond that, however, witnesses can be seen actively aiding the court in such aims as punishing perpetrators, and creating a historical record.[16] The Sonderkommando can be seen to be pursuing all of these purposes in their testimony. As people who had spent months and even years in the gas chambers, they were burdened with extremely painful memories but were also able to provide eyewitness accounts of crimes and give detailed explanations of how the process of mass murder worked.

Examining the role of the Sonderkommando in post-war trials therefore allows us to consider a number of questions. It provides an early example of how the Sonderkommando's witnessing met a public that was (to some extent) willing to receive it, and the significance that the

SK had for that public. It also makes clear how their significance operated differently in different contexts. Within the trial, their testimony formed part of a case against particular defendants or of a judgement on them and was scrutinized and questioned in its particularities by the defence. Beyond the courtroom, it featured in reports on and extracts from the trials. In their giving testimony at multiple trials, we can also see how their own self-understanding changed or moments at which it crystallized. In these shifting and contested contexts, different understandings were not simply brought to bear on the SK's testimony but were made possible by it too.

An account of post-war trials that focusses on the Sonderkommando necessarily has to look elsewhere than the two major trials usually cited in studies of Holocaust memory: the International Military Tribunal at Nuremberg (1945–1946) and the trial of Adolf Eichmann in Jerusalem (1961–1962).[17] Members of the SK were not among the small selection of eyewitnesses called at Nuremberg, nor did they take their place among the throng of survivors called by Gideon Hausner. However, they were present at a range of trials of lesser-ranking perpetrators, carried out by allied countries both immediately after the war and in West Germany some years later.

This chapter will place most of its focus on the immediate post-war period. It will consider the so-called Belsen trial held under a Royal Warrant in the British-controlled sector of Germany in Lüneburg, a trial which also considered the workings of Auschwitz, between September and November 1945,[18] and two of the seven trials conducted by the Supreme National Tribunal (Najwyższy Trybunał Narodowy, NTN) in Poland (of Rudolf Höss—the most famous commandant of Auschwitz—in Warsaw and of other Auschwitz personnel in Kraków) in 1947.[19] Indeed, there are links to be drawn between the NTN trials and the trials carried out by Western powers—they made use of many of the same legal concepts and reported to the same umbrella organization. Unlike the IMT at Nuremberg, these Polish and British trials both made extensive use of survivor testimony, including eyewitness accounts of Birkenau's gas chambers, both directly and indirectly from the Sonderkommando. We will also briefly discuss the Frankfurt Auschwitz trial (1963–1965), where the most extensive oral testimony from the SK was given. Of necessity, our readings of the testimony given at these trials rely on transcripts of the earlier trials and the audio recording of the Frankfurt Auschwitz trial. In the context of courtroom testimony,

Carlo Ginzburg notes that 'transcription is already interpretation, conditioning later interpretations undertaken in the near future [...] or the distant future'.[20] Transcriptions necessarily present some limitations in that information on the body language and tone of witnesses and lawyers, which can be very influential in terms of how testimony is received in the courtroom, is lacking. It is rare that the transcripts provide any sense of that reception although laughter in the room is referenced when a witness misspeaks during the Höss trial.[21]

While the early trials have been criticized for creating histories of the Holocaust that do not place enough emphasis on the specifically anti-Jewish nature of this crime, or on the fact that it occurred in other places than the concentration camp, there clearly was some attempt by people playing a role in the court (prosecutors and judges, as well, arguably, as some witnesses) to think through what the gas chamber represented. Its function as an instrument of extermination, and the fact that that policy was directed specifically at Jews, was clearly acknowledged, in both the British and Polish jurisdictions.

The Belsen Trial at Lüneburg (1945)

While known as the 'Belsen trial', the British prosecution of Commandant Josef Kramer and 44 others in a military court also took into account the fact that a number of personnel as well as inmates of Bergen-Belsen had come there from Auschwitz-Birkenau. Charges and testimony referred to and distinguished between these two sites.[22] Unlike Belsen, which had featured in newspaper headlines from the moment of its liberation, this was the first time that detailed information about Auschwitz-Birkenau was published in the UK, including detailed eyewitness accounts of its gas chambers and crematoria.[23]

The procedural difficulties with the trial, and patchy coverage in the press, have led Donald Bloxham to argue that covering both a concentration camp and a site of extermination in one case led to confusion between different kinds of camp and no distinct sense of the particular genocidal assault on Jews.

> [T]he homicidal gas chamber may well have entered western consciousness in 1945, but it did not signify the apparatus of total murder of a particular, racially defined victim group. Rather, and in no small measure as a result of the early trials, it remained bound up with ill-defined notions

of 'concentration camps' that could symbolize anything from the suffering of Jews to that of German prisoners to the threat posed by the Soviet Union.[24]

We would argue that 'western consciousness' is a rather difficult entity to describe coherently, and we are less inclined to consider it as a totality. What happened in the trial is perhaps better thought of as a set of potentialities that might, or might not, be activated, according to circumstances.

Testimonies at the trial about the gas chambers of Birkenau were given prominence and significance at different points, both in the arguments of the prosecution and in the press. What they meant changed at different points in the proceedings. Opening for the prosecution, Colonel Backhouse located the distinction between the concentration camp Bergen-Belsen and the extermination camp Auschwitz in the latter's having a gas chamber, used to 'exterminate all who were not fit to act as beasts of burden for Germany'. By the end of the trial, the gas chamber was more specifically figured as the instrument of a genocidal assault specifically on Jews.

In between, numerous Jewish survivors had given testimony, including a number who had seen the gas chambers. They included someone who identified himself as a member of the Sonderkommando, but he seems to have caused the prosecution some concern. His account of perpetrators had problems that the defence was able to point out, his affidavit giving details of the gas chamber itself was not included in the prosecution's case, and he was not singled out in the prosecution's closing arguments.[25]

However, two other witnesses, who did not identify as members of the SK, nonetheless could be said to have spoken on their behalf. The first Backhouse described in his opening statement as 'a doctor' who would tell the court 'that from records she has seen there were no less than 4,000,000 people cremated in that camp'. This was Ada Bimko, who had not seen official records, but rather ones that she said a member of the SK had shown to her. In affidavits taken before the trial, Bimko had stated that she 'had examined the records of the numbers cremated and I say that the records show that about 4,000,000 persons were cremated at the camp'.[26] Returning to this in a later deposition, she clarified: 'the records which I examined were not official records but were figures kept by prisoners who worked at the Crematorium'.[27] What is interesting here is the desire to give these 'records' a near official status. The Sonderkommando are figured as entirely objective witnesses, who are keeping records that might as well be those of a bureaucracy. The likelihood is that this was done in order to present the evidence as strongly as possible (whether by Bimko herself or by the investigator who deposed her). But even in the trial itself the term 'record' continued to be used, and it was picked up by the press. The special correspondent for *The Times* and *The Manchester Guardian* at the Lüneburg trial reported Bimko's testimony as the 'biggest moment of the trial' when she identified some of the accused. The report included references to the Sonderkommando as the record keepers on whom she relied for her figure of 4 million victims.[28]

The meaning that the trial was able to give to these documents (or perhaps, the meaning that emerged out of the trial process) was one of providing figures. As we will see, this was also a function given to the SK in the Polish trials. Of course, it is not possible to be an eyewitness to 4 million deaths, so some form of record keeping was the only way this claim could be plausible. It was also only because of the very different approach to hearsay evidence in the Royal Warrant from that usually taken by English criminal law that reports of the writings of the SK were admissible.[29]

A little more than a week later, Dr. Charles Sigismund Bendel, who had worked in the crematoria and at times tended to members of the SK, provided eyewitness testimony of a gassing and its aftermath. Asked about the day's work of one of the crematoria, Bendel explained how people arriving from a new transport were tricked into entering the gas chamber, and murdered. The rest of his description was structured around the actions of the Sonderkommando. When they 'started work' the doors of the gas chamber were opened, showing it to be 'filled to the height of one and a half metres with corpses'—a sight he could never forget. Shifting to the present tense, Bendel described how the 'proper work of the Zonder Kommando [*sic*] starts': dragging the bodies from the chamber and processing them. His account culminated with the following description:

> Now it is proper Hell which is starting. The Zonder Kommando tries to work as fast as possible. They drag the corpses by their wrists to which they attach something. They drag them along in furious haste. People who had human faces before I cannot recognise again. They are like devils.

A barrister from Salonika, an electrical engineer from Budapest, they are no longer human beings, because even during the work blows from sticks and rubber truncheons are being showered over them. During the time that this is going on they continue to shoot people in front of these ditches - people who could not be brought into the gas chambers because they were overcrowded. After an hour and a half the whole work has been done and a new transport has been dealt with in Crematorium No. 4.[30]

When Zalman Gradowski and Leyb Langfus wrote descriptions of the gas chambers, they were able to go into much greater detail about what they saw when the door was opened, describing the different postures and arrangements of bodies, noting individual characteristics as well as the mass of flesh compressed into the room. They even thought through their own feelings about what they saw. Bendel's account is different—more of an attempt to explain the entire functioning of the system, because that helps the court to see what happened in the crematoria overall. But within the space given to him by the court, he was able to do more than that. There was some room for his own sensibilities to be expressed. He explained how the abuse of Red Cross signs went against his own sense of medical ethics. After this, however, it becomes harder to see his own place in the description. Whatever feelings he has about the chamber are not described at length. He does say that anyone who has seen this sight will never forget it, but that of course also functions to validate his evidence: this is a sight that he cannot be accused of misremembering. The emotional weight of this terrible description, it seems to us, is carried by the Sonderkommando. They are mired in the 'proper hell', with their 'proper work'. The shift in tense to the present occurs with the description of the Sonderkommando.[31]

The figure of the gas chamber was far less under Bendel's control than it was in the testimony of Gradowski or Langfus. Its placement in the trial, its return in different contexts (and thus its place in a structure), was the product of different demands and personalities and interpretations: the prosecution, the judge advocate, the newspaper correspondents, and perhaps even the public attending the court. But that did not mean Bendel had no role in shaping the understanding of the gas chamber. The power of his description, achieved through 'literary' means of repetition and comparison, meant that it was taken up at other points in the trial and in press coverage of it. That was not just because of the content. It was because of the form he gave to it. That form was partly worked through the figure of the Sonderkommando.

Bendel's testimony clearly had a striking effect on the people in the court. *The Times* (and *Manchester Guardian*)'s special correspondent responded to it as follows: 'For sheer ghastliness nothing has equalled the description given in evidence to-day of the gas chambers and burning ghats of Auschwitz which were used as the chief instrument of Nazi policy for the mass extermination of the Jews'. The report also mentioned the SK, including their revolt, the burning of Crematorium 3 (IV), and the confusion that prevented much action in Crematorium 1 (II).[32]

When the prosecution made its closing arguments, Bendel's testimony was key to the way in which it characterized Auschwitz and its primary feature, the gas chamber: 'You heard that utterly foul picture painted by Dr. Bendel. Can you have any doubt about it?'[33] Backhouse also referenced as evidence the Soviet film taken on the camp's liberation, and other eyewitness reports, but Bendel's description of the work undertaken by the Sonderkommando functioned as the climactic piece of evidence, one that underpinned the impossibility of doubting what happened on the basis of its visceral, unsettling description of the pace at which the SK worked, the way in which they were transformed into 'devils'. The Judge Advocate, C. L. Stirling, too, gave the gas chamber central place in his understanding of the prosecution's case,[34] as characteristic of Auschwitz as 'wilful or culpable neglect' was of Belsen. The only quotation he included in his summing up was that from Bendel, although it ended just before the description of the work of the SK.

At the Belsen trial, the prosecution built a case in which the gas chamber was the central figure of Auschwitz. In part, this was because the prosecution wanted to argue that all the people involved in the running of the camp were aware of and part of the system that fed the gas chambers. The chamber therefore became the key that explained how Auschwitz worked, and the feature that distinguished it from a concentration camp like Belsen. This might be said to leave the two as still quite similar to each other, blending together different camps, or overweighting the importance of 'camps' themselves, but there was nonetheless within this treatment of the camps an acknowledgement of exterminatory intent against the Jewish people.

It was the Sonderkommando—eyewitnesses even if by hearsay—who provided the most powerful experience around the gas chamber. The Belsen trial allowed different versions of them to be presented without resolving them: objective recorders of facts and figures, as in Bimko's testimony, or figures whose moral and psychological abjection registered the horror of the gas chamber, as in Bendel's. Such contradictory conceptions had an afterlife up into the twenty-first century.

POLAND—TRIALS OF HÖSS AND AUSCHWITZ STAFF

The major trials held in Poland were under the auspices of the Supreme National Tribunal (Najwyższy Trybunał Narodowy, NTN), a special court set up in response to the London declaration by the allies. Of the seven trials that it held, the two to do with Auschwitz were the trial of Rudolf Höss held in Warsaw (11–29 March 1947), and the trial of forty members of the Auschwitz staff held in Kraków (24 November–16 December 1947).[35] Members of the Sonderkommando gave direct testimony at both trials, in a witness stand facing a two-feet high crucifix on the judges' bench, which cast its shadow on the panel of jurists behind. Arnošt Rosin and Henryk Mandelbaum spoke at both, while Filip Müller appears only to have given testimony in Kraków. Affidavits by the SK members Shlomo Dragon (named as Szlama Dragan), Henryk Tauber and Alter Feinsilber were also included as evidence.[36] Of the direct testimony, Mandelbaum's was, by a long way, the most extensive. The likelihood seems to be that Mandelbaum, as the Polish speaker (of Jewish heritage but Roman Catholic by declared religion) served as the person who was able to provide the background account (or the expert account) of the workings of the Sonderkommando for the Supreme Tribunal. His testimonies in both cases were heard before that of other members of the SK.[37]

The case for the prosecution made a distinction between the 'plan of total destruction of the Jews [*totalnej zagłady Żydów*]' and a 'plan of partial destruction of the Poles [*częściowej zagłady Polaków*]' both carried out for the most part in Oświęcim,[38] so once again witnesses to the gas chambers as the instruments of this plan were important. However, the Polish trials gave little room for the victim-witnesses from the SK to talk at length. Most of what they provided was specific testimony against (some of) the accused.[39] This could certainly be something that they themselves wanted to achieve. However, in each case, they also told the story, briefly but notably, of their entry into the Sonderkommando. This is particularly noticeable in the shorter testimonies provided by the Slovak witnesses. Arnošt Rosin's testimonies at Warsaw and Kraków, less than three typed pages, devoted half of its length to his first experiences of being in the SK.[40] Müller's testimony in Kraków, about three-and-a-half typed pages long, spent over half of his testimony on his first two days in the SK before providing examples of the behaviour of individual SS men from his whole time there.[41]

Focussing on this initial moment can be seen as serving a number of functions, some of them for the court, and some for the witness himself. Firstly, it grounded the testimony that the witness was about to give: it gave a clear sense of the position from which he was witnessing (i.e. from the SK and who the SK were), probably in a form that was as close to comprehensible as it could be made. The shock, bewilderment and suffering that each of them describes on entering the SK provide some way for the people hearing the testimony to enter imaginatively into that environment. It also served practical needs of providing reasonably precise dates (most of the SK could date when they were forced into its ranks), and memories that could plausibly be tied to them.[42] For the witnesses themselves, this was also probably a way to enter back into those experiences, and to work through some of the feelings associated with them.[43] While there is a good deal of overlap between these functions, they were not all in play at the same time. Henryk Mandelbaum, for example, gave an initial account of his entry into the SK that provided a slightly less good 'grounding' for his testimony against Höss, one that served primarily an expressive function:

> I thought I was in hell, because no one had ever seen this. Corpses, corpses and more corpses. At first I couldn't find my bearings [*Z początku nie orientowałem się*], because I was simply stunned [*oszolomiony*]. After a while I returned to a normal state and then I managed to observe how things worked. At that time nothing was burned in the ovens, but rather on pyres because mass transports were coming in, at that time transports from Hungary.[44]

In his later testimony, he described his reactions in almost exactly the opposite way:

> When I first went to work, I immediately realized where I was [*odrazu zdałem sobie sprawę, gdzie się znajduję*]. I thought that I was in hell – there were bodies everywhere, fire, and the place was crawling with SS men who guarded the laborers and hurried them on to remove the corpses of the gassed victims, for new transports were arriving all the time.[45]

There is little variance here (it seems to us) in terms of actual facts, but there is a small but direct contradiction, which makes them work quite differently as stories. In the first version, Mandelbaum took some time to be able to see what happened. In the second, he was able to work it out straight away. In the first, the emotional toll on him interferes (momentarily) with his ability to witness. In the second, it is part of what he bears witness to. It is, we think, entirely possible for someone to interpret the same experience in these two ways at different times, but the difference is telling nonetheless. This later testimony might then be called more 'streamlined', one that simply gets down to testimony of evidentiary value. Appearing in a different location but before the same people (much the same prosecutorial team and the same panel of judges), Mandelbaum may well have found it easier to give testimony the second time, or simply he had a better idea of what the court expected and how to fit his testimony to it. On his first appearance, the court did not permit him to express everything that he wanted: he was not allowed to talk about the experiences of his family under occupation.[46] In his testimony at the Kraków trial, Mandelbaum goes straight into his discussion of Auschwitz, and also straight into an account of what being in the SK was like. This is not to say that there is simply no room for discussion of what effect the sight had on him: he is still able to describe the experience as being in hell. But he makes this experience more part of explaining what he saw, how the system of the camp worked and how it related to the situation at the time.

The account of how people enter the gas chambers also changes from one testimony to the other. In the first, Mandelbaum tells more of a story: he explains how Otto Moll would give speeches to the newly arrived victims and quotes him directly:

> Mohl [*sic*] stood [*stanął*] on a bench – they had benches like this there – and launched into a sermon [*wygłosił kazanie*] to them: You have come to work, nothing bad will happen to you here, you will be given work and go to your quarters. But first please get undressed, have a shower, leave your clothes, you'll get new ones.[47]

In the second, he provides an overview:

> an average person could well believe that it was indeed a bath[room], especially if it was presented as such during the journey or after one's arrival at Auschwitz; the latter was the specialty of Hauptscharführer Mohl [*sic*],

who would launch into a sermon for the people [*wygłaszał ludziom kazanie*] and tell them that they had come to perform well-paid work. And although they had left valuable property behind, they would be able settle down here and earn new fortunes. Thereafter he instructed [*kazał*] them to undress, saying that they would receive fresh clothes because – since they were going to a place where cleanliness must be maintained – it was necessary to prevent the spread of disease.[48]

Moll's speech in the first instance is given with perfective verbs, indicating specific actions: Mandelbaum is telling of one time when a specific incident happened. In the second, the verbs are imperfective, indicating habitual action. It also uses indirect speech, not the direct speech of the first version. The second version is much less of a story, much more of an overall account of a system, explaining how the gas chambers operated and what people tended to do. The organizing language is oriented around explaining what happened, not following the experience of either Mandelbaum or the victims: 'Preparations for the incineration of gassing victims looked like this'; 'And now I will recount how transports were gassed during my period of incarceration'.[49]

These changes from one trial to another seem to show Mandelbaum finding solutions to the difficulties of what can happen at a trial, ones that apply to the Sonderkommando specifically. They were in a position to provide accounts of specific incidents, but also to speak from experience of how the system usually worked. There are narrative considerations here: does one provide a vivid example or a general account? But there are also juridical ones. In neither case was Otto Moll standing trial; he had already been executed for his actions in Dachau. In the first account, then, Mandelbaum was denouncing someone for his specific actions—a strategy that would have been more effective if Moll had been one of the defendants, or even still alive. In the second account, he was making these actions elements in a system in which the actual defendants had taken part. The shift between these two accounts thus shows Mandelbaum becoming a more effective juridical witness, and adopting different narrative strategies to do so.

Philippe Mesnard notes how one role the SK play in documentaries about the camps is that of technical specialists, who say little of their own feelings but rather simply explain how the machinery of death operated.[50] Mandelbaum shows that he wishes to do more than this, however. Even in his first account, when he lacks conventional Polish eloquence, using colloquialisms and stumbling into talking about a human body having four legs instead of limbs, he shows his ability to exercise agency on the witness stand and advance agendas of his own.[51] For example, he wants to explain the behaviour of the victims. After Moll finished his spiel, Mandelbaum goes on to explain: 'You know how folks are [*naród – jak naród*]. They went into the showers'. He adds slightly later in his testimony, 'That's how they hoodwinked these folks [*Tak tumanili ten naród*]'.[52] Here Mandelbaum is clearly using his testimony to explain why there was a lack of resistance from those murdered. They did not *realize* that there was a need to resist. Although he is nominally speaking as a Roman Catholic, he is defending the Jews (possibly as a people or nation—another meaning of *naród*), using the information he provides not just as evidence of crimes but as a means to illustrate deception so that he can then give an explanation as to why those about to be gassed did not rise up and fight.

Mandelbaum also seems keen to make it clear that the SK did show some resistance. He mentions that although the SK were instructed to work in a particular way when burning the bodies so as to be more efficient and therefore quicker, each man disregarded the directive: 'As he had to, he worked, but as slowly as he could so as to delay. The slower the work was done, the less transports could come' (154). He puts it on record that the SK were only superficially compliant even when not in open revolt. Linked with this emphasis on what might be called passive resistance, Mandelbaum explained how the prisoners informed the outside world, including the ways that they had buried documents and cameras (158). Documenting resistance was of interest to the court too. It was the chief prosecutor who asked Mandelbaum to provide an account of the Sonderkommando's uprising.

The statements provided by Dragon, Feinsilber and Tauber—as documentary evidence—provide fuller accounts of their time in the SK. Each is witnessed by the prosecutor Edward Pechalski and the investigative judge Jan Sehn. The statements were recorded by three different women, Krystyna Szymańska (for Dragon), Stefania Setmajer (for Tauber) and Jarosława Kocyłowska (for Feinsilber). These transcribers were tasked with transforming speech into writing, likely tidying up hesitations and repetitions, filtering out failures of fluency and grafting over periods of silence to provide the appearance of verbal continuity. The statements manifest in microcosm similar tensions between the need to provide a factual account of the extermination process and a wish to give additional information for other, often complex, reasons. Henryk Tauber, for instance, makes a point of stressing the goodness of the Kapo Władysław Tomiczek after detailing how he came to knew of his murder at the hands of the SS. Tauber states: 'He was a good person. He had concerned himself with our well-being. We had decided to incorporate him in our underground'.[53] Tauber does not need to reflect on the character of Tomiczek the man after explaining that he was killed. He clearly feels the need to do this. Tauber wants to honour the man's memory and make sure his good character is placed on record. This kind of divergence from the function of giving evidence to provide proof of a crime would probably not have been permitted on the witness stand.

Perhaps the most remarkable testimony to emerge as part of the judiciary evidence provided by the SK occurs in Dragon's statement. He details what it was like upon opening the gas chamber in the Bunkers after a gassing. His highly unsettling account employs simple language yet to powerful effect. Dragon observes that on first going into the chamber 'you could sense the gas and on the lips was left something sweet, almost pleasant'. A little later he remembers that 'a short time after the end of the gassing when we entered the chamber we could still hear some kind of groan [*jęk*]'. Gradowski's vivid account in *In the Heart of Hell* of the opening of the gas chamber in the crematorium asserts that a wave of death is expelled when the doors are opened.[54] He also recalls that on entering a faint sound, a light trickling, can be heard as bodies void their fluids. The groan or moan that Dragon describes, an unpleasant sound, is not the same as the exhalation Gradowski refers to, it is not the outrush of air once the hermetic doors are opened, nor is it the evacuating of fluids. As the sound is most evident when bodies are being grabbed to haul them out, it is possible that what has stuck in Dragon's mind is the sound of people who are unconscious but still alive (tellingly he then immediately goes on to describe finding a child beneath a pile of corpses that was still living).[55]

The level of detail in Dragon's description works to affirm the first-handedness of his account. It conforms to what is expected of him as a witness because he draws on the language of perception. Knowing the taste of the gas places him at the scene of the crimes. Taste is, of course, a proximate sense. Hearing the groans of the dying when moving them also situates him in the midst of the atrocity. This is not solely *eye*witness testimony. It is not detached in the way that Bendel's is at the Belsen trial. Dragon was implicated in the process of mass-killing in a way the medic was not. He was one of those who had to drag out the bodies, experiencing their dead-weight in his limbs on a daily basis, regularly tasting the residue of the deadly gas on his lips. He felt—as much as saw—the horrors of murder. His multi-sensory account contributes to buttressing the fact that he was there. This is not hearsay, this is direct testimony from the core of the death factory.

Yet there is a sense something more is going on in this description. That the gas tasted nice, for example, appears to present a difficulty for Dragon. He refers to it as *almost* pleasant. To say, the taste *was* pleasant would be to acknowledge there was something agreeable about it. At this moment, Dragon may realize that finding any kind of pleasure in the very substance used as a tool of murder is unconscionable. Here, buried in the legal testimony, there is a reference to sensual appreciation, to the (nearly) finding of sensual satisfaction where none would be thought possible. The qualifier Dragon uses registers his concern over what kind of language to use to communicate what he has experienced, over what it is appropriate to say. Mandelbaum apologizes in advance to the court for the graphic description he will go on to provide of the appearance of a gas chamber immediately after a gassing.[56] In the trial testimonies, the SK seem to be learning about what can be talked about, what should be talked about, and how it should be talked about. The SK are clearly already censoring dimensions of their personal and group experiences but some topics that will later become taboo are still admissible in this immediate post-war period. When Dragon later gives testimony to Gideon Greif in the 1990s, the reference to pleasantness is gone. He states simply 'you could sense the sweetish taste of the gas'.[57] It is also not some kind of groan but simply groaning. In this later testimony, there is no longer the same sense of searching for words to match with experiences. Things are more settled.

Only parts of the Sonderkommando's testimony were taken up by the court's judgement. Primarily they seem to have provided some way of estimating numbers, even though this was actually not something the SK were able reliably to do. The judgement of the court provided a detailed breakdown of its findings of fact. In these findings, references were made to witness statements, but the only reference to a member of the Sonderkommando was to Ludwik Nagraba, who provided the figure of deaths in the gas chamber of 2,550,000 (37). This was a figure the court accepted (39). However, the judgement also provided an account of the Sonderkommando's revolt:

In October 1944, the then prisoners of the 'Sonderkommando', who were informed that they would be transferred to another camp, which in reality meant to the gas chambers, carried out an uprising, after preparations made with the help of the wider resistance movement in the camp, in which they burnt one of the crematoria and wounded several SS men. The revolt was eventually crushed, with about 500 prisoners killed.[58]

No witness statement was referred to here, but the account was close to that provided by Mandelbaum.

There was, however, little interest in these trials in the west. In *The Manchester Guardian*'s report on the Höss trial in Warsaw, the correspondent noted a large Polish public presence in the court, but that 'the tables reserved for the foreign press are empty, with one or two exceptions', an absence of interest which caused surprise among 'Polish newspapermen'.[59]

Even so, the trials gave public space to the SK that they had not had before, one that channelled and shaped their testimony, but that did give some space for them to meet some of their own purposes too. It might also have helped establish ways of talking about their experiences that members of the SK drew upon for the rest of their lives: Filip Müller told the same story of his forced recruitment several times up to the interview with Claude Lanzmann in 1979[60]; Henryk Mandelbaum talked to Jan Południak about his entry into the SK in very similar terms in 1994.[61] The early conceptions of the crime as destruction of Jews specifically also provide important context and reinforcement for their testimony.

THE FRANKFURT AUSCHWITZ TRIAL (1963–1965)

The 'criminal case against Robert Mulka and others' held in Frankfurt between 20 December 1963 and 19 August 1965 has received considerably more attention than either the Royal Warrant or NTN trials. It involved some of the most extensive testimonies provided by members of the Auschwitz SK. Carried out under the West German legal system, and thus admitting no charges to be brought that were not in the German legal code at the time of the crime, the Frankfurt trial might be said to have been a rather more rigid application of the law to conceptualizing the crime than the more flexible approaches of the Allies. Nonetheless, like the trials of years before, Frankfurt had more than one purpose, with the prosecution attempting both to make a general case of perpetration as part of a system, but also, particularly because of the demands of German law, showing individual acts of killing that went beyond following orders. Systematic killing was difficult to prosecute, in that it was not readily classified as 'murder'. The perpetrators who followed orders in order to run the killing engines tended to be seen not as principal killers, but rather as accomplices. Only those who committed 'excesses' (*Exceßtäter*) were readily prosecutable as murderers.[62]

As eyewitnesses to the system of genocide (or at least its effects), the Sonderkommando were able to give detailed, first-hand accounts of how the machinery of mass murder operated, and the personnel who operated it on the ground. They were also able to testify to 'excesses'. Gas chambers were sites where excesses took place—ones that might be called more systematic (means to cow victims and force them to enter the gas chambers),[63] and ones that were more personally inventive (acts of sadism, e.g. those of Otto Moll).

Dov Paisikovic provided a detailed day-to-day account of what happened in the gas chambers and crematoria. Before examination by lawyers, he only talked about one incident: one of the SS men, Oswald Kaduk, drowning someone. Afterwards, when asked to identify people, he did identify several, mostly doctors, and fixed them to his story. The trial also revealed that he had kept a 'diary' in Birkenau, and that the magazine *Revue* published a story of him going to look for it.[64] *Revue*, it would appear, contacted Paisikovic because of the part that he was to play in the trial. Milton Buki provided a clear description of Kaduk's role in the process, as well as how the process worked. He had written a book in Yiddish about his experience.[65]

Even those witnesses who were less masterful were able to give testimony in the way that they wanted to, to some degree. When the judge Hofmeyer asked Milton Buki to explain in his own words how the crematorium operated, Buki said that he was too nervous to take responsibility for constructing the entire account himself. 'I can't speak freely', he said, 'but I can answer questions'.[66] Here the court's parameters function as an emotional support for Buki. He does not want to speak on his own terms, but to fit what he is saying to the needs of the court, what it wants to know. This takes some of the burden away from him. But it is also a format that he has chosen for himself. This process of negotiation takes away from the idea of a witness prevented from expressing his truth by terms dictated to him. Tailoring his speech to the needs of his audience is part of what allows him to testify.

Filip Müller's account of his first day in the Sonderkommando was more or less repeated between his testimony in Kraków in 1947 and his testimony in Frankfurt in 1964, with more emphasis placed upon the defendants of the particular trial: here Hans Stark rather than Aumeier and Grabner. As Peter Davies has shown, Müller's account had a dramatic power that impressed the judges with its truth, especially in his account of the actions of Stark.[67] The prosecution also described Müller's account as a 'particularly insistent and impressive statement'.[68] Another lawyer, Henry Ormond identified Müller as one of the most significant witnesses.[69] That power worked within the parameters provided by the court, as Davies has argued. But it functioned beyond the courtroom too: Peter Weiss's *The Investigation*, based on testimony at the Frankfurt trial, has only one canto named after a perpetrator, Canto 6 Unterscharführer Stark. While Stark's youth and sadism make him a striking case in itself, Müller's dramatic retelling of how he tortured and murdered victims on the threshold of the gas chamber must have played some part in Weiss's singling out of this particular case (from his own presence there, but also through consulting reports, particularly from Bernd Naumann), in which he makes use of Müller's testimony as Witness 7.[70]

Coming two decades after the liberation of Auschwitz, the Frankfurt trial could be seen as occurring at a very different time in Western Holocaust consciousness, after the publication of detailed historical scholarship (e.g. by Raul Hilberg), and at a point where more efforts were being made in West Germany to address its Nazi past. But it is also worth considering where it stood in the life cycle of the witnesses' testimony: at something like the mid-point of their telling these stories. All of the SK who bore witness on the stand had put their experience into some form immediately after (and in one case before) liberation: Paisikovic's diary, Buki's Yiddish memoir, Müller's testimony. Here the court was not simply generating testimony anew, but rather collecting it together, allowing it to be reheard, and redistributed. The use of Müller's words in Peter Weiss's play is the most striking example, but the interview with Paisikovic in *Revue* is also significant.[71]

Conclusion

The court testimony of the Sonderkommando thus functions in a number of different ways, which show different kinds of thinking and power relations at work in them. Members of the SK can be seen achieving ends that work in the same direction as the court: bringing particular perpetrators to justice and providing more general accounts. Survivors from the SK used the structures of the court to achieve those ends (Buki), adapted their testimony to fit the requirements of the court (Mandelbaum), and perhaps even founded some of their prime testimonial moments in the courtroom (Müller, talking about his first two days in the SK).

We also see stories from the SK operating even in their absence. This can range from the SK having an effect on the court (e.g. Filip Müller's powerful and dramatic account of Hans Stark), to that effect going beyond the court (e.g. Weiss's use of Müller's testimony), to that effect being registered in the courtroom proceedings and beyond (e.g. Bendel and Bimko speaking at Lüneburg on behalf of the SK—and their appearance in the newspapers). This functioning is not simply some reuse and repurposing of the testimony, but a response to the urgency and power of these particular stories. The later instance of the Frankfurt trial also shows that oral testimony of the SK was not a straightforward recollection of a previous moment, but was often bound up with previous tellings and recordings of what happened (Buki, Paisikovic), which sometimes fitted with what the court wanted and sometimes did not.

The SK's testimony (and accounts of them) was central to the accounts of the genocide that courts were beginning to piece together: the importance of the figure of the gas chamber, the importance too of stories of the revolt. These accounts were not fully 'successful' as accounts of the operation of the Final Solution, for reasons that scholars such as Bloxham and Wittman have shown. But they provided 'transitional truths' that gave opportunities for further attempts to think it through, whether in newspaper articles, or in plays such as Weiss's. Or in a film such as *Shoah*, which made use of the archive provided by the Frankfurt trial to identify one of its key witnesses: Filip Müller.

Notes

1. Proces Rudolfa Hoessa, Sygn. GK 196/93, NTN 93, Volume 1, 1946–1947. USHMM Accession Number 1998.A.0243. RG Number RG-15.167M.
2. For an insightful discussion of justice as improvisation, see Chapter 7 of Sarah Ramshaw's, *Justice as Improvisation: The Law of the Extempore* (Abingdon: Routledge, 2013).
3. Hannah Arendt, *Eichmann in Jerusalem: A Report on the Banality of Evil* (New York: Penguin, 1994).

4. Devin O. Pendas, *The Frankfurt Auschwitz Trial, 1963–1965: Genocide, History, and the Limits of the Law* (Cambridge: Cambridge University Press, 2006) and Rebecca Wittman, *Beyond Justice: The Auschwitz Trial* (Cambridge, MA: Harvard University Press, 2012).
5. Donald Bloxham, *Genocide on Trial: War Crimes, Trials and the Formation of Holocaust History and Memory* (Oxford: Oxford University Press, 2001).
6. The kind of testimony that is possible to articulate in courtrooms, for instance, is often restricted in significant part by questioning. As part of a discussion of the transmission of information between witness, counsel and magistrate in the British court system, Richard Mead observes that counsel exercise considerable control over testimony, lending it a 'tidied-up' quality that more resembles a performance than a naturally occurring conversation. Mead, *Courtroom Discourse* (Birmingham: University of Birmingham, 1985), pp. 32–33. Andrew E. Taslitz has examined how testimony given by an individual in private is often fuller than the account they provide in court because in private they can 'speak in [their] own fashion' whereas in court the defence counsel can employ 'courtroom language games' to disrupt the witness. Taslitz, *Rape and the Culture of the Courtroom* (New York: New York University Press, 1999), p. 10.
7. Arendt, *Eichmann in Jerusalem*. Lawrence Douglas considers Arendt's argument on what the point of a trial is (to render justice) to be 'a crabbed and needlessly restrictive vision of the trial as legal form' (*The Memory of Judgement: Making Law and History in the Trials of the Holocaust*. New Haven: Yale University Press, 2001), p. 2 and embraces instead what he calls 'didactic legality' (pp. 2–7).
8. Felman also relies on a rather schematic distinction between the Nuremberg trials (document-based trials) and the Eichmann trial of 1961. Nuremberg 'did not articulate the victims' story but subsumed it in the general political and military story of the war'. The Eichmann trial 'makes the victim's story *happen* for the first time, and happen as a legal act of *authorship of history*'. *The Juridical Unconscious: Trials and Traumas in the Twentieth Century* (Cambridge, MA: Harvard University Press, 2002), pp. 126, 129. See also Cathy Caruth, 'The Body's Testimony: Dramatic Witness in the Eichmann Trial,' *Paragraph* 40.3 (2017): 259–278.
9. Pendas, *The Frankfurt Auschwitz Trial*, pp. 161–168. Pendas suggests that giving testimony and being cross-examined was painful (and this was backed up by Tadeusz Cyprian's report on the Belsen Trial). The issue of the acknowledgment of trauma within the criminal justice system (as it intersects with more victim-centred approaches to legal processes) is still a major concern. See Louise Ellison and Vanessa E. Munro, 'Taking Trauma Seriously: Critical Reflections on the Criminal Justice Process,' *The International Journal of Evidence and Proof* 21.3 (2017): 183–208.

10. Pendas, *The Frankfurt Auschwitz Trial*, p. 162. Simon Gotland began by attempting to give his testimony in French, before settling on doing so primarily in Polish (although with multiple attempts to speak German). Actually, the Polish interpreter said that she could understand him perfectly well. Here a practical difficulty—finding a language which was mutually intelligible—and what might be called identity claims or desires (Gotland claiming French citizenship, claiming also to be able to speak German) are confused with (or blend into) the overarching claim of the Shoah's unspeakability. 70. Verhandlungstag (27 July 1964). Zeno.org: *Der 1. Frankfurter Auschwitz-Prozess*, p. 13299 (cp. AP096.027).
11. Mark Osiel, Lawrence Douglas, and Judith Shklar have a much less restrictive idea of what a human rights trial can achieve—it is a forum in which multiple goals are being aimed at. Mark Drumbl too, despite some scepticism about trials, sees them as attempting to achieve a range of goals. Osiel, *Mass Atrocity, Collective Memory and the Law* (Transaction, 1997). Douglas, ibid., Judith Shklar, *Legalism: Law, Morals and Political Trials* (Cambridge, MA: Harvard University Press, 1984), and Drumbl, 'Stepping Beyond Nuremberg's Halo: The Legacy of the Supreme National Tribunal of Poland,' *Journal of International Criminal Justice* 13 (2015): 903–932.
12. Pendas, *The Frankfurt Auchwitz Trial*, p. 4.
13. Daniela Accatino and Cath Collins, 'Truth, Evidence, Truth: The Deployment of Testimony, Archives and Technical Data in Domestic Human Rights Trials,' *Journal of Human Rights Practice* 8 (2016): 81–100.
14. For this point, we are particularly indebted to Peter Davies, 'What Can We Learn from Trial Testimony? Filip Müller's Sonderkommando Testimony to the Frankfurt Auschwitz Trial?' *Telling, Describing, Representing Extermination: The Auschwitz Sonderkommando, Their Testimony and Their Legacy*, Centre Marc Bloch, Berlin, 12 April 2018 [Video of this talk available at https://www.dailymotion.com/video/x6nkuyo].
15. Some legal theorists see this as part of the role of any human rights trial. See Mihaela Mihai, 'Socialising Negative Emotions: Transitional Criminal Trials in the Service of Democracy,' *Oxford Journal of Legal Studies* 31.1 (2011): 111–131.
16. For the first of these, see Davies, 'What Can Be Learned from Trial Testimony'.
17. The IMT trial at Nuremberg relied on Seweryna Szmaglewska to give a witness account of the ovens (based on her presence in Kanada) as part of an account of how children were treated (although she included other information about mistreatment). And for Treblinka on Samuel Rajzman—although he sorted the clothes, rather than being able to provide eyewitness accounts of the gas chambers. While there were significant

references to the Auschwitz Sonderkommando in the testimony of some witnesses at the Eichmann trial, no member of the Auschwitz SK testified. Yehuda Bacon, Raya Kagan, Vera Alexander, and Gedalia Ben Zvi all provided stories that they had been told by members of the SK. See http://www.nizkor.org/hweb/people/e/eichmann-adolf/transcripts/ (accessed 15 August 2018).

18. For the background to this and other British trials held under a Royal Warrant see A. P. V. Rogers, 'War Crimes Trials under the Royal Warrant: British Practice 1945–1949,' International and Comparative Law Quarterly 39.4 (1990): 780–800. Scans of trial records are available via http://www.legal-tools.org, transcripts via http://www.bergenbelsen.co.uk.

19. We provide NTN referencing for the relevant volumes of each of the trials. We accessed the trial material through the United States Holocaust Memorial Museum archives. Proces Rudolfa Hoessa (Sygn. GK 196), 1946–1947. USHMM Accession Number 1998.A.0243. RG Number RG-15.167M; Proces członków załogi Oświęcimia (Sygn. GK 196)—Trial Against the Staff of KL Auschwitz-Birkenau Accession Number 1998.A.0247. RG Number RG-15.169M. Witness testimonies from Henryk Mandelbaum, Filip Müller and Arnošt Rosin are also available as scans, transcriptions, and sometimes English translations at 'Chronicles of Terror,' http://www.zapisyterroru.pl (search by witness name). On the NTN trials in general see Alexander V. Prusin, 'Poland's Nuremberg: The Seven Court Cases of the Supreme National Tribunal, 1946–1948,' *Holocaust and Genocide Studies* 24.1 (2010): 1–25.

20. Carlo Ginzburg, *The Judge and the Historian*, trans. Antony Shuggar (London: Verso, 1999), p. 19.

21. Höss Trial, IPN GK 196/110, vol. 26, p. 154.

22. Here, it was not the same as other concentration camp trials. At the Ravensbrück trial Johann Schwarzhuber, who had been *Schützhaftlagerführer* of the men's camp in Auschwitz, was tried for his activities only in Ravensbrück. See the passing references to Schwarhuber's role at Auschwitz in the Judge Advocate's (again C. L. Stirling) summing up of this case Transcript of the 39th–44th days of the trial against Schwarzhuber et al., pp. 100–101. https://www.legal-tools.org/doc/84ff17/pdf/. Otto Moll, notorious as one of the most sadistic killers at the Birkenau crematoria was tried by an American military court solely for his actions in Dachau. References to Auschwitz were at a bare minimum in this trial, merely serving to indicate a wider criminal conspiracy beyond Dachau. *Trial against Martin Gottfried Weiss et al. Trial Reports Volume I (15 November 1945–13 December 1945)*, p. 141. Available at http://www.legal-tools.org/doc/3ddaef/pdf/.

23. Aside from a story from Reuters (summarizing Moscow radio's story from Pravda) carried in May 1945 by a handful of regional newspapers, the

first mention in major British newspapers of the Auschwitz camp seems to have been from testimony at the Belsen trial.
24. Bloxham, *Genocide on Trial: War Crimes, Trials and the Formation of Holocaust History and Memory* (Oxford: Oxford University Press, 2001), p. 226.
25. Roman Sompolinski's description of the gas chamber given in his affidavit does not match the generally agreed reconstruction of their form and adds detail that it is unlikely to have been simply misremembered (WO 235/24). The prosecution relied instead on the description of the gas chamber from Charles Bendel, as we will discuss. Questions were also raised both by the defence and by the Judge Advocate about Sompolinski's identification of perpetrators at Birkenau. It is possible Sompolinski briefly aided in the burning of bodies. Members of the *Leichenträgerkommando* (Corpse commando) came into contact with the SK in this way. In video testimony for the Shoah Foundation, Sompolinski refers to participating in corpse burning at Auschwitz. Roman Sompolinski interviewed by Beth Feldman on 7 December 1995. USC Shoah Foundation. Interview Code 9735. In testimony provided for the Holocaust Documentation and Education Center (Miami, Florida), however, he recalls hearing about the burning of bodies from others. Roman Sompolinski interviewed by Michael Spavin on 8 February 2002. USHMM Accession number 1995.A.1261.1125. RG-50.431.1125.
26. WO 235/24 9 May 1945.
27. WO 235/24 1 June 1945.
28. *The Times*, Saturday 22 September 1945, p. 3 (misspelled as Binko in their report). *The Manchester Guardian* carried the same report on 22 September, p. 6 (with correct spelling of Bimko's name). The *New York Times* also includes mention of the SK as 'the special group of prisoners assigned to work in the Oswiecim death-house' (22 September 1945, p. 5).
29. The Royal Warrant allowed the inclusion of 'any oral statement or any document appearing on the face of it to be authentic, provided the statement or document appears to the Court to be of assistance in proving or disproving the charge notwithstanding that such statement or document would not be admissible as evidence in proceedings before a Field General Court-Martial'. This included 'any diary, letter or other document appearing to contain information relating to the charge' [8(i)e]. The court was even allowed to accept, in the absence of the original, 'a copy of such document or other secondary evidence of its contents' [8(i)f]. John Cramer notes the importance of affidavits—one of the investigators writes to a colleague that the trial can't go ahead without them. Cramer, *Belsen Trial 1945: Der Lüneburger Prozess gegen Wachpersonal der Konzentrationslager Auschwitz und Bergen-Belsen* (Göttingen:

Wallstein, 2011), p. 191. The Judge Advocate was rather less enthusiastic. The affidavits, Stirling said, were 'somewhat of a novelty to me'. He strongly encouraged the court to regard them with scepticism. Day 51 (14 November 1945). http://www.bergenbelsen.co.uk/pages/TrialTranscript/Trial_Day_051.html.
30. Transcript of 13th day of trial (1 October 1945), pp. 4–5. http://www.legal-tools.org/doc/cf204c/pdf/.
31. In this testimony, Bendel stands apart from the group. He distances himself from the SK, observing them rather than participating in their work. But he identified himself with them as far as the revolt was concerned: 'we ourselves on the day of the revolution, on the 7 October, set fire to Crematorium No. 3'.
32. *The Times*, Tuesday 2 October 1945, p. 4 (dated October 1).
33. Day 50 (13 November 1945). http://www.bergenbelsen.co.uk/pages/TrialTranscript/Trial_Day_050.html.
34. Day 51 (14 November 1945). http://www.bergenbelsen.co.uk/pages/TrialTranscript/Trial_Day_051.html. The judge advocate was (and is) a feature of a British court-martial, who plays the same role as a judge in a Crown Court up to the sentencing stage.
35. Mark A. Drumbl 'Stepping Beyond Nuremberg's Halo'; Marcin Marcinko, 'The Concept of Genocide in the Trials of Nazi Criminals Before the Polish Supreme National Tribunal,' in *Historical Origins of International Criminal Law: Volume 2*, eds. Morten Bergsmo, Cheah Wui Ling, and Yi Ping, FICHL Publication Series No. 21 (Brussels: Torkel Opsahl Academic EPublisher, 2014).
36. For an account of the circumstances of these affidavits, see Andrea Rudorff, 'Early Testimony from Feinsilber, Dragon and Tauber: Moral Dimensions,' Unpublished Conference Paper, *Telling, Describing, Representing Extermination: The Auschwitz Sonderkommando, Their Testimony and Their Legacy*, Centre Marc Bloch, Berlin, 12 April 2018. [Video of this paper available at https://www.dailymotion.com/video/x6nl2pj].
37. Mandelbaum was called on 19 March 1947 for the Höss trial, five days before Rosin's testimony, and on 28 November 1947 for the Kraków trial, two weeks before Müller and Rosin. Polish witnesses were called before those of other nationalities.
38. Höss Trial, IPN GK 196/110 NTN 107, vol. 22, p. 8.
39. Both Mandelbaum and Rosin related specific accounts of Höss being personally involved with selections and burning bodies at Auschwitz. Müller gave evidence with examples of Aumeier and Grabner's actions.
40. Höss Trial: 24 March 1947 IPN GK 196/110 NTN 110, vol. 28, p. 45 (1164)-48 (1167). Kraków Trial: 11 December 1947 IPN GK 196/166 NTN 166, vol. 83, pp. 6–8.

41. Transcript of 16th day (11 December 1947). IPN GK 196/166 NTN 166, vol. 83, pp. 1–6. This story was repeated in his testimony at Frankfurt and again to Claude Lanzmann in *Shoah*. This may be because this story was always important to him, but telling it this way must have helped to establish it as important.
42. Defence counsel Ostaszewski tried to pin Henryk Mandelbaum down to dates when he had seen Höss at Birkenau, to claim that Höss could not have been there at that time. Höss Trial, IPN GK 196/110, vol. 26, pp. 150–153.
43. Note, for example, that when Primo Levi attempted to imagine the SK he did so mainly by envisioning the moment of entry into their ranks. See Dominic Williams, 'What Makes the Grey Zone Grey? Blurring Moral and Factual Judgements of the Sonderkommando,' in *Testimonies of Resistance: Representations of the Auschwitz-Birkenau Sonderkommando*, eds. Nicholas Chare and Dominic Williams (New York: Berghahn, 2019), in press.
44. IPN GK 196/108 NTN 108, vol. 26, p. 150.
45. IPN GK 196/162 NTN 162, vol. 79, p. 163.
46. Höss Trial, IPN GK 196/110, vol. 26, pp. 150–151.
47. Höss Trial, IPN GK 196/110, vol. 26, p. 149/838.
48. Kraków Trial, IPN GK 196/166, p. 166.
49. Ibid., pp. 163, 165.
50. Philippe Mesnard, 'The Sonderkommando on Screen,' in *Testimonies of Resistance: Representations of the Auschwitz-Birkenau Sonderkommando*, eds. Nicholas Chare and Dominic Williams (New York: Berghahn, 2019), in press.
51. Arlette Farge has examined how legal testimony manifests the agency of those invited to bear witness, displaying acts of improvisation and incorporating distinct ethical and stylistic traits. See Farge, *Le goût de l'archive* (Paris: Édition de Seuil, 1989), p. 110.
52. Höss Trial, IPN GK 196/110, vol. 26, pp. 151–152.
53. 'Protokół [Official Record]—Henryk Tauber', Proces Rudolfa Hoessa, Sygn. GK 196/93, NTN 93, Volume 11, 1946–1947. USHMM Accession Number 1998.A.0243. RG Number RG-15.167M, 122-149; 128 (1-28; 7).
54. Alexandre Prstojevic contrasts Gradowski's literary description of the process of mass murder at the crematorium with the judicial deposition provided by Dragon, which he finds soulless and factual. See Prstojevic, 'L'indicible et la fiction configuratrice,' *Protée* 37.2 (2009): 39–40.
55. Dragon may be referring to the sound of gas escaping from the dead but this appears unlikely given the context and what he states in later oral testimony.
56. Höss Trial, IPN GK 196/110, vol. 26, p. 152.
57. Greif, *We Wept Without Tears*, p. 136.
58. Kraków, IPN GK 196/166, vol. 32, pp. 37, 39, 43–44.

59. 'Hoess Admits His Guilt,' *The Manchester Guardian*, 17 March 1947.
60. See Chapter 7 of this book.
61. Jan Południak, *Sonder: An Interview with Sonderkommando Member Henryk Mandelbaum*, trans. Witold Zbirohowski-Kościa (Oświęcim: Frap-Books, 2008), p. 30.
62. Katrin Stoll, 'Producing the Truth: The Bielefeld Trial and the Reconstruction of Events Surrounding the Execution of 100 Jews in the Bialystok Ghetto following the "Acid Attack",' *Dapim* 25.1 (2011): 61–62, Rebecca Wittman, *Beyond Justice: The Auschwitz Trial* (Cambridge, MA: Harvard University Press, 2012), p. 101 and Michael S. Bryant, *Eyewitness to Genocide: The Operation Reinhard Death Camp Trials, 1955–1966* (Knoxville: University of Tennessee Press, 2014), p. 14. This is not to say that excessive acts were necessary to prove that someone was a principal murderer; if he could be shown to have treated the crime as if it were his own, he would count as more than an accomplice. Not surprisingly, however, this uniting of one's will with the instigator of the deed was not easy to prove.
63. E.g. the actions of Gustav Münzberger. Bryant, *Eyewitness to Genocide*, pp. 215–219
64. Paul Trunk, 'Wiedersehen mit der Hölle,' *Revue* 37, 13 September 1964. 98. Verhandlungstag (8 October 1964). Zeno.org: *Der 1. Frankfurter Auschwitz-Prozess*, p. 21050.
65. 127. Verhandlungstag (14 January 1965). Zeno.org: Der 1. Frankfurter Auschwitz-Prozess, p. 27859 (cp. AP261.005).
66. 127. Verhandlungstag (14 January 1965). Zeno.org: Der 1. Frankfurter Auschwitz-Prozess, p. 27859 (cp. AP261.005).
67. Peter Davies, 'What Can We Learn from Trial Testimony?'.
68. 155. Verhandlungstag (7 May 1965). Zeno.org: *Der 1. Frankfurter Auschwitz-Prozess*, p. 33049 (cp. AP368.071).
69. 97. Verhandlungstag (5 October 1964). Zeno.org: *Der 1. Frankfurter Auschwitz-Prozess*, p. 20603 (cp. AP180.044).
70. Peter Weiss, *Die Ermittlung* (Frankfurt: Suhrkamp, 2005), pp. 116–131. This canto also makes use of the testimony of Kazimierz Smoleń, which was much less animated. The contrast between the two might also be part of what attracted Weiss. The *Frankfurter Rundschau* also picked up on the power of Müller's testimony. In addition to his role in the SK, it was stories of atrocities on which the article focussed. Peter Miska, 'Den Kindern schlug das Herz noch,' *Frankfurter Rundschau*, Friday 9 October 1964, p. 11.
71. Particularly as these two were the survivors of the SK that Claude Lanzmann wished to include in *Shoah*. See Chapter 7 below.

CHAPTER 5

Figure Studies from the Grey Zone: David Olère

IN LINE WITH THE FACTS

Sometime after being liberated from the camp of Ebensee in 1945, the artist David Olère sketched a drawing entitled '*Memoires de 43-44-45*' which portrays Crematorium 2 (III) at Birkenau. The drawing has been dated to 1945.[1] The three-floor structure is shown in cross section with the undressing room and the gas chamber below ground, the ovens on the ground floor and an upper storey containing seated figures. To make sure that some of what he has drawn is readily understood, Olère has identified three of the parts of the building by name: the undressing room, the gas chamber and the ovens. The central figure in the composition is an SS guard shown forcing a group of victims closer together in the gas chamber. The victims are drawn with light pencil strokes, their limbs indistinct. Olère here presents a visual rendering of the expression 'packed like sardines' as a means to show how people appeared when jammed together in the chamber.[2] The guard is sketched in far sharper outline, using hard lines. He is also angular in contrast with the circles and slender cones that are used as shorthand for the victims. On the floor above, another SS guard (identifiable by his hat) is similarly sharply drawn. He seems to be observing the work taking place beside the ovens. A man adjacent to him, likely a third guard, is also sketched with force. Three members of the SK are visible to the far left of the room that contains the ovens. Two of them have a relatively sharp outline, the third

© The Author(s) 2019
N. Chare and D. Williams, *The Auschwitz Sonderkommando*, The Holocaust and its Contexts,
https://doi.org/10.1007/978-3-030-11491-6_5

much less so, his body traced with similar pressure to the rendering of the ovens themselves. Like this man, other members of the SK in the drawing are lightly sketched, faint and almost evanescent.

The pressure Olère exerts here to sketch the SS is comparable to the forceful penning of the initials SS in the written accounts of Zalman Lewental and Marcel Nadjary produced in 1944.[3] The extra pressure expended in producing these pointed figures betrays feelings of anger or hatred or a combination of both; certainly, it manifests an extra emotional charge. Here, however, two of the SK receive similar graphic treatment. It seems, therefore, that Olère is (consciously or not) thinking through questions of complicity in the drawing. He is trying to work out how he should view himself. Is he as one with the SS or distinct from them? In a more worked up, larger drawing of the same subject dated 1946, the difference in pressure used to form figures is less obvious. The victims are drawn with the same density as the perpetrators. There are, however, differences in terms of posture. The SS are all portrayed as upright, stiff. The SK shown at work in the upper storey and two prisoners descending the stairs to the undressing room are hunched, their backs bent. In this second—perhaps later—drawing, Olère appears to have decided that the SK clearly stand apart from the SS. They are posed unanimously as victims. Olère also offers a more factually accurate vision of the crematorium. There is no guard in the gas chamber. Instead, he stands outside the door. The SS did not enter the chamber leaving the SK to force the victims in and to empty it.[4] Olère also only shows three victims in the chamber, all against the back wall. They are of different heights, possibly an adult, an adolescent and a child. This decision not to show them as 'sardines' may be borne of an enhanced ethical sensibility. Olère wants to retain a level of individuality for the victims.

This drawing identifies far more of the crematorium by name. There are seventeen different parts of the structure labelled. As he has more space, Olère also depicts all five ovens rather than sketching two and then writing that there were five. The precision of this drawing and the volume of information it includes render it akin to the diagrams produced in 1945 for Jan Sehn by the engineer M. Nosal under guidance from Shlomo Dragon and included with Dragon's affidavit as trial testimony.[5] Nosal's sketches (as they are called) of Bunkers I and II and Crematorium 4 (V) are not cross sections but architectural plans of the buildings from above.[6] Both these sets of drawings can be read as diagrams, 'reductive renderings [...] supplemented with notations keyed to explanatory captions'.[7] Nosal's, however, are seemingly pared of the subjective.[8] Olère's, through the inclusion of figures and, in the 1946 cross section, of a lengthy title, do betray feelings. His more detailed second diagram is titled 'Human Abattoir "Crematorium" of Birkenau destroyed before our departure on 19 January 1945 for unknown destination'. Here, the designation, calling the crematorium an abattoir, already frames the reception of the diagram in a particular way. It signals that the SS viewed their victims as beasts and that this structure represents a slaughterhouse. Pointing out that the building was destroyed—that there was an effort to hide its existence and purpose—also foregrounds the testimonial value of the drawing. It can be read as an act of resistance to Nazi efforts to efface their crimes.

Olère and Dragon are not the only SK members to have produced or directed the production of diagrams. Dov Paisikovic also guided Tadeusz Szymański (in the presence of Jan Mikulski) to produce three drawings as part of testimony he provided in 1964 for the Auschwitz Museum detailing his experiences in the SK.[9] The three drawings are two views of the exterior of what is labelled as Bunker V and a diagram offering a bird's-eye view of the same Bunker. The exteriors, portrayed against a backdrop of trees, seem conceived to capture something of the innocent appearance of these buildings. David Nencel describes one of the bunkers as a 'little white house' and as 'an innocent looking farmer's house with a straw covered roof'.[10] The first drawing, showing three doors adjacent to three small, heavily shaded windows, might be said to manifest something sinister by way of the umbrageous elements yet the second drawing, in which the windows are absent, far less so. The third drawing includes trees—rough circles atop vertical lines, each vertical line having a horizontal line at its base to signify shadow and grant the tree mass—surrounding the Bunker on all sides, reinforcing its concealment.[11] The artist adds the words 'wooded area' [*teren zalesiony*] on three sides to explain what the few schematic trees signify, the seclusion of the structure. These drawings, like Dragon's, must be viewed as bound up with the verbal testimony that accompanies them.

The trees in the drawings by Szymański clearly possess foliage, dating the depictions to spring or summer. The solitary tree in the background of Olère's 1946 representation of the crematorium is leafless, he shows the building in autumn or winter. This seemingly innocuous detail does shift the reception of the image. The trees in the Paisikovic testimony work to reinforce the callous deception perpetrated by the Nazis.

In this idyllic woodland setting, mass murder is being perpetrated in these structures. Olère, by contrast, emphasizes coldness and absence of life by way of the solitary, bare tree. His cross section is about lifting the veil on the mechanisms behind mass murder not asserting that there was a veil. There is, however, another kind of veiling in operation in this drawing, one which becomes apparent when it is compared with the undated version of the same subject. In the undated drawing, three members of the SK are shown in an area of the building (beside the smokestack) where their living quarters was situated. They appear to be seated around a table in conversation. No guard is present. The hair combers are also shown to the right of this space, unguarded. In the drawing dated 1946, the SK living quarters is now depicted as a series of bunks viewed head-on, each filled with a circle which may be a sleeping person or a pillow. The hair combers are also shown again, this time guarded. The existence of leisure time for the SK has been excised. The relative autonomy of the men in the crematorium is downplayed. The place Olère represents seems distant from how Tauber described the crematorium and relations between the SS and the SK. He suggested the SS were kept at a distance—stating 'we did not allow anyone to spit in our buckwheat' [*sobie pluć w kaszę*] to describe relations between the two groups.[12] Tauber acknowledges that—at least for a time, in relative terms—the SK possessed a degree of autonomy.[13] This autonomy is visible in the less worked up drawing of the crematorium produced by Olère but absent from the one dated 1946. Like Dragon's testimony in the preceding chapter, these drawings can therefore be seen as embodying a hinge moment immediately post-war when SK survivors were thinking through their experiences and appropriate ways of bearing witness to them.

In the 1946 drawing, Olère wishes to render the Sonderkommando less ambiguously as victims and to suppress any information which might appear to suggest they had moments of relative freedom during their time working and living in the crematoria. There is nevertheless still some continuity between the two versions. When Olère writes of leaving the crematorium for an unknown destination, he does imply the crematorium was known, familiar. This familiarity can be seen in the apparently undated drawing through the way that many of the SK as figures are drawn with the same density of line as the structure itself, blending with its fabric. It is the SS who are set apart from the building through their darker, sharper modelling. As we have noted, this harder use of line likely registers Olère's emotional attitude to the SS. Nevertheless, it also makes the men, the guards, who were not quartered in the crematorium stand out. This was not their living space. The building was, however, home to the SK for a period of time. They knew it even if they abhorred it. Its destruction and the departure of the SK from Birkenau therefore registered as a displacement, one accompanied by the emergence of new fears and anxieties.

Read in this way, the two drawings taken together provide insights into how Olère as a survivor of Sonderkommando sought to articulate and process his experiences. These drawings are also clearly intended to transmit historical knowledge, designed to explain how mass murder at Birkenau was accomplished. In this, the second drawing has plainly been successful. It was included as evidence for the existence of a death camp at Auschwitz in the trial of Holocaust denier David Irving. In his account of the trial, Robert Jan van Pelt (who gave evidence) describes Olère's 1946 drawing as showing 'much information in an economical manner'.[14] One of the major pieces of information included by the artist is the four hollow wire-mesh columns that were used during the insertion of Zyklon B into the chamber. The existence of these columns and the holes in the roof that led to them cannot now be deduced from the fragmentary ruins of Crematorium 2 (III). Evidence therefore has to be sourced from photographs and from Olère's drawing.

It is clear from Olère's shifting perspectives on how and what he should describe of his time in the SK that despite the factual detail they include, the drawings also embody a subjective dimension. They might therefore seem unsuitable material for historians to study. The works are equally not readily assimilable into art history as it has traditionally been conceived. His art stands apart from hermetic histories of modernism that trace influences and reactions across and between avant-garde exhibitions and movements. His frequent embrace of figuration, particularly in the drawings, appears to embody a conscious rejection of twentieth-century modernist vocabularies of art-making of the post-war period. Olère cannot be readily absorbed into evolutionary narratives of modern art. This is not to say his work is unmarked by, in particular, German modernism. Olère, however, was not an avant-garde leader or innovator and did not seek to be one. In the pre-war years, he was a journeyman artist designing costumes and posters for Paramount. His corpus does not conform to what is selectively celebrated as modern art and as worthy of study within standard histories of modernism and the avant-garde.[15] Olère's avoidance of the tradition of abstract art, his preference for readily comprehensible cultural forms as a means to portray mass murder, might also explain a relative reluctance to engage with his oeuvre. In this chapter, however, we will demonstrate that despite his peripheral status within the history of art and the clearly subjective dimensions to his corpus, studying his works is of considerable value for both art history and history.

THE RECEPTION OF THE ARTIST

David Olère was born into a Jewish family in 1902 in Warsaw. He studied art at the Warsaw Academy of Fine Arts and, on completing his studies, moved to Danzig, then Berlin, and finally, in 1923, Paris, where he lived in Montparnasse and worked for Paramount designing film posters.[16] He became a French national in 1937 but would lose that nationality in October 1940 because of anti-Jewish laws introduced by the Vichy regime. On 20 February 1943, Olère was arrested during a round-up of Jews in Seine-et-Oise. He was deported to Auschwitz II-Birkenau from Drancy on 2 March 1943 on transport number 49. Upon arrival at Birkenau, he was one of 119 people from the roughly 1000 of the transport selected for 'work'. He was initially a general manual labourer before being assigned to the Sonderkommando. On 19 January 1945, he took part in the death march that followed the evacuation of Auschwitz. He was then interned at Mauthausen and Melk before finally being liberated from Ebensee on 7 April 1945. He began producing drawings based on his camp experiences upon his return to Paris in 1945, and the Holocaust would continue to form the overriding theme in his art until his death in 1985. He made the drawings for his wife Juliette Ventura in an effort to convince her that the stories he was recounting of his experiences were not fantasies.[17] He therefore viewed the visual as more compelling than the verbal. The drawings were collectively titled *MEMENTO*.

Three catalogues and a book have been published that are dedicated exclusively to Olère's art. *David Olère: The Eyes of a Witness* is a catalogue that offers a bilingual English and French overview of Olère's works.[18] It was published by the Beate Klarsfeld Foundation in 1989. Another bilingual catalogue (in English and Hebrew), *Out of the Depths: David Olère, an Artist in Auschwitz* was published in conjunction with an exhibition of Olère's works at Yad Vashem in 1997. *David Olère. The One Who Survived Crematorium III* accompanies a recent exhibition at Auschwitz-Birkenau (October 2018–March 2019).[19] *Witness: Images of Auschwitz* is a book that contains commentary on Olère's works provided by his son Alexandre Oler.[20] It was published in 1998. Olère's works also feature occasionally in general publications dedicated to art and the Holocaust. When his works are included, they are usually discussed briefly and uncritically.[21] Glenn Sujo's pointed remarks on Olère, which will be discussed later, form a rare exception.[22] Véronique Chevillon also provides a lengthier engagement with his oeuvre in her essay 'Entendre David Olère, entendre les prisonniers des *Sonderkommandos*' which was published as part of an edited collection on the Sonderkommando and *Arbeitsjuden*.[23] Susan Pentlin briefly discusses Olère's art as part of her essay on the Scrolls of Auschwitz. For Pentlin, the works are efforts by Olère to 'understand what has happened to him and to empathize with his victims'.[24] The most nuanced and detailed engagements with the artworks to date are Carol Zemel's essays 'Right After' and 'Enduring Witness'.[25] Zemel's measured exploration of the treatment of female subjects in Olère's work and of the psycho-sexual dynamics playing through these representations has been particularly inspiring to us.

In her essay, Chevillon draws attention to the relative neglect that Olère's work has been subject to. She links this to his membership of the Sonderkommando and to his post-war desire to bear witness to his experiences at Birkenau through his art. Chevillon suggests that Olère was possibly unique in that he worked in a number of different roles during his time in the SK rather than being restricted to one of the 'specialisations' members usually practised such as *Zahnarzt* (dentist) (extracting teeth from the mouths of the dead), *Schlepper* (emptying the gas chambers of corpses) or *Heizer* (burning bodies). Chevillon's analysis of Olère's oeuvre is brief and general as her main aim is to use Olère as an example to think through the broader neglect accorded to SK testimony. During her short discussion of his art, she makes a distinction between the drawings produced by Olère between 1945 and 1947 and later artworks. The former are claimed to possess 'exceptional documentary value'.[26] Echoing remarks made by Serge Klarsfeld about Olère's 'almost photographic memory', Chevillon here suggests the drawings should be considered akin to photographs.[27] For her, Olère shifts from expressing concrete facts in his drawings to engaging in allegory and interpretation in his later paintings.[28] The paintings explore feelings. The drawings comprise dispassionate documentation.

In the first part of this chapter, we will demonstrate that the absolute distinction that Chevillon makes between the roles of the earlier and later works is questionable. We will show that the drawings are also interpretative and heartfelt. We will also examine how the drawings, like the SK manuscripts and the photographs that we discussed in earlier chapters, sometimes raise troubling questions about how to bear witness to the experience of women in their final moments. The chapter will conclude with a brief consideration of how the paintings develop material explored in the drawings. Positioning Olère's work within the broader context of art of the Holocaust is beyond our scope. At times, however, we do consider Olère in relation to general questions about the issue of Holocaust representation. The primary aim is nevertheless to situate the artist's visual testimony in relation to other representations of the SK and consider how the artworks contribute to our understanding of life in the special squads.

The only Holocaust-related art that survives by Olère was produced retrospectively. No written or artistic testimony produced within Birkenau by Olère has been conclusively identified. It does, nevertheless, seem that during his incarceration he produced pictorial testimony and contributed to written efforts at bearing witness. Miklós Nyiszli makes reference to a four-page document detailing the murders perpetrated at Birkenau which was signed by all the members of the Sonderkommando who worked at Crematorium 1 (II) and was then hidden in a piece of furniture the squad were constructing for an SS guard, Oberscharführer Muhsfeldt. Nyiszli writes of the document's message: 'The Sonderkommando's editor, a painter from Paris, copied it in beautifully written letters, as was the custom with ancient manuscripts, using India ink so that the writing would not fade'.[29] Although this editor is not named, we can reasonably assume that it is Olère who is being referred to. Halivni recounts that in joint testimony given shortly after the war, Lemke Pliszko and Avraham Beril-Tokol 'relate that Oler, an artist from France sketched portraits of gased [sic] and shot corpses'.[30] None of these works which were produced within the crematoria to bear witness to Nazi atrocities seem to have survived.[31] Olère was also sought out for his skill at calligraphy by members of the SS who forced him to write letters home for them. Serge Klarsfeld describes these letters as including floral designs.[32]

While no works by Olère produced either for his captors or on behalf of the Sonderkommando are known, one buried document has been discovered, a letter, which was written by someone who arrived on the same transport from Drancy as Olère, now known to be Herman Strasfogel.[33]

The letter appears to make an oblique reference to Olère as the author states that he is one of only two people left from out of the 100 selected to work from his transport.[34] The author, like Olère, was born in Poland but subsequently settled in France.[35] In post-war legal testimony, Dov Paisikovic mentions Olère as a long-time member of the SK who was exempted from any task except producing paintings for the SS.[36] A drawing Olère made in 1946, entitled 'Pour un bout de pain à Birkenau' (for a piece of bread at Birkenau), shows him creating one such letter: his penmanship a precious commodity he can use to trade for food.[37] An officer stands over him, arms placed either side of Olère's shoulders, corralling him. The soldier's rifle is depicted at the same angle as the artist's pen, mirroring it. A tall guard clasping a glass of liquor stands in the background, presumably waiting his turn. Olère's oppressed status is tangible. He appears diminutive and confined. The two Germans dominate the picture space. The artist is portrayed as acting as the conduit for messages of love from these SS men. Olère must transcribe expressions of tenderness, of affection, on behalf of those who despise him. The retrospective image is a vehicle for displaying Olère's subjugation. It reveals a world of emotional extremes: men capable of incredible violence and hatred longing for their loved ones, manifesting a qualified softness.

Adopting drawing as the preferred artistic medium to begin his efforts to bear visual witness may derive from Olère's wish to give the testimony a sense of immediacy. The drawings can be taken for sketches from 'life': products of what the artist sees at a given moment. Olère might be seen to be saying: 'These are the sketches I would have carried with me from the camps if I could have'. Certainly, the content of Olère's later paintings invites us to read the drawings as, in some sense, preliminary. The earlier works become a means to document striking images and work out ideas that he will fully develop only subsequently. There is, however, no evidence to suggest Olère conceived of the works in this way. If the drawings were to end up being preparatory, they were so by accident.

Ilse Koch at Auschwitz

The choice of medium does more than create a sense of immediacy. Drawing is an intimate art form: the reception of drawings usually differs from those of paintings. Drawings held in archives are laid out, pored over. Drawings in galleries are frequently displayed in cases: looked down upon. There is a different power dynamic at work in their reception (and, indeed, their production) to, for instance, easel painting. Choosing small-scale figurative drawing as the means of representation also constitutes a rejection of the idea of unrepresentability which has a strong presence in thinking about the art of the Holocaust, particularly in relation to abstraction.[38] Unrepresentability is sometimes linked to the idea of the sublime. Murder on an industrial scale as it was perpetrated by the Nazis is a crime the enormity of which it is impossible to conceptualize and which cannot be represented rendering it sublime. Berel Lang suggests that 'the possibility that content may exceed any possible form has been cogently argued in accounts of the Sublime'.[39] Olère's drawings indicate a belief in the capacity of figuration to contain genocide and communicate it.[40] His small-scale works provide a marked contrast with large-scale abstract art that is interpreted as an expression of the seeming sublimity of the Holocaust.[41]

The content of Olère's drawings forms a combination of personal experience and of material gleaned from post-war accounts of the camps. The images Olère produces combine what he witnessed in the Sonderkommando with other events he could not have seen but must have heard about either during or after the war. Olère obviously endeavoured retrospectively to depict individuals he could not have encountered and events he could not have witnessed. A case in point is his sketch of the guard Ilse Koch examining the tattoos of inmates which is dated 1947. Koch was at Buchenwald not at Auschwitz. She was rumoured to have had lampshades and other items fabricated from the human skin of prisoners although this was not proven at either of her trials for war crimes.[42]

In the Klarsfeld Foundation catalogue of Olère's works, the disparity is explained in this way: 'Olère may have given the name of Elsa Koch of Buchenwald to a guard at Auschwitz who used the same methods'.[43] In the drawing, however, the face of the woman guard is not dissimilar to Ilse Koch's. Her hair is also close in style and length to Koch's at her trial before an American Military Tribunal in 1947. Koch provides a key example for Insa Eschebach of what she calls the stereotype of 'the attractive but vicious woman' as Nazi.[44] For Eschebach, the press was crucial in disseminating this stereotype which became a central means of representing Nazi crimes. It seems quite possible that the drawing was motivated, in part, by press accounts of the trial. There are also other works featuring a figure named Elsa Koch although the physical resemblance with the real-life Koch is less marked. One, from 1946, is titled

'Elsa Koch et ses victimes' (Elsa Koch and her victims). Another is titled 'Elsa Koch, un homme de moins, un abat-jour de plus et une bourse de plus...' (Elsa Koch, one man less, one lampshade and one purse more).

Other possible explanations for the artist's multiple representations of Koch are therefore that he had read about her and decided that he wanted to give a more general account of the horrors of the Holocaust so chose to depict purported events from Buchenwald or that he was simply mistaken and thought Koch had been a guard at Auschwitz and therefore felt that he ought to depict her even if he had never personally encountered her.[45] The works featuring Koch show that women as well as men in the camps were perpetrators.[46] It is noteworthy that none of the drawings of Koch are reproduced in *Witness: Images of Auschwitz* published in 1998. The drawings of Koch demonstrate that approaching Olère's work as straightforward pictorial autobiography or as bare fact is unwise. As we will show, this should nevertheless not detract from the testimonial value of the works.

An undated painting, titled 'Gardienne SS face au cadavre de son amant detenu qu'elle vient de tuer' (female SS guard facing the body of her prisoner lover whom she has just killed), is based on two drawings by Olère. One is 'Elsa Koch, un homme de moins' (Elsa Koch, one man less). The other depicts women prisoners assisting in the construction of Crematorium 2 (III) in 1943. It is dated 1945. The painting is reproduced in the 1989 catalogue. It shows an SS guard seated on her bunk with her head in her hands. She is clothed solely in a hat, stockings and a solitary boot (in the drawing the painting is based upon, she only wears a hat). A semi-clothed inmate lies supine on the ground in front of her. The pallor of the skin and the way the head is seemingly covered by a sheet suggests that the person is dead. That Olère also intended this painting to depict Koch or someone akin to her is clear from the lampshade in the top right corner with its tattoos including one of two hearts pierced by an arrow, overwritten with 'A Margot pour la vie' (to Margot for life). A prisoner's tattooed declaration of love here becoming decorative illustration on an object. The executed prisoner who lies at her feet had presumably been selected by the woman because they possessed a tattoo she wanted to add to her collection.

Additionally, the woman's state of undress suggests a sexual motive to the encounter.[47] The inmate is Jewish as is signalled by an overturned Kiddush cup.[48] The genitals of the body are, however, absent.

The crotch is a smooth expanse of flesh. Olère has castrated this figure. The groin area is reminiscent of the pubis of a woman as it is frequently rendered in classical statuary, devoid of genitalia.[49] This lack of any clear physical markers of sexual difference captures something of the complex experience of gender experienced by inmates at Auschwitz. With their shorn hair and emaciated bodies, they came to appear to each other as androgynous. An anonymous survivor at the *Women Surviving the Holocaust Conference* asserted in a question and answer session that asking how it felt to be a woman in the concentration camp was wrong-headed as 'after my hair was shaved, and after I no longer looked like a person, I no longer felt like a woman or a girl'.[50] As part of a discussion of Birkenau, Désiré Haffner makes a similar, if lengthier, observation:

> Women? What did they still possess that was feminine, human, those phantoms [*spectres*] that were terrifying to see? – their heads shaved, their skin weather-beaten, their skeletal bodies everywhere marked by atrocities perpetrated by the SS women, their arms tattooed, their hands frozen, their legs swollen, that was what women were [*c'était ça des femmes*]?[51]

At times in the concentrationary universe, it therefore seems a third sex emerged, one that fell outside everyday patterns of visual recognition, which refused categorization as either male or female. Judith Jack Halberstam has noted how heavily gender assignations rely on the visual.[52] Erna Low registers something of the visual confusion over gender that occurred at Auschwitz, writing about her transport's arrival in the camp 'Naked, we proceeded on this human assembly line until we reached a room that was filled to overflowing with other naked human beings. In my first horror I mistook them for men, only to realize a second later that they were my women companions from the cattle car with their heads shaved'.[53] Sarah Cushman writes of the impact on men of viewing 'women reduced to shapeless and pathetic skeletons, devoid of any semblance of gender'.[54]

This genderlessness (an absence of qualities associated with either sex) was tolerated by the Nazis but inmates whose appearance was gender non-conforming were subject to immense violence or death. Olga Lengyel writes of a '"man-woman,"' a person who might today identify as butch or trans*, who arrived dressed in men's clothing but wanted to be placed in the women's camp and then had to prove 'her' womanhood to the SS.[55] Halivni recalls of the selections:

I have seen an SS person select a woman for the gas chambers because she grew a slight beard. Whether the facial hair offended a sense of aesthetics, a sense of propriety, a sense of cosmic harmony, a notion of feminism [*sic*], I shall never know but I do know the blemish was corrected by gassing.[56]

Male inmates seemed more capable of retaining a visible semblance of masculinity although Olère's painting shows that they too could become visibly ambiguous, categorically inassimilable in terms of their gender. The corpse is not readily integrated into categories such as male and female. The dead body refuses to straightforwardly signify a sex. The dead prisoner's inmate number is, however, visible on their striped uniform. It is 106144. 106144 is Olère's number, a man's number.

With her shoulder-length golden hair and her left breast prominently exposed, the guard in Olère's artwork is readily identified as female.[57] Often, however, SS women guards were described as possessing masculine characteristics. Giuliana Tedeschi writes of such a guard, 'the ambiguous creature [watched] over us, with her matching skirt and jacket, tie, men's haircut, big boots, and hoarse, unpleasant voice, again like a man's, a drunk's'.[58] This framing of the SS women as excessively manly enabled female inmates to affirm their own femininity, to construct their gendered identity as female against their guards who were figured as embodying a negative form of female masculinity.[59] Beauty aesthetics were weaponized by the inmates as a means to attack their SS captors. In culture more broadly, it was also common to describe Nazi women in gender-ambiguous language. In his 1943 discussion of the Women's Branch of the Gestapo, Richard Baxter writes of two female Gestapo flanking a young woman who is about to be interrogated: 'Gaunt, forbidding women were these guards, big of limb, big of muscle, cruel, hard-faced creatures'.[60] Here, Baxter constructs the German women, the enemy, as bulky and phallic.[61] Olère's art sometimes adopts a comparable aesthetic attack although one not focussed on 'masculinizing' the women he represents. In the 1946 ink and wash drawing 'Elsa Koch et ses victimes' (Elsa Koch and her victims), for example, Koch has angular features, buck teeth and sagging breasts. She is portrayed as ugly, caricatured. In the painting of Koch, however, she is less emphatically rendered as unattractive.

Olère sometimes used his camp number as a second signature, writing it alongside his name in artworks.[62] This is the case, for example, in the undated painting 'L'ogre SS, ou l'ogre du Bois de Bouleaux' (the

SS ogre or the ogre from Birkenau).[63] Olère has signed his name in the bottom right corner below a pile of bones resting on a striped prisoner's uniform which has the number 106144 stitched on it. The combination of name and number could be seen to encapsulate Olère's distinctive status as a member of the Sonderkommando. Like other prisoners in the camp, he was subjected to Nazi efforts to depersonalize him. Unlike many prisoners, however, he was able to maintain a sense of self-identity. The Sonderkommando had numbers yet retained their names. Survivors sometimes used both their name and number when authoring testimony so another explanation is that Olère is reclaiming his name while not forgoing his past. The combination of name and number may, in this context, imply a conjoining of past and the present. In 'L'ogre SS', given the uniform is discarded, lying beneath a pile of bones, Olère is dead. He has been murdered by the ogre. In both paintings, Olère has perished.

In 'Gardienne SS face au cadavre de son amant detenu qu'elle vient de tuer', the presence of the number also means that the artist has castrated himself as the 'male' figure forms a self-portrait. Zemel reads the 'allegorical painting' as an 'inversion of masculine desire'. Once we recognize that the dead man murdered for his skin is none other than Olère, it becomes necessary to read the painting as a work of fantasy designed to act as allegory. Zemel, in fact, describes Olère's paintings in general as forming 'lurid allegories' that embody 'erotic fantasy'. The painting can be read, through its status as allegory, as one that visibly renders the feelings of emasculation felt by many of the members of the Sonderkommando. Something of the complexity of the masculinities of the SK is revealed even though the setting is a guard's quarters. The cause of the SK's emasculation is displaced onto a woman guard. She comes to stand for the SS men who supervised the crematoria. In a complex manoeuvre, then, Olère may retrospectively be bringing the masculinity of his oppressors into question.

The depiction of the building of the crematorium in the top left of the work shows what appears to be a group of women prisoners transporting bricks. Two lug a wooden pallet. Others carry piles of bricks gathered in their skirts. They are being attacked by a woman guard wielding a crop and a driving whip.[64] One woman has fallen to the ground and lies face down across the bricks she has dropped. A male guard with an Alsatian stands in front of her. The backdrop to the scene of the naked kapo and her dead lover is therefore one showing the violence endured by women prisoners in the camp. Through the way he depicts his dead body, Olère aligns himself with the women in the background. He portrays himself as similarly violated. The painting thus becomes one in which it is possible to see Olère placing himself in the stead of others. As will become clear, Olère performs this role of associating with another, of empathic identification, frequently.[65]

Sexual Violence

The theme of the sexual violation of women by members of the SS is a recurring one for Olère.[66] Mor Presiado associates depictions of sexual violence produced in the immediate aftermath of the camps with the art of women survivors rather than men.[67] Olère's work, the focus of which is unsurprising, belies this classification. As discussed in Chapter 2, the treatment of women sent to the gas chambers, including their forced undressing and the acts of sexual violation perpetrated against them by camp guards, caused many in the Sonderkommando significant distress. Olère retrospectively struggles with these memories of violation. He also presents images of children being separated from their mothers such as the ink and wash drawing 'Sa dernière tetée' (her last feeding) which shows an SS guard trying to pull a mother away from her suckling infant as her naked daughter looks on. As we will discuss in Chapter 6, memories of the mistreatment of children by the SS plagued survivors from the SK and often feature prominently in oral and video testimony.

In the introduction to the bilingual catalogue, Klarsfeld writes that 'it is not hard to understand why spectators would prefer to turn away and refuse to look at what David Olère saw with his own eyes at Auschwitz and which never ceased to haunt him'.[68] The reference to haunting implies traumatization, indicating the presence of an event that refuses to reduce in intensity, resisting becoming memory and therefore subject to forgetting. There is a compulsion to visually repeat scenes of abuse and humiliation running through Olère's oeuvre which can be read as symptomatic of the trauma he suffered from and also as evidence of ongoing efforts to both act out and work through that trauma. Zemel argues that the trauma is never resolved: 'Olère's pictures seem to signify his possession *by* as well as his attempt to master memory *of* the event'.[69]

An ink and wash work from 1948 called 'Birkenau. Il a déjà tout pris, mais il faut ça aussi…avant de les massacrer' (he has already taken everything, but has to have this too before slaughtering them) shows an SS guard who has removed his jacket confronting two naked women prisoners. The scene takes place in a room of a building situated near one of the crematoria. A smoking crematorium chimney can be seen through the window. A helmet on a shelf located above the women indicates that this room is used by guards. If Olère ever visited this place, it is unlikely he willingly did so while deeds like this were in progress. Olère's style in this picture, as with most produced in the late 1940s, mirrors that adopted during his forced creative labours at Birkenau in that he continues to combine text and images. In the drawings produced retrospectively, the visual far outweighs the written. When creating letters for the Germans, Olère's flowers were of secondary importance, functioning to figure feelings of affection, fondness, supplementing literary expressions of love. In these later drawings, writing is no longer privileged but still performs a crucial function, explaining the content and anchoring the emotional tenor of each picture. Olère seeks to guide our reception of his works through these titles. They operate to ensure clarity of interpretation and to guide feeling.

The title which Olère has noted in the bottom right corner on the drawing is informative in this context. The words ça aussi (this too) are underlined. Ça here stands for sex, possibly for virginity. There is a reluctance to name the crime of rape directly. This reticence prefigures Dario Gabbai's reluctance to name parts of the female anatomy in video testimony he gave, a reserve we examine in Chapter 6. Through using the word ça, Olère implies rather than names forced sex. Sexual violation is 'that'. Another survivor of the SK deported from France, Erko Hajblum, also uses the word 'ça' to refer to a traumatic experience, one clearly he views as beyond description. Hajblum was tasked with disinterring dead bodies near Bunkers I and II. He describes wading through mud and corpses to Maurice Garbarz, stating 'Ce que tu as subi Maurice n'est rien à côté de "ça"'[What you experienced, Maurice, is nothing compared to 'that'].[70] During a discussion of Sarah Kofman's *Rue Ordener, rue Labat*, Griselda Pollock writes of the word ça that it 'is the least descriptive, least referential indicator of something'.[71] She goes on to suggest:

> Perhaps it is akin to das Ding, la Chose, the Thing in Freudian-Lacanian psychoanalytical vocabulary, where it stands for a substance-less void before and beyond representation, the latter, in the form of the object, invisibly determined by this element of the unsignified Real. It is also, of course, the French term for Freud's id, the repressed element of the most intractable and infantile of psychic organizations and impulses.[72]

Ça is something that can be postulated retrospectively, discussed via symbols yet never accessed through them. Representation can point towards its existence yet cannot coincide with it. Pollock goes on to state that:

> Ça is also a signifier for what has none: trauma. Rather akin to the dark navel Freud postulates in his analysis of the dream of Irma in Interpretation of Dreams, that marks the limits of his interpretations of dreamwork, trauma confounds the interpretative enterprise as much as the representational one. It is, however, the structuring void that shapes the words curling around it.[73]

The most important thing in Olère's picture, the thing underlined, is therefore the thing that the work cannot signify. This beyond to representation is also signalled by the ellipses that separate 'ça aussi' from 'avant de les massacrer'. These elisions denote the unspeakable act of 'taking' that occurs subsequent to the scene we are presented with. They communicate the passage of time, the event that occurs between the women's undressing and their murder. The words denote what is not in the image, they fill in for the invisible 'between' of the two events shown in the picture, naked humiliation and, as the smoke from the chimney conveys, future annihilation. Trauma here is therefore rendered through abstraction, through a word and ellipses. Olère has encountered a limit he seemingly cannot ignore.

There is a drawing depicting the same jacketless guard which was produced a year earlier. The work is titled 'Et une heure plus tard, c'est fini' (and an hour later, it's over). It is set in a similar but seemingly not identical room. Here, as with 'Il a deja tout pris', an early part of the unfolding ordeal is recorded. A naked woman is shown on her knees pleading with the guard. A baby in swaddling, presumably the woman's, lies on a table nearby. The guard has seized her hands which are gripped in a pose of apparent supplication. This earlier work is more violent. The woman's hands are enlarged, as if the flesh of her forearms is being forced into them by the pressure of the guard's grip. The medium, a pen and ink drawing rather than the mix of ink and wash used in the later work, reinforces the sense of aggression. Given the context, the subject-matter, the twisting and turning lines used to sketch surfaces, substances and shadow, rapid, hard, come to possess a kind of violence in keeping with the event they delineate.[74] Hostility shapes the draughtsmanship, the inky marks.[75]

The technique attests to the violence as much as does the depiction itself. The unmarked paper which stands for the woman's skin as it is illuminated by the light from the window, particularly apparent at the backs of her thighs and across her upper right arm, stands in conspicuous contrast to the quick scribbling that signals the man's shadow cast across her quadriceps, belly and chest. The woman's vocalizations almost seem to push back the approaching, encroaching penmanship leaving an expanse of negative space, of white paper (far greater than that surrounding the guard's upper body), in front of her face. The act of violation is therefore potentially displaced onto the action of drawing.

Marked Men

Displacement also informs a watercolour and ink drawing from 1946 of two members of the SS administering a lethal injection to a naked woman. One holds her down while the other, standing between her thighs, injects her with a syringe just below the breast. A trickle of blood drips from the table. The drawing is called 'Piqûre mortelle' (lethal injection). Here, 'ça' is implied through the needle pricking the flesh.[76] 'Piqûre mortelle', like 'Et une heure plus tard, c'est fini', fosters a contrast of light and dark between victim and perpetrator. In the latter work, the body hair of the guard is captured through a series of small, tight curls of ink across the forearms, chest and back. This hair connotes the man's brutishness.

It is noteworthy that when Olère depicts himself or other members of the Sonderkommando shirtless they are not similarly hirsute. This may be because they were regularly shaved to prevent the spread of lice but it seems from the extreme hairiness of the SS that Olère exploits the contrast this provides to affirm difference. He used posture to similar effect in the diagram from 1946 that we discussed at the start of this chapter. Here, drawing figures on a larger scale, body hair (or its absence) becomes a means of distinguishing victim from perpetrator. In the pen and wash drawings 'SS Bewzinger. De la chambre à gaz au four' (SS Bewzinger, from the gas chamber to the oven) (1946) and 'In Crematorium No. III' (1945), the artist uses minimal lines to show the Sonderkommando displaying hairless, emaciated torsos. Other binaries also function across works to affirm differences between the aggressed and the aggressors, the oppressed and the oppressors. The blocky caricatures of the camp guards, for example, contrast with the more rounded features accorded to Olère and the other inmates. The Germans are visually affirmed as of a different order to those they oppress. As part of a broader critique of Olère's works, Sujo has written of their 'ambiguous or ill-defined relationships'.[77] To us, however, there appears to be a sustained effort to render relationships as clear and unambiguous as possible.

The contrasts disclose the structuring processes employed by Olère to make visual sense of his experiences. The drawings are witness accounts produced by eye and hand deriving inspiration from inherited visual vocabularies, such as the long-standing tradition of light signifying goodness and darkness and shadow signalling corruption and evil. The ink and wash version of 'Piqûre mortelle' (1946) shows a woman being injected by members of the SS. It exhibits this contrast. The men are uniformed, enabling Olère to aggressively shade their clothes and paint them. Much of the dead woman's body is left unpainted and unshaded. There is therefore a binary operating in these works, the bad are marked out by markings and the good are indicated through an absence of such markings.

In the context of Olère's status as a surviving member of the Sonderkommando, his efforts to retrospectively figure his experiences serve to instantiate secure borders between victims and perpetrators where, perhaps, the reality was more blurred. Seemingly, Olère forms one of those people who, in 'writing' a history of the Lager, exhibit the need Primo Levi identified: 'to separate evil from good, to be able to take sides, to emulate Christ's gesture on Judgment Day'.[78] Levi described the world of the Lager as comprising not two clearly demarcated groups but 'a grey zone, poorly defined, where the two camps of masters and servants both diverge and converge'.[79] Many of Olère's works, in their judicious figuring of good and evil, do not display the complicated formation Levi identifies. Where Levi says there is too much confusion to be able to judge, Olère adjudicates. His works often seem designed to resolve moral complexity and remove ambiguity.

This approach, one adopted by Levi himself in earlier works, can be understood as part of a post-war process of finding a moral footing. The Sonderkommando, as a key example or embodiment of the grey zone for Levi, were intimate with moral ambiguity and concerned by it. We know from Strasfogel's letter that there was unease among the Sonderkommando about how their actions would be perceived. They were afraid of being judged. They were not, however, fearful of judging.

Strasfogel writes: 'I ask you to never judge me badly as if among us there were good and bad I was certainly not among the latter'.[80] He makes it clear that he is not one of the unscrupulous members of the SK (what rendered some of the men unscrupulous must currently remain subject to conjecture but may conceivably be linked to sexual violence towards victims).

Olère similarly feels able to judge, incorporates judgments, through his figurative choices. Despite Olère's best efforts to distinguish victims and perpetrators, good and evil, as our discussion of the crematorium diagrams has already demonstrated, ambiguities do nevertheless surface. In 'SS Bewzinger. De la chambre à gaz au four' (to use the title Olère has inscribed at the bottom of the drawing), for instance, Olère has signed the work in the bottom right corner as is his usual practice. That corner is occupied by a club-wielding SS guard. The guard is, in a way, named as Olère. There is a faint annotation in ink at the base of the page (well below Olère's signature) which identifies the soldier as SS Bewzinger. There was an SS guard called Josef Benzinger at Auschwitz although little is known about him.[81] The positioning of Olère's signature could unconsciously reflect a moral complexity the work otherwise strives to deny. This lends support to Sujo's observation that 'an implicit problem in all Olére's [sic] work is his identification with figures of authority'.[82] Sujo does not develop this observation but he may possibly be referring to how the point of view offered by Olère is one that potentially replicates the objectifying gaze of the Nazis. In this sense, Olère struggles with similar issues to those we identified in Chapter 2 in relation to Gradowski's description of the murder of the women from the Czech family camp.

For his voluntary efforts to represent ça, to draw the trauma of his experiences at Birkenau into his works, Olère must choose specific forms of figuration. These forms direct how he tries to announce the presence of ça. A work in pen and watercolour from 1945, titled 'Le SS Moll abat et précipite des jeunes femmes dans une des fosses d'incinération du crématoire V' (the SS man Moll kills young women and hurls them into one of the burning pits at Crematorium 4 [V]), is informative in this context. The picture shows SS-Hauptscharführer Otto Moll, who was head of the crematoria in Birkenau from 1943 to 1945, aiming his pistol at two naked women who are facing an incineration pit. A third naked figure, a child who is lying face forward beside one of the women, seems to have already been shot by Moll. The Nazi officer is pointing his gun at the back of one of the women. She is on her knees, hunched over, with her head in her hands. The other woman, who will be next in line to be murdered, is standing. Her head is turned towards Moll. His gun is parallel with her genitals such that there is also a suggestion of sexual violence in the work. The picture is too posed to be read as a scene from life. The standing woman appears unperturbed by the flaming incineration pit, its scorching cinders. Olère's way of drawing the woman borrows from the traditional vocabulary of the female nude. Her posture is one that accentuates the curves of her body rather than encapsulating her pain and terror.[83] Her stance is not credible.[84] Van Pelt praises this drawing for the architectural exactitude of the portrayal of Crematorium 4 (V).[85] The depiction of the victims is, however, less studied. Olère is trying to portray naked women using the pictorial vocabulary of the nude. He is employing an iconography conventionally associated with titillation yet endeavouring to portray instances of violent humiliation.

Olère had previously produced paintings in the genre of the nude such as the circa 1925 'Nu endormi' (sleeping nude). 'Nu endormi' presents a languorous figure posed in such a way that her long, shapely legs and pert breasts are foregrounded. The woman is presented as an object to be viewed, a source of visual pleasure. Lynda Nead has described the nude as classically conceived as performing 'a kind of magical regulation of the female body, containing it and momentarily repairing the orifices and tears'.[86] In this understanding, the nude as a genre performs a regulating function in order to assuage anxieties regarding the female body and its potentially transgressive excretions and orifices. The conventional nude contains and protects. Nudes such as 'Nu endormi' conform to this tradition as do some post-war works such as 'Vous françaises, tu parles allemande?' (You French women, you speak German?) of 1947. This ink and wash drawing depicts a German soldier and three women inmates. Each of the women is downcast. One cowers in the background with their back turned. In the centre of the composition, another woman stands, her head bowed, concealing her breasts and vulva with her arms. The third woman is to her right. She sits, leaning against the back wall, drawing her body inwards, hiding as best she can from the soldier. He points at her. It is to her that the question from which the work takes its title is directed. The work strives to capture a sense of the shame of the women who are subject to the sadistic gaze of the SS man. It is, however, only partially successful.

The arms of the woman in the centre are posed similarly to those of the goddess in Sandro Botticelli's 'The Birth of Venus' (1484–1486).

The inmate is portrayed as demure rather than highly distressed. The woman the soldier points at could not easily be described as recoiling. She is rather modelled so as to be turned to the side, her left breast clearly visible, outlined, her pose drawn from the pictorial language of the coquette. An undated pastel work by Olère, 'Nu allongé', which was sold at auction in Paris in 2012, is composed in a comparable way.[87] In this work, a naked woman curls up, half covering her face with her right arm. In a counter-intuitive pose, her torso is twisted towards the viewer so that her breasts are both visible. The same pictorial vocabulary for depicting the naked female form also informs 'Jeunes filles cobayes' (young maidens guinea pigs), a pen and watercolour work from 1946. The central figure peers from behind folded arms which partially conceal her face. Her eyes and her body open towards the gaze. She is positioned to be admired, to entice the viewer.[88] Her body language is akin to 'Nu allongé'. It is difficult to detect the kind of repellence that Klarsfeld describes in works such as this. These women invite appreciation. They are composed by means that are usually employed to incite visual pleasure in the female form. Zemel describes depictions of dead women in Olère's drawings as 'comely'.[89] If such works are rebarbative, it is because of this beautification and the artistry. The pictures are not horrible enough. They display an abject insufficiency. There is too much that is pleasing in them.[90]

A Beautiful Death

Griselda Pollock has drawn attention to how women are the primary focus in efforts to represent the process of industrial murder in *Night and Fog* (Dir. Alain Resnais, France, 1955).[91] She connects this to a long-standing Western cultural tradition of linking death and the feminine. Similarly in Olère, at times, the figure of feminine beauty comes to stand for destruction. A 1946 pen and wash work depicting the recovery of teeth and hair in the gas chamber, 'Récupération des dents en or et des chevelures dans la chambre à gaz' (recovering gold teeth and hair in the gas chamber), centres upon a youthful woman whose hair is being clipped by shears. The English title translates 'chevelure' simply as 'hair'. 'Chevelure', however, is a term often used in the context of long or thick hair. This woman has been singled out because of her thick tresses. Her body is given a tangibility that the other corpses lack. They are misshapen, shapeless. Her form is scrupulously modelled as is that of the man who cuts her hair. His clothing, however, is composed of sharp, dark, dense concertinas of ink: his face a nose and a zigzag. Beauty here is seemingly asked to convey horror.

The same technique recurs in 'SS Bewzinger. De la chambre à gaz au four'. Here, the corpse of a young woman is dragged towards the ovens.[92] The member of the Sonderkommando also pulls a small child. The other dead are vague, diminutive forms in the background. They are a pile of anonymous corpses framed by the door of the recently opened gas chamber. The sight of the dead upon opening the gas chamber door is often referred to in testimony as beyond description. In *The Holocaust Odyssey of Daniel Bennahmias*, Sonderkommando, for example, the scene is termed a 'contorted mass' that formed 'an inabsorbable, inadmissible sight, too shattering for truth and too terrible for illusion'.[93] Henryk Mandelbaum stated in oral testimony that he didn't want 'even an enemy to see this view of those people who were murdered in the gas chamber'.[94] Olère attempts to provide an artistic rendering of this shocking spectacle. Once again, the horror of mass murder is condensed in the figure of a beautiful, naked woman, her body seemingly unsoiled despite the manner of her death. Another member of the SK, Marcel Nadjary, also produced a drawing of the aftermath of a gassing.[95] His sketch is intended to supplement his memoir, *Khroniko, 1941–1945*.[96] Unlike Olère, he chooses not to depict individuals. All his corpses remain vague. Nadjary crafts apparitions that spill forward out of the chamber, suggestions of bodies, careful uncertainties. His line is kept deliberately loose.

Nadjary's thumbnail sketch (it is literally of this scale) shows considerable skill. He fills the space behind the pile of bodies with pen strokes in order to signal a shadowy interior. Leaving the background blank or filling it entirely with black ink would prevent the viewer having any sense of depth. Nadjary includes an irregular zigzag—stark against the cream of the paper—that gives a sense of dimly illuminated space. More than the skill, what is of interest here is the refusal to include separate figures. His work represents the chamber prior to the commencement of separating the bodies. Through his close to formless rendering of mass murder, Nadjary provides a visual representation of the aftermath of a gassing that conforms to Leyb Langfus's description in *The Deportation* of a formless mass of human bodies.[97] The bodies became intertwined as people held each other or collapsed together. In video testimony, Daniel Bennahmias states that his specific task in the SK was to disentangle the dead after each gassing.[98] In trial testimony, Henryk Mandelbaum places considerable emphasis on this entanglement. He remarks that people were entwined [*spleceni*] and repeatedly refers to them holding each other. Shlomo Venezia states they appeared as if 'woven' [*interlacciato*] together.[99] Nadjary portrays this confusion, this tangle as do the bodies piled high in the background of Olère's drawing. Olère, however, also shows the process of the extraction of the bodies, their becoming separate again.[100] He put faces to two of the victims in 'SS Bewzinger' and also in his painting of a gassing which we will discuss later.

'SS Bewzinger' manifests compositional oddities. The woman's feet are positioned near the door to the gas chamber. Her left foot seemingly just behind the back leg of a member of the Sonderkommando who is seeking to pull out another body. He is diminutive in comparison with the member of the squad dragging the woman. The woman's feet are, however, depicted as if they are alongside this small figure in the background. There are distortions of scale at work. The woman's body is too big to fit the composition properly. She would be unfeasibly tall if she stood up. Elongating the proportions of nude female figures is not unusual. Jean Auguste Dominique Ingres famously added extra vertebrae to 'La Grande Odalisque' (1814). In the context of the gas chambers, however, this lack of anatomical realism is disquieting. The drawing does not strive for bodily veracity. The woman's body is drawn in a way that is studiedly incorrect. She is stretched, spread out. Such a disjuncture of scale possesses a powerful figurative potential. This female nude represented as flow rather than form signals the fate of the other corpses, holds their fate within it.

Olère's use of wash and of minimal wavy lines of ink suggests a pool of liquid on the floor. To claim the wash and sparse squiggles represent water would be to overstate things. Liquid is indicated rather than outlined. The depiction of water in the drawing is discussed in Shlomo Venezia's memoir *Inside the Gas Chambers*. Béatrice Prasquier asks Venezia about the strip of water in front of the ovens in Olère's picture. He explains that water was thrown into the passageway to make the bodies slip more easily.[101] The wash in the picture registers the effects of this practice. *Inside the Gas Chambers* is noteworthy as Olère's drawings are used to illustrate several of the experiences Venezia describes. The artworks are employed for their documentary value. There is, however, at one point a disjuncture between what Venezia describes and what the image by Olère depicts. The work 'Liquidation de la quarantaine des femmes – 24 décembre 1944 [*sic*]' is used to illustrate a section that discusses inmates who arrived at the crematoria by truck.[102] It is titled simply 'Naked women being unloaded' in the English translation of Venezia's memoir. It becomes clear from Venezia's account that usually trucks deposited fully clothed victims from the transports who were too weak to walk to a crematorium. Olère portrays an exceptional (and specific) event that is at odds with the everyday experience of the SK. He does not show what Venezia recounts. The drawing does, however, resonate powerfully with Venezia's description of how distressing undressing the prisoners and then taking them to their deaths was: 'for us, this was by far the most difficult task to accomplish'.[103] Venezia then gives the specific example of an old woman he had to undress who resisted. He had to forcibly remove her stockings.

Confronting the naked humiliation of victims was at the heart of the horror experienced by the SK. Both the drawing and Venezia's verbal account attest to this. In the drawing, a pile of thin, naked bodies, whose sex would be indeterminate was it not for Olère's title, spills from a truck. A figure who is half buried looks out from the pile towards a guard. She raises her hand, seemingly pleading for help. The guard's face is hidden from the viewer but his rigid stance bespeaks impassivity. This drawing is unlike the depictions of naked women discussed earlier in that there is no trace of the traditional vocabulary of the nude present. It is difficult to reconcile a work such as this with Sujo's charge that Olère identifies with the perpetrator. Similarly, his drawing of half-starved women from a work kommando, 'Détenues avalent leur repas' (prisoners gulp down their meal), is not redolent of sadism. As Emily Bilski observes, 'Olère's rendering of the women's hunched shoulders, their over-large hands clutching the precious bowls, and the intense concentration with which they devour their meagre food, impart a palpable sense of the starvation of the victims'.[104] Olère seems empathetic in his depiction rather than callous. His works are heterogeneous. He shifts position and varies approach as he exploits the field of visual possibilities available to him to work out how to respond to his experiences through his art. The drawing also does not seem to manifest the 'crass, even sentimentalised response to the victims' that Sujo also detects in Olère.[105] This is an unsparing vision of victimhood. These are not beautiful bodies. They are skin and bone. Olère has carefully contoured some of the bodies. The thick lines that border the bodies help to emphasize how thin their arms and legs are. He starkly underlines their suffering.

Out of Line

Lines, boundaries, are what ensure our psychic well-being as Marion Milner discusses in detail in *On Not Being Able to Paint*.[106] Line guarantees the tangible. Milner refers to outline as representing the world of fact.[107] In Olère's works, however, outline frequently assumes the role of fantasy, the beautiful feminine ideal, the crude caricature of evil. Line appears to be used as a means to affirm boundaries. The production of the drawings between 1945 and 1947 may therefore have held a therapeutic purpose. Through them Olère strived to assert differences, to find a clarity that was denied to him at Birkenau. It was a clarity at odds with his experience yet one that might have seemed necessary to his becoming a mentally healthy human being again. His art then does not simply reflect what he experienced or seek to remember it, it provides him with the forms and structures through which to re-find a stable selfhood. Outline, the giving of clear borders, is antithetical to the grey zone. It closes down the ambiguous. In this context, the beautiful nudes in Olère's works with their comely physiques perform a containing akin to that identified by Nead but here motivated by the artist's memories of the abject bodies he encountered in the crematoria, bodies of the kind described by Henryk Mandelbaum in his trial testimony: smeared with their own bodily fluids, often seeping blood, covered in puke and haemorrhaging. Mandelbaum, as we discussed in the previous chapter, felt obliged to apologize for this testimony. Olère, by contrast, shields us although that may not be his intention. He was motivated by a need to safeguard himself from such memories. Olère's nudes do not protect him from formlessness, they are efforts to re-find form.[108] This mending of violated bodies, however, is carried out by way of a troubling objectification. These are complex, conflicted works.

Olère's drawings taken as whole never escape the abject experience that was the grey zone of the crematoria. He attests to this abject in spite of himself by way of moments where outline falters, where line gives way, often causing representation to simultaneously falter. It is then that something of the horror Olère experienced emerges. This is not a claim for abstraction. It is in the interplay of outline and loosened line, loss of line, that something of the abject reality of the grey zone is registered. Olère's choice of wash as a technique is obviously noteworthy in this respect. Wash differs from watercolour in its restricted chromatic. A wash usually consists of only one or two colours. The drawings produced by

Olère that use this technique typically use a grey wash. This wash, an amorphous grey seethe, has the capacity to bleed or leak across carefully inked borders in the drawings. Like watercolour as Denise Brahimi has described it, it works against detail.[109]

In this context, the smoke in 'Il a deja tout pris' might perform a similar role, suggest a collapsing of boundaries. In 'Jeunes filles cobayes', despite the sure draughtsmanship, the anachronistic coyness, there are smears of wash which haemorrhage outwards from the sharp hatching and cross-hatching that seeks to set the tone of the work. These smears are coupled with the vertical striations of colour that stain the central figure. There is an unnerving excess to the carefully outlined testimony, the clear and clean pictorial vocabulary, which forms the rest of the drawing. This excess also inhabits the hatching, in which aggressive rhythms call into question the very forms they seek to substantiate. Determinate boundaries are continually troubled.

We want to argue that it is through such moments of breakdown in Olère's drawings that something of the horrors of working in the SK and of the complexities of the grey zone push to the fore. This can be seen, for instance, in 'Scène de torture par le SS Georges' (scene of torture by the SS Georges) (1945). The grey wash sweeps upwards mirroring the arc of the baton the SS officer is using to beat an inmate to death. It seeps into the weave of the paper giving the patches of watercolour uneven, ill-defined edges. The colour begins beneath the trough and the legs of the prisoner. Grey links guard and inmate: tinges them both. The two subjects, or the subject and the violently objectified, are chromatically bound together.

Collage

The paintings, which (along with his sculptures) are rarely discussed in the few engagements with Olère's work to date, can be seen to form a new stage in his efforts to work through the things he had lived through at Birkenau. The paintings are not history paintings—there is nothing noble or grand about them—but they are historical paintings. They provide an important form for thinking about the past. They seek to catch the feel of some of the horrific experiences Olère endured. In this, they can be read as providing a kind of graphic history of life in the SK and in Auschwitz-Birkenau more broadly. The paintings mark a significant departure from the drawings but not in the way Chevillon reads them. They are often intensely expressionistic, highly emotionally-charged. There are fantastic elements which resonate with aspects of surrealism. The works are also collagistic (in contrast to the drawings). In the paintings, events depicted in the drawings are combined with new imagery yet the two are not synthesized. The realistic portrayals associated with Olère's drawings make way for more nightmarish, surreal representations.

It is significant that in the paintings, Olère often depicts himself taking on the sufferings of others, enduring experiences he could not have personally been subjected to. As already discussed, this occurs in 'Gardienne SS face au cadavre de son amant detenu qu'elle vient de tuer'. The central figure in 'Gazage au Zyklon B, or A l'interieur de la chamber à gaz' may also be Olère. 'Gazage' (Gassing) is, perhaps, Olère's most well-known work. It depicts a scene he could never have seen. It shows people in their death throes. Olère would only have had visual knowledge of the lead up to a gassing and its aftermath. He would be familiar with the emptying of the gas chamber, with phenomena such as those described by Dragon in his trial testimony.[110] During a gassing, he would nonetheless potentially have been able to hear the death agonies of victims which may explain the strong emphasis given to the screams of the victims in the painting.[111] The pyramidal composition also echoes the circumstances in which people were found after a gassing, in a pile that resembled a pyramid, the shape caused by the dying clambering on top of each other in a desperate attempt to find uncontaminated air near the ceiling vent.[112] The tattoo of the central figure begins 1061 followed by what seems to be a 4. It would be in keeping with the other paintings if the figure were Olère himself. In such a reading of 'Gazage', Olère figuratively dies in the gas chambers. Like other representations of gassings such as Wiktor Simiński's *In the Gas Chambers* (1944), Olère's effort is highly problematic in that it is on some levels an imagining of an event. He could not have directly observed a gassing and, perhaps, therefore should not try to envision what one looked like.[113]

In other works, he paints himself as a spectral presence. This occurs, for example, in the undated painting 'Le Revier' which depicts Adolf Hitler dissecting a corpse with a wraith-like Olère looking over his shoulder. In 'La Massacre des innocents, ou La Mort SS' (The massacre of the innocents, or SS Death), a skeletal SS guard in a blood-spattered uniform stands on a pile of corpses. The ethereal face of Olère can be seen behind him. In 'L'orgie des SS, ou Les fosses ardentes' (The SS orgy, or the fiery pits), a disembowelled Olère observes the SS orgy through a barbed wire fence. He has two syringes sticking into him. One in his upper torso and one near his crotch. In the background, two incineration pits in the shape of the SS insignia can be seen. Similarly, complex gender dynamics to 'Gardienne SS face au cadavre de son amant detenu qu'elle vient de tuer' are at work here. The SS men are shown either semi- or fully clothed. They wear trousers and shirts or vests. The blonde female guards are naked except for their boots and, occasionally, their caps. They wear jewellery pilfered from Jewish victims. Olère seems unable to depict the Nazi men naked. This may be because the male nude was traditionally a symbol of heroism or, more likely, because the artist felt representing naked men might compromise his masculinity.[114] Only the bodies of the women are exposed to the spectator. Here, Olère continues to duplicate the power dynamic of his oppressors towards women even though he is portraying women oppressors. He also shows himself as, in a sense, penetrated. The painting is again a reflection on his emasculation. It also points towards the perverse pleasure some Nazis evidently took in perpetrating mass murder. The wordplay of the title, in which the pits are described as *ardentes*, a word that means both flaming and passionate, foregrounds a link between cruelty and sexual pleasure comparable to that discussed in relation to the Nazi gaze in Chapter 2.

These later works are complex efforts to negotiate feelings of anger and hatred towards the Nazis that are coupled with a sense of guilt over Olère's involvement in the genocide perpetrated against his people. The work '*Muselmänner* standing before the crematorium' based on an earlier drawing from 1946 depicts three emaciated men. They are, as the title implies, on their last legs. The central figure supports the other two whose heads are bowed. They look almost identical. They all have their eyes closed, with the two on the left looking as if they are concentrating instead on what they can feel of each other. A crematorium is visible in the background. Its chimney is belching fire and thick black smoke. The building's structure is rendered in such a way as to be reminiscent of a cross. The central figure, the figure of Christ, may well be Olère. Through his art, he takes on the suffering of those he watched go to their deaths. The flames emitted by the crematorium chimney form an arch shape around them, reminiscent of the central panel of many altarpieces, with two related scenes on either side. An SS guard, who seems to be Otto Moll, tortures and possibly murders hairless prone figures. The two versions of Moll's body cross into the canopy of flames. On the left, Moll's left boot is up against one central figure's right hip. On the right, another reaches down, with his left index finger virtually brushing against Moll's victim's left cheek. The composition is rather awkward (especially regarding the way that Moll's buttocks and legs cross into the canopy of flames), and it relies heavily on Christian imagery of triptychs and crucifixion scenes.[115] Olère's adaptation of Christian imagery is of course not new among Jewish artists, and Marc Chagall, especially, made repeated use of Judaized images of Jesus in imagery of antisemitic persecution.

This picture struggles to make meaning out of what Olère experienced. It seems animated by a desire to do more than simply attest to what he underwent, or even to what he saw. Rather it appears to be trying to 'raise' it to the level of its forebears in Christian art, and to use the conventions of this art to allow different scenes to be brought together. Placing himself in indirect contact, through a chain of touch, with both Moll and his victims suggests a contradictory sense of where he fits that echoes the earlier ambiguity in the drawings that he seemed to largely resolve concerning his status. Olère may also be striving to resurrect the dead, to provide the victims of Nazi genocide with a kind of afterlife through his art. Christian iconography provides him with a shorthand by which to explore themes of death and figurative resurrection. The cross becomes a scaffold through which Olère can point towards one of the key aims of his art: to resist the Nazi desire to obliterate all trace of their victims, their crimes.

A work such as '*Muselmänner* standing before the crematorium' can clearly not be understood as documentary. We have striven to demonstrate, however, that Olère's need to do more than simply record what he saw is present from the beginning in his artwork. In this, it is consonant with the writings produced by the Sonderkommando in the Scrolls of Auschwitz: they too tried to make some meaning of what they described, to form it into a composition that made some sense, and to think about their own position in relation to the process of genocide. Olère shows how difficult these tasks were. His turn to art historical precedents as a vocabulary on which to draw should not, however, be dismissed. In his undated paintings, the use of a kind of collage technique, which brings different scenes together from the drawings onto one canvas, could also be seen as following on from Leyb Langfus's later writings (especially 'Particulars') and as a precursor of the methods used by later writers and artists drawing upon the Scrolls themselves.

Notes

1. We view this date—given in *David Olère: The Eyes of a Witness*—as uncertain.
2. In a letter he composed in 1944 and buried in the grounds of the crematoria, Marcel Nadjary, for example, states the SS forced people 'to squeeze in so that they could fit as many as possible a real sardine tin of people after they sealed the door shut'. See 'The Letter of Marcel Nadjary,' trans. Ersy Contogouris, in *Testimonies of Resistance: Representations of the Auschwitz-Birkenau Sonderkommando*, eds. Nicholas Chare and Dominic Williams (New York: Berghahn, 2019), in press. Sardines as a metaphor for crowding are quotidian but its commonality in survivor testimony both of the SK and other camp survivors may be linked to the fact sardine tins were also regularly encountered in the camp. It is clear, for instance, that the SK had ready access to tins of sardines as Vitek Pavel who worked in the *Scheisekommando* remembers the SK giving them to his group. Pavel Vitek interviewed by Viera Rybarova on 21 August 1996. USC Shoah Foundation Interview Code 18769. Henry Levy, a survivor from Birkenau, recalls that there were sardines in a Red Cross parcel he was given just prior to his deportation from Salonika. See Levy, 'The Jews of Salonica and the Holocaust: A Personal Memoir,' in *Del Fuego: Sephardim and the Holocaust*, eds. Solomon Gaon and M. Mitchell Serels (New York: Sepher-Hermon Press, 1995), p. 229. In testimony to Gideon Greif, Abraham Dragon twice mentions that sardines were a foodstuff brought by deportees on transports from Holland. See Gideon Greif, *We Wept Without Tears* (New Haven: Yale University Press, 2005), pp. 145 and 152. It is possibly due to the inclusion of sardines in Red Cross parcels that Olga Lengyel recalls finding 'empty sardine cans' in the litter from the railway siding at Birkenau (p. 99). Lengyel also uses sardines as a metaphor to describe the transport of infirm inmates from the camp hospital to the crematoria: 'the "Red Cross" trucks would come and the sick would be packed into them like sardines' (p. 75). See Olga Lengyel, *Five Chimneys: A Woman Survivor's True Story of Auschwitz* (Chicago: Academy Chicago Publishers, 1995). Berry Nahmia mentions that canned sardines were found among belongings from the transports that were sorted at Kanada (p. 101). Nahmia uses sardines—'at night we

lay down in rows like sardines'—as a metaphor to describe the sleeping conditions on the transport that took her from Thessaloniki to Auschwitz (p. 37). See Berry Nahmia, *A Cry for Tomorrow 76859...* (Jacksonville: Bloch Publishing Company, 2011). Kitty Hart was caught smuggling a tin of sardines from Kanada to the main camp complex. See Kitty Hart, *Return to Auschwitz* (London: Granada Publishing, 1983), p. 157. The choice of metaphor to portray instances of crowding is, of course, not restricted to sardines. Morris K. refers to being put in cattle cars to be transported to Auschwitz as being 'packed up like chicken'. Morris K. interviewed by Lawrence Langer on 28 June 1989. Fortunoff Video Archive for Holocaust Testimonies, HVT-1431. Tape 1. 25:25. Olère's visual rendering potentially demonstrates how 'found' metaphors in the camps such as that of sardines carry into art as well as oral and written testimony. For further discussion of the metaphor of sardines, particularly in relation to the SK, see Nicholas Chare, Ersy Contogouris, and Dominic Williams, 'Disinterred Words: The Letters of Marcel Nadjary and Herman Strasfogel,' in *Testimonies of Resistance: Representations of the Auschwitz-Birkenau Sonderkommando*, eds. Nicholas Chare and Dominic Williams (New York: Berghahn, 2019), in press.
3. For a discussion of this phenomenon in Lewental and Nadjary, see Nicholas Chare and Marcel Swiboda, 'Introduction: Unforeseen Encounters,' *Liminalities* 14.1 (2018): 10–11.
4. Dario Gabbai explains 'We would push them in. The SS don't get [involved]'. Dario Gabbai interviewed by Stephen Smith on 1 May 2014. USC Shoah Foundation. Interview Code 142, Tape 5. 33:11. Halivni notes of Shlomo Dragon's testimony that although he 'admits that the prisoners helped with the unloading of the trucks and with the undressing of the victims he does not admit that they pushed them brutally into the gas chambers'. For Halivni, this is because there is a 'tendency among survivors to deny prisoners brutality'. Tzipora Hager Weiss Halivni Papers. USHMM Accession Number 2013.529.1. Box 19. Folder 3, sheet of printer paper paginated 8. Gabbai does not follow this tendency, refusing to sugar-coat the role of the SK in impelling victims into the gas chambers.
5. In some trials, figurative drawings (rather than diagrams) were presented as evidence. Some of the works of Violette Lecoq, for instance, were presented as evidence at the 1946 Ravensbrück trials. For a discussion of these drawings and others relating to Ravensbrück, see Catherine Quintal, 'De la déportation à l'expression; la femme et le témoignage dans les dessins clandestins de Violette Rougier-Lecoq et Jeanette L'Herminier', MA thesis, Université de Montréal, 2018.

6. For a discussion of the genesis of these drawing, see Robert Jan van Pelt, *The Case for Auschwitz: Evidence from the Irving Trial* (Bloomington: Indiana University Press, 2002), p. 188.
7. John Bender and Michael Marrinan, *The Culture of Diagram* (Stanford: Stanford University Press, 2010), p. 7.
8. It is possible the scale of the rooms as represented by Nosal in the diagram of Crematorium 4 (V) may be influenced to some extent by Dragon's emotions. It is also clear that the diagrams cannot be divorced from Dragon's transcribed oral testimony which serves to populate these seemingly empty structures with the dead.
9. Dov Paisikovic, 'Relacja' [Report], USHMM RG-15.205.
10. David Nencel interviewed by Joe Russin in 1996. USHMM Accession Number 2003.76. RG 50.560.0001 and David Nencel interviewed by anonymous woman on 25 June 1990. Yad Vashem Archive O3/6014. Tape 2, 36:00.
11. The trees, like those in the preceding two drawings, may manifest some effort to portray birches, the hardwood species from which *Birkenau* derives its name. The trees, for instance, are clearly not fir trees, trees which an artist might rapidly individually render by a line bisected by inverted v's.
12. 'We did not let people mess with us' might be the best way to translate this colloquial Polish expression into English. Tauber, 'Protokół', 2 (p. 123). NTN 93, Volume 11. Proces Rudolfa Hoessa (Sygn. GK 196), 1946–1947. USHMM Accession Number 1998.A.0243. RG Number RG-15.167M.
13. In an interview with Gideon Greif, Abraham Dragon describes negotiating working conditions with the SS. He also states that 'the Germans were afraid of the Sonderkommando; we were under no one's control'. See Greif, *We Wept Without Tears*, pp. 142 and 145. This relative independence is, it seems, initially visually depicted by Olère but then rejected in subsequent works. He, perhaps, came to view this pseudo-freedom as a potential liability, a possible way for the uninitiated to condemn the SK for their actions.
14. Van Pelt, *The Case for Auschwitz*, p. 174.
15. For a discussion of the particular sets of practices that govern the kinds of art and artists that are celebrated within modernist art history, see Griselda Pollock, *Vision and Difference: Femininity*, Feminism and the Histories of Art (London: Routledge, 1998).
16. Nadine Nieszawer, Marie Boyé, and Paul Fogel, *Peintres juifs à Paris 1905–1939* (Paris: Denoël, 2000), p. 272.
17. Carol Zemel, 'Right After: Aesthetics and Trauma in Survivor Narratives', in *The Holocaust, Art and Taboo: Transatlantic Exchanges*

on the Ethics and Aesthetics of Representation, eds. Sophia Komor and Susanne Rohr (Heidelberg: Universitätsverlag Winter, 2010), pp. 49–61 and 55.

18. Serge Klarsfeld, *David Olère: The Eyes of a Witness* (New York: Beate Klarsfeld Foundation, 1989).
19. Bella Shomer-Zaichik, *Out of the Depths: David Olère, an Artist in Auschwitz* (Jerusalem: Yad Vashem, 1997). Agnieszka Sieradzka, *David Olère. The One Who Survived Crematorium III* (Oświęcim: Auschwitz-Birkenau State Museum, 2018).
20. Alexandre Oler, *Witness: Images of Auschwitz* (1998). The French version of this book was titled *Un génocide en heritage* (Oler, 1999).
21. Four works by Olère are reproduced alongside some biographical information in the exhibition catalogue *Spiritual Resistance: Art from the Concentration Camps 1940–1945* (Dawidowicz, 1978). Exhibitions including Olère's work are referenced in the catalogue *The Last Expression: Art and Auschwitz* although no images by the artist are reproduced (Mickenberg, 2003), p. 149.
22. Glenn Sujo, *Legacies of Silence: The Visual Arts and Holocaust Memory* (London: Philip Wilson, 2001).
23. Véronique Chevillon, 'Entendre David Olère, entendre les prisonniers des Sonderkommandos,' in *Sonderkommando et Arbeitsjuden: Les travailleurs forcés de la mort*, ed. Philippe Mesnard (Paris: Éditions Kimé, 2015).
24. Susan Pentlin, 'Testimony from the Ashes,' p. 259. For us, Olère is himself a victim and his positioning of himself alongside other victims in some of his art is less an expression of empathy and more a portrayal of the collective suffering of the Jewish people.
25. Zemel, 'Right After' and Zemel, 'Enduring Witness: David Olère's Visual Testimony,' in *Testimonies of Resistance: Representations of the Auschwitz-Birkenau Sonderkommando*, eds. Nicholas Chare and Dominic Williams (New York: Berghahn, 2019), in press.
26. Chevillon, 'Entendre David Olère, entendre les prisonniers des Sonderkommandos,' p. 169.
27. Klarsfeld, *David Olère: The Eyes of a Witness*, p. 9.
28. Chevillon, 'Entendre David Olère, entendre les prisonniers des Sonderkommandos,' p. 169.
29. Miklós Nyiszli, *Auschwitz: A Doctor's Eyewitness Report*, p. 87.
30. Halivni renders Lemke as Leite. Halivni Papers. Box 18. File 1, sheet of printer paper numbered 2.
31. We can surmise that like most material gathered by the SK to bear witness to mass murder, the sketches were buried in the grounds of the crematoria although it is also possible that Olère either abandoned or destroyed them prior to the death march from Auschwitz.
32. Klarsfeld, *David Olère: The Eyes of a Witness*, p. 6.

33. On this attribution, see Andreas Kilian, 'Abschiedsbrief aus dem Krematorium: das verschollene Original und sein anonymer Verfasser,' *Mitteilungsblatt der Lagergemeinschaft Auschwitz/Freundeskreis der Auschwitzer* 38.1 (2018): 5–21.
34. In fact, six people from this transport are thought to have survived until the liberation of the camps. Strasfogel was, of course, not one of them.
35. For an extended discussion of this letter, see our book Chare and Williams, *Matters of Testimony*, pp. 154–182, and also Chare, Contogouris, and Willams, 'Disinterred Words: The Letters of Marcel Nadjary and Herman Strasfogel'.
36. Dov Paisicovic [*sic*], 'A Survivor of the Sonderkommando,' in *Auschwitz*, ed. Léon Poliakov (Paris: René Juillard, 1964), p. 164. Olère is also referenced in Leon Cohen's memoir where he mentions a Parisian, 'the painter Holler'. Cohen, *From Greece to Birkenau*, trans. Jose-Maurice Gormezano (Jerusalem: Graphit Press, 1996), p. 53.
37. The majority of the titles of Olère's drawings derive from text in French by the artist that forms part of them. The titles of many of Olère's paintings and a few of the drawings appear to have been devised after the artist's death. Where possible for the drawings, we have used French titles based on Olère's pencil inscriptions. For the paintings, we have used the English or French titles ascribed to these works by the various archives where they are now held. The archive titles occasionally differ from those used for the same works in previous literature on Olère's art.
38. See Mark Godfrey, *Abstraction and the Holocaust* (New Haven: Yale University Press, 2007). Godfrey is wary of too readily and rapidly linking abstraction with unrepresentability (pp. 4–9).
39. Berel Lang, *Holocaust Representation: Art Within the Limits of History and Ethics* (Baltimore: Johns Hopkins University Press, 2000), p. 124.
40. Mor Presiado identifies the artistic language of survivors producing paintings immediately after the war ended (1945–1949) as one characterized by realistic figuration. Olère's drawings broadly conform to this language. See Presiado, 'A New Perspective on Holocaust Art: Women's Artistic Expression of the Female Holocaust Experience (1939–1949),' *Holocaust Studies* 22.4 (2016): 418.
41. Mark Godfrey does not regard abstract art that takes the Holocaust as its theme as necessarily seeking to express the sublime. He positions himself against Jean-François Lyotard who he regards as an exponent of this view (*Abstraction and the Holocaust*, pp. 12–14). Lyotard forcefully links the unrepresentable and the sublime with modern art although the Holocaust is an implicit point of reference in his discussions linked to this theme. See, for example, his remarks on the differend and the sublime in *Lessons on the Analytic of the Sublime*, trans. Elizabeth Rottenberg

(Stanford: Stanford University Press, 1994), pp. 123–127 and his discussion of modern art and the sublime in the essay 'Answering the Question: What Is Postmodernism?,' in *The Postmodern Condition: A Report on Knowledge*, trans. Geoff Bennington and Brian Massumi, ed. Lyotard (Manchester: Manchester University Press, 1984), pp. 77–79. Lyotard's exploration of the philosophical significance of Auschwitz, *The Differend*, trans. George van den Abbeele (Manchester: Manchester University Press, 1988), refers only infrequently to the sublime although problems of expression are a key theme.

42. See the discussion of tattooed skin in Alexandra Przyrembel, 'Transfixed by an Image: Ilse Koch, the Kommandeuse of Buchenwald,' trans by Pamela Selwyn, *German History* 19.3 (2001): 383–384. See also Wendy Adele-Marie Sarti, *Women and Nazis*: Perpetrators of Genocide and Other Crimes During Hitler's Regime, 1933–*1945* (Bethesda: Academica Press, 2011), pp. 148–149 and 157.

43. Klarsfeld, *David Olère: The Eyes of a Witness*, p. 42.

44. Insa Eschebach, 'Interpreting Female Perpetrators: Ravensbrück Guards in the Courts of East Germany, 1946–1955,' in *Lessons and Legacies Volume V: The Holocaust and Justice*, ed. Peter Hayes (Evanston, IL: Northwestern University Press, 2002), p. 261.

45. He may, for example, have confused her with Irma Grese who had a reputation as a particularly sadistic guard at Auschwitz and who was reported to have slept with prisoners and to have raped them. Laura Sjoberg identifies Irma Grese and Dorothea Binz as particularly sadistic guards at Auschwitz (in reality Binz never worked at Auschwitz but was at Ravensbrück with Grese and is credited with having mentored her). See Sjoberg, *Women as Wartime Rapists: Beyond Sensation and Stereotyping* (New York: New York University Press, 2016), p. 104. Eschebach suggests that Grese and Binz are also major examples of the cliché of the attractive but vicious Nazi woman criminal. She sees the three women as having much in common: 'blond hair, youthful age, and reputed brutality'. Eschebach, 'Interpreting Female Perpetrators,' p. 261.

46. Wendy Lower foregrounds the gendered etymology of the term 'perpetrator' with its Latin roots in *pater* or father. As she explains, 'male agency is embedded in the term'. See Lower, 'German Women and the Holocaust in the Nazi East,' in *Women and Genocide: Survivors, Victims, Perpetrators*, eds. Elissa Bemporad and Joyce W. Warren (Bloomington: Indiana University Press, 2018), p. 118.

47. Koch was not known to sleep with inmates. At Auschwitz, however, Irma Grese was reported by Olga Lengyel to select male prisoners for her sexual pleasure. She mentions a Georgian man that Grese, 'like some

Eastern potentate, had picked [...] for herself'. Lengyel, *Five Chimneys*, pp. 201–202.
48. Despite the title of the work, the presence of the cup suggests the possible interpretation that the prisoner may have poisoned himself rather than submit to Koch's demands.
49. Nanette Salomon, 'The Venus Pudica: Uncovering Art History's "Hidden Agendas" and Pernicious Pedigrees,' in *Generations and Geographies in the Visual Arts: Feminist Readings*, eds. Griselda Pollock (London: Routledge, 1996), pp. 69–87. Griselda Pollock also discusses the classical female nude as a closed body with the genitals sealed. See Pollock, *After-affects/After-images* (Manchester: Manchester University Press, 2013), p. 52.
50. Esther Katz and Joan Ringelheim, *Proceedings of the Conference on Women Surviving the Holocaust*, eds. Esther Katz and Joan Ringelheim (New York: Institute for Research in History, 1983), p. 78.
51. Désiré Haffner, 'Birkenau,' in *Témoignages sur Auschwitz* (Paris: Éditions de l'amicale des déportés d'Auschwitz, 1946), p. 67.
52. Judith Halberstam, *In a Queer Time and Place: Transgender Bodies, Subcultural Lives* (New York: New York University Press, 2005), p. 104.
53. Erna Low, 'I Was in Oswiecim,' Unpublished manuscript, circa 1952. USHMM Accession number 2017.466.1, p. 3.
54. Sarah Cushman, *The Women of Birkenau*, PhD thesis, Worcester, MA: Clark University, 2010, p. 256.
55. Lengyel, *Five Chimneys*, p. 199.
56. Halivni Papers. Box 17. Folder 6, loose leaf p. 12.
57. Female perpetrators were, however, as Wendy Lower notes, sometimes referred to as 'she-men' suggesting that they too troubled common gender categories. Lower, 'German Women and the Holocaust in the Nazi East,' p. 121.
58. Giuliana Tedeschi, *There Is a Place on Earth: A Woman in Birkenau*, trans. Tim Parks (London: Lime Tree, 1993), p. 24.
59. For a discussion of female masculinities, see Judith Jack Halberstam, *Female Masculinity* (Durham: Duke University Press, 1998).
60. Richard Baxter, *Women of the Gestapo* (London: Quality Press, 1943), p. 9.
61. Jennifer Craik notes that denouncing women in uniform (her example is policewomen) as butch and unfeminine was still common as recently as the 1980s because, for some men, the female gender continued to be perceived as 'problematic in occupational roles of authority, security and forcefulness'. Craik, *Uniforms Exposed: From Conformity to Transgression* (Oxford: Berg, 2005), p. 134.

62. Olère's signature varies in his works. Those produced in 1945 sometimes include the accent grave on the first e in his name. From 1946 onwards, however, Olère no longer accents his signature. Works from 1945 are also either dated '45' or '1945'.
63. 'Bois de bouleaux' means birch woods and is a reference to Birkenau (which takes its name from the birch trees that grow in that location).
64. Irma Grese was reputed to have keenly used her whip on prisoners, sometimes for her sexual excitement. Gisella Perl gives a particularly disturbing account of Grese becoming sexually excited and slavering while watching surgical operations being performed on women whose breasts she had injured with her whip. Perl, *I Was a Doctor in Auschwitz* (New York: Arno, 1979 [1948]), p. 62.
65. For a nuanced discussion of empathy and identification, see Susan Gubar, 'Dis/Identifications,' *Signs* 28:1 (2002).
66. Sonja Hedgepeth and Rochelle Saidel have suggested that sexual violence towards women 'began to be mentioned in some memoirs, documentary films, literature, and reports right after the Holocaust' (Hedgepeth and Saidel, 2010, p. 1). The art of Olère could be added to this list. Additionally, Zoë Waxman notes the absence of descriptions of sexual abuse in concentration camp testimony which has led to the belief that such abuse was relatively rare (Waxman, 2006, p. 138). Olère's art suggests that it was a familiar event in the extermination camp.
67. Presiado, 'A New Perspective on Holocaust Art,' p. 419.
68. Klarsfeld, *David Olère: The Eyes of a Witness*, p. 9.
69. Emphases are in the original. Zemel, 'Right After,' p. 58.
70. Erko Hajblum cited in Maurice Garbarz and Elie Garbarz, *Un Survivant – Auschwitz-Birkenau-Buchenwald* (Paris: Ramsay, 2006), p.115.
71. Griselda Pollock, 'Art as Transport-Station of Trauma? Haunting Objects in the Works of Bracha Ettinger, Sarah Kofman and Chantal Akerman,' in *Representing Auschwitz: At the Margins of Testimony*, eds. Nicholas Chare and Dominic Williams (Houndmills: Palgrave Macmillan, 2013), p. 205.
72. Ibid.
73. Ibid.
74. Lisa Tickner examines how artistic technique can come to embody aggression in her inspiring reading of Walter Sickert's *La Hollandaise* (c. 1906), writing of 'the slashing strokes of the brush, conjuring limbs and torso into being but seeming to cut across and erase the features above them, already imply[ing] a kind of violence to the figure they represent'. Tickner, *Modern Life and Modern Subjects: British Art in the Early Twentieth Century* (New Haven: Yale University Press, 2000), p. 20.

75. Wash is also occasionally exploited by Olère to reinforce a sense of violence as is the case with the 1945 artwork 'Jusqu'au dernier souffle. Georges' in which the SS officer Georges is shown using a truncheon to beat a man to death. The man's head is immersed in a tub, his back exposed across the tub's rim. The wash follows the trajectory of the truncheon as Georges raises it, bringing a strong feeling of physical force to the depiction. The significant quantity of negative space in the work reinforces the victim's exposure, his helplessness.
76. A second smaller version of this subject from the same year is more explicit with the injection occurring between the woman's legs.
77. Sujo, *Legacies of Silence*, p. 88.
78. Primo Levi, 'The Grey Zone,' in *The Drowned and the Saved* (London: Abacus, 1989), p. 37.
79. Levi, 'The Grey Zone,' p. 42. For an in-depth discussion of the grey zone as conceived by Levi and others, see Dominic Williams, 'What Makes the Grey Zone Grey? Blurring Moral and Factual Judgements of the Sonderkommando,' in *Testimonies of Resistance: Representations of the Auschwitz-Birkenau Sonderkommando,* eds. Nicholas Chare and Dominic Williams (New York: Berghahn, 2019), in press.
80. Herman Strasfogel, 'The Letter of Herman Strasfogel,' trans. Ersy Contogouris, in *Testimonies of Resistance: Representations of the Auschwitz-Birkenau Sonderkommando*, eds. Nicholas Chare and Dominic Williams (New York: Berghahn, 2019), in press.
81. It seems therefore that Olère has misspelled the name although 'bewzinger' is close to the German word *bezwinger* meaning conqueror or captor and the mistake is therefore potentially revealing.
82. Sujo, *Legacies of Silence*, p. 88
83. Bella Shomer-Zaichik notes the beauty of many of the women Olère depicts, drawing attention to his idealizing tendencies. Shomer-Zaichik perceives a link between Olère's film posters and his art. See Shomer-Zaichik, 'The Transition from Reality to Imagination in the Work of David Olère,' in *Out of the Depths: David Olère, an Artist in Auschwitz*, p. 14.
84. The 1946 ink and wash work 'Le SS Georges execute une femme' is similarly unrealistic.
85. Van Pelt, *The Case for Auschwitz*, p. 180.
86. Lynda Nead, *The Female Nude: Art, Obscenity and Sexuality* (London: Routledge, 1992), p. 7.
87. The inclusion of the accent grave in Olère's signature suggests that this is a pre-war work.
88. Olère's works frequently represent female sexuality on patriarchal terms, objectifying women. We are not suggesting, however, that they are

pornographic. As Feona Attwood has noted, the meanings that accrue to practices of objectification are variable, context-specific and not always bound to pornography. Olère objectifies women yet often with a tenderness that disrupts any ready identification of his female figures as simple scenery for the projection of male sexual fantasies. See Attwood, 'Pornography and Objectification,' *Feminist Media Studies* 4.1: 7–19.
89. Zemel, 'Enduring Witness,' in press.
90. In this context, it is noteworthy that Olère's wife posed as a model for some of the drawings. See Bella Shomer-Zaichik, 'The Transition from Reality to Imagination in the Work of David Olère,' p. 14.
91. Griselda Pollock, 'Death in the Image: The Responsibility of Aesthetics in *Night and Fog* (1955) and *Kapò* (1959),' in *Concentrationary Cinema: Aesthetics as Political Resistance in Alain Resnais's Night and Fog*, eds. Griselda Pollock and Max Silverman (New York: Berghahn, 2011), pp. 285–288.
92. Ziva Amishai-Maisels sees the woman as still being alive in this drawing, increasing the horror of the scene. See Amishai-Maisels, *Depiction and Interpretation: The Influence of the Holocaust in the Visual Arts* (Oxford: Pergamon Press, 1993), p. 48. The drawing is titled 'Ouverture de la chambre à gaz' in *David Olère: The Eyes of a Witness*.
93. Rebecca Camhi Fromer, *The Holocaust Odyssey of Daniel Bennahmias*, Sonderkommando (Tuscaloosa: The University of Alabama Press, 1993), p. 39.
94. Henryk Mandelbaum interviewed by Elliott Perlman. USHMM Accession Number 2006.201. RG Number RG-50.634.0001. 2:12:45.
95. Nadjary worked with Daniel Bennahmias emptying the gas chamber. See Fromer, *The Holocaust Odyssey of Daniel Bennahmias, Sonderkommando*, p. 45n2.
96. Marcel Nadjary, *Khroniko 1941–1945* (Thessaloniki: Etz Kaim, 1991).
97. Langfus, 'The Deportation' [96] 107–[97] 108)]. See Chare and Williams, *Matters of Testimony*, pp. 106–107.
98. Daniel Bennahmias interviewed by Beatrice Netter, Lisa Barnett and Ilana Braun on 12 November 1991. USHMM Accession Number 1999.A. 0122.661. RG-50.477.0661.
99. Shlomo Venezia interviewed by Manuela Consonni on 13 December 1987, USC Shoah Foundation, Interview Code 36179. Tape 10. 27:30.
100. Ana Firoiu and Fleur Kuhn suggest that Zalman Gradowski's writings can be understood as performing what might be viewed as a comparable process of separating, a returning of individuality to victims transformed into 'an indistinct mass' [*une foule indistincte*]. The mass they describe is not restricted to the aftermath of a gassing but that sight might be viewed as representing the apotheosis of Nazi efforts at

de-individualizing and de-humanizing the victims. See Firoiu and Kuhn, 'Au coeur de l'enfer de Zalmen Gradowski: Expérience collective et subjectivité dans le témoignage immédiat de la Shoah,' in *La Psychologie de masse, aujourd'hui*, eds. Michel Gad Wolkowicz, Thibault Moreau, Alexis Nouss, and Gérard Rabinovitch (Paris: Des Rosiers, 2012), p. 82.

101. Shlomo Venezia, *Inside the Gas Chambers*: Eight Months in the Sonderkommando of Auschwitz, trans. Andrew Brown (Cambridge: Polity, 2009), p. 71
102. This liquidation actually took place in 1943. Olère has misdated it in the pencil notation he has made on the drawing.
103. Venezia, *Inside the Gas Chambers*, p. 77.
104. Emily Bilski, 'Art During the Holocaust,' in *Kunst und Holocaust: Bildliche Zeugen vom Ende der westlichen Kultur*, eds. D. Hoffmann and K. Ermert (Rehburg-Loccum: Evangelische Akademie Loccum, 1990), p. 41.
105. Sujo, *Legacies of Silence*, p. 88.
106. Joanna Field (Marion Milner), *On Not Being Able to Paint* (New York: Jeremy P. Tarcher, 1957).
107. Ibid., p. 17.
108. In this, they can be read as akin to Charlotte Delbo's poetic prose as Chare discusses it in *Auschwitz and Afterimages*. They are efforts from within abject experience to reappropriate symbolic language.
109. Denise Brahimi, *La Peinture au féminin: Berthe Morisot et Mary Cassatt* (Paris: J-P Rocher, 2000), p. 41.
110. See our discussion of Dragon's affidavit in the preceding chapter.
111. We are grateful to Martine Saint-Cyr for drawing this to our attention.
112. We are grateful to Élisabeth Pagé for drawing this to our attention.
113. For a thoughtful engagement with the complexities of Siminski's *In the Gas Chamber*, see Amishai-Maisels, *Depiction and Interpretation*, p. 45.
114. For a discussion of the male nude, including its association with heroism and its erotic connotations, see Abigail Solomon-Godeau, *Male Trouble* (London: Thames & Hudson, 1997), pp. 177–224.
115. Olère borrows from several forms of Christian iconography in his work. 'Her Last Nursing,' for example, evokes 'a traditional Madonna-and-child' design. See Zemel, 'Right After,' p. 57.

CHAPTER 6

Matters of Video Testimony

Listening and Resistance

The Sonderkommando revolt of 7 October 1944 plays a major part in a significant discussion of the nature and value of Holocaust video testimony. In his well-known essay 'Bearing Witness or the Vicissitudes of Listening', the psychoanalyst and child survivor Dori Laub focusses on an account given by a woman survivor of the SK uprising as a means to examine the relationship between testimony and historical truth.[1] This woman, whom Laub describes as 'slight, self effacing [and] almost talking whispers', gives an impassioned account of the rebellion.[2] Laub suggests that as she 'was relating her memories of the Auschwitz uprising; a sudden intensity, passion and colour were infused into the narrative':

> She was fully there. 'All of a sudden,' she said, 'we saw four chimneys going up in flames, exploding. The flames shot in the sky, people were running. It was unbelievable.' There was a silence in the room, a fixed silence against which the woman's words reverberated loudly, as though carrying along an echo of the jubilant sounds exploding from behind barbed wires, a stampede of people breaking loose, screams, shots, battle cries, explosions. It was no longer the deadly timelessness of Auschwitz. A dazzling brilliant moment from the past swept through the frozen stillness of the muted, grave-like landscape with dashing meteoric speed, exploding it into a shower of sights and sounds.[3]

This testimony, Laub writes, is subsequently screened at a conference and historians criticize the account for its lack of accuracy, a lack which, for them, considerably undermined its credibility. Laub, who is present, disagrees vehemently and argues that 'the number [of chimneys] mattered less than the fact of the occurrence. The event itself was almost inconceivable'.[4] For him, the feelings of the woman are highly insightful. The historians, over-focussed on objectivity, overlook or reject this insight about the revolt, this emotional truth.

Laub's critique of the wrong-headed reception of video testimony by a group of positivist historians has been highly influential.[5] The summary of the testimony and of the reactions to it was taken as fact, followed on faith. Through inspiring archival work, Thomas Trezise, however, sought out the testimony Laub references and also more details on the conference the psychoanalyst attended.[6] He discovered that there is no solitary testimony that conforms to the description Laub provides. The psychoanalyst has, rather, composed a composite account of what are likely three interviews with different women conducted on the same day. There is also seemingly no conference with multiple historians in attendance that Laub also participated in within the correct time frame. Based on the specific reference to four chimneys, Trezise established that the main interviewee's testimony which Laub refers to is that of Serena N. The other two interviews which feature in his composite are Serena N.'s sister Irene W. and their aunt Rose A. The three women were barracked together at Auschwitz and then Birkenau where they worked in Kanada.

Kanada was the colloquial name for the *Effektenlager*, the warehouses where the possessions of those transported to Auschwitz were gathered together (often in bundles) stored and sorted.[7] The complex known as Kanada II was in close proximity to Crematorium 3 (IV). Workers there, like members of the SK, engaged in shift work. The kommando was made up of men and women employed in different tasks. There were day and night shifts. Day shifts involved working indoors in the warehouses, whereas during night shifts inmates laboured outdoors. Like the SK, workers in Kanada had many privileges in comparison with the general camp population, particularly once they were housed in barracks in Kanada itself.[8] Kitty Hart remarks on how luxurious the huts were there with inmates allocated 'well-filled straw mattresses and two blankets each'.[9] The kommando also enjoyed daily showers (sometimes with warm water).[10] Hart, who worked on the night shift for a period of time, recalls that 'on fine days we lay outside on the lovely lawn that surrounded our hut, sunbathing and splashing ourselves with water to cool off'.[11] She also describes spending 'many hours reading the books that [she] had found while making up the bundles'.[12] The task of sorting through possessions, however, sometimes exacted 'a heavy mental price'.[13] The sight of items linked with babies, for example, was particularly distressing. The relationship with objects was sometimes complex. Berry Nahmia, for instance, describes inventing stories for the materials she handled, imagining backstories for their former owners.[14]

Hart also describes a cultural life in Kanada that involved the staging of plays. She writes:

> This was surely the craziest set-up in the whole world. All around us were screams, death smoking chimneys making the air black and heavy with soot and the smell of burning bodies. I think our main fight was for sanity and so we laughed and sang with the burning hell all around us.[15]

Here cultural activities, like the writings of the SK, seem employed in complex ways to safeguard identity and process traumatic experiences. It is clear that some inmates working in Kanada felt conflicted about their actions. Hart believed that by sorting possessions she was, in some way, 'helping the Germans'.[16] At the same time, she also engaged in acts of defiance recalling that any banknotes that were found were used as toilet paper rather than surrendered to the SS.[17] Those in Kanada could source clothing and food from abandoned belongings and were therefore, like the SK, able to maintain their health better than some inmates.

The workers in Kanada also feared a similar fate to the SK who regularly had their ranks pared and then reinforced. Hart observes that there 'was the constant fear that our *Kommando*, like the *Sonderkommando*, would be exchanged, burned. Everyone was convinced that the Germans would never let us out alive, for we knew too much, being direct witnesses of mass murders'.[18] Those who worked at Kanada II often saw transports arriving and people being ushered to their deaths. They also heard cries and screams from the burning pits. Although the Nazis strove to prevent anxiety and resistance from those arriving transports by using subterfuge, the need to use the burning pits during the Hungarian Aktion meant those sent to Crematoria 3 (IV) and 4 (V) were sometimes well aware of their fate. The pits were located out of sight, surrounded by trees, but the heat, smell and smoke emitted by them would have been perceived by anyone in their vicinity.[19] Weiss recalls in testimony for the Shoah Foundation that at night the flames from the pits were particularly noticeable. This meant that 'people who came at night actually saw this who were heading into the crematorium and they would scream, they would scream, blood curdling screams'.[20] In her testimonies, Irene Weiss provides insight into the kind of bizarre and outlandish sights that greeted those being sent to their deaths when the pits were in operation. Weiss spotted someone from her hometown among the SK in the yard of Crematorium 3 (IV), an eighteen-year-old man called Joel (Yoel) Moskowitz. She says that covered as he was with soot from the pits, 'he was almost black'. Weiss goes on to explain that his appearance made him seem dark-skinned to her.[21] In this context, colour therefore became a key measure of difference, the semiotics of racial difference supplementing familiar class and gender categories (Moskowitz came from a working-class family, whereas Weiss's background was what nowadays might be referred to as middle-class).[22] Given how blackness was frequently understood in Europe at this time (equated with savagery and evil), the men presented a spectacle that, if ever encountered by people arriving on transports, quite possibly registered as terrifying.[23] We can also assume that this forced appropriation of blackness contributed to the SK men's alienation from themselves and each other, and that it played a part in the SS's view of them too: not as the (pseudo-)colleagues of Primo Levi's imagining, but as objects of disgust and perhaps even amusement.

Weiss's account, like many others from women who worked in Kanada, provides insights into the operation of the death factory that can go beyond her own perspective. Although no testimony has survived produced directly by women sent to their deaths in the crematoria, women who worked in Kanada have been able to bear witness to the process of mass murder. In Chapter 2, we discussed how the SK strove to speak for women and children sent to their deaths, even sometimes to allow women to speak through their writings. To a degree, the testimony of workers in Kanada gives voice to the men of the SK. Joel Moskowitz, for example, does not feature in the list of SK members included in Eric Friedler et al.'s *Zeugen aus der Todeszone*.[24] It is through Weiss's testimony that his name, the name of a Hungarian Jewish member of the SK, is known to us and that he becomes singularized. Weiss also recalls Moskowitz throwing a note over the fence to her aunt Perl, a note which detailed the circumstances of her father's death, shot by the SS for refusing to work in the SK.[25] Nahmia reproduces from memory a note she says Marcel Nadjary threw over the fence to his cousin Sarika la Evréa (who worked in Kanada) advising them to prepare for the impending revolt. We also know from the women of Kanada that in the immediate aftermath of the revolt, among them, there was no feeling of elation, only of tragedy at the deaths of the men who worked opposite them. The testimonies from Kanada provide accounts from the outside of the crematoria, looking in. The testimonies from the SK, which sometimes mention Kanada, were produced from the inside looking out. These testimonies, however, frequently connect and weave into each other.

We want to argue that understanding the testimony of the three women from Kanada who were interviewed by Laub is impossible if the importance of the Sonderkommando for their accounts is not adequately addressed. Laub vehemently denies that the account referenced in *Testimony* is a composite of the testimonies of Rose A., Serena N. and Irene W.[26] He insists that his summary is solely based on Serena N.'s interview. She is the woman who is 'slight and self effacing'.[27] Having viewed the testimonies, however, it is difficult to disagree with Trezise's conclusion that Laub has fashioned a composite. The principal influence upon this composite appears to us, contra Laub and Trezise, to be Rose A. Rose A. conforms to the age of the survivor Laub describes: she is a woman in her late sixties (born in 1916), and her tone is relatively unvaried, close to affectless.[28] She also, Trezise notes, describes more than one crematorium exploding: 'And one crematorium blew and the other crema, so…'.[29] As she relates this event, each reference to an exploding crematorium is accompanied by a sweeping upward gesture of the arm to signal its destruction. For Rose A., this part of her account is quite animated, much more noticeably so than for Serena N., Rose A. also has difficulty discussing the name of her Kommando. The following exchange takes place:

> *Dori Laub*: You were in, was it the Kanada commando that you were in? The one that…
> *Rose A.*: I was not in… Only men were in the Sonderkommando. I was…
> *DL*: No, I'm asking about…
> *Sergio Rothstein*: Kanada
> *DL*: Kanada
> *RA*: No.
> *DL*: You weren't called the Kanada commando. I mean those were took over here.

SR: It was about the nickname for that group of people that sorted the...
RA: Oh, that was...
SR: Kanada, no?
RA: Yeah, yes, there was red kerchiefs and white kerchiefs, some of them were during the day, some of them were during the night.[30]
DL: But was it the Kanada called?
RA: That's right.
DL: The Kanada commando.[31]

It seems clear to us that this is the exchange Laub has in mind when he writes:

I asked her if she knew of the name of the commando she was serving on. She did not. Does the term 'Canada commando' mean anything to her? I followed up. 'No' she said, taken aback, as though startled by my question.[32]

Rose A. is clearly not startled but there is confusion when she is asked about Kanada. She begins to give an explanation for the Kommando's name that is linked to the colour of the headscarves of the day and night shifts (red or white). This linking of the name Kanada with headscarves that mirror the colours of the Canadian flag differs from the usual explanation that the nickname arose because the *Effektenlager* was perceived as a land of plenty.[33] It is an important observation that the two men miss. In their testimonies, Rose A.'s two nieces have no difficulty referring to Kanada. If we accept Trezise's supposition, however, which we are minded to, it seems that Rose A.'s responses here can be interpreted not so much as a disavowal of her time in that commando but, potentially, as a symptom of some kind of unprocessed feelings regarding the SK. She mishears Laub, substituting Sonderkommando for Kanada commando.

The Sonderkommando also appear highly important in relation to Serena N.'s account of her experiences at Birkenau. This reality is ignored by both Trezise and Laub. They overlook the importance of the fact that Serena N.'s own father was, as she recounts, briefly a member of the SK. He could not stand the work and was therefore shot soon after joining the squad. Her aunt learnt his fate from Joel Moskowitz. Serena N. relates of her father:

He found the...the bodies of his own family, his children and my mother. So he couldn't stand it mentally and they shot him. Everybody else who could stand it – usually they changed the Sonderkommando every three months.[34]

On two occasions, Laub has to prompt Serena N. to use the word Sonderkommando (although after the first prompt she does later use the word spontaneously). It is not Kanada that she represses, as Laub claims, but the name of the SK, the name of the group of slave labourers of which her father was briefly a part. The failures of memory in relation to the SK in these interviews are noteworthy. Rose A., for instance, twice mispronounces the Sonderkommando calling them the 'Zonekommando' and the 'Zeldakommando'. Across the three testimonies, it is the Sonderkommando who form a traumatic kernel, for it was there that Rose A.'s brother, Serena N.'s and Irene W.'s father, Meyer F., met his death. Each of the women, in their different ways, has trouble naming this group. Rose A. contorts the term, Serena N. has to be repeatedly prompted to use it, and Irene W. avoids using it at all. The potential reasons for this reluctance or refusal are multiple but one possible explanation is clearly that the term has become bound up with their sense of loss for Meyer F.

In a summary of Serena N.'s testimony that he provided to the United States Holocaust Memorial Museum (USHMM), Lawrence Langer does note some of her silences, picking up on the fact she never refers to the gas chambers, only the crematoria. This choice of wording is likely influenced by the specifics of what Serena N. was capable of seeing from Kanada. For her, the crematorium existed more as a site for the burning of bodies, a place of fire, smoke, and stench. She does, anyway, refer to gassing, if not to the 'gas chamber', as Langer acknowledges. Langer, like the historians described by Laub, finds Serena N.'s testimony 'suspect' because of her description of the four crematoria blowing up simultaneously.[35] The only crematorium Serena N. would have a direct view of was Crematorium 3 (IV), which was damaged by fire in the revolt, and it seems she inferred from what she did see that the other crematoria had suffered a similar fate (or she later heard anecdotally that they had).[36] She actually says 'we saw the gates, yes, the gates open, men running from there and all the four crematoria at one time blew up'.[37] It is therefore not even clear if she is claiming to have *seen* this 'blowing up' (as Laub's summary has it). She saw a gate open and men running. That the women in Kanada heard explosions seems plausible.[38] It is quite possible the SS used grenades during their efforts to suppress the uprising and the SK may have been able to use some improvised weapons such as Molotov cocktails.

At least four men (but probably many more) ran into Kanada to try and hide (three who were caught and shot and one, Isaak Venezia, who was concealed and then able to rejoin the SK a few days later).[39] Rose A. mentions that 'one man ran into our barrack and he was schlepped out and killed'.[40] She adds 'I mean I didn't see all [of] them killed because we were inside and they chased us to the barrack'.[41] Here Rose A. appears to be retroactively seeking to explain how she could claim to Laub that she saw the crematorium blow up when she was inside the barracks.[42] She suggests she was outside but then shepherded inside mid-revolt. This is highly unlikely as the SS would be preoccupied with containing the uprising. In reality, with the passage of time the ordering (but not the reality) of events for Rose A. has become confused. It seems to us that what is actually happening here is that as the testimony goes on her recall is improving. She has 'warmed up' so to speak and is growing into the past at this point, remembering more.[43] She now recognizes that when the revolt broke out she was inside her work barrack but for her narrative to cohere, she has to make this emergent insight fit with her previous remarks.[44]

Rose A.'s mode of recall conforms to the constructive process of remembering identified by memory theorists such as, most notably, Frederic Bartlett.[45] This constructive process means that the retrieval of memory can be influenced by established beliefs (such as that Rose A. was outside when the revolt began) to the extent that new recollections must be made to adapt to pre-existent beliefs about past events, assimilated to them. Other survivors of Kanada confirm that during the day the work of sorting was done inside. It was only at night time that the women worked outside (women did sometimes sneak between barracks but it was fraught with risk to do so). The blowing up of the crematoria/crematorium is focussed on by Laub et al. at the expense of another element of the account that is consistently remarked upon across the testimonies: the open gate—the breached boundaries between Kanada and Crematorium 3 (IV). Irene Weiss has remarked of this event: 'The gate [was] open, [something] which we never saw, just open'.[46] Giving greater thought to Serena N.'s specific location within Birkenau and to how that influenced her perceptions renders her account more comprehensible.

In his response to Trezise's initial article regarding his use (and perceived abuse) of testimony, Laub cautions about the need 'to strike a balance between the close examination of specific excerpts and the larger view of the testimony as a whole'.[47] He does not seemingly recognize how a witness's location within a specific setting will inform their perception. Laub is apparently accusing Trezise of creating what might be termed 'bleeding chunks' of oral history, 'nuggets' of the kind much desired by the USHMM when they initially began to record video testimony.[48] Donald Tovey used the phrase 'bleeding chunks' in an essay on Anton Bruckner's Symphony Number 4 as part of a criticism of the tendency to single out the choice cuts of operas and perform them as standalone pieces.[49] Out of context, such excerpts or 'highlights' lose their integrity musically. Laub argues that a similar problem arises when Trezise fails to adequately position Serena N.'s remarks on the Sonderkommando revolt within her overall testimony. He suggests that 'the testimonial excerpt in question was in my mind deeply connected to the interview in its entirety since I was the one who did the interview'.[50] Here Laub wishes to foreground the qualitative difference between conducting and listening to an interview. In asserting, it was *his* interview; however, he also simultaneously sidelines Eva Kantor who was the co-interviewer of Serena N. In the early stages of the interview, it is Kantor who takes the lead. Despite this retrospective lapse, during the interview itself Laub displays a strong wish to protect women's achievements.

Laub does not rectify Serena N.'s error about the detail of the destruction of the four crematoria but he does interrupt her to emphatically correct her testimony later. She claims that the explosives procured by the SK were bought from a German. Laub interjects:

> *Dori Laub*: Do you know that Jewish girls worked in an ammunition factory, in a grenade [*sic*], and smuggled out the powder that was used for that?
> *Serena N.*: No. We knew there was an ammunition factory but we thought only men worked…I thought only men worked the…[cut off by Laub]
> *DL*: Jewish girls in their vag…in their vaginas…
> *SN*: Is that right?
> *DL*: and in their mouths smuggled out…
> *SN*: I did not know how it went – I only know that it happened.[51]

It is difficult to know what to make of this exchange, in which Laub suddenly takes it upon himself to fill in gaps in Serena N.'s knowledge, to correct her about the source of the explosives. Here he goes into what, in the context of the rest of his interventions in the interview, is a remarkable level of detail. It is part of Fortunoff Archive guidelines that interviewers 'address historically inaccurate information or myths' but this is meant to be done through posing questions such as 'How do you know that?'.[52]

Laub's corrective is historically accurate. The vagina was one way (among several) that small wrapped packages of powder were smuggled out.[53] The orifice was probably perceived as less likely to be searched than any clothing the women were wearing. Vaginal searches were, nonetheless, a clear possibility.[54] There are numerous accounts of such examinations occurring either just prior to deportation or immediately upon arrival at various camps. Raizel Tabakman, who worked at the Union Factory, recounts having her vagina searched at the transit camp of Malines.[55] Prior to her deportation from the Chust ghetto, Cecilie Klein-Pollack describes having a stick poked in her vagina to verify there were no valuables concealed in it.[56] Aranka Siegal also endured a vaginal search just prior to her deportation to Auschwitz from the brick factory at Beregszász which served as a ghetto.[57] For her, this was less of a torment than watching her mother, 'a religious lady' having to go through 'such a terrible ordeal'. Laub's decision to name the vagina without much hesitation may stem from his role as a psychoanalyst. Both the mouth (oral fixation) and the vagina (genital fixation) feature in Sigmund Freud's ideas about psychosexual development. It is clear from testimonies of some members of the Sonderkommando which we will go on to examine that directness of the kind shown by Laub in relation to naming the vagina is not uniform in the presence of women in the context of video testimony.

The open reference to the vagina can therefore be understood as drawing attention to the psychoanalytic interests of many of the interviewers working on Yale's video testimony programme. Kantor, for instance, completed psychoanalytic training as well as undertaking a Ph.D. in clinical psychology. Laub was a practising psychoanalyst until his death in 2018. This dimension to the personal histories of the interviewers causes some of the interviews to take on the character of an analytic session. In the early days of the Yale initiative, the fixed time which was dedicated to each testimony was reminiscent of the fifty-minute session of Freudian psychoanalysis with the major difference that there was no opportunity to continue in a future session (except as a clinical patient—during his interview with her, Laub asks Irene W. if she has considered a course of therapy). The part-mirroring of the analytic situation can lead to unfortunate situations of the kind experienced by Rose A. Her interview ends like this:

> *Rose A.*: So by the time I reached home, I had no desire to live.
> *Sergio Rothstein*: OK, thank you very much.
> *RA*: Did I over... [looks at watch]. Too much, too much talk.
> *Dori Laub*: Not enough.[58]

Here the listener-viewer is much inclined to agree with Laub. Thanking a survivor just after they have articulated their suicidal tendencies seems inexcusable (even if these feelings of despair had already been expressed earlier in the interview).

The influence of analysis also explains why sometimes in the Yale interviews the interviewers offer 'interpretations'. There are several examples of this in Serena N.'s interview. Kantor and Laub are good listeners and their interjections are minimal. Aside from questions, Kantor only seems to proffer a single interpretation, observing of when Serena N. lost sight of her father upon arrival at Auschwitz: 'It was like he disappeared'.[59] Laub interprets more although his efforts invariably fall flat; often he seems to be talking at cross purposes with Serena N., the two on different wavelengths (at least as far as the manifest content of the interview is concerned). For example, Serena N. questions her sister's memory of events at Auschwitz: 'She remembers certain things...uhm... wrong, not, not factually so much. Because she was that much younger and insists that it happened. And I insist that it didn't happen'.[60] For Laub, Serena N.'s insistence on the youth of her sister—her mistakenly claiming Irene W. was 12½ and not 13½—is an attempt to diminish the younger woman's capacity to remember.[61] Laub asserts: 'She must be wrong!'[62] Serena N., however, does not understand what he is getting at. Eventually, he offers a gloss on his earlier comment: 'She must not remember right because she must have been years a little child'.[63] Serena N. disagrees, affirming that her sister does remember many things with accuracy. It is exchanges such as these which prompt Langer to state in a summary of this testimony he provided to the USHMM that 'the rapport between [the] witness and one interviewer breaks down as survivor testimony, perhaps unintentionally, becomes a kind of therapy session'.[64] He detects a tension developing between Laub and Irene W. as well.[65]

At the end of the interview, Laub offers another comment that is, if not rejected, only cautiously embraced:

Eva Kantor: We will have to stop here. Thank you very much.
Serena N.: How much did we take [glances at watch] – a long time...
Dori Laub: Not long enough.
SN: Pardon?
DL: Not long enough, perhaps.
SN: Long enough.
DL: Not long enough.
SN: No, I know, there are many things that happened [...].[66]

In a sense, Laub's subsequent textual analysis can be seen to provide the very prolongation he clearly believed was necessary. The end of the interview is also notable for the physical interactions between the participants. Serena N. nearly forgets the photographs she brought with her to show her interviewers. These were securely stowed in an envelope in her handbag. The envelope has, however, fallen out and lies on the floor. Kantor notices this—saying 'Don't forget your pictures!'—and picks the packet up, trying to place it in Serena N.'s hand but it falls to the floor again.[67] At her second attempt, Kantor successfully delivers the pictures. Once Kantor has removed Serena N.'s microphone, the survivor stands up and what seems to be a set of keys that were resting on her lap fall to the floor. Laub stoops to pick them up but Serena N. retrieves them herself. In a sense, this unsuccessful gesture of help encompasses in condensed form the tenor of much of the interview. To someone watching at a distance, analysing the video rather than being physically present, it feels very much as if these bungled actions figure something of the nature of the interview as a whole. The interview is characterized by missed connections, by failures to unlock the significance of specific actions and utterances, a situation most notable in relation to Serena N.'s apparent reluctance to say the word 'Sonderkommando'. No link is made between this disinclination and Meyer F.'s fate. Serena N. is therefore perhaps able to 'smuggle' the enduring pain of the loss of her father past Kantor and Laub.

This is not to say the interview is a failure. Serena N. is clearly appreciative and sensitive to the exertion involved in receiving her testimony: 'So you have an exhausting day – all of you – with these stories'.[68] There is, however, a sense of lost opportunity, one common in (the experience of viewing) many video testimonies. This sense can be particularly forceful in the case of the Sonderkommando as there were so few survivors of the group and so many myths that have come to circulate regarding them that risk becoming concretized. In what follows, we engage with many of the extant testimonies with SK survivors, testimonies that derive from the main video testimony archives of the Fortunoff, the USHMM and the Shoah Foundation but also from smaller-scale archives and recordings. Drawing on Noah Shenker's inspiring work on the framing practices that inform the production and reception of video testimony, we explore how a number of such practices register in testimonies of the SK focussing, in particular, on issues of age and gender and on the nature of video as a medium. In this last context, we analyse ways in which recording technology intervenes in the production of testimony. These interventions foreground the materiality and mediated quality of the testimony.

Carolyn Steedman writes of historians engaging with literature that they are more likely to plunder writings 'for content – for quotations to support the historical argument they are making – than they are to pay attention to them as forms of composition'.[69] There is a similar tendency in relation to video testimony: already often divided into easily searchable segments of information that encourage the search for 'bleeding chunks', survivor testimonies are frequently reduced to so many footnotes used to support or contest specific arguments. The ways in which the testimonies are composed and articulated not solely by the interviewer(s) and the interviewee but also by way of the recording technology itself rarely attract attention, although Shenker's work now provides an important foundation for such an exploration.[70] Additionally, we also consider issues of reception, transcription and translation. We continue to make occasional reference to the testimonies of Rosa A., Serena N. and Irene W. when relevant. Our approach here consciously seeks to avoid drawing on the video testimonies solely or simply as sources of information about the SK; we do not view them only as so much data to be mined.[71] We also intermittently look beyond historical issues, striving to capture something of their individual personalities as they emerged through the interview encounters.

AGE AND GENDER: DARIO GABBAI AND DANIEL BENNAHMIAS

Dario Gabbai, a Greek Sephardi Jew who was deported to Auschwitz in 1944 and joined the SK shortly thereafter, was interviewed twice by the USC Shoah Foundation, first in 1996 by Carol Stulberg and then again in 2014 by Stephen Smith. These two interviews provide a useful comparison. The style of the Shoah Foundation is designed to solicit details and clarifications and this can cause a bittiness or fragmentariness to the exchanges. This is initially the case with Gabbai and Stulberg although they gradually find a rhythm. It is a rhythm that likely emerges in part because Gabbai makes it clear his memory does not lend itself to detailed chronological reminiscing. When Stulberg asks Gabbai to tell her step by step what happened on the ramp when he arrived at Auschwitz, he responds: 'I really don't remember step by step'.[72]

Gabbai reaffirms the stereotypical view of the SK as unfeeling and machinelike. He asserts that as a means to survive he transformed himself into an automaton: 'I said to myself I am a robot and I did just this to my mind'.[73] He then makes a gesture twice, bringing his hands to the sides of his face and twisting the skin at the edge of each of his eyes with his index fingers so his face around his eyes becomes distorted. He continues: 'And I said from now on close your eyes and do whatever is to be done without asking too much'.[74] Becoming a robot here is closely linked with ways of seeing; it clearly involves perfecting a look that does not see. In his subsequent interview with Smith, Gabbai states: 'My mind was blind'.[75] How all encompassing this unemotional demeanour was is, however, undercut by Gabbai's discussion of what caused him the most distress during his time working as a member of the SK.[76] As with many members of the SK, it was violence against women or against children that he found particularly hard to shut out.[77] Gabbai recounts, for example, how Otto Moll would come and select the '*most beautiful girls*' and then, as 'a good marksman', shoot (Gabbai says 'marks') them in 'the more sensitive places of their body'.[78] Here, Gabbai gives a very vague word for the kind of wounds inflicted and does not go into specifics about such places. He avoids using words such as 'breasts'.[79]

This reticence also occurs elsewhere in the interview with Stulberg. Gabbai explains at one point that deportees often concealed valuables in different places on their person.[80] Stulberg asks 'What kind of places?' and Gabbai simply nods repeatedly and remains silent.[81] His silence, however, as an act of clear self-censorship gestures to the kinds of places he is referring to. He knows his silence communicates a clear message. He is then coaxed into saying more and observes 'Different places… Especially after they were dead…a lot of things were found in ears, I can't even mention…' Here he again returns to silence, his refusal signalling that he is referring to the anus and the vagina. He tells without telling.[82] His reluctance to name the places is likely not solely because he regards it as indecorous to do so in Stulberg's presence but also because to name the place is additionally to confirm where the Sonderkommando had to put their hands. They had to search the orifices of the corpses of both men and women. Gabbai tells Stulberg this but without naming the cavities in question. Gabbai, like any survivor of the SK, cannot, however, be taken as representative of the group as a whole. Morris Venezia, for instance, has no qualms about telling Stulberg: 'Even in the woman's body they were hiding something in the genitoral [*sic*] places'.[83]

The violence that appears to particularly disturb Gabbai is enacted against *beautiful* young women, whom he refers to as girls. This is then not simply an attack on femininity but specifically an attack on feminine beauty. Morris Venezia also draws attention to beauty, describing 'three beautiful Hungarian girls, young, beautiful Hungarian girls' who were placed in a line and shot with a single bullet.[84] The destruction of beauty, a trait associated with youth by the men, amplifies the horror of acts of individual aggression by the SS and of mass murder. Daniel Bennahmias provides examples of the obliteration of a different kind of beauty, the shooting of an opera singer and of a boy who is humming The Blue Danube Waltz.[85] What is most shocking about these examples for Bennahmias is that the SS appear to possess some kind of aesthetic appreciation. The singer is accorded special status, a final cigarette, and the guard who shoots the boy then takes up the tune. The singling out of women perceived as beautiful also signals a kind of atrocious aesthetics at work.

As well as linking youth with female beauty, Gabbai recognizes that male beauty is also bound up with youthfulness. In his subsequent testimony with Smith, he expresses what seems like vanity about his appearance, mentioning how he is often taken for being much younger than his actual age.[86] Certainly, in 1996, he belies his seventy plus years and is still a handsome man by standards of masculine beauty of the time.[87] Pairing Gabbai's two testimonies as the Shoah Foundation has done, however, serves to strongly foreground the ageing process. If the testimonies are watched back to back, the physical changes between Gabbai in 1996 and Gabbai in 2014, nearly twenty years later, are disconcerting. Gabbai is clearly a man who takes great pride in his physical appearance. In 2014, in his nineties, his looks have faded. He has a plaster on his arm, an unintended signifier of vulnerability (whatever the actual reason for it). In the context of contemporary aesthetics of masculinity, he appears visibly diminished.

To us, the justification for this second interview is highly questionable.[88] The USHMM has a screening process which involves, among other things, assessing whether a 'witness's health and age would enable him or her to endure the interview process'.[89] The Shoah Foundation does not officially possess such a process. There is, however, a responsibility of any archive not just towards the memory of the Shoah but towards the memory of the survivor (of which these testimonies form an important part). The extra information gleaned from the second interview with Gabbai is minimal and, at times, Smith appears frustrated. He sighs and sounds despondent when his interviewee seemingly does not 'remember' in the way he would like him to. The interviewer's mood may, in part, not have been helped by recurring technological difficulties with the audio. These likely knocked him off his stride (but then they would also have disrupted the interview for Gabbai).

Smith speaks the language of a twenty-first-century Holocaust researcher with his talk of 'sexual violence' and the significant emphasis he places on multi-sensory detail.[90] A more euphemistic approach to issues of sexual violence against men and women might potentially have generated a productive response. Stulberg's chosen vocabulary for her questions was smarter, more accessible. Smith, clearly influenced by the approach of the Fortunoff Archive, also endeavours to be an analyst. Shortly after Gabbai observes that he 'got involved with a few young girls, you know' and that always 'she was 25 years younger that [sic] I was', Smith clumsily seeks to link the survivor's womanizing with his Holocaust experiences.[91] Gabbai, denying any such connection, responds: 'Always I had sexual. I was very good on that'.[92] Here Gabbai closes down efforts to link his post-liberation experiences with the Holocaust implying that his womanizing was present prior to the event and continued after it. The revelation of Gabbai's preference for younger women, however, does raise the question as to whether he appraised Stulberg's attractiveness in their interview.[93]

Interviewees do size up their interviewers. When Judith Meisel is interviewed by Linda G. Kuzmack for the USHMM Oral History Project, for example, the interviewer explains that she will be off camera: 'My stomach rumbles so we don't put a camera on me'.[94] Meisel responds: 'I wish I had your figure…' She shows that she has noted Kuzmach's physical appearance and that she believes it renders Kuzmach photogenic. Given Kuzmach's reference to being hungry, the comment may also index Meisel's connecting of food (or its absence) with a desirable physique.[95] Kuzmach's pleasing figure, her conforming to contemporary beauty ideals, may function as a status cue in the interview with Meisel.[96] Unsurprisingly, neither Gabbai nor Stulberg comment on each other's appearance (Meisel's remark is likely made possible by her talking woman to woman) yet that is not to say how they look to one another does not have effects. Stulberg, youthful, well manicured with polished nails, blonde, with voluminous hair, conforms to long-standing beauty ideals.

There is a lack of recognition in much of the extant literature on video testimony surrounding the potentially complex influences of physical attractiveness and/or sexual appeal upon interviewer–interviewee interactions in the giving of testimony.[97] Beauty, whether it is perceived as a status cue or (probably more rarely given the age differentials involved) as sexual desirability, potentially impacts the ways interviews unfold. Research has indicated, for instance, that people viewed as 'beautiful' are more likely to be seen to possess outlooks in accord with those who hold such a perception.[98] They are also seen to be more attentive (as better listeners) in interview situations.[99] Physical attractiveness also informs perceptions of credibility.[100] The effects of ageing upon Gabbai's physical appearance likely impacts the reception of his testimony in negative ways.[101] At the least, the possibility of such unconscious influences upon its reception needs to be acknowledged and carefully thought about. Gabbai's own rakish good looks, his status cue, potentially cease to register in the second interview thereby altering how his account will be received.

The advance of time changes not just the kinds of questions that are posed to Gabbai but also how he is addressed. For Stulberg, Dario Gabbai remained 'Mr. Gabbai' throughout their interview. For Smith, he is 'Dario' from the outset. This use of the forename implies an intimacy that may be real but which appears out of place. David Morand has noted how modes of address form 'only brief moments of interaction' but 'are nevertheless critical events that are key to defining ensuing role orientation'.[102] The choice of using Gabbai's forename functions as a leveller of status difference.[103] Stulberg's more deferential tone seems better judged. In this context, the lengthy interview between the former Sonderkommando member Shlomo Venezia and the academic Manuela Consonni (also for the Shoah Foundation) is enlightening.[104] Consonni begins the interview addressing Venezia as 'Signor Venezia'. After a considerable period of time and numerous tape changes, when Venezia describes arriving at Auschwitz, she starts to refer to him as 'Shlomo'. Here it seems that an intimacy has developed yet only from within the interview itself, Consonni has 'earnt' the right to address Venezia by his forename and, to our minds, there is no sense of a reduction in the latter's status.

The fact that Gabbai is interviewed by a man for his 'follow-up' interview clearly does produce a different dynamic than existed with Stulberg. A side to Gabbai which was concealed from her emerges, or, perhaps, it would be more precise to say another Dario Gabbai is revealed. Nikolas Rose has drawn attention to how subjectivity is multiple and malleable, shifting according to specific circumstances.[105] Here a change of interviewer, of situation, causes Gabbai to become 'one of the boys' whereas in his interaction with Stulberg he was a 'gentleman'. Towards the end of the interview with Smith, for example, Gabbai moves his leg and this shifts the microphone impairing the sound quality. The camera person has to intervene: 'Just one second...' He explains what has occurred and Gabbai says jocularly: 'Why don't you tell me don't move your fucking leg!'[106] He swears again shortly afterwards. This banter, which causes Smith to crack up, would likely have appeared out of place to Gabbai in the interview with Stulberg. Swearing in the presence of a 'lady' would be improper. Swearing in the company of men is, however, acceptable. The exchange demonstrates that often, for the interviewee, their audience as they conceive it is simply the person interviewing them and any helpers they might have with them. The survivor does not think outside the immediacy of the moment that is the interview. This reality is revealed by Gabbai's willingness to go into more detail about where Moll shot 'nice beautiful young [...] girls'. He explains it was in the breasts. Any listener to Stulberg's interview would, nonetheless, already have a good idea that this was the case. Subjecting Gabbai to a second interview reveals how gendered discourses shape the kind of testimony he delivers but provides little in terms of additional historical insights regarding his time in the SK.[107]

Another member of the SK who was interviewed on separate occasions by interviewers of different sexes was Daniel Bennahmias. Bennahmias, who was born in Salonika, Greece, in 1923 was captured and imprisoned in the Haidari concentration camp near Athens in March 1944. He was deported to Auschwitz a month later where he was selected to join the Sonderkommando shortly afterwards. He survived the war and subsequently immigrated to the USA. Bennahmias gave audio testimony to Joel Neuberg for the Bay Area Oral History Project on 24 June 1986. On 12 November 1991, he was again interviewed for the Bay Area Holocaust History Project, this time in the form of video testimony. His interviewers were Beatrice Netter, Lisa Barnett and Ilana Braun. The camera operator was Laurie Sosna. Neuberg seemingly has more knowledge of the history of Greece and of the Holocaust than the later interviewers. Throughout most of the second interview, which sometimes involves repetitive questions and in which the interviewers occasionally display a tenuous grasp of Greek history, Bennahmias nonetheless remains patient and good-natured.

A rare moment when he seemingly displays a measure of hostility, a measured hostility, in the video interview is when he questions the use of giving testimony and recounts atrocities he has witnessed that have particularly marked him. Prior to describing two horrific events, Bennahmias makes an observation that undermines the very testimony he is about to deliver in the sense that he draws attention to the futility of description. He states of his experiences in the SK: 'It's something that you cannot describe, yeah you can describe but somebody will say "Oh how horrible!" but that [*sic*] you don't see it yet. You can't'.[108] He then details two events. The first is of children being thrown into the gas chamber onto people who are already standing, crammed inside. The second: 'I've seen some German officer kill a baby of three month, four month, I don't know what it is, in his hand and let it go on the cement floor'.[109] He continues: 'If you don't see, then you don't believe those things'.[110] After this, there is a period of silence and then he softly says 'So ask questions...'[111]

There is a conscious wish to shock here and for a moment the bonhomie which characterizes much of the interview is, understandably, entirely absent. Bennahmias's motives for foregrounding the two events are complex. He wants to show the three women—who, from their voices and their modes of expression, reveal that they are younger than him—that there are limits to what any testimonial endeavour can accomplish and also, from other observations in the interview, that there are no limits to a human being's capacity for cruelty. If the examples Bennahmias provides are compared with the earlier interview with Neuberg, it seems, however, that he is toning down the horror of what he has seen. There is far more detail in the earlier account he provides:

> I saw with my eyes a German officer with a baby, three months, I don't know what it was, four months, shooting it in the eye and then once in the ear and the baby was moving still in his hand and then once more and he dropped it on the cement.[112]

It is possible the more succinct account evinces the vagaries of memory but, to us, it seems conceivable that Bennahmias is self-censoring his later account because he does not want to overly distress a specific audience. The truncated version may be influenced by the combined factors of the age and gender of his interviewers. It is possible to interpret this moment as influenced by gender stereotypes held by Bennahmias. He feels a male interviewer can better handle the gruesome details or he is more willing to inflict those details on another man. Bennahmias is, however, possibly showing compassion here within an account of its antithesis. His ostensible aim is to indicate that what he has lived through is too horrible to comprehend yet he finds himself moderating that horror. For him, based on views he expresses elsewhere in his testimony, this capacity to refrain from being horrible is not somehow proof that he is good where others are bad. For Bennahmias, all people, including himself, are capable of untold cruelty in certain circumstances. Yet the interview clearly does not constitute such a circumstance: he is showing care and restraint for those listening. Through the events that he selects to illustrate atrocity, he also reveals that even at the heart of the death factory, horrible events could be qualitatively distinguished. The two occurrences he chooses to detail, each featuring very young children as victims, marked him.

Both Bennahmias's testimonies and those of Gabbai reveal how factors such as age and gender potentially influence the quality and kind of testimony that is given by members of the Sonderkommando (and, potentially, by survivors more broadly). Shenker has drawn attention to how individual frameworks already influence the nature of testimony prior to any encounter with institutional frameworks. Institutional preferences shape 'the conditions of possibility for giving and receiving testimonies' but 'they cannot account for the diverse backgrounds, experiences and identities – including those of gender (among other considerations) – that impact witnesses' experiences throughout their lives, including those of giving testimony'.[113] The only individual mode of framing Shenker identifies is gender. He does not, however, tease out how gender inflects the ways in which institutional frameworks are implemented or resisted in interview scenarios. Langer has also recognized that gender can be conceived as an important consideration when analysing video testimony.[114] He urges caution in applying (essentialist) ideas about gender to such testimony but does not consider how gender potentially registers not solely at the level of content but in the interactions between interviewer(s) and interviewee.

Memory in the Frame: Technique and Technology

James Young has described video testimony as forming a 'celluloid *megilla*' because it involves stitching together 'broken fragments of memory' into 'a continuously unfurling scroll'.[115] Here, Young is thinking of a scroll as a roll of paper or parchment. We, however, would like to consider how video testimony might also bear comparison with the Scrolls of Auschwitz, the writings we focussed on in Chapter 2. As we explored in that chapter (and elsewhere), the SK manuscripts attest to the experience of the death factory not simply through the words inscribed upon them but by way of their physical characteristics. We believe a similar argument can be made for video testimony. Young openly compares video testimony to writing as a means to distinguish the two media, suggesting 'where writers necessarily break silence in order to represent it, in video testimony silence remains as much a presence as the words themselves; silence that cannot exist in print except in blank pages is now accompanied by the image of one who is silent, who cannot find the words'.[116] For him, unlike writing, video testimony 'can also represent *not* telling a story, the point at which memory will not enter speech'.[117] We are not so sure that writing is incapable of representing the refusal or incapacity to tell a story but what interests us more here is how contingency sometimes impacts video testimony in comparable ways to the SK manuscripts, at times impairing the clarity of testimony and lending it another level of power and effectiveness. Additionally, we want to examine how gesture, also crucial for interpreting, contributes to the impact of video testimony featuring members of the Sonderkommando.

The Scrolls of Auschwitz all manifest the conditions in which they were written and also, sometimes, the effects of their concealment. Even though some are now held in archives in Israel and Russia, far from Poland, Birkenau persists in their pages. They are physically marked by times and by place. These material indices were not intended by the authors of the manuscripts. Video testimony is similarly often marked by time and place, and equally, the registration of these attributes is frequently unmotivated, accidental. In the same way that dirt and the blurring and decompositional effects of humidity now form a kind of 'visual noise' in some of the Scrolls, literal noise occasionally disrupts video testimonies. Gabbai's mobile phone, for instance, goes off during the testimony with Smith. This was something unforeseeable in 1996 and likely unforeseen in 2014. The ringtone disrupts the testimony but also works to ground it in a particular historical and technological moment.

In the second testimony given to the Bay Area Project, Sosna films Bennahmias, who has a seemingly swollen face, in close-up with a shallow depth of field. The image of him, dressed in a blue-striped shirt and beige jacket, is sharp but the background is fuzzy. The mise-en-scène appears designed to accord him no specific location. The audio, however, picks up incidental sounds that occasionally puncture this effort at positioning Bennahmias in a 'placelessness'. Sirens and car horns can be heard, along with what seems like a motorbike accelerating, the soundscape of an urban environment. These noises signal the world off-camera, beyond the frame. They intrude upon this spoken account of past, signalling not simply where the testimony is taking place but also, to a degree, when.[118] Such sounds are, of course, not uncommon in video testimony. They clearly do not contribute significantly to our understanding of what Bennahmias has to say and they add nothing to our thinking about his time as part of the SK. They do, however, ground the testimony, audibly distancing the listener from Birkenau, from the place Bennahmias's words seek to conjure in the present.

Sometimes noises can take on a more influential role in relation to the reception of testimony. In the oral testimony that Bennahmias gave to Neuberg, for instance, there is a moment of noisy contingency which, while accidental, inflects the testimony in a way that lends it additional eloquence. A glitch in the recording causes what sounds like a heartbeat—an effect that is perhaps produced by electromagnetic interference influenced by the revolving reels—to register noticeably for several minutes beneath the verbal exchange and alongside the constant hiss caused by the magnetic particles used to make the tape. This includes during a discussion of the SK revolt:

> The motivation for the Sonderkommando, the revolution is very simple – we were never expected to live. Because their method was such that every once in a while you take Sonderkommando people and make a transport

and disappear them. So we knew that...and the fact that they had us isolated from the camp, it was an obvious reason why they would not let us live. So for us to be into a revolt condition – it was simple because, because we didn't have anything to lose anyway. So the fact is they, they finished there in Auschwitz. There was no question about it and they want to eliminate us so they could clear all the traces there.[119]

Here the revolt is explained as motivated by a sense of fatalism regarding the SS's intentions towards the men. The talk about perceived impending death takes place against what sounds like a heart pulsating, this (unintended) underlying signifier of 'life' coming to stand for that which the SK believed would soon be extinguished. The fortuitous sound of 'life' that contrasts with the 'death' being discussed by Bennahmias also figures as a kind of resistance to the action of erasure planned by the Nazis because we link the beat with the man being recorded, and it becomes his heartbeat. Bennahmias, through his ability to attest, embodies the failure of the Nazi's plan to erase all evidence of their crimes. Here an accidental noise, an inadvertent 'life sign', does not interrupt the narrative but contributes to its effect. In this, it can be viewed as playing a role akin to the rust-coloured staple bleeds in Zalman Lewental's account of the SK revolt, bleeds that form a kind of accidental metaphor for injury, violence.[120] The strange acoustic contamination can either be viewed as foreign, corrupting, and as something to be filtered out, or be accepted as a particularly foregrounded dimension of the recording process, a reminder of technological mediation that also possesses its own context-specific evocative power. Something comparable occurs in the testimony of Morris Venezia to Carol Stulberg, as he recounts of people being gassed—'They were calling God...crying and screaming'—there is a harsh sound as the Venezia's microphone is displaced, a chance acoustic violence that assails the ear.[121]

Sound in video testimony does not respect the limits imposed by the visual frame of a given shot. The choice of shot greatly influences the kind of visual information that is recorded. The 'talking head' shot or medium close-up, for instance, risks obscuring gestural content in a testimony. The shot favoured by a given camera person and/or institution shapes 'the interpretative possibilities of testimony'.[122] The 'gestures' of the camera have a similar shaping influence. The Fortunoff Archive, for instance, draws attention to the zoom as both an enabling tool and a hindrance.[123] Zooming in may function as an emotional cue for the viewer yet also serves to foreground the technical apparatus that is the camera. It draws attention to the camera itself and potentially distracts the listener-viewer.

At the start of Serena N.'s testimony, Laub employs a technological metaphor (one that was in common use among the Yale interviewers) to explain the kind of testimony he hopes to elicit: 'Just assume that you're looking at photographs and begin describing a little bit about the background'.[124] As he utilizes the image of the photograph as a spur to recollection, the camera person is simultaneously focussing the camera, zooming into Serena N.'s face and out repeatedly, so she appears blurred then sharply defined then blurred once more. Here, as with the 'heartbeat' in Bennahmias, the accidental assumes a figurative power. In this instance, it becomes a trope for the nature of memory as it will be revealed in the subsequent testimony, with events that stand out and others that remain hazy, and also for the listener-viewer's experience of Serena N. herself. We catch glimpses of who she is but much is also withheld.

Additionally, the focussing makes the camera the focal point, the role of the camera in the testimonial process made visible through a series of failures of vision. It is noteworthy that this moment in the testimony is 'concealed' in the digital version which is primed to begin a couple of minutes after the camera actually began filming. The listener-viewer has to pull the recording back to the actual (rather than preferred) start in order to view this 'hidden' history of the interview. There are also examples of focussing that occur in the middle of testimony. Judy (Iboya) F., for example, shows her interviewers her Auschwitz tattoo. The camera person focusses on the tattoo and then has to refocus on Judy F.'s face, enabling the presence of the camera to manifest itself, drawing attention to the mediated nature of the testimonial act.[125] The testimony of Judy F. is also notable as once the interview has officially (if not literally) concluded and filming has stopped it is clear from the audio-track that she nearly leaves with her microphone still attached. Against the backdrop of colour bars, Judy F. can be heard saying: 'Almost walked away *Organisierung* something you know!'. The joke is noteworthy because in her testimony she affirms that she thought for a long time after Auschwitz that she would never laugh again.

The Shoah Foundation favours the use of medium close-up without the use of zoom.[126] This approach allows some, although not all, of the gestures used by survivors during their testimony to be seen. Often recollections are articulated by way of both words and gestures. In the testimony of Gabbai to Stulberg, gestures which centre on his face or torso are clearly visible. When Gabbai describes using a cane to pull corpses out of the gas chamber, he gestures towards his neck and then puts his fingers around his own throat.[127] A part of *his* body, the neck, here stands in for one of the victims he pulled out of the gas chamber, representing someone dead. Another body part, the hand, is used to represent the technology used to facilitate dragging a body, a technology originally designed to aid walking but repurposed in the crematoria to assist in the disposal of the bodies of those murdered (or, as Morris Venezia relates, used as a tool by the SS to beat the SK).[128] Gabbai will repeat this gesture in the second interview conducted by Smith.[129] In an effort to *show* the practice of removing bodies from the gas chamber, both times Gabbai improvises a cane with his hand. His body, through gesture, becomes a technology of witnessing.

As Philippe Mesnard has noted, documentaries featuring the Sonderkommando often render testimony purely as expertise. For Mesnard, once the SK member is reduced to a specialist he is made to appear bereft of feeling, pared to his skills.[130] Mesnard recognizes that an emphasis on the technical aspects of mass murder offers a kind of safety to the SK, a 'refuge' as he calls it, allowing these men to lose themselves in a surfeit of detail, to become, to a degree, detached from the horrors they are recounting. This focus on the technical, on the skills needed to get the job done, likely also assisted the SK while they were at work in the death factory. Shlomo Venezia described it to Consonni as like working 'at a butcher's shop' [*a la macellaria*] and said he became accustomed to the work.[131] The image of the butcher's is graphic but also normalizing. Venezia's report of the technique of placing a body in the oven signals how this habituation became possible. In focussed, unemotional testimony (punctuated by hand gestures to clarify technique), he recounts the practicalities of using a stretcher to tip corpses into the oven, explaining that it had to be put into the oven at speed and then almost immediately pulled backwards [*'in forno va subito "ta ta" e tira a fuori'*].[132] There is something unnerving about Venezia's calmness as he shares the intricacies of atrocity yet perhaps the importance of such testimony is that it reveals both the need for the SK to perfect an 'efficiency' and the fact they gained the necessary practice to achieve it. The technical is not fetishized but rather the precision and stream-lining reinforce the enormity of the crime.

Gabbai, as Sarah Gregory has observed, is also composed while giving much of his testimony.[133] He holds himself together, just, while describing events in which the SK are forced to participate in unusually close ways (even for them) in the process of mass murder. When smaller groups of people arrived at the crematorium, gassing was deemed uneconomical. The SS would then shoot people individually inside the building. Although the SK helped push victims into the gas chamber (as mentioned in Chapter 5, Gabbai reports members propelled people in while the SS looked on, his testimony contradicting other members such as David Nencel who state the SS did the pushing), the gassings themselves took place out of sight, behind walls.[134] The shootings were in full view and an SK member had to hold each victim:

> You have to pick it up by the ear [briefly holds his own ear] – bring then that and keep them by the ear [lightly touches his ear] and the SS would be behind shooting them [moves his head to indicate a presence behind him]. [...]. They would go down [looks down]. Somebody would pick it up and then we had to clean up the blood.[135]

Here, the forced intimacy of the SK with the mass murders perpetrated by the SS is at its greatest. Members had to literally hold the victims at the point of death. The difficulty of confronting this proximity may inform Gabbai's description of a person as 'it' rather than 'he' or 'she'. Linguistic factors may also need considering but there does seem to be a verbal effort at distancing, at dehumanizing the victims. In this context, however, Gabbai's gestures are remarkable. When he illustrates the action of holding the victim's ear, his own body becomes both victim and SK member. His body embodies the victim's humanity.

Morris Venezia also gives two accounts of this method of killing. These are, in some ways, even more complex and disturbing than Gabbai's. The first account is a general overview of the killing technique:

> One of us used to hold the prisoner from the ear [touches his own ear] and tell, tell him because they didn't know what was going on and now they were going to kill. Holding the ear [briefly holds his own ear] like this and the hiding gun of the, of the German just shoot them in the back of the head [touches the back of his head]. And, of course, when they shooted someone in the back of the head, the knees bended and the body goes in the back, not in the front. That's why the one that's holding the guy by the hair [sic] when the German was shooting him, he used to push him like this [makes a shouldering motion] so the body was going at the front.[136]

Here, the technical dimension to the method of execution is accorded greater detail than in Gabbai's account. This focus on technique is, however, being emphasized not to distance Venezia from the event that he is describing (as Mesnard would have it), or not only for that reason, but also in order to illustrate the difficulty of taking on a role in the SK that one was unfamiliar with.[137] Venezia did not usually hold the victims but was once asked to do so. He did not realize that it was necessary to shoulder the falling victim and failed to carry out this action, causing the dead person to fall backwards, their blood spattering the SS man doing the shooting. Venezia begins his account of this (almost fatal) mistake in this way:

> I hold his, his ear [his right hand comes into frame, briefly moving in the direction of his ear before disappearing again] of the guy and I told him 'Look, look, look' [points to a space off camera in front of him], the guy to look in front of him, bam [makes his hand into a gun], they shot.[138]

Here, now he is not talking in general terms but about *his own behaviour specifically*, Venezia does not actually hold his own ear. He keeps his distance from the victim. He does, however, still provide the distraction that he gave. At this moment, the usual, broad subterfuge of the shower is condensed into a brief gesture to grab someone's attention, a pointing to a non-event. The victim dies deceived, looking at a nothing. Venezia, by mimicking the act of shooting, comes to stand in the stead of the SS guard, the murderer. Gabbai adopted the role of victim and SK member; Venezia alternates between SK member and SS killer. The gestural dynamics of the two testimonies incarnate something of the complex situation of the Sonderkommando, of victims forced to facilitate murder. The gestures as a technology of witnessing point towards the horror of the situation, the choiceless choices, imposed upon these men. Gesture, as much if not more so than words, gives insight into the trapping roles that characterized their impossible circumstances.

Ethics and Reception: Segmentation, Transcription and Interpretation

As many, including Young, have observed, the video medium informs how testimony is produced and received. In terms of reception, Amit Pinchevski claims the emergence of 'deep memory', memory of the kind Langer accords great value to in video testimony, is made possible by the ability to 'pause, rewind and play' the recorded histories.[139] Laura Mulvey's work on how digital technology has changed the way people view films, enabling a kind of acoustic and optical unconscious to register which would hitherto likely have passed unnoticed, is equally applicable to video testimony which is now often digitized and even more easy to view and review.[140] Digital versions of analogue testimony often (but not always) respect the length of the original videotapes which usually lasted about half an hour. The testimony is therefore broken down into a series of half-hour segments. The interviewers were acutely aware of the need to try and work to the half-hour limit for each tape and to avoid having to interrupt survivors as they were recounting particularly important or distressing events. Nevertheless, sometimes the tape reached its end at highly inopportune moments.

Shlomo Venezia's testimony to Consonni does not follow the standard format for Shoah Foundation footage as it is extremely long (comprising over eight hours of film shot over two days). Consonni also refrains from barraging her interviewee with questions (as can sometimes happen in testimonies made by the Shoah Foundation). She, rather, allows Venezia to take his time and only asks questions once he has finished speaking. It is clear from the brief off-camera exchanges at the beginning of each tape that before filming starts interviewer and interviewee agree what they will discuss for each section but once filming starts Consonni is happy to adopt a relatively passive role. As already discussed, the considerable length of the interview also enables an intimacy to develop between Consonni and Venezia that is less evident in some shorter video testimonies. At one point, Consonni develops a cough and Venezia instructs someone off camera (perhaps his wife) to give her some sweets.

It is rare that Venezia becomes visibly distraught. Like many testimonies of the SK and other survivors, it is during a discussion of close family that he becomes most distressed. As part of a conversation about his post-war life, Venezia recounts going to meet his sister Rachel, who also survived, in Israel in 1957. When he saw her, he saw her as both his sister and his dead mother. Venezia began speaking to her: '*e continua a piangere e parlare, piangere e parlare*' [and kept crying and talking, crying and talking].[141] As he utters the final 'parlare', his voice is fading as he is overcome with that same intense emotion again. He continues his account of their meeting but Consonni must stop him as the tape is at an end. He has tears in his eyes as he is interrupted and explains he has just a little more to say and makes a gesture bringing his fingers close together to signal how short he will be.¹⁴² As the new tape starts, there is no discussion between the two of them but once the camera is rolling Consonni simply states '*Mi scusi*' [I'm sorry].¹⁴³ There is very little she can say but the minimal apology is clearly heartfelt. She is here apologizing for interrupting a moment of considerable emotional distress, apologizing for her actions but also, in a sense, for the testimonial format, for the technology that brought about the need to interrupt. She is saying sorry for video technology and its sometimes violent, even violating limitations. It is a touching moment. Consonni's upset is palpable. In the interim, Venezia has composed himself and finishes the story of the meeting relatively untroubled.

This kind of occurrence could happen in any video testimony but within the specificity of Venezia's account, the account of a former member of the Sonderkommando, it cannot be divorced from the kind of investment in technical specialization identified by Mesnard as a defensive trait in SK testimony. Venezia does place considerable emphasis on the technical aspects of his role in his testimony. Here, however, in a rare moment of emotion, he abandons such succour in expertise. He, perhaps, demonstrates something of the character of life in the SK. Even if the men threw themselves into their work, there were always moments, fleeting but crucial, where the pain of loss or other emotions intruded on their horrific everyday. In this, Venezia's testimony mirrors the Scrolls of Auschwitz, showing the persistence, but likely not continuous presence, of complex sets of feelings in the men.

Mesnard's account also implies that the SK survivors exploit their expertise to avoid confronting their feelings. Here the cruelty of the interruption to Venezia's expression of grief is once more revealing. It is technology itself which works to silence him, curtailing his agency. The technology, unlike the interviewer, is unfeeling. It is equally possible that the technology of mass murder employed at Birkenau had a similar impact on agency, the work shaping the individual. The men became part of the killing apparatus, unwilling cogs in a larger process. Their expertise was not chosen but imposed and, in a sense, if they still remember through the technical this is because they were made to embody such technique but, as Venezia's tears demonstrate, never to the extent it totally 'owned' them.

Finally, Mesnard does not consider how ideas about masculinity might influence recourse to the technical. In a sense, showing technological expertise for some of these men including Gabbai and the Venezia brothers may be bound up with their ideas of how to behave as men. Patriarchal ideology in nineteenth- and twentieth-century Europe led to the notion that there was a clear association between technology and manliness. Unconsciously, developing technical expertise may have been a means to shore up the masculinity of the men. Ideas about masculinity also govern how the men appear in testimony. Displays of upset are likely viewed by the Southern European Jews as unmanly. It is to the credit of Consonni and Stulberg that they fostered conditions in which the men felt able to subvert masculine stereotypes and show distress, even if only briefly. That Gabbai retains his composure throughout his interview with Smith yet not with Stulberg may be linked to his reluctance to show emotion in front of men. We are not suggesting here that women make 'better listeners' but we are proposing that that stereotype and a host of other gender stereotypes are being lived out through these interviews.

As already mentioned, there is a gentle choreographing at work at the beginning of each tape in Consonni's interview with Venezia. In other SK testimonies, this choreographing is less respectful. An interview with the SK survivor David Nencel which is held in the USHMM collection, for instance, was always intended to be deposited there but was filmed so that excerpts could be used in a planned documentary. The format of the interview, which is very disjointed, featuring three different mise-en-scènes, reflects its purpose. The crew who are filming expect to extract 'choice' bits and do not foresee it being viewed in its entirety as testimony. They nevertheless make clear efforts to govern the chronology of the account and its quality. Nencel is made to repeat sections more than once and is also discouraged from talking about certain topics too early. This creates some tensions such as when, for example, an event the interviewer thinks should be discussed later seems important for Nencel as he strives to explain why the unloading ramp was built adjacent to Crematorium 1 (II) when, prior to that, those who were to be gassed were brought on trucks.

> *David Nencel*: It happens when one transport that came, we had, they had American passports...
> *Joe Russin*: Hold up, don't...
> *DN*: Yeah, that transport...
> *JR*: Don't [forcefully], don't tell me about that yet.

DN: Yah [tetchily], ok, but from that time when they had the... [Pointing finger at JR]. They, they gave them problems right by unloading...
JR: Yeah, hold on to that for the next tape.[144]

Clearly, in Nencel's mind, the change in procedure, the use of a ramp beside the crematorium, was influenced by the actions of this particular transport which began to resist from the moment of unloading. He is, however, prevented from articulating this.

Nencel also resists the interviewer's efforts to use everyday language to describe the crematoria. For Nencel, common terms such as 'work' do not translate to the specific slave labour of the SK as the following exchange demonstrates:

> *Joe Russin*: What was it like to work in the oven room?
> *David Nencel*: I don't want you to use the word 'work'. Can you use something else? [Silence]. Forced labour, ok, you can apply [the term 'work'] to a lot of forced labour, but this...
> *JR*: OK, what was it like to be forced to put bodies in the oven?
> *DN*: But this is a devilish thing, it's a devilish thing, to take people, gas them, burn them, get finished of them, children, innocent children, you want to use the word of 'work'? That's a... I can't, I can't get it out.
> *JR*: No, but what I want you to tell me is, as you were doing this, what was it like to do it? Make me understand being there.
> *DN*: No, you can't understand. If you would [be] able in any sense [to] understand that – it's something not normal.[145]

For Nencel, the SK did not do 'work'. The word is too prosaic, too detached to be appropriate for their circumstances. In his testimony, he also tends to resist providing technical detail demonstrating that video testimony of SK survivors is heterogeneous with different approaches adopted by specific individuals to communicate their experiences. Nencel, like Bennahmias, also foregrounds what he perceives to be the limits of video testimony. For him, it will not generate an *understanding* of what it was like in the crematoria. Again, a specific word used by the interviewer is found wanting. To understand is to possess comprehension. It is to claim a kind of ownership over an experience that can never adequately be communicated in testimony. The experience is not there to be grasped but is, instead, gestured towards.

The Fortunoff Archive, in contrast to interviews of the kind conducted with Nencel, consciously adopts an approach that strives to maximize the agency of witnesses. There is clearly an ethical imperative in the desire, discussed by Shenker, not to appropriate survivor experiences, the wish to engage and invest without seeking to direct or demand, to overwrite with preconceived ideas and agendas.[146] The idea that video testimony will lead to an understanding of the process of murder structures the kinds of questions Russin poses to Nencel. Approaching an interview with no preconceived agenda is, nevertheless, an ideal rather than an achievable aim. The tendency of some Yale interviewers such as Laub to offer interpretations in the interviews, for example, betrays a therapeutic agenda. Interpretations impose meaning on the words and gestures of survivors. This imposition even manifests at a micro-level in transcriptions of interviews. Trezise is critical of Laub precisely because he does not take advantage of the easy repeatability of excerpts of witness accounts to correct his errors of transcription or memory failures. Trezise's own version of Serena N.'s testimony is closer by far to the actual account she gave but it is also open to question in terms of its precision (as is any summary, including our own, of a given video testimony).

Here is Serena N.'s account of the revolt as it is summarized by Trezise:

> *Serena N.*: All of a sudden we saw the gates open...
> *Dori Laub*: You saw...
> *SN*: The men, we saw the gates, yes, the gates open, men running from there and all the four crematoria at one time blew up. And of course these men knew that this would probably be the end for them, but they thought they perhaps they might prolong the fight a little bit if the outside, the others will help. But there was no chance. Instantly they descended, you know, the Germans, the SS, with machine guns and everything. They killed out every man. Two SS died in that incident.

The exchange as we hear it is:

> *SN*: All of a sudden we saw the gates open and...
> *DL*: You saw?
> *SN*: Men, we saw the gates, yes, the gates open, men running from there and all the four crematoria at one time blew up... And... And of course they, these men, knew that this **will** probably be the end for them but they thought that perhaps they might prolong the fight a little bit if the outside, the others will help. But there was no chance. Instantly

they descended, you know, the Germans, the SS, with machine guns and everything. They killed out every man. Two SS **dies** in the, in that **incidence**.[147]

We have reproduced in bold three moments where our hearing differs to Trezise's. The tidying up by Trezise of some of the words that are used by Serena N. glosses over the reality that she is not speaking her first language, or, indeed, simply the fact that she is speaking. His transcriptions, like ours, are acts of interpretation that potentially condition subsequent interpretations. The shift from 'will' to 'would' by Trezise, for instance, reorients the temporality of the account from one that is briefly, even if unintentionally, in the present and forward-looking 'we will likely die' to one that is in the past 'they knew they would likely die'. This example demonstrates Trezise's own judgements about how to 'receive' Serena N.'s testimony as they manifest through his decisions regarding how to transcribe the testimony.

Many survivors who provide testimony do so in languages that are not their mother tongue. Gideon Greif writes of the Greek Sonderkommando member Shaul Chazan, 'I interviewed [him] in Hebrew, a language that he had never really mastered'.[148] Greif then observes that Chazan gave his oral testimony in 'simple terms' which reflected his personality, one not tending to 'lofty rhetoric'.[149] This simplicity is interpreted as expressing Chazan's desire not to 'prettify the ghastly reality' of the extermination process.[150] Such an extrapolation is, however, highly problematic given the admission Chazan was not at home in Hebrew. In his first language, speaking more easily, it is possible that he might have been florid. Reading into the modes of expression of those speaking in their second, third or fourth language is fraught with difficulty. Many oral and video testimonies are in English despite this not being the interviewee's mother's tongue. Young suggests that survivors favour English as it is regarded by them 'as a neutral, uncorrupted, and ironically amnesiac language'.[151] There also seems to be a pressure to record interviews in English to maximize their circulation.

In his interview with Stulberg, Morris Venezia implores: 'Excuse of English, Carol, because it is not my native language. I can express myself in my native language better'.[152] Here it does seem as if he would prefer to speak in Italian or, possibly, Ladino. In his interview with Phyllis Dreazen, Leon [Lajzer] Welbel, a Polish Jew recruited to the SK shortly after his arrival at Auschwitz who describes ending up working as an assistant to the Kapo of Crematorium 4 (V), often turns to his wife asking her to translate from Yiddish for him.[153] Survivors (such as Morris Venezia and Welbel) who speak in their second or third language when they are interviewed will frequently hesitate as they search for specific words, or will use 'incorrect' words or use words 'improperly'. They also, on occasion, display eccentric syntax. There is a tendency to tidy up these 'mistakes' in summaries and transcripts (Welbel's testimony is not yet transcribed) yet the verbal slips also possess a testimonial value. Transcription is therefore bound up with ethical questions surrounding fidelity to the oral record.

Welbel's switching between English and Yiddish is not just evidence of missing vocabulary in a language learned later in life. At one point, he explains the behaviour of prisoners in Auschwitz by claiming 'mir [we] was not people, we was animals', before giving it added emotional emphasis in Yiddish: 'khayes, gevorn khayes'.[154] His limited palette of English words also allows him to state quite starkly how the plans for a revolt failed to concretize: 'mir was talking about uprising and talking and talking between us'.[155] The alienness of English to him may actually help him to speak in a more forthright way, even to the extent of making a grotesque joke about extracting teeth from dead bodies. This forthrightness also allows aspects to come out that other members of the SK played down: tensions between Litvaks and Galitsianers, and even romantic or sexual relationships within the camp.[156]

Much of the materiality of memory embodied in the testimonies is also unavoidably lost when we read of them rather than view them. In Trezise's summary of Serena N.'s testimony and also in Laub's, her gestures are absent. It is noteworthy that she looks up twice in transcribed section, as she says 'we saw the gates open' and as she says 'men running from there'. Each time she looks up it is clear she is again placing herself in Kanada and that 'there', Crematorium 3 (IV), existed first and foremost as its chimney. From Kanada, Serena N. daily looked up to 'death'. The revolt, however, produced smoke of a different kind, signalling desperate resistance. The chimney had a symbolic as much as functional value and the SK were able to visibly disrupt that symbolism for those close enough to see the precise source of the smoke. Something of this act of resistance written across the sky is lost when the gestures of Serena N. are divorced from her words.

Transcription, of course, also excises the work of the camera. Shlomo Venezia's testimony is not transcribed but it is unlikely any reference would be made to behaviour of the camera at the interview's conclusion. As his testimony draws to a close, Venezia thanks Consonni telling her that if it was not for her understanding (*simpatia*) and her know-how (*saper fare*) he would not have been able to make it to the end.[157] There is a sincerity to his words. As he says this, the camera pulls back, visually giving Venezia space, symbolically freeing him from the act of testifying. After a pause, he ends by saying 'OK', the word clearly indicating that it is time to move on.[158]

Notes

1. Dori Laub, 'Bearing Witness or the Vicissitudes of Listening,' in *Testimony: Crises of Witnessing in Literature, Psychoanalysis and History*, eds. Shoshana Felman and Dori Laub (New York: Routledge, 1991), pp. 57–74.
2. Ibid., p. 59.
3. Ibid.
4. Ibid., p. 60.
5. His conception of history has, however, also been criticized. Karyn Ball suggests that '[t]he problem with Laub's analysis is that it leaves us with a reductive opposition between factual and psychoanalytic definitions of truth and thus ignores the ways in which the discipline of history relies on a narration of events that poetically configures it moral impact'. Ball, 'Unspeakable Differences, Obscene Pleasures,' p. 24.
6. Thomas Trezise, *Witnessing Witnessing: On the Reception of Holocaust Survivor Testimony* (New York: Fordham University Press, 2013). His findings were first published as 'Between History and Psychoanalysis: A Case Study in the Reception of Holocaust Survivor Testimony,' *History & Memory* 20.1 (2008): 7–47. Laub replied to this article in 'On Holocaust Testimony and Its "Reception" Within Its Own Frame, as a Process in Its Own Right: A Response to "Between History and Psychoanalysis" by Thomas Trezise,' *History & Memory* 21.1 (2009): 127–150.
7. For a history of Kanada including the establishment of Kanada I and Kanada II, see Andrzej Strzelecki, 'The Plunder of Victims and Their Corpses,' in *Anatomy of the Auschwitz Death Camp*, eds. Yisrael Gutman and Michael Berenbaum (Bloomington: Indiana University Press, 1994), pp. 250–253.
8. Before the workers were housed at Kanada, they were also able to smuggle items out of Kanada regularly and either gift or trade them. Krystyna Żywulska describes placing orders with workers from Kanada for specific

articles. She was also given 'beautiful silk nightgown' from one of the Hungarian transports as a present. This gift-giving was a kind of resistance which ensured that high-quality articles were not sent to Germany but rather used to benefit inmates. Żywulska, *I Survived Auschwitz*, trans. Krystyna Cenkalska (Warsaw: tCHu Publishing House, 2004), p. 163. Once the workers were barracked in Kanada, moving around the camp was still possible but required bribes. Lisa Pinhas recalls that for 100 marks or a tin of sardines an inmate could buy passage to another part of the camp. Pinhas, *A Narrative of Evil* (Athens: Jewish Museum of Greece, 2014), p. 188.
9. Kitty Hart, *Return to Auschwitz* (Frogmore: Granada Publishing, 1983), p. 149.
10. Ibid., p. 164. Susan Cernyak-Spatz noted of her time in Kanada: 'the members of the detail had the luxurious privilege of a shower every night in the big Sauna with as much hot water as one wanted'. Cernyak-Spatz, *Protective Custody: Prisoner 34042* (Cortland: N & S Publishers, 2005), pp. 203–204. According to Józef Garliński, the SK had similar opportunities. He writes that 'each man had a comfortable bed with a down quilt, slept in pyjamas from *Canada*, could use the showers as often as he wished and in his spare time could read books, of which there were many'. Garliński, *Fighting Auschwitz: The Resistance Movement in the Concentration Camp* (Greenwich: Fawcett Crest, 1975), pp. 322–323. Even if this is exaggerated, Garliński's claim at least gives us an idea of how the SK were perceived in Auschwitz.
11. Kitty Hart, *I am Alive* (London: Abelard-Schuman, 1961), p. 92.
12. Ibid. If reading took place, however, it was not during a shift. Serena Neumann and Irene Weiss recall a young woman from Holland who started to read a book during a shift and was severely beaten by a kapo. Personal correspondence from Lesley Weiss, 21 July 2018.
13. Irena Strzelecka, 'Women' in *Anatomy of the Auschwitz Death Camp*, eds. Yisrael Gutman and Michael Berenbaum (Bloomington: Indiana University Press, 1994), p. 408.
14. Nahmia, *A Cry for Tomorrow 76859...*, trans. David Weinberg (Jacksonville: Bloch Publishing, 2011), p. 105.
15. Hart, *I Am Alive*, p. 92.
16. Hart, *Return to Auschwitz*, p. 152.
17. Ibid., p. 153.
18. Hart, *I Am Alive*, p. 91.
19. Ya'akov Gabbai discusses the location of the burning pits in relation to Crematoria 3 (IV) and 4 (V) in an interview with Gideon Greif. See Greif, *We Wept Without Tears* (New Haven: Yale University Press, 2005), p. 187.

20. Irene Weiss interviewed by Ileane Kenney on 26 July 1996. USC Shoah Foundation Interview Code 17212. Tape 4. 5:13.
21. Irene Weiss interviewed by Nicholas Chare, 8 July 2018, 1:15:50.
22. For a discussion of how colonial discourse had shaping effects on racial difference as it was encountered in terms of colour, see Griselda Pollock, 'Proximity and the Color of Desire: The Laboring Body and Its Sex,' in *Looking Back to the Future: Essays on Art, Life and Death*, ed. Griselda Pollock (Amsterdam: G+B Arts International, 2001), pp. 179–182.
23. Compare also Krystyna Żywulska's description of the SK in *I Survived Auschwitz*, p. 250. Franz Fanon provides a good understanding of European attitudes to blackness in the immediate post-war period in his 1952 book *Peau noire, masques blancs* [*Black Skin, White Masks*]. Fanon, *Peau noire, masques blancs* (Paris: Éditions de Seuil, 1952). Amber Jamilla Musser explores the links between Jewishness and blackness in Fanon's work in *Sensational Flesh: Race, Power, and Masochism* (New York: New York University Press, 2014), pp. 104–105. At the burning pits, the Nazis created a situation in which Jewish prisoners literally became blackened, their bodies made to figure a different ethnic background to their own, made to look racially Other to those arriving on the transports.
24. Eric Friedler, Barbara Siebert, and Andreas Kilian, *Zeugen aus der Todeszone: Das Jüdische Sonderkommando in Auschwitz* (Munich: Deutsche Taschenbuch Verlafg, 2005).
25. Irene Weiss interviewed by Nicholas Chare, 8 July 2018, 1:17:35.
26. Irene W. interviewed by Dori Laub and Sergio Rothstein on 7 November 1982. Fortunoff Video Archive for Holocaust Testimonies. Interview Code HVT-65.
27. Serena N.'s demeanour, which is a point of contention between Laub and Trezise, seemed, to us, to be somewhere in between their characterizations of timidity and confidence. Serena N. is clearly nervous towards the beginning of the interview, she appears a little hunched and her hands can be seen at one point fiddling anxiously with her glasses (which she does not wear). The black leather or faux leather armchair she is made to sit in also seems oversized for her frame and is positioned in a corner so that when the camera occasionally pulls back to include Kantor and Laub in shot, Serena N. appears hemmed in. Laub may unconsciously have been influenced in his judgement of Serena N. by the set-up of the room and by the furnishings.
28. Rose A.'s lack of animation may be partly attributable to the arduous conditions in which the interview was recorded. Irene Weiss, who gave testimony for the Yale project at roughly the same time as Rose, recounts that there were 'enormous hot lamps' when she gave testimony

that left her 'drenched' in sweat. She states 'it was so painful, it was absolutely excruciating'. Rose A. likely faced similarly difficult conditions. Irene Weiss interviewed by Nicholas Chare, 8 July 2018, 1:39:40.
29. Trezise hears this slightly differently as 'And one crematorium blew, and another'. Trezise, *Witnessing Witnessing*, p. 229n.6. Rose A. interviewed by Sergio Rothstein and Dori Laub on 7 November 1982. Fortunoff Video Archive for Holocaust Testimonies. HVT-183. Tape 2. Segment 11. 19:58. All tape and segment numbers refer to the digital version of each testimony. At the time of writing, in the case of Rose A.'s testimony, there is an error in the ordering of the segments which run from 1–12 and then 7–12 instead of 1–18. For segments after the first twelve, we use the Yale numbering and add what would be the proper sequential number in brackets.
30. Here Rose A. seems to take the question as being about the origin of the name Kanada commando and links it with the different kerchiefs worn by the workers. Various other explanations have also been offered for the origins of this name.
31. Rose A. Tape 2. Segment 12 (18). 40:27.
32. Laub, 'Bearing Witness,' p. 60.
33. For an extended discussion of the naming of Kanada, see Joseph Steinitz, *What's Metaphor Got to Do with It? Troping and Counter-Troping in Holocaust Victim Language*, Unpublished PhD thesis, The University of Iowa, 2015, pp. 159–173.
34. Serena N. interviewed by Eva Kantor and Dori Laub on 7 November 1982. Fortunoff Video Archive for Holocaust Testimonies. HVT-179. Tape 2. Segment 10. 21:02.
35. Correspondence and Analysis of Fortunoff Archive Testimonies from Lawrence Langer to Michael Berenbaum, 18 February 1991. USHMM; Institutional Archives; Research Institute; Subject Files of the Director Michael Berenbaum; 1989–1997; 1988-011, Box 20; Lawrence Langer.
36. It is clear that despite later claims Crematorium 3 (IV) was dynamited, some inmates at Birkenau who were not members of the SK were aware it was actually damaged by fire. In his 1946 essay Birkenau, for example, the French survivor Désiré Haffner writes that 'on Saturday 7th October, the men of the special squad set ablaze (*incendient*) Crematorium no. 3 which was completely destroyed by the flames'. Désiré Haffner, 'Birkenau,' in *Témoignages sur Auschwitz* (Paris: Éditions de l'amicale des déportés d'Auschwitz, 1946), p. 76. Interestingly, Haffner also refers to a kapo being thrown into an oven alive and to an SK member successfully escaping. The legend (if it is that) of 'the one that got away' features in several survivor testimonies. See also Abe Korn, 'Fate,' unpublished manuscript, c1969. USHMM Collection Number RG-02.191, p. 102.

37. Serena N. Tape 2. Segment 13. 28:55.
38. Irene Weiss recalls being in the barracks sorting and hearing 'huge explosions'. Weiss interviewed by Chare, 1:02:50. For many of the women, it is clear that the revolt was more an acoustic than a visual phenomenon. In this sense, the early Yale approach with its emphasis on visualizing the past (which we go on to discuss in this chapter) manifests its limits. Those testifying are encouraged to extrapolate images from what they have heard.
39. In addition to the account of a man who runs into a warehouse in Kanada that we go on to discuss in this chapter, Berry Nahmia writes of two or three members of the SK seeking refuge in the warehouse she worked in: 'Suddenly, two or three prisoners burst into our barrack begging us for help and imploring us girls to hide them someplace... Soon armed officers followed them.' Nahmia, *A Cry for Tomorrow 76859...*, pp. 117–118. Morris Venezia recounts that Isaak Venezia (no relation) escaped from the burning building of Crematorium 3 (IV) and then took refuge in Kanada. Morris Venezia interviewed by Carol Stulberg on 27 October 1996. USC Shoah Foundation. Interview Code 20405. Tape 6. 9:25. There were 30 barracks at Kanada II. There were around sixty people employed in any given barrack. Approximately 800 women and 600 men worked there at its peak.
40. Rose A. Tape 2. Segment 11. 21:06.
41. Ibid., 21:11.
42. This initial claim occurs at 20:20 of Tape 2.
43. In many testimonies, the first half hour to hour can seem lacklustre. The reasons for this are likely manifold depending on factors such as whether an interviewee has been interviewed before or is familiar with the interviewer. We are grateful to Monika Vrzgulová for sharing considerable insights regarding the interview process in video testimony.
44. In her written account of the revolt, Nahmia states 'we heard shots and machine-guns outside while working in the barrack'. Nahmia, *A Cry for Tomorrow 76859...*, p. 117.
45. For a discussion of memory as constructive process, see Nicholas Chare and Dominic Williams, 'Questions of Filiation: From the Scrolls of Auschwitz to *Son of Saul*,' *Mémoires en jeu* 2 (2016), pp. 63–72.
46. Irene Weiss interviewed by Nicholas Chare, 8 July 2018, 1:12:50.
47. Laub, 'On Holocaust "Testimony",' p. 129.
48. See Shenker's discussion of the USHMM approach to oral and video testimony. Shenker cites Martin Smith, who was director of exhibitions at the museum, insisting on the need for 'little nuggets'. Shenker, *Reframing Holocaust Testimony*, p. 75.
49. D. F. Tovey, *Symphonies and Other Orchestral Works: Selections from Musical Analysis* (New York: Dover, 2015), pp. 254–255.

50. Laub, 'On Holocaust "Testimony",' p. 129.
51. Serena N. Tape 2. Segment 13. 31:05.
52. Shenker, *Reframing Holocaust Testimony*, p. 32.
53. The gunpowder was smuggled in various ways including in the mouth and the vagina but also between the breasts, in the hair, under the armpit and in the hems of dresses and inside pieces of bread. See our Introduction and also Harran, 'The Jewish Women at the Union Factory, Auschwitz 1944,' p. 50. John Sack suggests the hair, mouth and vagina as common hiding places used by the women of the Union Factory. See Sack, *An Eye for an Eye* (New York: Basic Books, 1993), p. 27.
54. Lisa Pinhas who worked in the Union Factory states that in August 1944 searches became more thorough as the Nazis had become suspicious of the women. Lisa Pinhas, *A Narrative of Evil* (Athens: The Jewish Museum of Greece, 2014), p. 110.
55. Raizel Tabakman, 'My Husband, a Flitzer, Was Gassed Upon Arrival Together with All Other Flitzers,' in *The Union Kommando in Auschwitz: The Auschwitz Munition Factory Through the Eyes of Its Former Slave Laborers*, ed. Lore Shelley (Lanham: University Press of America, 1996), p. 41. This book has a foreword by Dori Laub.
56. Cecile Klein-Pollack interviewed by Linda G. Kuzmack on 7 May 1990. Oral History Interview. United States Holocaust Memorial Museum. Accession Number 1990.383.1. RG Number: RG-50.030.0107. Judith Meisel was also subjected to a vaginal search upon her arrival in Stutthof. See Judith Meisel interviewed by Linda G. Kuzmack on 25 January 1990. Oral History Interview. United States Holocaust Memorial Museum. Accession Number 1990.340.1. RG Number: RG-50.030.0157.
57. Aranka Siegal, *Upon the Head of the Goat: A Childhood in Hungary 1939–1944* (London: J.M. Dent & Sons, 1982), p. 213.
58. Rose A. Tape 2. Segment 12 (18). 44:53.
59. Serena N. Tape 2. Segment 8. 11:35.
60. Ibid. Tape 2. Segment 18. 52:36. It is noteworthy that here, within her own testimony, Serena N. is calling into question the veracity of some eyewitness testimony. She is, in a sense, prefiguring the response of the historians described by Laub. For her, as for the historians, the truth of testimony resides in its factual accuracy.
61. Ibid. Tape 2. Segment 18. 54:58.
62. Ibid. Tape 2. Segment 19. 55.27.
63. Ibid. Tape 2. Segment 19. 55:38.
64. Correspondence and Analysis of Fortunoff Archive Testimonies from Lawrence Langer to Michael Berenbaum, 18 February 1991.

65. Correspondence and Analysis of Fortunoff Archive Testimonies from Lawrence Langer to Michael Berenbaum, 4 April 1991. USHMM; Institutional Archives; Research Institute; Subject Files of the Director Michael Berenbaum; 1989–1997; 1998-011, Box 26; Folder 9; Oral History-Fortunoff Archives-Yale.
66. Serena N. Tape 2. Segments 19–20. 57:10.
67. Ibid. Tape 2. Segment 20. 57:42.
68. Ibid. Tape 2. Segment 20. 58:21.
69. Carolyn Steedman, *Poetry for Historians or W.H. Auden and History* (Manchester: Manchester University Press, 2018), p. 7.
70. For an important discussion of other aspects of Holocaust testimony, especially the role played by the language of the interview, see Hannah Pollin-Galay, *Ecologies of Witnessing: Language, Place and Holocaust Testimony* (New Haven: Yale University Press, 2018).
71. On the question of how one should listen to the multitude of video testimonies now accessible to researchers, see Todd Presner, 'The Ethics of the Algorithm: Close and Distant Listening to the Shoah Foundation Visual History Archive,' in *Probing the Ethics of Holocaust Culture*, eds. Claudio Fogu, Wulf Kansteiner, and Todd Presner (Cambridge, MA: Harvard University Press, 2016), pp. 150–175.
72. Dario Gabbai interviewed by Carol Stulberg on 7 November 1996. USC Shoah Foundation. Interview Code 142. Tape 2. Segment 42. 10:45.
73. Ibid. Tape 2. Segment 50. 18:53.
74. Ibid. Tape 2. Segment 50. 18:57.
75. Dario Gabbai interviewed by Stephen Smith on 1 May 2014. USC Shoah Foundation. Interview Code 142. Tape 6. 36:05.
76. Gabbai's brother Ya'akov (who also worked in the SK) did not think Dario would survive stating 'Truth to tell, I didn't think he'd make it. He was a sensitive man [...].' Gideon Greif, *We Wept Without Tears*, p. 189.
77. See also, for instance, Moses Mizrahi's description of having to witness a mother and her children being shot and then cremate the bodies: 'Then, uh, I took, it was I took inside, I put inside the fire [purses lips, overcome with emotion]'. Moses Mizrahi interviewed by Elizabeth Yonan on 7 May 1996. USC Shoah Foundation. Interview Code 15146. Tape 2. 14:18. See also Morris K.'s interview with Lawrence Langer from 28 June 1989. Fortunoff Archive for Holocaust Testimonies. HVT-1431.
78. Our emphasis. Dario Gabbai interviewed by Carol Stulberg. Tape 2. Segment 51. 19:38.
79. Gabbai will later reveal to Smith, after considerable hesitation, that Moll shot the women in the breasts. Dario Gabbai interviewed by Stephen

Smith. Tape 6. Segment 193. 59:17. It is possible he also shot them in the genitals and Gabbai finds himself unable to reveal this to either interviewer. There are (at least anecdotal) precedents of soldiers inflicting such violence on women.
80. Dario Gabbai interviewed by Carol Stulberg. Tape 3. Segment 69. 6:34.
81. Ibid. Tape 3. Segment 69. 6:37.
82. Halivni is similarly reticent, referring to those on the transports arriving with 'precious jewellery hidden in all imaginable places on their bodies'. USHMM Tzipora Hager Weiss Halivni Papers Box 19, File 2. Loose leaf lined paper numbered 51.
83. Morris Venezia interviewed by Carol Stulberg on 27 October 1996. Interview Code 20405. Tape 5. Segment 23. 0:50.
84. Ibid. Tape 5. Segment 26. 10:53.
85. Daniel Bennahmias interviewed by Beatrice Netter, Lisa Barnett and Ilana Braun on 12 November 1991. USHMM Accession Number 1999.A.0122.661 RG-50.477.0661.
86. Dario Gabbai interviewed by Stephen Smith. Tape 6. Segment 217. 1:23:47.
87. In the 1980s, leanness (which Gabbai exhibits) was a key standard of male attractiveness. See Cheryl Law and Magdala Peixoto Labre, 'Cultural Standards of Attractiveness: A Thirty-Year Look at Changes in Male Images in Magazines,' *Journalism & Mass Communication Quarterly* 79:3 (2002): 697–711.
88. Although for an attempt to see what else might be learnt from this second interview, see Dawn Skorczewski, '"You Want Me to Sing?" Holocaust Testimonies in the Intersubjective Field,' *Dapim* 32.2 (2018): 125–126. In her comparison of the two interviews with Gabbai, Skorczewski erroneously states Gabbai was first interviewed by Yitzchak Kerem rather than Carol Stulberg.
89. Shenker, *Reframing Holocaust Testimony*, p. 78.
90. Dario Gabbai interviewed by Stephen Smith. Tape 6. Segment 195. 1:01:33.
91. Ibid. Tape 6. Segment 217. 1:22:55; 1:23:20.
92. Ibid. Tape 6. Segment 222. 1:28:20.
93. He also likely unconsciously sized-up Smith. Smith's appearance, however, if deemed pleasing would likely register as a status cue rather than as desirability.
94. Here Kuzmack's comment about her noisy stomach seems more connected with a microphone than a camera. Mics do pick up the sounds of stomachs rumbling in interviews, particularly the early Yale interviews where, perhaps, the pressure of conducting multiple interviews in

a single day led to skipped meals. These sounds lend an oddly reassuring corporeality to the interviews they occur in.
95. In the context of a Holocaust survivor, of course, food is a loaded subject. The Auschwitz survivor Judy F. remarks in video testimony that 'I got very screwed up in this area, in [the] food area, because after Auschwitz I ate an awful lot. […]. I have problems with my eating habits and I know it happened because [of] that knowledge after I came home [that] now I can have everything I want foodwise'. Judy [Iboya] F. interviewed by Susanna Neumann and Robert Prince. HVT-211. 31 October 1982. Tape 1. Segment 13. 41:26.
96. For a discussion of beauty as a status cue, see Murray Webster and James E. Driskell, 'Beauty as Status,' *American Journal of Sociology* 89.1 (1983): 140–165.
97. Just as there has been a tendency to homogenize the camp experience as desexualized (a desexualization that, as we have already discussed in previous chapters, is not all encompassing), the potential play of sexual desire in some interviews has not been widely acknowledged. Towards the beginning of the emergence of initiatives to videotape survivor testimony, the age differentials between interviewer and interviewee were, however, sometimes not that great, increasing the likelihood of such play. Dylan Kwart, Tom Foulsham and Alan Kingstone speculate that 'when younger individuals view older adults they may make stigmatisations or judgements differently from the way in which older viewers rate similarly aged faces'. It is possible that a reduced age differential increases the likelihood of attractiveness registering with an interviewer or an interviewee. Clearly, this can also apply to the judgements made retrospectively about an interviewee (or an interviewer—if they are visible) by listener-viewers of the testimony. See Kwart, Foulsham and Kingstone, 'Age and Beauty Are in the Eye of the Beholder,' *Perception* 41.8 (2012): 936. In Claude Lanzmann's interviews with women survivors, there sometimes seem to us to be at least an element of flirtation, in, for example, his statement at the beginning of his interview with Paula Biren that he wants to 'make her nervous', or in the gallant way he apologizes to Ruth Elias for asking her age. Only the former of these moments appears in *The Four Sisters* (dir. Claude Lanzmann, 2017). Interview with Biren, USHMM RG-60.5001, Film ID: 3105 (03:00:30); interview with Elias USHMM RG Number: RG-60.5003, Film ID: 3112 (01:04:30). https://collections.ushmm.org/film_findingaids/RG-60.5003_01_trs_en.pdf, p. 2.
98. See Norman Cavoir and Paul R. Dokecki, 'Physical Attractiveness, Perceived Attitude Similarity, and Academic Achievement as Contributors

to Interpersonal Attraction Among Adolescents,' *Developmental Psychology* 9.1 (1973): 44–54.
99. Chris L. Kleinke, Richard A. Staneski, and Dale E. Berger, 'Evaluation of an Interviewer as Function of Interviewer Gaze, Reinforcement of Subject Gaze and Interviewer Attractiveness,' *Journal of Personality and Social Psychology* 31.1 (1975): 115–122.
100. See Gordon Patzer, 'Source Credibility as a Function of Communicator Physical Attractiveness,' *Journal of Business Research* 11.2 (1983): 229–241.
101. Attractiveness as an attribute declines less rapidly for men than for women but it declines nevertheless. See Francine M. Deuisch, Carla M. Zalenski and Mary E. Clark, 'Is There a Double Standard of Ageing?' *Journal of Applied Social Psychology* 16.9 (1986): 771–785.
102. David Morand, 'What's in a Name?: An Exploration of the Social Dynamics of Forms of Address in Organizations,' *Management Communication Quarterly* 9.4 (1996): 423.
103. Ibid.
104. Shlomo Venezia interviewed by Manuela Consonni on 11 December 1997. USC Shoah Foundation. Interview Code 36179. Shlomo Venezia also provided a written account of his Holocaust experiences *Inside the Gas Chambers*. Additionally, a summary of his time in the Sonderkommando is included in Roberto Olla, *Le non persone: Gli Italiani nella Shoah* (Rome: RAI Radiotelevisione Italiana, 1999), pp. 35–68.
105. Nikolas Rose, 'Identity, Genealogy, History,' in *Identity: A Reader*, eds. Paul du Gay et al. (London: Sage, 2000), pp. 321–322.
106. Dario Gabbai interviewed by Stephen Smith. Tape 6. Segment 230. 1:36:17.
107. Bos discusses how gendered discourses inform the construction and shaping of memory in her essay 'Women and the Holocaust'.
108. Daniel Bennahmias interviewed by Beatrice Netter, Lisa Barnett and Ilana Braun on 12 November 1991. USHMM Accession Number 1999.A.0122.661. RG-50.477.0661. Tape 1. 1:27:41.
109. Ibid. Tape 1. 1:28:43.
110. Ibid. Tape 1. 1:29:04.
111. Ibid. Tape 1. 1:29:15.
112. Daniel Bennahmias interviewed by Joel Neuberg on 24 June 1986. USHMM Accession Number 1999.A.0122.1160. RG-50.477.1160. 1:11:44.
113. Shenker, *Reframing Holocaust Testimony*, p. 13.
114. Langer, 'Gendered Suffering? Women in Holocaust Testimonies,' in *Women in the Holocaust*, eds. Dalia Ofer and Lenore J. Weitzman (New Haven: Yale University Press, 1998), pp. 351–363.

115. James Young, *Writing and Rewriting the Holocaust: Narrative and the Consequences of Interpretation* (Bloomington and Indianapolis: Indiana University Press, 1988), p. 157.
116. Ibid., p. 161.
117. Ibid. Young's emphasis.
118. The language used by the interviewers also 'dates' the interview. One, likely Lisa Barnett, asks 'Were your friends, your schoolmates, the people you sort of hung out with, were they primarily Jewish?' Another, perhaps Netter, states; 'I want to get more flavour [...] of what your life was like in Auschwitz.' This kind of phraseology foregrounds the relative youthfulness of the women.
119. Daniel Bennahmias interviewed by Joel Neuberg. 1:01:03.
120. See the discussion of the staples in Nicholas Chare, 'Material Witness: Conservation Ethics and the Scrolls of Auschwitz,' *symplokē* 24:1–2 (2016): 81–97.
121. Morris Venezia interviewed by Carol Stulberg. Tape 4. Segment 22. 23:17.
122. Shenker, *Reframing Holocaust Testimony*, p. 27.
123. Ibid.
124. Serena N. Tape 1. Segment 1. 1:41.
125. Tape 2. Segment 22. 0:51.
126. Shenker, *Reframing Holocaust Testimony*, p. 130.
127. Dario Gabbai interviewed by Carol Stulberg. Tape 2. Segment 58. 26:58.
128. Morris Venezia interviewed by Carol Stulberg. Tape 4. Segment 21. 18:05.
129. Dario Gabbai interviewed by Stephen Smith. Tape 6. Segment 184. 49:59.
130. Philippe Mesnard, 'The Sonderkommando on Screen,' in *Testimonies of Resistance: Representations of the Auschwitz-Birkenau Sonderkommando*, eds. Nicholas Chare and Dominic Williams (New York: Berghahn, 2019), in press.
131. Shlomo Venezia interviewed by Manuela Consonni on 11 December 1997. USC Shoah Foundation. Interview Code 36179. Tape 10. Segment 278. 16:00.
132. Ibid. Tape 10. Segment 280. 19:00.
133. Sarah Gregory, 'To Pass, To Last, To Cast Aside: The Testimonies of Two Auschwitz-Birkenau Sonderkommando Survivors, the Gabbai Brothers,' *History in the Making* 2.2 (2013): 30–40 and 38.
134. Gabbai responds to Smith's question 'Did you have to force people to go in?' in the following terms: 'Yeah. [makes push gesture]. If there's not enough room [makes push gesture] you used to push'. Dario Gabbai interviewed by Stephen Smith. Tape 6. Segment 166. 32:16.

135. Dario Gabbai interviewed by Carol Stulberg.
136. Morris Venezia interviewed by Carol Stulberg. Tape 4. Segment 21. 16:40.
137. While the way that Dawn Skorczewski characterizes the difference between Dario Gabbai and Morris Venezia's accounts (the former more focussed on the technical details, the latter on what happened to the victims as people) might be seen as at odds with our reading here, in fact it is consistent with it. Venezia gives detail at this point because of its personal significance. Skorczewski, 'You Want Me to Sing?' 122–124. Skorczewski does not consider the potential influence of gender on the way SK interviewees respond in video testimony.
138. Morris Venezia interviewed by Carol Stulberg. Tape 4. Segment 21. 18:54.
139. Amit Pinchevski, 'The Audiovisual Unconscious: Media and Trauma in the Video Archive for Holocaust Testimonies,' *Critical Inquiry* 39 (2012): 155. Langer discusses 'deep memory' in *Holocaust Testimonies: The Ruins of Memory* (New Haven: Yale University Press, 1993), pp. 1–38.
140. See Laura Mulvey, *Death 24× a Second: Stillness and the Moving Image* (London: Reaktion, 2006).
141. Shlomo Venezia interviewed by Manuela Consonni. Tape 16. Segment 467. 28:50.
142. Ibid. Tape 16. Segment 468. 29:09.
143. Ibid. Tape 17. Segment 469. 0:19.
144. David Nencel interviewed by Joe Russin in 1996. USHMM Accession Number 2003.76. RG-50.560.0001. Tape 8. 24:03.
145. Ibid. Tape 8. 18:03.
146. Shenker, p. 23.
147. Serena N. Tape 2. Segment 13. 28:55.
148. Greif, *We Wept Without Tears*, p. 258.
149. Ibid.
150. Ibid.
151. Young, *Writing and Rewriting the Holocaust*, p. 160.
152. Morris Venezia interviewed by Carol Stulberg. Tape 1. Segment 4. 15:45.
153. Leon Welbel interviewed by Phyllis Dreazen on 30 March 1995. USC Shoah Foundation. Interview Code 1770. Henry Fuchs [Henryk Tauber] identifies Leizer as being a Kapo in his video testimony for the Shoah Foundation. Despite his elevated status, however, Fuchs calls Leizer 'one of us'. Henry Fuchs interviewed by E. Tina Tito on 22 July 1996. USC Shoah Foundation. Interview Code 17625. Tape 4. 12:38. Perhaps inevitably, however, not everyone felt that way. Leon Lewin,

who like Welbel (and Zalman Gradowski) was a Betarist from Łunna, gave a less complimentary assessment of him as a 'bitch' when he was in the SK (Segment 15). Leon Lewin interviewed by Mildred Gelfand on 19 September 1996. USC Shoah Foundation. Interview Code 20004.
154. Welbel, Segment 74.
155. Welbel, Segment 118.
156. Welbel, Segments 78 and 98.
157. Shlomo Venezia interviewed by Manuela Consonni. Tape 17. Segment 479. 11:28.
158. Ibid. Tape 17. Segment 479. 11:40.

CHAPTER 7

The Voice of Bronze: Filip Müller and *Shoah*

Telling for the Last Time

It was a story he had told several times before he told it to Claude Lanzmann in late spring of 1979[1]: to Ota Kraus and Erich Kulka for their book *The Death Factory* (1946); in the morning of 11 December 1947 at the trial of Auschwitz personnel in Kraków[2]; on 5 October 1964 at the trial of other Auschwitz personnel in Frankfurt,[3] and in his book *Sonderbehandlung*, published sufficiently earlier that year for Lanzmann to have read it and for a copy to be available for them to peruse together.[4] He was in Block 11 of Auschwitz I. He was thirsty and went searching for tea to drink. He was caught. He and six other prisoners were taken to the crematorium, forced to undress bodies and to man the ovens. In attempting to work the fans, they caused a fire. Later that night they loaded the unburnt bodies onto trucks and were taken somewhere near Birkenau, where they dumped the corpses into flooded pits. They were beaten and some of them were shot, but were too exhausted to carry on. The following day they were taken back and forced to complete their task.

In their edit for *Shoah*, Lanzmann and Ziva Postec left almost all of these elements in.[5] In voice-over, Lanzmann addresses someone as Filip, who says he was twenty when he came to Birkenau. The date is made specific: a Sunday in May. On the screen, snow falls; the entire sequence seems to have been shot in winter. The camera starts with a shot of the death wall at Block 11 in Auschwitz I, pulling back to reveal the doorway into the courtyard that contains it.[6] It then goes on to replicate the movements described by the speaker: it walks towards the crematorium, 'sees' it at the same time as he describes it, goes past the back door while he mentions it and enters the crematorium at the same time as he says: 'we go into the corridor'. Just before then, the subtitles inform us that this is Filip Müller of the special squad, survivor of five selections. The camera continues to move round within the building, a continuous shot except for two subtle, unobtrusive cuts. It appears more or less to be following what Müller is saying, although it also has something of the feel of a tourist looking round an interior and trying to piece together what is was used for. As Müller describes the work he did, we see him for the first time, sitting on a sofa in front of a window with a Venetian blind, a man now in his late fifties, wearing a short-sleeved white shirt. He begins to describe being told to 'stir the corpses' (*die Leichen rühren*). He gestures repeatedly to demonstrate how a rod (*Stange*) was used to do this (his hand coming up into the frame of the close-up) while Lanzmann, checking the meaning of the word *Stange*, causes Müller to repeat it: 'an iron rod' (perhaps hearing '*Was für eine Stange?*' for '*Was ist eine Stange?*'). He also demonstrates the rotation of the fan with his hand. As Müller explains that they caused a fire in the chimney, the film cuts back to an exterior shot of the crematorium and its chimney, replicating the first mention of the building.[7]

Cut to a shot of a field, with the camera panning left, over rural-looking buildings, trees and electricity lines and pylons before the gate to Birkenau comes into frame as Müller says its name. Müller talks about taking the corpses to the field, probably, he says, in Birkenau. Editing simplifies his story into an account of stopping when night came, which is matched to a night-time shot of the moon over Birkenau and loud noises of wildlife. The story of the following day, with its emphasis on working in water and mud, plays over a shot of a pond in Birkenau next to Crematorium 3 (IV), with the camera turning again from the ruins of the crematorium to the pond. The account ends with a return to Müller, again gesturing to show how he found it difficult to carry and move wet bodies.[8] Capping this sequence, dialogue in voice-over between Lanzmann and Müller establishes some context: that the crematoria in Birkenau did not exist at this time. A static camera zooms in on the notice board next to Crematorium (1) II, while Müller explains what these new crematoria were like.

What does this give us that the previous versions did not? The film editor of *Shoah*, Ziva Postec, described what she did with this sequence as follows:

Filip Muller's march: a traveling shot from the executions wall in Block 11 in Auschwitz - the central camp - into the inner parts of the crematorium. [...]

Only his voice is heard, speaking without any anecdote (or emotion), a voice describing the essentials: the street, the gate, the building, the chimney, the door, the entrance. We walk with him. Past mixes with the present. And we are there. These moments of truth were created on the editing table - as collages. I sometimes looked for a sentence, a word, from other and sometimes remote places in the interview. In spite of the overwhelming scope and breadth of the footage, it was necessary to grasp the essence of each and every interview. For example, in the original text, Muller says: 'all of a sudden I saw a building in front of me'. But the image shows a building with a chimney, and I wanted Muller to also mention the chimney, for we viewers already know about the chimney for some time and I wanted that knowledge to be tapped into and dramatized. It was important that we - editors and viewers - should be able to meticulously follow and accompany the process of terrible discovery, which Muller went through as he walked for the first time in his life towards the crematorium.

So when Muller reiterates that it was 'a flat building', I pasted the words 'with a chimney' taken from another part of the interview. The rhythm of his steps, too, had to be reconstructed in a synthetic, fictional way. I had to put myself in the boots of the protagonist to enact it, that is to say, to add those elements and that rhythm that would express Filip Muller's terrible experience, to which he was only partly aware. I found an 'inner rhythm' that allowed me to relive the scene[.][9]

Postec describes here a number of important innovations and differences. Most important is the presence of visual elements, footage recorded by Lanzmann and his team in Auschwitz itself. Müller's testimony is contrasted with and matched to that, at times subordinated to it. She is also quite explicit at how extreme that editing process on Müller's words was at times: splicing together utterances which were made at very different times in the interview, giving what he said quite a different rhythm from the way in which he was recorded.[10] On top of this (a part that Postec does not mention) is the contrast between these moments and those where Müller speaks in person, where his voice is located in his body, and is matched with gestures that he makes.[11] All of this suggests that Müller was perhaps less in control of this testimony than any he had made before. To be sure, none of Müller's previous testimony was entirely produced on his own terms. In cases of what he wrote, he is likely to have been edited, while his court testimony was guided by the presiding judges (and in the trial at Kraków does not appear to be spontaneous speech). However, here more than in any other case, his testimony appears to have been taken away from him and repurposed.

This chapter will consider the ways in which *Shoah* makes use of Müller's testimony, considering the editing of his voice-over, the images and their relation to his words, as well as the moments where he is physically present. We will show that this use of his testimony stems not simply from Müller's personal position as a witness, but also from the particular situation of the Sonderkommando at Auschwitz, as opposed to their equivalents in other camps. Auschwitz-Birkenau, we will argue, plays a contradictory role in *Shoah*: both as the culmination of the exterminatory apparatus and as a site that does not quite fit into the explanatory framework that Lanzmann advanced for his film.

SHAPING THE VOICE

Claude Lanzmann repeatedly indicated that what marked Müller out as a witness was his voice.[12] He describes it in his autobiography as '*cette voix de bronze*' ['this voice of bronze']. For Lanzmann, Müller's voice is therefore stentorian, incredibly powerful. Hera is described in the Iliad as shouting in the guise of Stentor, whose brazen voice has the force of fifty men. In French translation, this brazen voice is rendered as '*la voix de bronze*'.[13] Aristotle mentions the voice of Stentor in Book 7 of the *Politics*, asking of an extremely crowded city 'who will be the general of an overly excessive number, or who will be a herald, unless he has the voice of Stentor?'[14] Müller's voice in *Shoah* is burdened with speaking for the close to a million Jews murdered in the gas chambers at Auschwitz, tasked with communicating the hell of the crematoria. He is also the sole representative of the Auschwitz SK to speak in the film and therefore acts as their only spokesperson. Lanzmann had initially also wanted to include Dov Paisikovic in *Shoah*, but he died before he could be filmed.[15] Müller's voice, wrote Lanzmann, had 'a resonant and reverberating timbre that hung in the air long after each of his frank, dramatic utterances'.[16] Its significance for him thus also lay in its relationship with silence. But, as he indicates (giving Postec as little place in the process as her account gives to him), that relationship was the product of editing as much as of the actual way Müller spoke.

> I edited his words, his voice, setting them over the contemporary landscapes, constantly moving back and forth from synch-sound to voice-over.

When I used voice-over, the difficulty was to preserve the interior rhythm of the voice even as I refined it.[17]

This method of refinement often results in slowing down the way Müller speaks. In the march to the crematorium in Auschwitz I, for example, the pace of speaking is more than a third slower than the pace at which he tells the story in the unedited footage, giving his voice-over a more epic quality.[18]

In other places, the process of editing is even more interventionist. The final shot of Müller's first appearance, in which he explains when the new crematoria were built, is made up of phrases and even single words that Müller uttered at very different times in the interview. It is put together as follows:

reel 3	Damals war Birkenau noch nicht ausgebaut	Birkenau still wasn't completely set up.
	war noch bloß der Lager B1 der da später als Frauenlager war |	Only Camp B1, which was later the women's camp, existed.
reel 7	Im Frühjahr 1943 |	It wasn't until the spring of 1943
reel 19	Facharbeiter	that skilled workmen
	und andere, unqualifizierte Arbeiter, |	and unskilled laborers,
?	Juden, |	all Jews,
reel 19	müßten hier arbeiten	must have [sic] gone to work here
	und die vier Krematorien bauen |	and built the four crematoriums.
reel 7	je ein Krematorium | ... die hatten |	Each crematorium
	15 Öfen	had 15 ovens,
	Eine [sic] große Auskleiderungsraum [sic] von etwa 280 Quadratmeter, |	a big undressing room, around 280 square metres,
	und eine große Gaskammer wo man bis 3000	and a big gas-chamber where up to 3000 people
	auf einmal |	at once
reel 4	vergast |	were gassed
reel 7	hat.[19]	

When Lanzmann called the film a fiction of the real, he was not exaggerating. At times, Müller's testimony is almost a set of phonemes from which is constructed the background of Auschwitz-Birkenau.

In the second part of the film (the 'Second Era'), where the story goes 'inside' the gas chambers for part of it, Müller expands in much greater detail on the operations of the crematorium and what the inside of the gas chamber looked like. The sequence begins with a four-minute pan around the model of Crematorium 1 (II) at Birkenau which is located in the Auschwitz Museum, with Müller providing a description.[20] This model was built by the artist Mieczyslaw Stobierski based, in part, on the trial testimony of SS guards. Müller's account therefore overlays a vision of the crematorium provided by perpetrators of mass murder.[21] He might be seen to be vocally reclaiming the memory of the crematorium for the SK.[22] However, his words are just as spliced together as they were for his previous explanation of the workings of the gas chamber.[23] The voice-over mechanically repeats some of the points, down to using a re-edited version of recordings used previously.

eine [*sic*] große Auskleideraum,	a big undressing room,
von etwa 280 Quadratmeter,	around 280 square metres,
und eine große Gaskammer	and a big gas-chamber
wo konnte man bis 3000 Menschen	where up to 3000 people
auf einmal vergasen.	at once could be gassed.[24]

Although much of the second version looks like a repetition, it is actually a heavily edited reconstruction of the original. The last two lines are almost entirely taken from different pieces of footage, with the following time codes in the archive:

04:01:49:06	konnte man
02:27:43:03	bis drei
03:13:15:21	tausend Menschen
03:29:04:16	auf einmal
02:17:37:25	vergasen

The first three lines are replayed from the original recording, but even here, they are edited. In this second version, the extra syllable 'rungs' is cut out from 'Auskleiderungsraum'. As far as we can tell, this is the most extreme piece of editing to which Müller's words were subjected. They are a recapitulation of words he is already made to utter earlier in the film, following much the same syntax and expressions, albeit with small changes. The replacement words are taken from very different contexts: 'konnte man' from an explanation of how many bodies it was possible to burn in a pit; 'tausend Menschen' from a point where he talks about 2000 people being gassed; 'auf einmal' from a description of Crematorium 4 (V), whose three gas chambers operated simultaneously and 'vergasen' from the story of the women who learned about her fate from one of the Sonderkommando crying out 'me vet undz fargazn'.[25]

Such heavy-handed altering and repurposing of a witness's words (and, at one point, of a witness's relaying of the words of a victim) seem to violate all ethical obligations to the witness, as expressed in Dori Laub's idea of the receiver of testimony as a 'companion on the eerie journey' of the survivor.[26] It makes a mockery of Lawrence Langer's valorization of oral testimony where 'every word spoken falls directly from the lips of the witnesses' against written testimony 'that is openly or silently edited'.[27]

In some ways, the approach is of a piece with other aspects of Lanzmann's project. In its wilful departure from the form in which a survivor chooses to tell their own story, it is similar to the more famous moments of 'incarnation': triggering traumatic episodes by getting them to re-enact the most difficult parts of their experience and break through previous 'habits' of telling. It also fits with Francine Kaufman's sense that Lanzmann was trying to film his witnesses repeating details and indeed words that he had recorded them uttering two or three years previously.[28] Both of these bespeak a process of manipulation, of Lanzmann having an idea of the kind of testimony that he wanted and trying to get his witnesses to produce it.

On the other hand, it is clearly different from these two examples because it was carried out post factum. In the other cases, the witnesses have some opportunity (albeit limited by the pain and shock caused by the memories and the demands being made of them) to react to what is being asked of them, to resist or assent and to respond in their own way. In the editing suite, they were not even aware of what was being done. Here, control seems to have passed entirely to the film-maker, with Müller simply becoming a resource to be quarried.

We do not want to scant these ethical problems, and in Müller's case, they seem to be particularly cogent. After his interview with Lanzmann, he refused to give any more testimony.[29] That seems more likely to be a response to the editing than anything that he was made to do in the interview. That Müller was an attentive listener is clear from testimony he provides in *Shoah* such as when he listens to the exchanges between members of a transport arriving at the crematorium at Auschwitz I. He makes a circular gesture with his hand at head height to signal the inner workings of the mind as he recounts that the words of the people indexed their emotions. Shortly afterwards, he observes that their 'conflicting words echoed the conflict in their feelings'. Müller obviously recognizes the affective as well as informational insights that are afforded by speech in a given context. He knows the rich potential of speech as an expressive medium. He is therefore likely to have noted and responded negatively to having his own words manipulated.

The extraordinary (perhaps even reckless) willingness to take and repurpose words in this scene was probably underpinned by the fact that it was done to reconstitute a sentence that Müller had actually spoken. But the need to do it is also very suggestive. Firstly, it indicates an extreme self-consciousness about the repetition of this section. It appears to have been designed to function as both a repetition and a variation on Müller's words describing Crematorium 1 (II) earlier in the film. The words are deliberately kept close to their original statement (what might be called the 'theme'), but they are made to sound different, by replacement and subtraction. That suggests that a wholesale repetition was both not what Lanzmann and Postec wanted and something they felt the audience might perceive. If that is so, then they might also be said to have expected that the parts that are actual repetitions would be (on some level) perceived too, especially the use of 'vergasen'/'fargazn', which returns fifteen minutes later. Secondly, the fragments that were chosen strike us as having very distinctive intonation, each having some sonic quality that made them stand out in the editing process, with the high pitched fragments ('konnte man', 'tausend Menschen' and 'vergasen') alternating with the lower register ones ('eine große Gaskammer', 'bis drei' and 'auf einmal') in what sounds like a conscious patterning. Lanzmann and Postec appear to have believed that they had spotted something in the way that Müller talked, something that could be extracted from his accounts, sonic moments that did something other than simply carry the meaning of what he was saying.

That Lanzmann and Postec felt able to treat Müller's voice in this way may have been due to its being recorded rather than 'live'. As Amy Lawrence has noted, 'the possibilities of ownership, repetition, and control increase the potential identification of the recorded voice as object and fetish'.[30] That automatized element is discernible in some of the ways he is allowed to speak. The contours of intonation in much of the voice-over often feel quite unnatural. Even with a small edit, in which Müller's original words are reordered from 'war es also alles auf einer Ebene' to 'alles war auf einer Ebene' ('everything was on one level'—with a change of syntax and not of meaning), the splicing of the earlier word into the later part of the utterance makes it jump from high to low intonation and back again.[31] Glitches between other different parts can be heard, once one is aware of it, for example the words 'vergast hat' at the very end of the first sequence with Müller. Müller's role in these voice-overs is to explain the technology of Auschwitz, but his voice too becomes an effect of technology, even to the extent of taking on an inhuman quality. Unlike the examples of the SK acting as 'technical specialists' that we examined in the previous chapter, this is a role that seems to have little to do with Müller's own choices in self-presentation, but is rather a technologized self that has been created by the process of editing.

Such a collage process is not unique to Lanzmann and Postec. Peter Weiss also made a collage out of Müller's words, as we discuss in Chapter 4. Additionally, the artist Peter Krausz employs Müller's statement 'It was impossible' (a reference to the impossibility of becoming habituated to the sight of corpses in the gas chamber) and other quotations from witnesses in *Shoah* in his artwork *Night Train* (1990).[32] But perhaps a closer parallel is to Steve Reich's use of recorded testimony in *Different Trains*, his piece for string quartet and tape. Reich took speech fragments from testimony and made them the basis of his composition, where the melody as much as the semantic content of speech fragments is highlighted by their being played repeatedly and doubled by instruments.[33]

In his essay on *Different Trains*, Stephen Frosh says that Reich's technique

> disembodies the voice and converts it into a sound pattern that undoubtedly carries meaning; yet this meaning is no longer that of the story told by the survivors in their Holocaust testimony [...] It is rather a kind of evocation of a "more than," an excess that is stage-managed in Reich's piece, a flow of echoes back and forth, sometimes static and sometimes propelled violently forward, in which the uncanny nature of repetition and narrative irresolution underpinned by the thick texture of musical sound replaces any simple linear reconstruction of what a witness might say.[34]

Müller's voice-over is an 'acousmatic' voice, a voice whose origin is indeterminate. Mladen Dolar calls this kind of vocal sounding 'a voice in search of an origin, in search of a body, but even when it finds its body, it turns out that this doesn't quite work, the voice doesn't stick to the body'.[35] While Dolar's paradoxical point is that all voices fail to some degree to 'stick' to their bodies, it is true of Müller in a far more obvious way: his voice-over is not the voice that comes out of his body. Its cadences and inflections are those of the editing suite, indexed in part to the movements of the camera, not to the gestures that work alongside it in the sequences where he is shown speaking to Lanzmann. This hearing of the voice aside from its meaning, aside from the body that produces it, is a frequently used technique in Lanzmann's film: from the beginning where voices off-screen in Polish respond to the voice of Simon Srebrnik,[36] to the end where Antek's (Itzhak Zuckerman) words play over a close-up of his face (with a complex relationship of word and body here, because he describes the body that is seen—the face of a heavy drinker). With Müller, this detachment and reattachment of voice to body is taken to its extreme.

Embodiment

Marianne Hirsch and Leo Spitzer claim that women's voices in *Shoah* are usually detached from their bodies whereas male voices are 'embodied and authoritative'.[37] This is a valid assertion, but it does not quite describe the full spectrum of what male voices do. It might be better to say that while male voices often are detached from the bodies that produce them, they are eventually grounded in those bodies again. In Müller's case, his bodily presence is certainly significant. As the first sequence shows, he often makes use of gestures, with some of them likely to have been used to help Lanzmann to understand.[38] In *Orality and Literacy*, Walter Ong recognizes how crucial gesture is to speech, drawing attention to the way 'spoken words are always modifications of a total, existential situation, which always engages the body'.[39] When Müller explains how he saw Aumeier, Grabner and Hössler persuade Jews to undress and enter the gas chambers, he animates this section as its story teller, his bodily gestures replicating those of the SS men as they spoke from the roof of the crematorium to the Polish Jews below and acting out their dialogue.[40] Müller even gestures to show what happened in the gas chamber itself, indicating the layers of bodies (with his hand out, palm down), people trying to break through the door (he swings his left fist outward), babies' skulls being crushed (he touches his head). He enacts how he considers people acted and suffered within this space.

Embodiment presses much more heavily on these sequences than on accounts from others. Only Müller 'embodies' the gas chamber in this way. The other people able to bear witness to the aftermath of gassing like this are the survivors from Chełmno, Mordechai Podchlebnik and Simon Srebrnik. Podchlebnik cries as he says that he saw his own family had been gassed. The extreme close-up on his face (chosen to capture these emotions) conceals what his gestures are (although they seem minimal) and gives little indication that Lanzmann is sitting next to him and holding his shoulder (as the outtakes show much more explicitly).[41] Srebrnik also describes bodies coming out of the gas van, but says that he felt nothing. He is shown in full shot walking round the site of cremation, where nothing is left, not recreating or indicating what was there.[42] Only Müller is shown in medium close-up, registering his gestures, a choice that may simply stem from the fact that he makes gestures, but also from the fact that he is less emotionally expressive than Podchlebnik, and not filmed in any significant setting like Srebrnik.

Hirsch and Spitzer's comment also overlooks the forms of embodiment that are created in the dialectic between voice and camera. In the case of Müller, the camerawork itself often replicates, or can be read as, bodily movement, sometimes his own, sometimes that of the perpetrators he describes. The sequence describing his entry into the SK uses a mobile camera, whose operator walks to the crematorium in the same way that Müller did.[43] In the moment when Hössler et al. are able to deceive the Jews into getting undressed, the camera moves round the crematorium building of Auschwitz, getting onto the roof in the same way as the SS men. Here, the camera looks down to where the crowd from the transport would be, assuming the position of the SS officers, replicating their Nazi gaze. The cobbled space is, however, empty. There is nothing to visually objectify, and it is left to Müller's words and (later) gestures to repopulate the scene.

The camera also semi-enacts the route he describes people taking through the crematoria in Auschwitz, after the shot depicting the model of Crematorium 1 (II). It walks into the ruins of the crematorium, descending the steps, manoeuvring over the rubble in the undressing room and clambering onto the collapsed roof to look at the gas chamber.[44] As Müller compares Crematoria 3 (IV) and 4 (V), the camera passes through Crematorium 4 (V), slight jolts indicating again that it is being carried by someone walking (which rhymes too with the footprints in the snow).[45] The camera indicates bodily movements as it enters and moves around these spaces, even if some of that movement (e.g. climbing over ruins) is entirely different from what victims at the time would have done. These bodily movements are readable and/or necessary because of the camera operator's interaction with the remains of Auschwitz.[46]

Embodiment, we would therefore suggest, is a much more complicated process than Hirsch and Spitzer make it. Müller's embodiment and gestural economy come about from his personal dispositions but also Lanzmann's own imperfect grasp of German, the fact that he is indoors rather than outdoors, his own relationship with what he saw and choices about how to film him, possibly based on his own affective regime. It is also the result of the situation of the environment of Auschwitz itself, a location that contains many remains that affect the way that it is filmed and that calls attention to the body of the person filming it. Bringing these elements together is what gives Müller his bodily presence in *Shoah*.

Müller's Unique Position

Müller's story is given significance in its placement in relation to other testimonies. Lanzmann tended to group him with Abraham Bomba, Richard Glazar and Rudolf Vrba as the heroes of his film. But Müller is placed in such a way that his testimony often fits with that of what might be called 'technical specialists', people explaining the workings of the systems of extermination: the SS guard Franz Suchomel and the historian Raul Hilberg. Müller is the last of the 'heroes' to appear in the film.[47] He takes his place in the fourth circle of chaos and invention, rather than the third of the shock of arrival.[48] Richard Glazar appears after half an hour, Abraham Bomba after fifty minutes. Müller does not appear until well over two hours into the film. Glazar and Bomba, both woven together with the words of bystanders such as Czesław Borowy and the semi-participant Henryk Gawkowski,[49] tell a story of arriving at Treblinka and of being selected to be part of the workers in the death camp. This story of arrival is much the same: their seeing commandos of Jews with armbands, standing naked and being pulled out of the line, learning that everyone who had come with them was dead, spending the first night in the barracks when some people committed suicide. There is also some reference to Auschwitz, but the equivalent of this story of arrival is provided by Rudolf Vrba.

All of these moments of arrival are indexed to transport technology, especially trains of course but also linked to movements of cars. The entire sequence about arrival is woven through with Henryk Gawkowski driving the train that Lanzmann hired, as well as cameras moving along rails, such as those leading up to the gates of Birkenau. In addition, cars stand in for or call to mind trains, especially up the track to Treblinka where there are no longer any rails (with sound as well as speed indicating that this is a vehicle).[50] But it works at other points too. Lanzmann is shown driving past the sign for Treblinka and parking next to the rail lines while Bomba talks about the Jewish dream for freedom, his experience in the ghetto and being transported by rail.[51] Even the shots from a car driving round Manhattan or over Brooklyn Bridge seem chosen to evoke rail travel, the girders at the side of and above the roadway rhyming with the rail tracks, while Rudolf Vrba speaks about trains arriving at Birkenau.[52] Hand in hand with these technologized movements through landscape are the camera movements that are ones of panning and zooming, especially around the field of Treblinka, turns to the right and left and zooms in, almost always fixing on the giant monument in the centre of the field, marking the Jews of Warsaw at the location of the gas chamber. Also linked to these ideas are a firm distinction on the inside and outside of the 'camp'. With Mr. Piwoński at Sobibór, Lanzmann, the camera operator and the interpreter Barbara Janicka walk in and out of the space where the Sobibór camp existed: one side (outside) is the Polish side, and the other side (inside) is death.[53]

The recreation of Müller's entry into the Auschwitz SK takes quite a different form. His arrival at the camp does not coincide with his selection for the SK. He moves *out* of the camp in order to enter the crematorium. He does so on foot. And, of course, there are buildings that still remain that he describes (even if that description is sometimes tailored to the sights, rather than the other way round). His speaking goes at the same pace as the camera moves, word and image indexed to each other in a much more literal way than when the film has to respond to spaces where the specific things being discussed are no longer present. Some of these differences stem from the different nature of Auschwitz, as a concentration camp as well as a death camp. With Treblinka and Sobibór, the entry to the camp can parallel the entry into the gas chamber. With Auschwitz, this is less straightforward—even though for many this was their experience. But Auschwitz is also different in what remains. Here, the talk of language animating an empty landscape is far less appropriate than the way Treblinka, Chełmno, Sobibór and Bełżec are filmed.[54] The Auschwitz crematorium is (in some sense) still there and does not need to be evoked in the metonymic/metaphorical way that the gas chambers of Treblinka are.

When Müller appears alongside Raul Hilberg and Franz Suchomel, he provides knowledge of how the perpetrators improvised and improved upon their technology of murder and systems of processing victims. In this sequence, he is the only survivor who speaks. When he talks over the model of Crematorium 1 (II) in the Second Era, he only describes the layout and logic of the crematorium, showing how the improvisation and invention discussed in First Era has reached its culmination in the design of this building.[55] Apart from the mention of SS men at the beginning, the only references to people are in terms of capacity. It is purely a systematic account of how the crematorium was designed. The nearest equivalent to this is Suchomel pointing out areas on a map of Treblinka, although that map is shown in a much more piecemeal style. The model of the crematorium is dwelt on at length, the camera lingering over its representations of dead and dying people in the gas chamber. It is Müller who provides the impersonal facts while the model populates it.

It is also possible to compare the way that Müller's speech is matched to images to one of Lanzmann's other witnesses. Both Müller and Rudolf Vrba speak over a pan over Stobierski's model of Crematorium 1 (II).[56] The camera moves somewhat more quickly the second time, taking under two minutes to traverse the space that previously took two- and three-quarters. The footage seems to have been sped up, as the camera movements in both shots match exactly. This greater speed, although not really noticeable in a normal viewing after so much time between the first showing and its repetition, is nonetheless noteworthy in tandem with an awareness of the heavy editing of Müller's words in the previous version. The soundtrack was, it would seem, not cut straightforwardly to fit with the pictures. Lanzmann and Postec were prepared to play with the speed of camera movement to fit the words spoken. In the second case, Vrba's higher-pitched, sardonic tones (ironically accusing himself of 'anarchic and individualistic activity' in escaping from Auschwitz) seem to have been met with a faster rhythm of both sound and picture editing. It is also likely that Müller's words are made to play so slowly to fit with the tempo of his voice-overs over the terrain of Auschwitz and Birkenau.

What happens with Müller, far more than any other witness, is that his words cause us to enter the crematorium buildings again and again. This constant repetition plays out conceptually, but also in visual parallels and replayings, and aural/verbal parallels and replayings. In his first appearance, he speaks of his first entrance into the Auschwitz I crematorium.

The word 'Schornstein' is repeated. His contextualization, an explanation of what the later Birkenau crematoria were like, is accompanied with a zoom in on the ruins of Crematorium 1 (II) and an information sign displaying a reproduction of a Nazi-era photograph of the building and plan of its layout. These words are recycled in his explanation in Second Era of the layout of the crematoria. The structure of this sequence is to enter the building twice: in the explanation and then in the description of how people came through the murder process. The fact that he describes both the layout of 1 (II) and 2 (III) and that of 3 (IV) and 4 (V) means that the camera enters one and then the other. As he describes the fate of the Czech family camp, we enter the ruins of Crematorium 1 (II) again, with him going into the gas chamber. And as he leaves us, immediately after his last words, the camera pans once more over the model of Crematorium 1 (II), going 'into' the undressing room.

This repetition is the form that much of the film takes: trains, signs, railway tracks and gateways. But Müller more than anyone else is the figure who causes, enables and is subjected to the repeated entry into the crematoria and gas chambers. This is an effect of the technology of the film, of the material fact of sound recordings that are repeated, recontextualized and repurposed. But it is also an effect of what happened in Auschwitz as opposed to the other camps. Müller survived for long enough to become an expert in the ways that the crematoria operated and so was able to talk repeatedly and in detail about them. It is this role of 'technical specialist' that the film partly edits into being, but that can also be seen in the transcripts of the interview he gave to Lanzmann.

Going Back to the Archive

Although Müller's part in *Shoah* is given much of its meaning by the shape of the film, it is not fully defined by it. The film's shape inevitably threatens to collapse all the time. The size of it means that it is difficult to stand back and see what that overall shape is. The experience of duration (if it is watched all at once) inevitably means that attention wanders, that not everything can be noticed and that, inevitably, will mean that the linking concepts will not always be clear. For example, when Müller mentions the Jews of Corfu, and the film then moves to Corfu, that mention is several minutes before and is not really the focus of his point. Indeed, the film encourages and exploits that inability to follow by making some of its narratives illogical. The logic of what Müller says (especially in these points where he is edited into saying it) makes little sense apart from the pictures. Why discuss the SS men and dogs outside the crematoria before simply going on to talk about the building? Why go into such detail about the design of the Birkenau crematoria when he has simply been asked if there were no crematoria in Birkenau in May 1942? Inevitably, then, the film becomes separate moments that detach themselves in the viewers' consciousnesses from the rest of the film, or rather a relationship of separation and similarity, both a background which feels interminable and moments of extreme emotional pain. In that sense, *Shoah* might be said to be operate not just as a work of art, but also rather like an archive, a collection through which people search to find items of interest.[57]

With the 'outtakes' and transcripts collected and now available online, this archival element to *Shoah* is even more clearly visible or audible. It is possible to see the constructed nature of Müller's voice-overs. And it is also possible to see what was left out of the film. Müller's moment of 'incarnation' now looks even more of an editorial decision: the following reel shows him going back and retelling the story. It is probable that Müller did not appreciate Lanzmann's decision to include this footage of him in a state of heightened emotion as he recalls his decision to join members of the Czech family camp in the gas chamber and to die with them. Of the two versions Müller gave of this event, the later one is far more controlled. As he likely felt keeping control of his voice, of its emotional timbre, was bound up with masculinity, he would no doubt have preferred the second telling to be retained.[58] The transcript of his entire testimony to Lanzmann makes it clear that he was highly uncomfortable in the presence of men betraying extremes of emotion. Müller names one of the victims of the family camp as Jana. He describes visiting Jana's sweetheart Sascha, a Russian 'tough boy', to tell him of Jana's murder and to present him with the golden necklace she had bequeathed to him. Müller leaves once the man starts to cry, stating 'I couldn't stand to hear anymore'.[59] He leaves at the moment when emotional breakdown is registered acoustically, a moment when Sascha loses his voice, speech replaced by sobbing. In viewing *Shoah*, Müller is forced to encounter himself reduced to a state akin to that of Sascha, likely a state he viewed as emasculating.[60]

This breakthrough into incarnation can be read, therefore, as being profoundly gendered. The film has worked up to this point to associate Müller with two masculine roles: as specialist who can explain the workings of Auschwitz and as storyteller who can bring moments there to life. As Hirsch and Spitzer argue, part of what makes Müller and others who fulfilled similar roles is their masculinity. Their maleness is figured in the film as part of their being directly in contact with death (and in the case of most of his key witnesses, of being able to converse directly with Lanzmann). They show how women feature in multiple ways as mediators: as interpreters, as generators of pathos and harbingers of death without rebirth.[61] To this, we could add the way that women survivors feature primarily as transitional moments between different parts. They provide the frame round those moments which are about getting back. Women cannot 'go back'—either literally in the case of Paula Biren, or in being able to 'incarnate'.

An examination of the archive shows that this lack of mediation for men is constructed by the film. While Müller's own book goes unmentioned, Mordechai Podchlebnik does mention books, only to say that he does not read them (the one mention by a survivor of 'research' that is left in).[62] It also shows that the interview with Müller inhabits the memory of a death camp more intensely than those filmed with others. The filming process with him seems to have been far more concentrated than for other people who dealt with death. The recordings of Richard Glazar, Abraham Bomba, Simon Srebrnik and Mordechai Podchlebnik all include talk about their life before and after the 'camp'. They were also filmed in more familial locations: Srebrnik with his family in Israel, pushing some of his grandchildren on a swing, for example, or Glazar with his pet dog sitting next to him on the sofa. And all of them are at least partly filmed in an open-air location. Glazar and Bomba are both framed for part of their interview with some view of the outdoors. With both of them, a boat sailing by attracts the attention of the camera operator. Müller is indoors all the time. With Müller, the entire discussion is of nothing but Auschwitz—there is no before and no after. The whole filming session seems to have had a claustrophobic intensity that matches the subject of his discussion. This may be that Lanzmann and his team had a clear idea of what the role for Müller should be, but it also fits with (and so may be the result of) Müller's own record of giving his story. With most of the other witnesses, some element of easing into the subject takes place. Lanzmann talks to Bomba about his life in Israel or Glazar about his life before the war. With Müller, the fact that he had told this story many times before might itself have functioned as a kind of 'comfort zone'.

Lanzmann and Postec's editing decisions concentrated much more heavily on the elements recorded earlier: the majority of what appears in the first half of the transcript and only a few snippets from the later material. These are points, especially at the beginning, where Müller tells the story the way that he has done it before. What goes into the film seems therefore to be partly dictated by the existing archive, by what Müller himself had written and testified to previously. The outtakes show many ways in which memory is mediated, the past not simply relived in the present. Key to these, we would suggest, are the moments we highlighted in *Matters of Testimony*: the points when Lanzmann and Müller read through and look at texts.[63] One of them is the story of the '600 Boys' from the Scrolls of Auschwitz, which Müller reads aloud and finds very difficult to finish. The other is their looking through a book—the English translation of Müller's own book—that includes plans of the crematoria and photographs, including one of the four taken by 'Alex'.

Müller is shown, therefore, relying on the archive to prompt and inform his memory, and even, we would argue, 'incarnating' someone else's memory, with some of that incarnation actually created by the process of transmission rather than simply the originary event: his hesitations and stumbles speak of psychological pain, but also of material damage to the manuscript. There is, therefore, an immense network of mediation (and thus of transmission) in the moments of 'incarnation' that occur in the film. In addition to the technologies of editing and filming that we have discussed above, we could also include the architecture of Auschwitz, and the means by which its remains were/are tended to, and indeed representations, both those that figure in the film (such as the plan, photograph and model of Crematorium 1 (II) that Lanzmann films in Birkenau and Auschwitz)[64] and those that do not (such as the plans and photographs reproduced in Müller's own book).

The editing works to conceal this: Müller's own book, the photographs and the story from the 'Scrolls of Auschwitz' were all left out, while almost everything else from the first eighteen reels is left in. As a result, we might say that at one and the same time, Müller's testimony is the most shaped (edited into a form different from what he actually said) and the most shaping (following the form of what he had written before). The question of control is important here, but we also wish to note that *both* of these elements are reliant upon technologies of transmission and mediation. Müller's impersonal role of specialist is edited into being (while also reliant on elements of his own experience and personality). And his ability to tell some of these stories relies on his having written them, worked them through perhaps, before. This form of mediation is figured as feminine in the film, but it is in fact present all the way through—at times hidden in plain sight or in plain hearing.

Conclusion

The existence of mediation in plain sight in Müller's stories, descriptions and moment of incarnation is also, we would argue, present in perhaps the most famous scene in *Shoah*: Abraham Bomba being filmed in a barber's shop while telling of his experience cutting women's hair in the gas chambers of Treblinka. As with many other points, it is an encounter with women, one between a friend of his and his relatives that reaches the point of indescribability. After about two minutes of silence, and Lanzmann pleading with him to go on, Bomba continues his testimony. Just before he does, he murmurs two sentences in Yiddish to his friend in the barber's chair. Sue Vice reads his speaking in Yiddish as 'consitut[ing] the moment of Bomba's being taken over by the past, just as his recovery and return [...] can only be signalled in the English of his post-war life'.[65] However, the content of what Bomba says does not quite match this reading. On repeated listening to the Yiddish words that Bomba speaks, we believe that they are: 'At such a point I have to collapse. The same as in the in the Düss- in the in the court in in Germany, too' (*'Aza min, in aza min portsye muz ikh tsuzamenbrekhn. Di zelbe zakh af di af di Duess- af di af di sond in in Daytshland oykhet'*).[66] This reference to the court in Germany is, we believe, the second Treblinka trial in Düsseldorf in 1964, where Bomba gave testimony.[67] At this trial, having borne witness, Bomba was in the audience while another survivor told of his family's suffering. Bomba himself is reported to have fled the courtroom at this point, crying.[68]

To our eyes, Bomba looks to be speaking to his friend, who does not speak English. Bomba is therefore not likely to be saying anything about particular details he has mentioned before to Lanzmann, but could well be simply saying something about his own behaviour, explaining himself or perhaps even reassuring the friend. Bomba seems, therefore, not to be (simply) back in the gas chamber of Treblinka, but to be (also) reliving his experience of bearing witness at a previous time: a point about fifteen years before. If that is so, it may well be this remembered moment that supports him in bearing witness again as much as anything provided for him by Lanzmann and his film crew. Rather than this being a collapse together of two moments (the past and present as Lanzmann phrases it), the two moments are mediated by a third, a transitional time that makes their meeting possible. Bomba's own post-war life history, therefore, entirely excluded from the film when Lanzmann is aware of it, manifests in this moment in the film, in a language that lies beyond Lanzmann's control. And it is part of Bomba's way of remembering, giving him a stepping stone on his way back to (or perhaps back from) this memory.[69]

Our argument in this chapter has been that this is true of Müller too, that his past is mediated by multiple strategies, including moments where he gave testimony before. And, we would argue, one of the mediators is the site of Auschwitz itself: not a non-place in the way that Sobibór and Bełżec feature in the film, but a site that materially, and patently, works to transmit memory.[70] This material existence of the site impinges on its chief witness, Müller, both his voice, whose tempo is moulded to fit its remnants, and even his bodily presence, constructed in the dialectic between voice-over and synch sound, camera movement and physical gesture. The memory of the Auschwitz Sonderkommando constructed by *Shoah* is therefore not the same as that of their equivalents in other sites. It is one that is much less under their own control, because of the nature of the site itself and its history.

Part of that history is the presence of other prisoners, other stories about the SK. As we argued in the introduction and in Chapter 6, this was more salient for the Sonderkommando of Auschwitz than their equivalents at other sites. Both male and female survivors were able to bear witness to what Birkenau was like and even to their encounters with members of the SK. Whereas Abraham Bomba is left to speak (so far as he can) for the women who were victims at Treblinka, women survivors from Birkenau did have stories that could be linked to those of the SK. This includes the stories from the women of Kanada commando that we discussed in the previous chapter. But there is a female survivor who could have taken a similar role in *Shoah* too. Ruth Elias, a survivor of Auschwitz and Theresienstadt, is the person who starts telling the story of the Czech family camp and the liquidation of half of its inhabitants in March 1944. Elias speaks for only the first four minutes of the approximately half-hour long sequence. After that, the story is handed on to Rudolf Vrba and Filip Müller.[71] Vrba provides the overview and even what might be called theorization; Müller's role is to be the witness, including the moment of 'incarnation' which is its climax. The role given to Elias by the editing of *Shoah* is one of ignorance and incredulity: 'I didn't know about Auschwitz anything', 'we didn't believe'.[72] The latter of these statements is edited to put more emphasis on the fact that she is told that Auschwitz is a '*Vernichtungslager*' (extermination camp) by 'men': points where she calls them 'people' in the original recording are edited out.[73]

Examination of the outtakes, and of the recent use of her testimony to form one of the films from *The Four Sisters* (2017), shows that Elias has her own story about what happened in March 1944, including hearing 'Hatikvah' and 'Kde domov můj', the Zionist (later Israeli) and Czech anthems, that Müller reports hearing in *Shoah*. A more complex relationship between belief, knowledge, denial and hope, what Elias calls the 'struggle in believing', is further brought out in the more recent edit.[74] Elias interweaves this story of the murder of her fellow Czechs in the gas chambers with an account of the experience of life in the family camp, including pointless labour, minimal rations, sexual violence and her own pregnancy. None of this kind of knowledge counts for *Shoah*. What does count is the eyewitness testimony borne by Müller himself from within the chamber, grounded in his familiarity with its technical workings and given weight by his emotional breakdown. Such a breakthrough from 'masculine' expertise to the symbolic emasculation of silence figures trauma as an assault on emotionally restrained masculinity. Masculinity is, therefore, central to *Shoah*'s schema of representation. Trauma is made to manifest its power in its capacity to break Müller as a man.[75]

As Shoshana Felman points out, Müller's breakdown is a moment of bearing witness on behalf of women.[76] However, as we have shown, his witnessing contains much more of the 'feminine' (in the film's terms) than that. One moment in particular might sum this up: the splicing of the words 'vergasen'/'fargazn' into one of Müller's technical descriptions of the gas chambers, which the film works to associate with a masculine position. In its original context, Müller is citing the terrified words of someone else, a woman who was told by one of the SK that she was going to die and ran round telling everyone else. Müller even seems to quote her in Yiddish, rather than German: '*Men vet undz hargenen ... me vet undz fargazn*' ['They're going to murder us ... they're going to gas us']. That moment, chosen (it would seem) for its sonic quality, haunts the supposedly objective description of the gas chamber, the sound of it and the language of it, infusing it with the lament (which also transmits objective information) of a woman. Here, Müller's seemingly dispassionate account of his former workplace, the site of his slave labour, retains an echo of one of the Jewish women he witnessed murdered there. The voice of bronze carries a memory of the woman's last moments, of Müller's recognition of her perturbed emotions, enabling both his feelings and hers to still register amid the facts.

Notes

1. The transcript of Lanzmann's interview with Müller is available at: https://collections.ushmm.org/film_findingaids/RG-60.5012_01_trs_de.pdf.
2. Scan, transcript and translation of testimony available at: https://www.zapisyterroru.pl (search: Filip Müller).
3. Transcript and recording of testimony available at: http://www.auschwitz-prozess.de/ (Day 97).
4. Filip Müller, *Sonderbehandlung: Drei Jahre in den Krematorien und Gaskammern von Auschwitz*, literary collaboration with Helmut Freitag (Munich: Steinhausen, 1979), pp. 9–44 and Müller, *Eyewitness Auschwitz: Three Years in the Gas Chambers*, trans. Susanne Flatauer (Chicago: Ivan R. Dee, 1999), pp. 1–26. The English translation was published before the German version and had certainly been printed by the time Lanzmann interviewed Müller, as they were filmed looking through a copy of the book together. The edition was published in the UK in 1979 by Routledge and Kegan Paul, under the title *Auschwitz Inferno*. We are grateful to Andreas Kilian for identifying this book for us.
5. Lanzmann edited out the story of the tea, but Müller included it in his interview with him as he had done at all his other times. This was the moment where, perhaps, he could have acted differently and not ended up in the Sonderkommando—at least in his understanding of the event.
6. This wall, as Georges Didi-Huberman notes, is not the original but a reconstruction. *Écorces* (Paris: Minuit, 2011), p. 24. Didi-Huberman is critical of the authorities of Auschwitz for not including a sign foregrounding this reality.
7. The chimney and the furnaces are reconstructions as the Nazis dismantled these once mass killing was transferred to Birkenau. Indeed, Müller himself explained this at the Frankfurt Auschwitz Trial, saying that the original chimney was round. 1. Frankfurter Auschwitz-Prozess »Strafsache gegen Mulka u.a.«, 4 Ks 2/63 Landgericht Frankfurt am Main 97. Verhandlungstag, 5.10.1964.
8. For further discussion of the significance of gesture in this description by Müller, see Nicholas Chare, 'Gesture in *Shoah*,' *Journal for Cultural Research* 19.1 (2015): 37–39.

9. Ziva Postec, 'As Editor: *Shoah* Paris 1979–1985'. http://www.posteczivа.com/Shoah.php (accessed 29 January 2019).
10. Rémy Besson discusses how towards the end of 1981 much footage was shot at Auschwitz to use with this section of the interview. The filming was consciously structured around Müller's account, but when *Shoah* was edited, it was easier to alter the soundtrack rather than the visuals. Besson speaks of cuts in the soundtrack but, as he goes on to briefly discuss, the process of linking Müller's words with the images of Auschwitz was much more complex than this. Besson, *Shoah: Une double reference? Des faits au film, du film auz faits* (Paris: MkF, 2017), pp. 107–108.
11. See Chare, 'Gesture in *Shoah*' for a discussion of gesture's significance in addition to words and as a possible form of 'working through' the past.
12. Claude Lanzmann, *Le Lièvre de Patagonie* (Paris: Folio, 2010), p. 607. Claude Lanzmann, *The Patagonian Hare*, trans. Frank Wynne (London: Atlantic, 2012), p. 422.
13. Lanzmann, *The Patagonian Hare*, p. 422. Lanzmann, *Le Lièvre de Patagonie*, p. 607.
14. Homère, *L'Iliade*, trans. Eugène Lasserre (Paris: Garnier, 1965), p. 105. Lanzmann has discussed *Shoah* in relation to Greek mythology, suggesting the film could be viewed as akin to the Delphic oracle. Claude Lanzmann, 'Autoportrait à quatre-vingt-dix ans,' in *Claude Lanzmann: Un voyant dans le siècle*, ed. Juliette Simont (Paris: Gallimard, 2017), p. 277.
15. Book 7, Chapter 4, Aristotle, *Politics*, 2nd ed., trans. Carnes Lord (Chicago: Chicago University Press, 2013), p. 195.
16. Lanzmann planned to film Paisikovic fishing in silence and provide his story in voiceover. Lanzmann would therefore lend his own voice to a man he described as 'a slab [*un bloc*] of silence'. *Patagonian Hare*, p. 422 (*Lièvre de Patagonie*, p. 608).
17. Marc Chevrie and Hervé Le Roux, 'Site and Speech: An Interview with Claude Lanzmann About *Shoah*,' in *Claude Lanzmann's Shoah: Key Essays*, ed. Stuart Liebman (Oxford: Oxford University Press, 2007), p. 45.
18. What Müller tells in about a minute and fifteen seconds in the unedited footage takes a minute and thirty-five in the final cut, even though what he says has been edited down from 110 to 84 words. https://collections.ushmm.org/search/catalog/irn1003921 (1.10.32–1.11.45—including a question from Lanzmann) *Shoah* Disc 1, 2.14.46–2.16.20. Overall, this means a change from 90 words to 54 words per minute.
19. German text adapted from Claude Lanzmann, *Shoah*, trans. Nina Börnsen and Anna Kamp, Kindle ebook (Reinbek bei Hamburg: Rowohlt, 2011), with reference to the transcript. Vertical lines indicate cuts in the soundtrack tape. English text from *Shoah: The Complete Text of the Acclaimed Holocaust Film*, trans. A. Whitelaw and W. Byron, with corrections by Claude Lanzmann (Boston: Da Capo, 1995), pp. 50–51.

20. *Shoah* Disc 3, 49.40–53.55.
21. The United States Holocaust Memorial Museum (USHMM) would subsequently commission Stobierski to build a similar model for them. The model corrects some minor inaccuracies that are present in the version displayed at the Auschwitz Museum. The cover image for this book is a detail of the USHMM version of the model.
22. Briefly, the camera also zooms in on members of the SK in the model working at the ovens. Müller's voice is here given a 'body', albeit a body with its back turned to the camera.
23. The first two paragraphs use material from pp. 25, 37, 35, 33, 45, 34, 45 and 33 of the transcript (in this order).
24. The French publication of *Shoah* uses the exact same phrasing for these two moments, albeit with different lineation. Claude Lanzmann, *Shoah* (Paris: Gallimard, 1985), pp. 94 and 177. The German indicates the difference (although it tidies up Müller and Lanzmann's German). Lanzmann, *Shoah*, trans. Börnsen and Kamp, locations 1045–1053 and 2216–2224.
25. We transcribe these last words as Yiddish, because it seems to us that Müller is closer to Yiddish than German here. 'Bis drei' comes from the original statement but is edited in a different way from the first version. In the original, Müller repeats the word 'bis' (up to). The first version uses one of these utterances, the second the other.
26. Laub, 'An Event without a Witness: Truth, Testimony and Survival,' in *Testimony: Crises of Witnessing in Literature, Psychoanalysis, and History*, eds. Shoshana Felman and Dori Laub (New York and London: Routledge, 1992), p. 76.
27. Lawrence Langer, *Holocaust Testimonies: The Ruins of Memory* (New Haven: Yale University Press, 1991), p. 210n.18. While Langer in fact acknowledges in the following endnote that he has learnt that Müller's statements were edited, he characterizes this as caused by the fact that Müller 'stammers' (n. 19). This (at least second-hand) explanation is not an accurate account of how Müller speaks in the recordings, and by describing Lanzmann's actions as 'patiently edit[ing] out the speech impediments', it implies that he was removing obstacles from Müller's self-expression.
28. Francine Kaufmann, 'Interview et interprétation consécutive dans le film Shoah, de Claude Lanzmann,' *Meta* 38.4 (December 1993): 665. See also André Habib, 'Delay, Estrangement, Loss: The Meanings of Translation in Claude Lanzmann's *Shoah* (1985),' *SubStance* 44.2 (2015): 108–128.
29. He also appears to have rejected Lanzmann's subsequent efforts to contact him. Claude L. says of Müller post the release of *Shoah*, 'I phoned him but I lost his trace' (39:57). Claude L. interviewed by Dori Laub and Laurel Vlock on 5 May 1986. Fortunoff Video Archive for Holocaust Testimonies. HVT-700.

30. Amy Lawrence, *Echo and Narcissus: Women's Voices in Classical Hollywood Cinema* (Berkeley: University of California Press, 1991), p. 23.
31. In fact, some of the 's' from 'alles' is perceptible after the 'war' and before the 'auf' in the reconstituted utterance.
32. The quotations are each etched onto individual sheets of copper which bear oil paintings of landscapes inspired by *Shoah*. There are fourteen paintings in total. The entire work is held at the Jewish Museum in New York.
33. Even Reich, however, argues that phrases from Holocaust survivors 'cannot be "played" with in the same manner' as other speech recordings and that 'it seemed appropriate *not* to repeat what was said'. Steve Reich, 'Answers to Questions About Different Trains,' in *Writings on Music 1965–2000*, ed. Paul Hillier (Oxford: Oxford University Press, 2002), p. 182. This is not to say that there are repetitions in the second movement, but that they are less frequent than in the other two.
34. Stephen Frosh, 'Different Trains: An Essay in Memorializing,' *American Imago* 74.1 (Spring 2017): 18.
35. Mladen Dolar, *A Voice and Nothing More* (Cambridge, MA: MIT Press, 2006), pp. 60–61. Cited in Frosh, 'Different Trains'. The term 'acousmatic' comes from Michel Chion, *L'audio-vision: Son et image au cinéma* (Paris: Armand Colin, 1991). See also Marianne Hirsch and Leo Spitzer, 'Gendered Translations: Claude Lanzmann's *Shoah*,' in *Claude Lanzmann's Shoah: Key Essays*, ed. Stuart Liebman (Oxford: Oxford University Press, 2007), pp. 175–190.
36. We use the spelling in line with what Srebrnik himself used rather than the spelling in the film.
37. Hirsch and Spitzer, 'Gendered Translations,' p. 188n.8.
38. Lanzmann says that 'I could only speak to them in a foreign language; this estrangement — another term for the distance I spoke of earlier — was for me, paradoxically, a necessary condition to approach the horror'. *Patagonian Hare*, p. 422 (*Lièvre de Patagonie*, p. 607).
39. Walter Ong, *Orality and Literacy* (London: Routledge, 2002), p. 67.
40. Bomba also provides dialogue in direct speech, but it is much less dramatized, with much less of an attempt to characterize the speakers. Disc 1, 1:46:35–1:47:10.
41. *Shoah* Disc 1, 21:15–22:20.
42. *Shoah* Disc 2, 1:45:40–1:46:40. His gestures in this sequence are mostly out of frame and are used to indicate what he saw in the Łódź ghetto.
43. Here, the motion of the camera replicates the part that is semi-imaginable: entry into the SK. The rest of the sequence has a greater deal of impersonality.
44. *Shoah* Disc 3, 54:13-56-57:12.
45. *Shoah* Disc 3, 58:36–59:56.

46. Jan Karski's testimony also involved some replication of his speech by the camera, but to a far lesser extent: going through a gateway and looking at some buildings on the site of the Warsaw Ghetto (Disc 4 around 1.03). Karski's gestures are also significant. He re-enacts the actions of the Bund leader, a member of the Hitler Youth and a dying man in the ghetto. In later films, *Sobibor* (2001) relies much more (perhaps too much) on this re-enactment of Yehuda Lerner's words. In *The Last of the Unjust* (2013), Lanzmann's own body acts out some of the described movement in the spaces of Theresienstadt.
47. In 1983, Lanzmann conceived of five individuals as recurring characters in the film (Suchomel, Bomba, Müller, Vrba and Glazar). Suchomel is therefore intended as the regular villain of the piece. These five names were inscribed on a whiteboard in the cutting room for *Shoah* as can be seen in film footage David Perlov shot of his daughter Yael Perlman at work helping Postec with editing. 'Claude Lanzmann, Ziva Postec, and Yael Perlman editing *Shoah* 1983' USHMM RG-60-0151. Film ID: 4271. Accessed at USHMM. Courtesy of Re-Voir.
48. Postec identified the first four circles organizing the film as: first circle: 'the difficulty to talk' and 'erasing traces' (45 minutes); the second circle: 'the absence of Jews, or the Polish memory'; the third circle: 'The first shock of the Jews'; the fourth circle: 'the Nazis get organized - the initial chaos, followed by a pioneering and inventive mind!' Postec, 'As Editor'. See also Besson, *Shoah*, pp. 83–86.
49. Here, we follow the standard Polish spellings of Borowy and Henryk, rather than those given in the film.
50. *Shoah* Disc 1, 1.22.52–1.24.42.
51. *Shoah* Disc 1, 50.53–52.39.
52. *Shoah* Disc 1, 1.31.35–1.32.31. The sound is again very important and kept high in the mix.
53. Lanzmann, *Shoah*, p. 64.
54. Bełżec appears late on in the film, in Disc 4, 1:42:04–1:44:10, during Raul Hilberg's discussion of Adam Czerniaków's knowledge of death camps.
55. *Shoah* Disc 2, 49:40–53:32. See also Suchomel's comparisons between Bełżec, Treblinka and Auschwitz. *Shoah* Disc 2, 2:04–3:05.
56. *Shoah* Disc 3, 33:21–35:16.
57. Indeed, Dominick LaCapra's interpretation of it might be said to indicate that fact. He suggests that readings that focus on Vrba and Glazar would be different from ones that focus on the moments of incarnation. LaCapra, 'Lanzmann's *Shoah*: "Here There Is No Why",' in *Claude Lanzmann's Shoah: Key Essays*, ed. Stuart Liebman (Oxford: Oxford University Press, 2007), pp. 225–226n.19.

58. In *The Human Voice*, Anne Karpf draws attention to the pressure on men to suppress '"unmasculine" qualities in their voice'. Masculine voices are associated with authority and power. See Karpf, *The Human Voice* (New York: Bloomsbury, 2006), p. 163.
59. Müller Interview with Lanzmann Transcript, p. 76.
60. His emotional breakdown is prompted by the memory of members of the Czech family camp singing in defiance shortly before their deaths, by an acoustic memory. This is not the only reference to singing in his testimony. He also mentions Greek members of the SK signing as they pulverized ashes. Their songs were, however, monotonous [*monotonen Lieder*]. To his ear, they confirmed the unhappiness of the men. The songs were laden with negative affect. This mention of singing does not feature in *Shoah*, yet it does contribute to our emotional understanding of the SK.
61. Hirsch and Spitzer, 'Gendered Translations'. Jennifer Cazenave frames her reading of the role of women's voices in *Shoah* as a rejoinder to Hirsch and Spitzer, but it strikes us more as an extension and elaboration of their argument. Cazenave, *Genèses des figurations de la femme dans la Shoah: Voix féminines et représentations de l'Holocauste (1946–1985)*, Unpublished PhD dissertation, Northwestern University, 2011.
62. *Shoah* Disc 1, 13:23–13:30 (in Yiddish); 13:35–13:40 (translated into French). Zuzana Jurgens and Magdalena Marszałek argue that Richard Glazar also virtually quotes from his written memoir at points in his testimony. 'Zeugen und Erben der Geschichte: Der Holocaust in der tschechischen Literatur (Richard Glazar und Jáchym Topol),' in *Nach dem Vergessen*, eds. Magdalena Marszałek and Alina Molisak (Berlin: Kulturverlag Kadmos, 2010), pp. 222–223.
63. Chare and Williams, *Matters of Testimony*, pp. 217–220.
64. This image depicts the construction of Crematorium II. A copy is held by Yad Vashem, Album Number FA157/387, Item ID 66599. Again, this is not exclusive to Müller but seems to us to be most present there. Suchomel and Alfred (misnamed in the film as Anton) Spiess (a prosecutor at the Treblinka trial) both speak in front of a plan of Treblinka. Kazik and Antek speak over photographs and models of the Warsaw ghetto in the Ghetto Fighters House.
65. Sue Vice, *Shoah* (L3:05 London: BFI, 2012), p. 57. Vice probably takes the idea that Bomba repeats his words about bags in Yiddish from the French text of *Shoah*. Lanzmann, *Shoah* (French), p. 168.
66. 'Sond' is a Yiddish dialect word for court (cp. Polish *sąd*). Compare the meaning given to them by Anna Gonshor: 'In such a place one must come apart/collapse… It was the same thing at the, at the_____ in

Germany too' (quoted in Habib, 'Delay, Estrangement, Loss,' p. 126). Gonshor appears to have heard 'in aza min plats', rather than 'port-sye'. The word, 'dues', is not recognizable as a Yiddish word. The most likely explanation is that Bomba started saying something like 'at the Düsseldorf trial' before switching to 'at the court in Germany'. Thanks to Zsombor Hunyadi, Monika Polit, Alina Bothe and Hannah Pollin-Galay for discussing possible renderings of what Bomba says. While we have taken on board suggestions from them (as well as Anna Gonshor's version) about the words Bomba speaks, any errors here are our responsibility.

67. The fact Lanzmann's questioning prompts Bomba to remember his hearing courtroom testimony, specifically testimony the giving of which caused a witness distress, is noteworthy. David Perlov, who visited the cutting room for *Shoah* and filmed his daughter Yael Perlman working there, described Lanzmann's approach as 'dry, unemotional, like that of a legal prosecutor'. Lanzmann does not attend to Bomba's emotion, ignoring his entreaties to allow him to stop, subjecting him to a similarly difficult questioning. 'Claude Lanzmann, Ziva Postec, and Yael Perlman editing *Shoah* 1983' USHMM RG-60-0151. Film ID: 4271. Accessed at USHMM. Courtesy of Re-Voir.

68. Fritz Mörschbach, 'Der Zeuge stürzte weinend aus dem Gerichtsaal,' *Frankfurter Rundschau*, Tuesday, 22 December 1964, p. 3. Cited in Michael S. Bryant, *Eyewitness to Genocide: The Operation Reinhard Death Camp Trials, 1955–1966* (Knoxville: University of Tennessee Press, 2014), p. 105. The witness, Moses Rapaport, fainted shortly after. The incident happened on December 7. See 'Kollaps in Treblinka-Prozeß,' *Ludwigsburger Kreiszeitung*, 8 December 1964, p. 7 and 'U.S. Witness Collapses on Stand at Nazi Trial,' *New York Times*, 8 December 1964.

69. For a detailed reading of Bomba's testimony in *Shoah* as well as in the Shoah Foundation video archive, and discussion of his use of Yiddish, see Alina Bothe, *Die Geschichte der Shoah im virtuellen Raum: Eine Quellenkritik* (Berlin: De Gruyter, 2019), pp. 156–180.

70. For a discussion of Lanzmann's treatment of place that resists the idea of the killing sites as non-places, see George Didi-Huberman's essay 'Le lieu malgré tout' (1995). For Didi-Huberman, place persists in spite of everything in *Shoah*, functioning to bring the past into dialectical relation with the present. 'The Site, Despite Everything,' in *Claude Lanzmann's Shoah: Key Essays*, ed. Stuart Liebman (Oxford: Oxford University Press, 2007), pp. 113–123.

71. Indeed, the fact that Müller's testimony is woven together with that of Rudolf Vrba also shows the difference between Birkenau and Treblinka or Chełmno. Glazar and Bomba's, or Podchlebnik and Srebrnik's stories

are only supplemented by perpetrators and bystanders. Only Müller's testimony is matched with that of another prisoner who was not working the machinery of death. Lanzmann did film testimony from male and female survivors of Sobibór, but even in revisiting these recordings, he kept them separate: Yehuda Lerner [who is the sole witness of *Sobibór, October 14, 1943, 4 p.m.* (2001)] and Ada Lichtman [the sole witness of *The Merry Flea*, one of the films in *The Four Sisters* (2017)].
72. *Shoah* Disc 4, 0:02:57–0:03:00; 0:03:50.
73. Transcript of interview with Ruth Elias. https://collections.ushmm.org/film_findingaids/RG-60.5003_01_trs_en.pdf, p. 31. The fuller version is kept in *The Hippocratic Oath* (39:20–39:25).
74. Transcript of interview with Ruth Elias. See especially, p. 33. This particular phrase is not included in *The Hippocratic Oath*.
75. The process reveals something about Lanzmann's own masculinity and his idea of what it means to be a man. His actions towards Müller and other men in *Shoah* manifest violence. Raewynn Connell suggests that violence emerges through a relation between bodies and that questions of embodiment are therefore crucial to its understanding. This seems true of *Shoah* in which it is through visible displays of emotion prompted by Lanzmann's pressing that something of the gender dynamics of trauma as the film conceives it is brought to the fore. The director's aggressive probings express his own vision of masculinity. Connell, 'On Hegemonic Masculinity and Violence,' *Theoretical Criminology* 6.1 (2002): 94.
76. Shoshana Felman, 'In an Era of Testimony: Claude Lanzmann's *Shoah*,' *Yale French Studies* 79 (1991): 77–79.

Bibliography

Accatino, Daniela, and Cath Collins. 'Truth, Evidence, Truth: The Deployment of Testimony, Archives and Technical Data in Domestic Human Rights Trials,' *Journal of Human Rights Practice* 8 (2016): 81–100.
Adele-Marie Sarti, Wendy. *Women and Nazis: Perpetrators of Genocide and Other Crimes During Hitler's Regime, 1933–1945*. Bethesda: Academica Press, 2011.
Améry, Jean. *At the Mind's Limits*, trans. Sidney Rosenfeld and Stella P. Rosenfeld. London: Granta, 1999.
Amishai-Maisels, Ziva. *Depiction and Interpretation: The Influence of the Holocaust in the Visual Arts*. Oxford: Pergamon Press, 1993.
Arendt, Hannah. *Eichmann in Jerusalem: A Report on the Banality of Evil*. New York: Penguin, 1994.
Aristotle. *Politics*, 2nd ed., trans. Carnes Lord. Chicago: Chicago University Press, 2013.
Attwood, Feona. 'Pornography and Objectification,' *Feminist Media Studies* 4.1 (2004): 7–19.
Axelrod, Toby. *In the Camps: Teens Who Survived the Nazi Concentration Camps*. New York: Rosen Publishing, 1999.
Baer, Ulrich. *Spectral Evidence: The Photography of Trauma*. Cambridge, MA: MIT Press, 2002.
Ball, Karyn. 'Unspeakable Differences, Obscene Pleasures: The Holocaust as an Object of Desire,' *Women in German Yearbook* 19 (2003): 20–49.

Bar-Itzhak, Haya. 'Women in the Holocaust: The Story of a Jewish Woman Who Killed a Nazi in a Concentration Camp: A Folkloristic Perspective,' *Fabula* 50.1/2 (2009): 67–77.

Barad, Karen. 'Posthumanist Performativity: Toward an Understanding of How Matter Comes to Matter,' *Signs* 28.3 (2003): 801–831.

Baxandall, Michael. *Patterns of Intention: On the Historical Explanation of Pictures.* New Haven: Yale University Press, 1985.

Baxandall, Michael. *Giotto and the Orators: Humanist Observers of Painting in Italy and the Discovery of Pictorial Composition 1350–1450.* Oxford: Clarendon Press, 1986.

Baxandall, Michael. *Painting and Experience in Fifteenth-Century Italy*, 2nd ed. Oxford: Oxford University Press, 1988.

Baxter, Richard. *Women of the Gestapo.* London: Quality Press, 1943.

Bazyler, Michael J., and Frank M. Tuerkheimer. *Forgotten Trials of the Holocaust.* New York: New York University Press, 2014.

Bender, John, and Michael Marrinan. *The Culture of Diagram.* Stanford: Stanford University Press, 2010.

Benjamin, Walter. 'The Work of Art in the Age of Mechanical Reproduction,' in *Illuminations*, ed. Hannah Arendt, trans. Harry Zorn. London: Pimlico, 1999, pp. 211–244.

Bergen, Doris. 'Sexual Violence in the Holocaust: Unique and Typical?' in *Lessons and Legacies VII: The Holocaust in International Perspective*, ed. Dagmar Herzog. Evanston: Northwestern University Press, 2006, pp. 179–200.

Besson, Rémy. *Shoah: Une double reference? Des faits au film, du film aux faits.* Paris: MkF, 2017.

Bettelheim, Bruno. *The Informed Heart.* London: Penguin, 1986.

Bilski, Emily. 'Art During the Holocaust,' in *Kunst und Holocaust: Bildliche Zeugen vom Ende der westlichen Kultur*, eds. D. Hoffmann and K. Ermert. Rehburg-Loccum: Evangelische Akademie Loccum, 1990, pp. 29–72.

Bilsky, Leora. 'The Eichmann Trial: Towards a Jurisprudence of Eyewitness Testimony of Atrocities,' *Journal of International Criminal Justice* 12 (2014): 27–57.

Bloch, Claudette. 'Les femmes à Auschwitz,' in *Témoignages sur Auschwitz*. Paris: Éditions de l'amicale des déportés d'Auschwitz, 1946, p. 22.

Bloch, Marc. *The Historian's Craft*, trans. Peter Putnam. New York: Vintage, 1953.

Bloxham, Douglas. *Genocide on Trial: War Crimes, Trials and the Formation of Holocaust History and Memory.* Oxford: Oxford University Press, 2001.

Bloxham, Donald. 'British War Crimes Trial Policy in Germany, 1945–1957: Implementation and Collapse,' *Journal of British Studies* 42.1 (January 2003): 91–118.

Bloxham, Donald. 'From Streicher to Sawoniuk: The Holocaust in the Courtroom,' in *The Historiography of the Holocaust*, ed. Dan Stone. Basingstoke: Palgrave Macmillan, 2004, pp. 397–419.
Bondy, Ruth. 'Women in Theresienstadt and Birkenau,' in *Women in the Holocaust*, eds. Dalia Ofer and Lenore J. Weitzman. New Haven: Yale University Press, 1998, pp. 310–327.
Bos, Pascale Rachel. 'Women and the Holocaust: Analyzing Gender Difference,' in *Experience and Expression: Women, Nazis, and the Holocaust*, eds. Elizabeth R. Baer and Myrna Goldenberg. Detroit: Wayne State University Press, 2003, pp. 23–50.
Bothe, Alina. *Die Geschichte der Shoah im virtuellen Raum: Eine Quellenkritik*. Berlin: De Gruyter, 2019.
Brahimi, Denise. *La Peinture au féminin: Berthe Morisot et Mary Cassatt*. Paris: J-P Rocher, 2000.
Brink, Cornelia. 'Secular Icons: Looking at Photographs from the Nazi Concentration Camps,' *History and Memory* 12.1 (2000): 135–150.
Bryant, Michael S. *Eyewitness to Genocide: The Operation Reinhard Death Camp Trials, 1955–1966*. Knoxville: University of Tennessee Press, 2014.
Carey, Maddy. *Jewish Masculinity in the Holocaust*. London: Bloomsbury, 2017.
Caruth, Cathy. *Unclaimed Experience: Trauma, Narrative, and History*. Baltimore: Johns Hopkins University Press, 1996.
Cavoir, Norman, and Paul R. Dokecki. 'Physical Attractiveness, Perceived Attitude Similarity, and Academic Achievement as Contributors to Interpersonal Attraction Among Adolescents,' *Developmental Psychology* 9.1 (1973): 44–54.
Cazenave, Jennifer. *Genèses des figurations de la femme dans la Shoah : Voix féminines et représentations de l'Holocauste (1946–1985)*, Unpublished PhD dissertation, Northwestern University, 2011.
Cernyak-Spatz, Susan. *Protective Custody: Prisoner 34042*. Cortland: N & S Publishers, 2005.
Chare, Nicholas. 'Puncture/Punctum: Out of Shot,' in *Conceptual Odysseys: Passages to Cultural Analysis*, ed. Griselda Pollock. London: I.B. Tauris, 2007, pp. 91–102.
Chare, Nicholas. *Auschwitz and Afterimages: Abjection, Witnessing and Representation*. London: I.B. Tauris, 2011.
Chare, Nicholas. 'On the Problem of Empathy: Attending to Gaps in the Scrolls of Auschwitz,' in *Representing Auschwitz: At the Margins of Testimony*, eds. Nicholas Chare and Dominic Williams. Houndmills: Palgrave Macmillan, 2013, pp. 11–32.
Chare, Nicholas. 'Gesture in *Shoah*,' *Journal for Cultural Research* 19.1 (2015): 30–42.
Chare, Nicholas. 'Material Witness: Conservation Ethics and the Scrolls of Auschwitz,' *Symplokē* 24.1–2 (2016): 81–97.

Chare, Nicholas, Ersy Contogouris, and Dominic Williams. 'Disinterred Words: The Letters of Marcel Nadjary and Herman Strasfogel,' in *Testimonies of Resistance: Representations of the Auschwitz-Birkenau Sonderkommando*, eds. Nicholas Chare and Dominic Williams. New York: Berghahn, 2019, in press.

Chare, Nicholas, and Dominic Williams. *Matters of Testimony: Interpreting the Scrolls of Auschwitz*. New York: Berghahn, 2016.

Chare, Nicholas, and Dominic Williams. 'Questions of Filiation: From the Scrolls of Auschwitz to *Son of Saul*,' *Mémoires en jeu* 2 (2016): 63–72.

Chare, Nicholas, and Marcel Swiboda. 'Introduction: Unforeseen Encounters,' *Liminalities* 14.1 (2018): 1–25.

Chatwood, Kirsty. 'Schillinger and the Dancer: Representing Agency and Sexual Violence in Holocaust Testimonies,' in *Sexual Violence Against Jewish Women During the Holocaust*, eds. Sonja Hedgepeth and Rochelle Saidel. Waltham: Brandeis University Press, 2010, pp. 61–74.

Chéroux, Clément. 'Photographies de la résistance polonaise à Auschwitz,' in *Mémoire des camps: Photographies des camps de concentration et d'extermination nazis (1933–1999)*, ed. Clément Chéroux. Paris: Éditions Marval, 2001, pp. 86–91.

Chevillon, Véronique. 'Entendre David Olère, entendre les prisonniers des *Sonderkommandos*' in *Sonderkommando et Arbeitsjuden : Les travailleurs forcés de la mort*, ed. Philippe Mesnard. Paris: Kimé, 2015, pp. 165–182.

Chevrie, Marc, and Hervé Le Roux. 'Site and Speech: An Interview with Claude Lanzmann About *Shoah*,' in *Claude Lanzmann's* Shoah: *Key Essays*, ed. Stuart Liebman. Oxford: Oxford University Press, 2007, pp. 37–49.

Chion, Michel. *L'audio-vision: Son et image au cinéma*. Paris: Armand Colin, 1991.

Chisholm, Dianne. 'Violence Against Violence Against Women: An Avant-Garde for the Times,' in *The Last Sex: Feminism and Outlaw Bodies*, eds. Arthur Kroker and Marilouise Kroker. New York: St. Martin's Press, 1993, pp. 29–66.

Cohen, Elie A. *Human Behaviour in the Concentration Camp*. London: Free Association Books, 1988.

Cohen, Leon. *From Greece to Birkenau*, trans. Jose-Maurice Gormezano. Jerusalem: Graphit Press, 1996.

Cohen, Nathan. 'Diaries of the Sonderkommandos,' in *Anatomy of the Auschwitz Death Camp*, eds. Yisrael Gutman and Michael Berenbaum. Bloomington: Indiana University Press, 1994, pp. 522–534.

Cohen, Sande. *History Out of Joint: Essays on the Use and Abuse of History*. Baltimore: Johns Hopkins University Press, 2006.

Connell, R. W. 'On Hegemonic Masculinity and Violence: Response to Jefferson and Hall,' *Theoretical Criminology* 6.1 (2002): 89–99.

Connell, R. W. *Masculinities*, 2nd ed. Cambridge: Polity, 2005.

Craik, Jennifer. *Uniforms Exposed: From Conformity to Transgression*. Oxford: Berg, 2005.
Cramer, John. *Belsen Trial 1945: Der Lüneburger Prozess gegen Wachpersonal der Konzentrationslager Auschwitz und Bergen-Belsen*. Göttingen: Wallstein, 2011.
Crenshaw, Kimberlé Williams. 'Mapping the Margins: Intersectionality, Identity, Politics, and Violence Against Women of Colour,' *Stanford Law Review* 43.6 (1991): 1241–1299.
Cushman, Sarah. *The Women of Birkenau*, PhD thesis, Worcester MA: Clark University, 2010.
Davies, Peter. *Witness between Languages: The Translation of Holocaust Testimonies in Context*. Rochester, NY: Camden House, 2018.
Dawidowicz, Lucy. *Spiritual Resistance: Art from the Concentration Camps 1940–1945*. New York: Union of American Hebrew Congregations, 1981.
Des Pres, Terrence. *The Survivor: An Anatomy of Life in the Death Camps*. Oxford: Oxford University Press, 1976.
Deuisch, Francine M., Carla M. Zalenski, and Mary E. Clark. 'Is There a Double Standard of Ageing?' *Journal of Applied Social Psychology* 16.9 (1986): 771–785.
Didi-Huberman, Georges. *Images malgré tout*. Paris: Éditions de Minuit, 2003.
Didi-Huberman, Georges. 'The Site, Despite Everything,' in *Claude Lanzmann's* Shoah: *Key Essays*, ed. Stuart Liebman. Oxford: Oxford University Press, 2007, pp. 113–123.
Didi-Huberman, Georges. *Écorces*. Paris: Minuit, 2011.
Didi-Huberman, Georges. *Sortir du noir*. Paris: Les Éditions de Minuit, 2015.
Didi-Huberman, Georges. 'Out of the Plan/Out of the Plane' English translation of Letter 4 of 'Sortir du Plan,' forthcoming in *Testimonies of Resistance: Representations of the Auschwitz-Birkenau Sonderkommando*, eds. Chare and Williams. Berghahn, 2019.
Dolar, Mladen. *A Voice and Nothing More*. Cambridge, MA: MIT Press, 2006.
Douglas, Lawrence. *The Memory of Judgement: Making Law and History in the Trials of the Holocaust*. New Haven: Yale University Press, 2001.
Drumbl, Mark A. 'Stepping Beyond Nuremberg's Halo: The Legacy of the Supreme National Tribunal of Poland,' *Journal of International Criminal Justice* 13 (2015): 903–932.
Ellis, Mark S. 'Assessing the Impact of the United Nations War Crimes Commission on the Principle of Complementarity and Fair Trial Standards,' *Criminal Law Forum* 25 (2014): 191–222.
Erll, Astrid. 'Travelling Memory,' *Parallax* 17.4 (2011): 4–18.
Eschebach, Insa. 'Interpreting Female Perpetrators: Ravensbrück Guards in the Courts of East Germany, 1946–1955,' in *Lessons and Legacies Volume V: The Holocaust and Justice*, ed. Peter Hayes. Evanston, IL: Northwestern University Press, 2002, pp. 255–267.
Fanon, Franz. *Peau noire, masques blancs*. Paris: Éditions de Seuil, 1952.

Farge, Arlette. *Le Goût de l'archive*. Paris: Éditions de Seuil, 1989.
Felman, Shoshana. 'In an Era of Testimony: Claude Lanzmann's *Shoah*,' *Yale French Studies* 79 (1991): 39–81.
Felman, Shoshana. *The Juridical Unconscious: Trials and Traumas in the Twentieth Century*. Cambridge, MA: Harvard University Press, 2002.
Felstiner, John. *Paul Celan: Poet, Survivor, Jew*. New Haven: Yale University Press, 1995.
Field, Joanna. (Marion Milner). *On Not Being Able to Paint*. New York: Jeremy P. Tarcher, 1957.
Firoiu, Ana, and Fleur Kuhn. '*Au coeur de l'enfer* de Zalman Gradowski: expérience collective et subjectivité dans le témoignage immédiat,' in *La psychologie de masse, aujourd'hui*, eds. Michel Gad Wolkowicz et al. Paris: Des Rosiers, 2012, pp. 81–104.
Fleming, Katherine E. *Greece: A Jewish History*. Princeton: Princeton University Press, 2008.
Flusser, Vilém. *Gestures*, trans. Nancy Ann Roth. Minneapolis: University of Minnesota Press, 2014.
Freud, Sigmund. *The Psychopathology of Everyday Life: Penguin Freud Library*, Vol. 5, trans. Alan Tyson. London: Penguin, 1991.
Friedländer, Saul. *Nazi Germany and the Jews: Years of Extermination, 1939–1945*. New York: Harper Collins, 2007.
Friedler, Eric, Barbara Siebert, and Andreas Kilian. *Zeugen aus der Todeszone: Das Jüdische Sonderkommando in Auschwitz*. Munich: Deutsche Taschenbuch Verlafg, 2005.
Fromer, Rebecca Camhi. *The Holocaust Odyssey of Daniel Bennahmias, Sonderkommando*. Tuscaloosa: The University of Alabama Press, 1993.
Frosh, Stephen. 'Different Trains: An Essay in Memorializing,' *American Imago* 74.1 (Spring 2017): 1–22.
Garbarz, Maurice, and Elie Garbarz. *Un Survivant – Auschwitz-Birkenau-Buchenwald*. Paris: Ramsay, 2006.
Garliński, Józef. *Fighting Auschwitz: The Resistance Movement in the Concentration Camp*. Greenwich: Fawcett Crest, 1975.
Gilbert, Martin. *The Holocaust: The Jewish Tragedy*. London: Fontana, 1987.
Ginzburg, Carlo. *The Judge and the Historian: Marginal Notes on a Late-Twentieth-Century Miscarriage of Justice*, trans. Antony Shugaar. London: Verso, 1999.
Glowacka, Dorota. *Disappearing Traces: Holocaust Testimonials, Ethics, and Aesthetics*. Washington: University of Washington Press, 2012, pp. 12–13.
Godfrey, Mark. *Abstraction and the Holocaust*. New Haven: Yale University Press, 2007.
Goldberg, Amos. *Trauma in First Person: Diary Writing During the Holocaust*. Bloomington: Indiana University Press, 2017.

Goldberg, Vicki. *The Power of Photography: How Photographs Changes Our Lives.* New York: Abbeville Press, 1991.
Gradowski, Zalman. *In Harts Fun Gehenem.* Tel Aviv: Wolnerman, n.d. [1977].
Gradowski, Zalman. *Au Cœur de l'enfer,* trans Batia Baum. Paris: Éditions Kimé, 2001.
Gradowski, Zalmen. *From Heart of Hell: Manuscripts of a Sonderkommando Prisoner, Found in Auschwitz,* trans. Barry Smerin and Janina Wurbs. Oświęcim: Auschwitz-Birkenau State Museum, 2017.
Gradowski, Salmen. *Die Zertrennung: Aufzeichnungen eines Mitglieds des Sonderkommandos,* ed. Aurélia Kalisky, trans. Almut Seiffert and Miriam Trinh. Frankfurt: Suhrkamp, 2020, forthcoming.
Gregory, Sarah. 'To Pass, To Last, To Cast Aside: The Testimonies of Two Auschwitz-Birkenau Sonderkommando Survivors, the Gabbai Brothers,' *History in the Making* 2.2 (2013): 30–40.
Greif, Gideon. *We Wept Without Tears: Testimonies from the Jewish Sonderkommando from Auschwitz,* trans. Naftali Greenwood. New Haven: Yale University Press, 2005.
Grosz, Elizabeth. *Volatile Bodies: Toward a Corporeal Feminism.* Bloomington: Indiana University Press, 1994.
Gubar, Susan. 'Dis/Identifications: Empathic Identification in Anne Michaels's *Fugitive Pieces*: Masculinity and Poetry After Auschwitz,' *Signs* 28:1 (2002): 249–276.
Habib, André. 'Delay, Estrangement, Loss: The Meanings of Translation in Claude Lanzmann's *Shoah* (1985),' *SubStance* 44.2 (2015): 108–128.
Haffner, Désiré. 'Birkenau,' in *Témoignages sur Auschwitz.* Paris: Éditions de l'amicale des déportés d'Auschwitz, 1946, pp. 57–79.
Hakim, Catherine. *Erotic Capital: The Power of Attraction in the Boardroom and the Bedroom.* New York: Basic Books, 2011.
Halberstam, Judith. *Female Masculinity.* Durham: Duke University Press, 1998.
Halberstam, Judith. *In a Queer Time and Place: Transgender Bodies, Subcultural Lives.* New York: New York University Press, 2005.
Halivni, Tsiporah Hager. 'The Birkenau Revolt: Poles Prevent a Timely Insurrection,' *Jewish Social Studies* 41.2 (1979): 123–154.
Halivni, Tsiporah Hager. 'Preparation for Revolt in Auschwitz-Birkenau: Heroes and Martyrs,' *Proceedings of the World Congress of Jewish Studies* Volume Division B, Volume II (1989): 403–410.
Harren, Ronnen. 'The Jewish Women at the Union Factory, Auschwitz 1944: Resistance, Courage and Tragedy,' *Dapim: Studies on the Holocaust* 31.1 (2017): 45–67.
Hart, Kitty. *I Am Alive.* London: Abelard-Schuman, 1961.
Hart, Kitty. *Return to Auschwitz.* Frogmore: Granada Publishing, 1983.

Hedgepeth, Sonja, and Rochelle Saidel, eds., *Sexual Violence Against Jewish Women During the Holocaust*. Waltham: Brandeis University Press, 2010.
Helmerdig, Silke. *Fragments, Futures, Absence and the Past: A New Approach to Photography*. Bielefeld: Transcript Verlag, 2016.
Heywood, Leslie. *Bodymakers: A Cultural Anatomy of Women's Bodybuilding*. New Brunswick: Rutgers University Press, 1998.
Hills, Helen. *The Matter of Miracles: Neapolitan Baroque Architecture and Sanctity*. Manchester: Manchester University Press, 2016.
Hirsch, Marianne. 'Family Pictures: *Maus*, Mourning and Post-memory,' *Discourse: Journal for Theoretical Studies in Media and Culture* 15.2 (Winter 1992–1993): 3–29.
Hirsch, Marianne. 'Surviving Images: Holocaust Photographs and the Work of Postmemory,' *The Yale Journal of Criticism* 14.1 (2001): 5–37.
Hirsch, Marianne. *The Generation of Postmemory: Writing and Visual Culture After the Holocaust*. New York: Columbia University Press, 2012.
Hirsch, Marianne, and Leo Spitzer. 'Gendered Translations: Claude Lanzmann's *Shoah*,' in *Claude Lanzmann's Shoah: Key Essays*, ed. Stuart Liebman. Oxford: Oxford University Press, 2007, pp. 175–190.
Homère, *L'Iliade*, trans. Eugène Lasserre. Paris: Garnier, 1965.
Hördler, Stefan, Christoph Kreutzmüller, and Tal Bruttman. 'Auschwitz im Bild: Zur kritischen Analyse der Auschwitz-Alben,' *Zeitschrift für Geschichtswissenschaft* 63.7/8 (2015): 609–632.
Horowitz, Sara R. 'Women in Holocaust Literature,' in *Women in the Holocaust*, eds. Dalia Ofer and Lenore J. Weitzman. New Haven: Yale University Press, 1998, pp. 364–377.
Huberband, Shimon. *Kiddush Hashem: Jewish Religious and Cultural Life in Poland During the Holocaust*, trans. David E. Fishman. New York: Yeshiva University Press, 1987.
Hutton, Margaret-Anne. *Testimony from the Nazi Camps: French Women's Voices*. London: Routledge, 2005.
Jockusch, Laura. *Collect and Record!: Jewish Holocaust Documentation in Early Postwar Europe*. Oxford: Oxford University Press, 2012.
Jurgens, Zuzana, and Magdalena Marszałek. 'Zeugen und Erben der Geschichte: Der Holocaust in der tschechischen Literatur (Richard Glazar und Jáchym Topol),' in *Nach dem Vergessen*, eds. Magdalena Marszałek and Alina Molisak. Berlin: Kulturverlag Kadmos, 2010, pp. 219–232.
Kant, Immanuel. *Critique of Judgement*, trans. Werner S. Pluhar. Indianapolis: Hackett, 1987.
Karpf, Anne. *The Human Voice*. New York: Bloomsbury, 2006.
Karpf, Anne. 'Chain of Testimony: The Holocaust Researcher as Surrogate Witness,' in *Representing Auschwitz: At the Margins of Testimony*, eds.

Nicholas Chare and Dominic Williams. Basingstoke: Palgrave Macmillan, 2013, pp. 85–103.

Katz, Esther, and Joan Ringelheim, eds., *Proceedings of the Conference on Women Surviving the Holocaust*. New York: Institute for Research in History, 1983.

Kaufmann, Francine. 'Interview et interprétation consécutive dans le film Shoah, de Claude Lanzmann,' *Meta* 38.4 (December 1993): 664–673.

Kilian, Andreas. 'Zur Autorenschaft der Sonderkommando-Fotografien,' *Mitteilungsblatt der Lagergemeinschaft Auschwitz – Freundeskreis der Auschwitzer* 35 (2016): 9–19.

Kilian, Andreas. 'Abschiedsbrief aus dem Krematorium: das verschollene Original und sein anonymer Verfasser,' *Mitteilungsblatt der Lagergemeinschaft Auschwitz / Freundeskreis der Auschwitzer* 38.1 (2018): 5–21.

Klarsfeld, Serge. *David Olère: The Eyes of a Witness*. New York: Beate Klarsfeld Foundation, 1989.

Kleinke, Chris L., Richard A. Staneski, and Dale E. Berger. 'Evaluation of an Interviewer as Function of Interviewer Gaze, Reinforcement of Subject Gaze and Interviewer Attractiveness,' *Journal of Personality and Social Psychology* 31.1 (1975): 115–122.

Kozman, Peter. 'I Could Hold onto That Camera...,' in *We Saw the Holocaust*, ed. Monika Vrzgulová. Bratislava: Milan Šimečka Foundation, 2005, pp. 29–40.

Kracauer, Siegfried. *History: The Last Things Before the Last*, trans. Paul Oskar Kristeller. New York: Oxford University Press, 1969.

Krystal, Henry. 'Studies of Concentration Camp Survivors,' in *Massive Psychic Trauma*, ed. Henry Krystal. New York: International Universities Press, 1968, pp. 23–46.

Krystal, Henry. 'What Cannot Be Remembered or Forgotten,' in *Loss of the Assumptive World: A Theory of Traumatic Lossi*, ed. Jeffrey Kauffman. New York: Brunner-Routledge, 2002, pp. 213–219.

Krystal, Henry. 'Resilience: Accommodation and Recovery,' in *Living with Terror, Working with Trauma: A Clinician's Handbook*, ed. Danielle Knafo. Lanham: Jason Aronson, 2004, pp. 67–82.

Kuby, Emma. 'In the Shadow of the Concentration Camp: David Rousset and the Limits of Apoliticism in Postwar French Thought,' *Modern Intellectual History* 11.1 (2014): 147–173.

Kuhn-Kennedy, Fleur. '"Écoute, mon ami, ce qui se passe ici": Autour de Zalmen Gradowski et du témoignage comme espace d'interlocution,' *Plurielles 20* (2017): 63–70.

Kwart, Dylan, Tom Foulsham, and Alan Kingstone. 'Age and Beauty are in the Eye of the Beholder,' *Perception* 41.8 (2012): 925–938.

LaCapra, Dominick. 'Lanzmann's *Shoah*: "Here There Is No Why",' in *Claude Lanzmann's Shoah: Key Essays*, ed. Stuart Liebman. Oxford: Oxford University Press, 2007, pp. 191–229.

Landsberg, Alison. *Prosthetic Memory: The Transformation of American Remembrance in the Age of Mass Culture*. New York: Columbia University Press, 2004.

Landsmann, Stephen. 'The Eichmann Case and the Invention of the Witness-Driven Atrocity Trial,' *Columbia Journal of Transnational Law* 51.69 (2012): 69–119.

Lang, Berel. *Holocaust Representation: Art Within the Limits of History and Ethics*. Baltimore: Johns Hopkins University Press, 2000.

Langbein, Hermann. *Against All Hope: Resistance in the Nazi Concentration Camps 1938–1945*, trans. Harry Zohn. New York: Paragon, 1994.

Langer, Lawrence. *Holocaust Testimonies: The Ruins of Memory*. New Haven: Yale University Press, 1993.

Langer, Lawrence. 'Gendered Suffering?: Women in Holocaust Testimonies,' in *Women in the Holocaust*, eds. Dalia Ofer and Lenore J. Weitzman. New Haven: Yale University Press, 1998, pp. 351–363.

Lanzmann, Claude. *Shoah*. Paris: Gallimard, 1985.

Lanzmann, Claude. *Shoah: The Complete Text of the Acclaimed Holocaust Film*, trans. A. Whitelaw and W. Byron, with corrections by Claude Lanzmann. Boston: Da Capo, 1995.

Lanzmann, Claude. *Le Lièvre de Patagonie*. Paris: Folio, 2010.

Lanzmann, Claude. *Shoah*, trans. Nina Börnsen and Anna Kamp, Kindle ebook. Reinbek bei Hamburg: Rowohlt, 2011.

Lanzmann, Claude. *The Patagonian Hare*, trans. Frank Wynne. London: Atlantic, 2012.

Lanzmann, Claude. 'Autoportrait à quatre-vingt-dix ans,' in *Claude Lanzmann : Un voyant dans le siècle*, ed. Juliette Simont. Paris: Gallimard, 2017, pp. 247–286.

Laska, Vera. 'Auschwitz: A Factual Deposition,' in *Women in the Resistance and in the Holocaust: The Voices of Eyewitnesses*, ed. Laska. Westport: Greenwood Press, 1983, pp. 169–185.

Laub, Dori. 'Bearing Witness or the Vicissitudes of Listening,' in *Testimony: Crises of Witnessing in Literature, Psychoanalysis and History*, eds. Shoshana Felman and Dori Laub. New York: Routledge, 1991, pp. 57–74.

Laub, Dori. 'An Event Without a Witness: Truth, Testimony and Survival,' in *Testimony: Crises of Witnessing in Literature, Psychoanalysis, and History*, eds. Shoshana Felman and Dori Laub. New York and London: Routledge, 1992, pp. 75–92.

Laub, Dori. 'On Holocaust Testimony and Its "Reception" Within Its Own Frame, as a Process in Its Own Right: A Response to "Between History and Psychoanalysis" by Thomas Trezise,' *History and Memory* 21.1 (2009): 127–150.

Law, Cheryl, and Magdala Peixoto Labre. 'Cultural Standards of Attractiveness: A Thirty-Year Look at Changes in Male Images in Magazines,' *Journalism and Mass Communication Quarterly* 79.3 (2002): 697–711.

Lawrence, Amy. *Echo and Narcissus: Women's Voices in Classical Hollywood Cinema*. Berkeley: University of California Press, 1991.
Lengyel, Olga. *Five Chimneys: A Woman Survivor's True Story of Auschwitz*. Chicago: Academy Chicago Publishers, 1995.
Levi, Primo. 'The Grey Zone,' in *The Drowned and the Saved*, trans. Raymond Rosenthal. London: Abacus, 1988, pp. 22–51.
Levy, Henry. 'The Jews of Salonica and the Holocaust: A Personal Memoir,' in *Del Fuego: Sephardim and the Holocaust*, eds. Solomon Gaon and M. Mitchell Serels. New York: Sepher-Hermon Press, 1995.
Lewental, Zalman. 'Addendum to the Łódź Manuscript,' in *The Scrolls of Auschwitz*, ed. Ber Mark, trans. Sharon Neemani. Tel Aviv: Am Oved, 1985, pp. 236–240.
Lingens-Reiner, Ella. *Prisoners of Fear*. London: Victor Gollancz, 1948.
Lower, Wendy. 'German Women and the Holocaust in the Nazi East,' in *Women and Genocide: Survivors, Victims, Perpetrators*, eds. Elissa Bemporad and Joyce W. Warren. Bloomington: Indiana University Press, 2018, pp. 111–136.
Lyotard, Jean-François. *The Postmodern Condition: A Report on Knowledge*, trans. Geoff Bennington and Brian Massumi. Manchester: Manchester University Press, 1984.
Lyotard, Jean-François. *The Differend*, trans. George van den Abbeele. Manchester: Manchester University Press, 1988.
Lyotard, Jean-François. *Lessons on the Analytic of the Sublime*, trans. Elizabeth Rottenberg. Stanford: Stanford University Press, 1994.
Malgouzou, Yannick. *Les Camps nazis: Réflexions sur la reception littéraire française*. Paris: Classiques Garnier, 2012.
Marcinko, Marcin. 'The Concept of Genocide in the Trials of Nazi Criminals Before the Polish Supreme National Tribunal,' in *Historical Origins of International Criminal Law: Volume 2*, eds. Morten Bergsmo, Cheah Wui Ling, and Yi Ping. FICHL Publication Series No. 21 (2014). Brussels: Torkel Opsahl Academic EPublisher.
Mark, Ber. *Megiles Oyshvits*. Tel Aviv: Yisroel Bukh, 1977.
Mark, Ber. *The Scrolls of Auschwitz*, trans. Sharon Neemani. Tel Aviv: Am Oved, 1985.
McCaughey, Martha. *Real Knockouts: The Physical Feminism of Women's Self-Defense*. New York: New York University Press, 1997.
McClintock, Louisa Marie. *Projects of Punishment in Postwar Poland: War Criminals, Collaborators, Traitors, and the (Re)construction of the Nation*, Unpublished PhD, University of Chicago, 2015.
Mead, Richard. *Courtroom Discourse*. Birmingham: University of Birmingham, 1985.
Mesnard, Philippe. 'The Sonderkommando on Screen,' in *Testimonies of Resistance: Representations of the Auschwitz-Birkenau Sonderkommando*, eds. Nicholas Chare and Dominic Williams. New York: Berghahn, 2019, in press.
Mickenberg, David, Corinne Granof, and Peter Hayes, eds., *The Last Expression: Art and Auschwitz*. Evanston, IL: Northwestern University Press, 2003.

Mihai, Mihaela. Socialising Negative Emotions: Transitional Criminal Trials in the Service of Democracy,' *Oxford Journal of Legal Studies* 31.1 (2011): 111–131.
Morand, David. 'What's in a Name?: An Exploration of the Social Dynamics of Forms of Address in Organizations,' *Management Communication Quarterly* 9.4 (1996): 422–451, 423.
Müller, Filip. *Sonderbehandlung: Drei Jahre in den Krematorien und Gaskammern von Auschwitz*, literary collaboration with Helmut Freitag. Munich: Steinhausen, 1979.
Müller, Filip. *Eyewitness Auschwitz: Three Years in the Gas Chambers*, trans. Susanne Flatauer. Chicago: Ivan R. Dee, 1999, pp. 87–88.
Mulvey, Laura. *Death 24x a Second: Stillness and the Moving Image*. London: Reaktion, 2006.
Musser, Amber Jamilla. *Sensational Flesh: Race, Power, and Masochism*. New York: New York University Press, 2014.
Nadjary, Marcel. *Khroniko 1941–45*. Thessaloniki: Etz Kaim, 1991.
Nadjary, Marcel. 'The Letter of Marcel Nadjary,' trans. Ersy Contogouris, in *Testimonies of Resistance: Representations of the Auschwitz-Birkenau Sonderkommando*, eds. Nicholas Chare and Dominic Williams. New York: Berghahn, 2019, in press.
Nahmia, Berry. *A Cry for Tomorrow 76859...*, trans. David R. Weinberg. Jacksonville: Bloch Publishing, 2011.
Nead, Lynda. *The Female Nude: Art, Obscenity and Sexuality*. London: Routledge, 1992.
Nieszawer, Nadine, Marie Boyé, and Paul Fogel. *Peintres juifs à Paris 1905–1939*. Paris: Denoël, 2000.
Nyiszli, Miklós. 'Journal d'un médecin déporté d'un crematorium d'Auschwitz,' *Les Temps modernes*, trans. Tibère Kremer 6.65 (March 1951): 1655–1672 & 6.66 (April 1951): 1855–1886.
Nyiszli, Miklós. 'SS Obersturmführer Doktor Mengele,' *Merlin* 3 (1952–1953): 158–171.
Nyiszli, Miklós. *Im Jenseits der Menschlichkeit: Ein Gerichtsmediziner in Auschwitz*, trans. Angelika Bihari, ed. Andreas Kilian and Friedrich Herber. Berlin: Karl Dietz, 2005.
Nyiszli, Miklós. *Auschwitz: A Doctor's Eyewitness Report*, trans. Tibere Kremer and Richard Seaver. London: Penguin, 2012.
Oler, Alexandre. *Witness: Images of Auschwitz*. N. Richland Hills, TX: Westwind, 1998.
Olivier, Laurent. *Le sombre abîme du temps : Mémoire et archéologie*. Paris: Éditions du Seuil, 2008.
Ong, Walter. *Orality and Literacy*. London: Routledge, 2002.
Osiel, Mark. *Mass Atrocity, Collective Memory and the Law*. Transaction, 1997.

Paisicovic, Dov. 'A Survivor of the Sonderkommando,' in *Auschwitz.*, ed. Léon Poliakov. Paris: René Juillard, 1964, pp. 159–171.
Patterson, David. *The Holocaust and the Nonrepresentable: Literary and Photographic Transcendence.* New York: SUNY, 2018.
Patzer, Gordon. 'Source Credibility as a Function of Communicator Physical Attractiveness,' *Journal of Business Research* 11.2 (1983): 229–241.
Pawełczyńska, Anna. *Values and Violence in Auschwitz: A Sociological Analysis*, trans. Catherine S. Leach. Berkeley: University of California Press, 1979.
Pendas, Devin O. *The Frankfurt Auschwitz Trial, 1963–1965: Genocide, History, and the Limits of the Law.* Cambridge: Cambridge University Press, 2006.
Pentlin, Susan. 'Testimony from the Ashes: Final Words from the Auschwitz-Birkenau Sonderkommando,' in *The Genocidal Mind*, eds. Dennis Klein et al. St. Paul: Paragon, 2005, pp. 245–262.
Perl, Gisella. *I Was a Doctor in Auschwitz.* New York: Arno Press, 1979.
Pinchevski, Amit. 'The Audiovisual Unconscious: Media and Trauma in the Video Archive for Holocaust Testimonies,' *Critical Inquiry* 39 (2012): 142–166.
Pinhas, Lisa. *A Narrative of Evil.* Athens: Jewish Museum of Greece, 2014.
Pollin-Galay, Hannah. *Ecologies of Witnessing: Language, Place and Holocaust Testimony.* New Haven: Yale University Press, 2018.
Pollock, Griselda. 'Killing Men and Dying Women,' in *Avant-Gardes and Partisans Reviewed*, eds. Fred Orton and Griselda Pollock. Manchester: Manchester University Press, 1996, pp. 219–294.
Pollock, Griselda, *Vision and Difference: Femininity, Feminism and the Histories of Art.* London: Routledge, 1998.
Pollock, Griselda. 'Proximity and the Color of Desire: The Laboring Body and Its Sex,' in Pollock, *Looking Back to the Future: Essays on Art, Life and Death.* Amsterdam: G+B Arts International, 2001, pp. 177–226.
Pollock, Griselda. *Encounters in the Virtual Feminist Museum: Time, Space and the Archive.* Abingdon: Routledge, 2007.
Pollock, Griselda. 'Death in the Image: The Responsibility of Aesthetics in *Night and Fog* (1955) and *Kapò* (1959),' in *Concentrationary Cinema: Aesthetics as Political Resistance in Alain Resnais's Night and Fog*, eds. Griselda Pollock and Max Silverman. New York: Berghahn, 2011, pp. 258–302.
Pollock, Griselda. 'Photographing Atrocity: Becoming Iconic?' in *Picturing Atrocity: Photography in Crisis*, eds. Geoffrey Batchen et al. London: Reaktion Books, 2012, pp. 64–78.
Pollock, Griselda. *After-Affects/After-Images: Trauma and Aesthetic Transformation in the Virtual Feminist Museum.* Manchester: Manchester University Press, 2013.
Pollock, Griselda. *Art in the Time-Space of Memory and Migration: Sigmund Freud, Anna Freud, and Bracha L. Ettinger in the Freud Museum: Artwriting After the Event.* Leeds: Wild Pansy Press, 2013.

Pollock, Griselda. 'Art as Transport-Station of Trauma? Haunting Objects in the Works of Bracha Ettinger, Sarah Kofman and Chantal Akerman,' in *Representing Auschwitz: At the Margins of Testimony*, eds. Nicholas Chare and Dominic Williams. Houndmills: Palgrave Macmillan, 2013, pp. 194–221.

Pollock, Griselda. 'To Play Many Parts: Reading Between the Lines of Charlotte Salomon's/CS's *Leben? oder Theater?*' *RACAR* 43 (2018): 63–80.

Pollock, Griselda, and Max Silverman, eds., *Concentrationary Cinema: Aesthetics as Political Resistance in Alain Resnais's Night and Fog (1955)*. New York: Berghahn, 2011.

Postec, Ziva. 'As Editor: *Shoah* Paris 1979–1985,' http://www.posteeziva.com/Shoah.php.

Presiado, Mor. 'A New Perspective on Holocaust Art: Women's Artistic Expression of the Female Holocaust Experience (1939–1949),' *Holocaust Studies* 22.4 (2016): 417–446.

Presner, Todd. 'The Ethics of the Algorithm: Close and Distant Listening to the Shoah Foundation Visual History Archive,' *Probing the Ethics of Holocaust Culture*, eds. Claudio Fogu, Wulf Kansteiner, and Todd Presner. Cambridge, MA: Harvard University Press, 2016, pp. 150–175.

Prstojevic, Alexandre. 'L'indicible et la fiction configuratrice,' *Protée* 37.2 (2009): 33–44.

Prusin, Alexander Victor. 'Poland's Nuremberg: The Seven Court Cases of the Supreme National Tribunal, 1946–1948,' *Holocaust and Genocide Studies* 24.1 (2010): 1–25.

Przyrembel, Alexandra. 'Transfixed by an Image: Ilse Koch, the Kommandeuse of Buchenwald,' trans. Pamela Selwyn, *German History* 19.3 (2001): 369–399.

Quigley, Paxton. *Stayin' Alive: Armed and Female in an Unsafe World*. Bellevue: Merrill Press, 2005.

Quintal, Catherine. 'De la déportation à l'expression; la femme et le témoignage dans les dessins clandestins de Violette Rougier-Lecoq et Jeanette L'Herminier,' MA thesis, Université de Montréal, 2018.

Ramshaw, Sara. *Justice as Improvisation: The Law of the Extempore*. Abingdon: Routledge, 2013.

Reason, J. T. 'The Psychopathology of Everyday Slips: Accidents Happen When Habit Goes Haywire,' *The Sciences* 24.5 (1984): 45–49.

Reich, Steve. 'Answers to Questions About Different Trains,' in *Writings on Music 1965-2000*, ed. Paul Hillier. Oxford: Oxford University Press, 2002, pp. 180–183.

Ringelheim, Joan. 'Women and the Holocaust: A Reconsideration of Research,' *Signs* 10.4 (1985): 741–761.

Ringelheim, Joan. 'The Split Between Gender and the Holocaust,' in *Women in the Holocaust*, eds. Dalia Ofer and Leonore J. Weitzman. New Haven: Yale University Press, 1999, pp. 340–350.

Rifkin, Adrian. *Ingres Then, and Now*. London: Routledge, 2000.
Rogers, A. P. V. 'War Crimes Trials Under the Royal Warrant: British Practice 1945–1949,' *International and Comparative Law Quarterly* 39.4 (1990): 780–800.
Rose, Nikolas. 'Identity, Genealogy, History,' in *Identity: A Reader*, eds. Paul du Gay et al. London: Sage, 2000, pp. 313–326.
Rose, Sven-Erik. 'Auschwitz as Hermeneutic Rupture, Differed, and Image *malgré tout*: Jameson, Lyotard, Didi-Huberman,' in *Visualizing the Holocaust*, eds. David Bathrick, Brad Praeger, and Michael Richardson. Rochester: Camden House Press, 2008, pp. 114–137.
Roskies, David. 'Wartime Victim Writing in Eastern Europe,' in *Literature of the Holocaust*, ed. Alan Rosen. Cambridge: Cambridge University Press, 2013, pp. 15–32.
Sack, John. *An Eye for an Eye*. New York: Basic Books, 1993.
Salomon, Nanette. 'The Venus Pudica: Uncovering Art History's "Hidden Agendas" and Pernicious Pedigrees,' in *Generations and Geographies in the Visual Arts: Feminist Readings*, ed. Griselda Pollock. London: Routledge, 1996, pp. 69–87.
Schweitzer, Petra. *Gendered Testimonies of the Holocaust: Writing Life*. Lanham: Lexington Books, 2016.
Scott, James C. *Weapons of the Weak: Everyday Forms of Peasant Resistance*. New Haven: Yale University Press, 1985.
Seaver, Richard. *The Tender Hour of Twilight: Paris in the '50s, New York in the '60s: A Memoir of Publishing's Golden Age*, ed. Jeannette Seaver. New York: Farrar, Straus and Giroux, 2012.
Shenker, Noah. *Reframing Holocaust Testimony*. Bloomington: Indiana University Press, 2015.
Shik, Na'ama. 'Sexual Abuse of Jewish Women in Auschwitz-Birkenau,' in *Brutality and Desire: War and Sexuality in Europe's Twentieth-Century*, ed. Dagmar Herzog. Houndmills: Palgrave Macmillan, 2009, pp. 221–246.
Shklar, Judith. *Legalism: Law, Morals and Political Trials*. Cambridge, MA: Harvard University Press, 1984.
Shomer-Zaichik, Bella, ed., *Out of the Depths: David Olère, an Artist in Auschwitz*. Jerusalem: Yad Vashem, 1997.
Shomer-Zaichik, Bella. 'The Transition from Reality to Imagination in the Work of David Olère,' in *Out of the Depths: David Olère, an Artist in Auschwitz*. Jerusalem: Yad Vashem, 1997, pp. 14–15.
Siegal, Aranka. *Upon the Head of the Goat: A Childhood in Hungary 1939–1944*. London: J.M. Dent and Sons, 1982.
Sieradzka, Agnieszka. *David Olère: The One Who Survived Crematorium III*. Oświęcim: Auschwitz-Birkenau State Museum, 2018.

Simpson, Kevin E. *Soccer Under the Swastika: Stories of Resistance and Survival.* Lanham, MD: Rowman and Littlefield, 2016.

Sinnreich, Helene. '"And It Was Something We Didn't Talk About": Rape of Jewish Women During the Holocaust,' *Holocaust Studies* 14.2 (2008): 1–22.

Sjoberg, Laura. *Women as Wartime Rapists: Beyond Sensation and Stereotyping.* New York: New York University Press, 2016.

Skorczewski, Dawn. '"You Want Me to Sing?" Holocaust Testimonies in the Intersubjective Field,' *Dapim* 32.2 (2018): 112–127.

Smith, Marquard. 'Observance, Notes Towards Decipherability,' *Journal of Visual Culture* 17.1 (2018): 68–96.

Solomon-Godeau, Abigail. *Male Trouble: A Crisis in Representation.* London: Thames & Hudson, 1997.

Sommer, Robert. '*Pipels*: Situational Homosexual Slavery of Young Adolescent Boys in Nazi Concentration Camps,' in *Lessons and Legacies XI: Expanding Perspectives on the Holocaust in a Changing World*, eds. Hilary Earl and Karl A. Schleunes. Evanston, IL: Northwestern University Press, pp. 86–101.

Sontag, Susan. *Regarding the Pain of Others.* London: Hamish Hamilton, 2003.

Spiegel, Gabrielle M. 'History, Historicism and the Social Logic of the Text in the Middle Ages,' *Speculum* 65 (1990): 59–86.

Steedman, Carolyn. *Poetry for Historians or W.H. Auden and History.* Manchester: Manchester University Press, 2018.

Stengel, Katharina. *Hermann Langbein: Ein Auschwitz-Überlebender in den erinnerungspolitischen Konflikten der Nachkriegszeit.* Frankfurt: Campus Verlag, 2012.

Stoll, Katrin. 'Producing the Truth: The Bielefeld Trial and the Reconstruction of Events Surrounding the Execution of 100 Jews in the Bialystok Ghetto following the "Acid Attack",' *Dapim* 25.1 (2011): 11–64.

Stone, Dan. 'Chaos and Continuity: Representations of Auschwitz,' in *Representation of Auschwitz*, ed. Yasmin Doosvy. Oświęcim: Auschwitz-Birkenau State Museum, 1995, pp. 25–33.

Stone, Dan. 'The Sonderkommando Photographs,' *Jewish Social Studies* 7.3 (2001): 132–148.

Stone, Dan. *Constructing the Holocaust: A Study in Historiography.* London: Vallentine Mitchell, 2003.

Stone, Dan. *History, Memory and Mass Atrocity: Essays on the Holocaust and Genocide.* Elstree: Vallentine Mitchell, 2006.

Stone, Dan. 'The Harmony of Barbarism: Locating the Scrolls of Auschwitz in Holocaust Historiography,' in *Representing Auschwitz: At the Margins of Testimony*, eds. Nicholas Chare and Dominic Williams. Basingstoke: Palgrave Macmillan, 2013, pp. 11–32.

Stone, Dan. 'Excommunicating the Past? Narrativism and Rational Constructivism in the Historiography of the Holocaust,' *Rethinking History* 21.4 (2017): 549–566.

Strasfogel, Herman. 'The Letter of Herman Strasfogel,' trans. Ersy Contogouris, in *Testimonies of Resistance: Representations of the Auschwitz-Birkenau Sonderkommando*, eds. Nicholas Chare and Dominic Williams. New York: Berghahn, 2019, in press.

Struk, Janina. *Photographing the Holocaust: Interpretations of the Evidence*. London: I.B. Tauris, 2004.

Struk, Janina. 'Images of Women in Holocaust Photography,' *Feminist Review* 88 (2008): 111–121.

Strzelecka, Irena. 'Women,' in *Anatomy of the Auschwitz Death Camp*, eds. Yisrael Gutman and Michael Berenbaum. Bloomington: Indiana University Press, 1994, pp. 393–411.

Strzelecki, Andrzej. 'The Plunder of Victims and their Corpses,' in *Anatomy of the Auschwitz Death Camp*, eds. Yisrael Gutman and Michael Berenbaum. Bloomington: Indiana University Press, 1994, pp. 246–266.

Suderland, Maja. 'Männliche Ehre und menschliche Würde. Über die Bedeutung der Männlichkeitskonstruktionen in der sozialen Welt der nationalsozialistische Konzentrationslager,' in *Prekäre Transformationen: Pierre Bourdieus Soziologie der Praxis und ihre Herausforderungen für die Frauen- und Geschlechterforschung*, eds. Ulla Bock, Irene Dölling, and Beate Krais. Göttingen: Wallstein, 2007, pp. 118–140.

Sujo, Glenn. *Legacies of Silence: The Visual Arts and Holocaust Memory*. London: Philip Wilson, 2001.

Sundquist, Eric. 'The Historian's Anvil, the Novelist's Crucible,' in *Literature of the Holocaust*, ed. Alan Rosen. Cambridge: Cambridge University Press, 2013, pp. 252–267.

Świebocka, Teresa, and Renata Bogusławska-Świebocka. 'Auschwitz in Documentary Photographs,' in *Auschwitz: A History in Photographs*, ed. Teresa Świebocka. Bloomington: Indiana University Press, 1993, pp. 33–216.

Tabakman, Raizel. 'My Husband, a Flitzer, Was Gassed Upon Arrival Together with All Other Flitzers,' in *The Union Kommando in Auschwitz: The Auschwitz Munition Factory Through the Eyes of Its Former Slave Laborers*, ed. Lore Shelley. Lanham: University Press of America, 1996, pp. 39–43.

Tagg, John. *The Burden of Representation: Essays on Photographies and Histories*. Minneapolis: University of Minnesota Press, 1993.

Taslitz, Andrew E. *Rape and the Culture of the Courtroom*. New York: New York University Press, 1999.

Tedeschi, Giuliana. *There Is a Place on Earth: A Woman in Birkenau*, trans. Tim Parks. London: Lime Tree, 1993.

Tickner, Lisa. 'The Body Politic: Female Sexuality and Women Artists Since 1970,' in *Framing Feminism: Art and the Women's Movement, 1970–1985*, eds. Rozsika Parker and Griselda Pollock. London: Pandora, 1987, pp. 263–276.

Tickner, Lisa. *Modern Life and Modern Subjects: British Art in the Early Twentieth Century*. New Haven: Yale University Press, 2000.

Tomai, Photini. *Greeks in Auschwitz-Birkenau*. Athens: Papazisis Publishers, 2009.
Trezise, Thomas. 'Between History and Psychoanalysis: A Case Study in the Reception of Holocaust Survivor Testimony,' *History and Memory* 20.1 (2008): 7–47.
Trezise, Thomas. *Witnessing Witnessing: On the Reception of Holocaust Survivor Testimony*. New York: Fordham University Press, 2013.
Turda, Marius. 'The Ambiguous Victim: Miklós Nyiszli's Narrative of Medical Experimentation in Auschwitz-Birkenau,' *Historein* 14.1 (2014): 43–58.
Uriah, Vivian. 'Photography During the Holocaust,' in *Flashes of Memory: Photography During the Holocaust*. Jerusalem: Yad Vashem, 2018, pp. 12–16.
Van Pelt, Robert Jan. *The Case for Auschwitz: Evidence from the Irving Trial*. Bloomington: Indiana University Press, 2002.
Venezia, Shlomo. *Inside the Gas Chambers: Eight Months in the Sonderkommando of Auschwitz*, trans. Andrew Brown. Cambridge: Polity, 2009.
Waxman, Zoë. *Writing the Holocaust: Identity, Testimony, Representation*. Oxford: Oxford University Press, 2006.
Waxman, Zoë. *Women in the Holocaust: A Feminist History*. Oxford: Oxford University Press, 2017.
Webster, Murray, and James E. Driskell, 'Beauty as Status,' *American Journal of Sociology* 89.1 (1983): 140–165.
Wellers, Georges. 'Révolte du sonderkommando à Auschwitz,' *Le Monde juif* 18 (1949): 17–18.
Wieviorka, Annette. 'Justice, histoire et mémoire. De Nuremberg à Jérusalem,' *Droit et société* 38 (1998): 59–67.
Williams, Dominic. 'Figuring the Grey Zone: The Auschwitz Sonderkommando in Contemporary Culture,' *Holocaust Studies* (2018). https://doi.org/10.10 80/17504902.2018.1472880.
Williams, Dominic. 'What Makes the Grey Zone Grey? Blurring Moral and Factual Judgements of the Sonderkommando,' in *Testimonies of Resistance: Representations of the Auschwitz-Birkenau Sonderkommando*, eds. Nicholas Chare and Dominic Williams. New York: Berghahn, 2019, in press.
Willis, Ika. *Reception*. London: Routledge, 2018.
Wittman, Rebecca. *Beyond Justice: The Auschwitz Trial*. Cambridge, MA: Harvard University Press, 2012.
Wobovnik, Claudia. 'These Shoes Aren't Made for Walking: Rethinking High-Heeled Shoes as Cultural Artefacts,' *Visual Culture and Gender* 8 (2013): 82–92.
Wünschmann, Kim. 'Männlichkeitskonstruktionen jüdischer Häftlinge in NS-Konzentrationslagern,' in *Männlichkeitskonstruktionen im Nationalsozialismus: Formen, Funktionen und Wirkungsmacht von Geschlechterkonstruktionen im Nationalsozialismus und ihre Reflexion in pädagogischen Praxis*, eds. Anette Dietrich and Ljiljana Heise. Frankfurt: Peter Lang, 2013, pp. 201–219.

Young, James. *Writing and Re-writing the Holocaust: Essays on the Nature of Holocaust Literature and Its Critical Interpretation*, PhD thesis, Santa Cruz: University of California, 1983.

Young, James. *Writing and Rewriting the Holocaust: Narrative and the Consequences of Interpretation*. Bloomington, Indianapolis: Indiana University Press, 1988.

Zemel, Carol. 'Emblems of Atrocity: Holocaust Liberation Photographs,' in *Image and Remembrance: Representation and the Holocaust*, eds. Shelley Hornstein and Florence Jacobowitz. Bloomington: Indiana University Press, 2003, pp. 201–219.

Zemel, Carol. 'Right After: Aesthetics and Trauma in Survivor Narratives,' in *The Holocaust, Art, and Taboo*, eds. Sophia Komor and Susanne Rohr. Heidelberg: Universitätsverlag Winter, 2010, pp. 49–62.

Zemel, Carol. 'Enduring Witness: David Olère's Visual Testimony,' in *Testimonies of Resistance: Representations of the Auschwitz-Birkenau Sonderkommando*, eds. Nicholas Chare and Dominic Williams. New York: Berghahn, 2019, in press.

Żywulska, Krystyna. *I Survived Auschwitz*, trans. Krystyna Cenkalska. Warsaw: tCHu, 2004.

Index

A
aesthetics, 20, 90, 97, 141, 161, 162, 168, 185
'Alex' (Greek Jewish prisoner, possibly Alberto Errera), 17, 72
allegory, 92, 135, 142
Améry, Jean, 47, 68
archive, 5, 6, 14, 48, 51, 66, 67, 79, 84, 87, 89, 92, 94, 95, 99, 121, 123, 124, 127, 137, 160, 163, 180, 183, 186, 191, 193, 201, 207, 208, 210, 211, 216, 224, 233–236, 242, 246
Arendt, Hannah, 2, 11, 96, 103, 121, 122
Ash, 86, 245
Auschwitz Album, 82, 84, 97
Auschwitz museum, 58, 62, 63, 84, 131, 224, 242
Auschwitz trial (Kraków, 1947), 20, 62, 103, 105, 118, 122, 240

B
Backhouse, T.M. (Col.), 107, 110
Ball, Karyn, 64, 205
Bar-Itzhak, Haya, 25, 58, 99
Baxandall, Michael, 48, 68, 80, 83, 97
Baxter, Richard, 141, 165
Belsen trial (Trial of Josef Kramer and 44 others, Lüneburg, 1945), 105, 106, 110, 122, 125
Bendel, Charles Sigismund, 108–111, 125, 126
Benjamin, Walter, 77, 79, 96
Bennahmias, Daniel, 151, 168, 183, 185, 188–190, 192–194, 201, 212, 214, 215
Bergen, Doris, 31, 40, 42, 62, 66, 67
Bergen-Belsen, 67, 106, 107, 125
Bettelheim, Bruno, 2, 26–28, 59
Bełżec, 21, 52, 55, 231, 238, 244
Bimko, Ada, 107, 108, 111, 121, 125

© The Editor(s) (if applicable) and The Author(s), under exclusive license to Springer Nature Switzerland AG, part of Springer Nature 2019
N. Chare and D. Williams, *The Auschwitz Sonderkommando*, The Holocaust and its Contexts, https://doi.org/10.1007/978-3-030-11491-6

Birkenau
  Block 2, 41
  Block 6, 68
  Block 10, 39
  Block 13, 41
  Block 25, 50
  Bunkers, 130
  crematoria, 1, 2, 13, 15, 41, 88, 101, 106, 119, 124, 132, 144, 148, 159, 162, 178, 220, 223, 233, 234, 236
  Crematorium 1 (II), 223, 236
  Crematorium 2 (III), 129, 133, 139
  Crematorium 3 (IV), 172, 178, 208, 220
  Crematorium 4 (V), 130
  Czech family camp, 35, 57, 84, 148, 233
  Gypsy camp, 38
  Kanada, 9, 13, 18, 23, 39, 41, 66, 159, 172, 176, 178, 208, 209
  Sauna, 22
Bloch, Marc, 16, 21, 24, 56, 70, 123, 126
Bloxham, Donald, 103, 106, 122
Bomba, Abraham, 230, 235, 237, 238
Bos, Pascale, 35, 64, 66, 214
Buchenwald, 138, 139
Buki, Milton, 119–121

C
ça, 144, 146, 148
Caruth, Cathy, 14, 96, 122
Chatwood, Kirsty, 25–28, 58, 59
Chazan, Saul, 203
Chevillon, Véronique, 135, 156, 162
children, 9, 31–34, 44, 85, 123, 143, 174, 176, 184, 189, 190, 201, 211
chronology, 5, 52, 200
clothes, 8, 22, 29, 43, 49, 84, 98, 113, 114, 123, 139, 147, 153

Cohen, Elie, 56, 70
Cohen, Leon, 163
Cohen, Nathan, 34, 63
concentration camps, 2, 5, 20, 21, 23, 25, 32, 34–36, 39, 41, 42, 44, 47, 58, 64, 66, 67, 78, 106, 107, 110, 140, 188, 231
Consonni, Manuela, 168, 187, 195, 198–200, 205, 214–217
corpses, 4, 27, 71, 73, 81, 89, 108, 112, 116, 125, 135, 136, 141, 144, 150–152, 156, 157, 185, 195, 205, 219, 220, 227
court (of law), 2, 14, 18, 54, 102–104, 106, 107, 109–113, 115, 117–122, 124–126, 164, 221, 237, 245, 246
Crenshaw, Kimberlé, 37, 65
crime
  effacement of, 87, 131
  evidence of, 62, 71, 93, 115, 143, 193
  and Nazis, 15, 16, 87, 138, 164, 193
Cushman, Sarah, 31, 62, 140, 165
Cyrankiewicz, Józef, 79–81

D
Dachau, 114, 124
Davies, Peter, 120, 123, 128
dead bodies. *See* corpses
death camp, 16, 19, 37, 41, 42, 44, 63, 67, 70, 128, 133, 205, 206, 230, 231, 235, 244, 246
deception, 90, 115, 131
dehumanisation, 42, 54, 77, 196
Didi-Huberman, Georges, 71, 73, 74, 76, 77, 81, 82, 84, 86, 87, 91–94, 97, 98, 100, 240, 246
Dinoor, Yehiel (KaZetnik), 103
Dolar, Mladen, 227, 243

Dragan, Shlomo, 41, 66, 71, 111
Drancy, 134, 136
Dutch women, 38

E
Ebensee, 129, 134
Eichmann, Adolf, 16, 17, 105, 121, 122
emotions
  detachment and, 83
  extremes of, 234
  fear, 82
  horror, 16
  shame, 8
empathy, 4, 90, 99, 162, 166
Errera, Alberto, 17, 72, 93
Escape, 17, 52, 58, 72, 154, 209
Eschebach, Insa, 138, 164
ethical sensibility, 53, 130
ethics, 48, 77, 97, 109, 162, 163, 197, 211, 215
evidence, 2, 3, 7, 16, 18, 40, 43, 54, 63, 69, 71, 72, 80, 81, 84, 91, 93, 95, 97, 101–103, 108–111, 115, 116, 122, 123, 125, 126, 133, 137, 160, 204

F
Fajnzylberg, Alter. *See* Feinsilber, Alter
fantasy, 142, 154
fear. *See* emotions
feelings. *See* emotions
Feinsilber, Alter, 26, 38, 58, 71, 111
Felman, Shoshana, 103, 122, 205, 239, 242, 247
femininity, 27, 30, 31, 34, 35, 38, 43, 60, 61, 141, 161, 185
fetish, 30, 47, 195, 226
figuration, 133, 138, 148, 163, 245
Firoiu, Ana, 34, 63, 68, 95, 168

Flusser, Vilém, 73, 94
Fortunoff Video Archive for Holocaust Testimonies, 66, 160, 183, 208, 211
Foucault, Michel, 90
France, 37, 62, 93, 136, 137, 144, 150
Frankfurt Auschwitz trial (1963-65), 105, 118, 122, 123
French Jews, 20, 134, 222
Freud, Sigmund, 75, 94, 99, 180
Friedlander, Henry, 36
Friedländer, Saul, 5, 21
Friedler, Eric, 174, 207

G
Gabbai, Dario, 53, 144, 160, 183–188, 190, 192, 195–197, 200, 211, 214–216
gas chambers, 1–3, 13–15, 35, 38, 41, 44, 48, 49, 54, 57, 59, 70, 79, 84, 89–91, 104–111, 113, 114, 116–121, 123, 125, 129, 130, 141, 143, 146, 150–152, 156, 160, 168, 169, 177, 189, 195, 196, 214, 222–224, 227–229, 231–234, 237, 239, 240
gassing, 20, 62, 75, 81, 108, 114, 116, 117, 141, 151, 152, 156, 168, 177, 196, 228
Gawkowski, Henryk, 230
gaze
  male, 15, 33, 43, 47–50, 69, 90
  Nazi, 15, 16, 43–47, 51, 56, 57, 68, 90, 97, 148, 229
  sadistic, 46–50, 57, 68, 149
gender, 6, 9, 15–18, 25, 27, 30, 31, 34–37, 41, 57, 60, 61, 64, 67, 140, 141, 157, 164, 165, 174, 183, 188, 190, 191, 200, 214, 216, 243, 245, 247

gesture, 75, 82, 94, 147, 175, 182, 184, 191, 193–197, 199, 201, 202, 204, 215, 220, 221, 225, 228, 229, 238, 240, 243, 244
ghettos, 21, 27, 28, 65, 180, 231, 244, 245
Gilbert, Martin, 5, 21
Ginzburg, Carlo, 106, 124
Glazar, Richard, 230, 235, 244–246
Gradowski, Zalman
  Czech transport, account of the, 34, 35, 43, 44, 48, 50, 56
  In the Heart of Hell, 10, 25, 34, 48, 50, 51, 58, 64, 75, 88, 90, 99, 116
  masculinity, 31, 33–35, 49, 64, 65, 69
  sadism, reflections on, 15, 16, 46, 57
Greece, 20, 93, 163, 188, 189, 206, 210
Greek Jews, 37, 71, 72
Gregory, Sarah, 196, 215
Greif, Gideon, 5, 6, 20, 61–63, 117, 127, 159, 161, 203, 206, 211, 216
Grese, Irme, 38, 164, 166
grey zone, 2–5, 21, 23, 147, 154, 155, 167

H
Haidari, 188
hair, 1, 29–31, 44, 52, 64, 132, 138, 140, 141, 146, 150, 151, 164, 187, 196, 210, 237
Hajblum, Erko, 144, 166
Halberstam, Judith (Jack), 140, 165
Halivni, Tziporah Hager, 6–13, 21–23, 60, 62, 89, 90, 92, 99, 136, 140, 160, 162, 165, 212

Hart, Kitty, 40, 66, 160, 172, 173, 206
Hartman, Geoffrey, 16, 24
hearing. *See* senses
Hebrew, 58, 70, 134, 203
hell, 81, 88, 108, 109, 112, 113, 173, 222
Herman, Chaim, 33
Hilberg, Raul, 2, 11, 120, 230, 232, 244
Hirsch, Marianne, 14, 72, 85, 86, 88, 89, 228–230, 235
historians, 5, 7, 12, 22, 23, 45, 77, 82, 103, 133, 172, 177, 183, 210, 211
historiography, 5, 11, 21, 37, 56, 76, 77, 95, 97
Hofmeyer, Hans, 119
homosexuality, 40
Höss (Hoess), Rudolf, 26, 71, 81, 101, 105, 111, 124, 126, 127
  trial of (Warsaw, 1947), 71, 101, 111
humiliation, 8, 9, 27, 42, 44, 45, 47, 52, 57, 68, 90, 143, 145, 149, 153
Hungarian Jews, 82, 89

I
iconography, 74, 149, 158, 169
icons, secular, 78, 96
imagination, 4, 69, 167, 168
incarnation, 225, 234, 236–238, 244
incineration pits, 73, 92, 148, 149, 157
ink and wash, 141, 143, 145, 147, 149, 167
intersectionality, 37, 65
intonation, 226
irony, 52, 54
Irving trial, 161

J

Jewish identity, 11
Judy F., 40, 66, 194, 213

K

Kant, Immanuel, 77, 95
Kantor, Eva, 179–182, 207, 208
Karl Höcker Album, 82
Karpf, Anne, 14, 24, 85, 98, 245
Kilian, Andreas, 20, 63, 71, 92, 93, 163, 207, 240
Koch, Ilse, 137–139, 164
Korn, Abe, 42, 67, 208
Krause, Kurt, 27
Kraus, Ota, 219
Krausz, Peter, 227
Krystal, Henry, 44, 67, 85, 98
Kuhn, Fleur, 34, 63, 68, 95, 168
Kulka, Erich, 5, 6, 21, 23, 219
Kuzmach, Linda G., 186, 187
Kłodziński, Stanisław, 79–81

L

LaCapra, Dominick, 244
Landsberg, Alison, 14, 24
Langbein, Hermann, 4, 5, 12, 21, 26, 59, 62, 104
Lang, Berel, 65, 138, 163
Langer, Lawrence, 160, 177, 191, 208, 210, 211, 216, 225, 242
Langfus, Leyb
  'The 600 Boys', 32, 33
  The Deportation, 10, 151
  'The 3000 Naked Women', 21, 32, 33, 50, 51, 56
  'Notes', 52
  'Particulars', 51, 52, 159
  sadism, reflections on, 15, 56
Lanzmann, Claude, 14, 68, 118, 127, 128, 213, 219–223, 225–238, 240, 241
Laub, Dori, 14, 18, 23, 171, 172, 175–182, 194, 202, 204, 205, 207–210, 225, 242
Lengyel, Olga, 20, 38, 39, 65, 66, 140, 159, 164, 165
lesbianism, 36, 40
Les Temps modernes, 1, 2, 19, 20
letters, 15, 16, 24, 32, 33, 62, 63, 71, 72, 125, 136, 137, 144, 147, 159
Levi, Primo, 2–5, 21, 127, 147, 167, 174
Levy, Henry, 39, 66, 159
Lewental, Zalman
  addendum to the Łódź diary, 26, 58
  history of the revolt of 7 Oct, 81
  photographs, 81
Low, Erna, 40, 66, 140, 165

M

Majdanek, 52
Maków Mazowiecki, 86
Mandelbaum, Henryk, 92, 111–115, 117, 118, 126, 127, 151, 154, 168
Mann, Franceska, 26–28, 60
Mark, Ber, 5, 6, 21, 22, 33, 34, 58
Mark, Esther, 22, 69
masculinity, 26, 27, 33–37, 49, 65, 69, 141, 142, 157, 185, 199, 200, 234, 235, 239, 247
materiality, 98, 183, 204
Mauthausen, 134
Meisel, Judith, 186, 187, 210
Melk, 134
Mesnard, Philippe, 114, 127, 162, 195, 197, 199, 215
Milner, Marion, 154, 169
modernism, 133
Moll, Otto, 113–115, 119, 124, 148, 149, 158, 184, 188, 211

Müller, Filip, 18, 20, 23, 26, 29, 30, 41, 44, 47, 48, 60–62, 68, 111, 112, 118, 120, 121, 123, 126, 128, 220–236, 238–242, 245–247
Mulvey, Laura, 198, 216
Muselmänner, 157, 158
music, 179, 227, 243

N

Nadjary, Marcel
  drawings, 130, 151, 152
  Khroniko, 1941–1945, 151, 168
Nagraba, Ludwik, 117
Nahmia, Berry, 99, 159, 160, 173, 174, 206, 209
nakedness, 42, 44, 46, 52, 75
Nencel, David, 26, 30, 61, 62, 86–88, 94, 99, 131, 161, 196, 200, 201, 216
nude (art), 149, 152, 157, 165, 169
Nuremberg trials, 17, 105, 122
Nyiszli, Miklós, 1–3, 6, 12, 13, 19, 20, 22, 136

O

objectification, 46, 47, 50, 75, 76, 92, 154, 168
objects, 7, 12, 18, 27, 30, 31, 43, 47, 77, 84, 85, 87, 89, 95, 96, 139, 144, 149, 166, 173, 174, 226
observing. *See* witnessing
Olère, David, 18, 129–158, 160–163, 166–169
Ong, Walter, 228, 243

P

Paisikovic, Dov, 20, 62, 119, 120, 131, 137, 161, 222, 241
passivity, 2, 11, 59, 69
Pawełczyńska, Anna, 39, 40, 64, 66

pen and wash. *See* ink and wash
Pendas, Devin O., 103, 122, 123
Pentlin, Susan, 34, 63, 135, 162
Perl, Gisella, 38, 66, 90, 99, 166, 174
perpetrators, 26, 52, 56, 71, 82, 93, 103–105, 107, 119–121, 125, 130, 139, 146–148, 153, 164, 165, 224, 229, 232, 247
Perrin, Alban, 71, 72, 93
photographs
  and ethics, 77
  and improvisation, 61
  and postmemory, 14, 17, 72, 86
  and retouching, 89
  by 'Alex', 17, 72, 74–76, 81, 86, 89–92
physical feminism, 30, 61
Pinchevski, Amit, 197, 216
Polish Jews, 228
Polish resistance, 7, 10, 17, 52, 81
Pollock, Griselda, 20, 43, 67, 68, 90, 97, 99, 144, 145, 150, 161, 165, 166, 168, 207
possessions. *See* objects
Postec, Ziva, 219–222, 226, 227, 232, 236, 241, 244, 246
postmemory, 14, 17, 72, 84–86, 89, 98
proof. *See* evidence
Prstojevic, Alexandre, 127

Q

Quackernack, Walter, 25, 29, 30

R

rape, 42, 144
Rassenschande, 28, 40
reader, 8, 33, 53, 80, 82, 88
  emotional responses of, 52
  gender of, 9
Red Cross, 109, 159
Reich, Steve, 227, 243

resistance
  acts of, 26, 49
  masculinity and, 26, 49
  passive, 49, 115
  revolt. See Sonderkommando
Ringelheim, Joan, 15–17, 24, 26–28, 32, 33, 36, 40, 41, 43, 59, 60, 62, 66, 67, 165
Robota, Roza, 9
Romania, 6, 10
Rose A., 172, 175–178, 181, 183, 207–210
Rosin, Arnošt, 111, 126
Rousset, David, 2, 3, 20

S
sadism, 16, 46, 47, 51, 52, 54–57, 90, 119, 120, 153
sardine, 129, 130, 159
Schillinger, Josef, 25–31, 42, 47, 49, 58–60, 62, 88
Scott, James C., 49, 69
Scrolls of Auschwitz, 10, 17, 18, 20–22, 25, 31, 33, 34, 40, 63, 67, 73, 86, 97, 99, 135, 158, 191, 199, 209, 215, 236
selections, 8, 38, 64, 105, 126, 140, 220, 231
senses. See also witnessing
  hearing, 116
  seeing, 45, 77
  smell, 173
  touch, 158
Serena N., 172, 175–179, 181–183, 194, 202–204, 207–211, 215, 216
sexual appeal, 187
sexual difference, 9, 36, 48, 140
sexuality, female, 27, 61, 68, 167
sexual relationships, 40, 204

sexual violence, 15, 17, 23, 25–27, 31, 36, 41, 42, 47, 48, 50, 53, 57, 58, 62, 64, 66, 67, 143, 148, 149, 166, 186, 239
shame. See under emotions
Shenker, N., 183, 190, 202, 209, 210, 212, 214–216
Shoah (Claude Lanzmann)
  camera, 220, 230, 238
  editing, 221, 222, 225, 239
  embodiment, 230
  model of Crematorium 1 (II), 229
  Müller, Filip, 18, 44, 219, 222, 225, 227, 230, 234, 239
  voice-over, 220, 222, 238
Shoah Foundation, 66, 68, 125, 159, 160, 168, 174, 183–187, 194, 198, 207, 209, 211, 214–216, 246
Siebert, Barbara, 174, 207
silences, 19, 103, 115, 171, 177, 184, 189, 191, 222, 237, 239
Sinnreich, Helene, 42, 67
Slovakia, 10, 41
Slovak Jews, 38, 40
Smell, 173
Smith, Stephen, 183
Sobibór, 4, 21, 231, 238, 247
Sonderkommando
  masculinity and, 31
  psychological damage/suffering, 4
  revolt of 7 Oct, 81
  self-image, 18
song
  Czech anthem, 48, 239
  Hatikva, 48
  the Internationale, 48
Sontag, Susan, 78, 80, 96
sound, 48, 116, 127, 171, 186, 188, 192, 193, 212, 213, 226, 227, 231–233, 238, 239, 244

Srebrnik, Simon, 228, 229, 235, 243, 246
SS, 1, 3, 8, 9, 12, 15, 20, 25–30, 34, 35, 40–48, 52–54, 56, 61, 62, 68, 70, 82, 88, 90, 97, 112, 116, 118, 129–133, 136, 137, 139–143, 146, 148, 149, 151, 152, 155–157, 159–161, 167, 173, 174, 177, 178, 185, 193, 195–197, 202, 224, 230, 234
Steedman, Carolyn, 183
Stirling, C.L., 110, 124, 126
Stone, Dan, 17, 21, 71, 76–80, 82–84, 92–98, 238
Strasfogel, Herman, 63, 147
Stulberg, Carol, 183–188, 193, 195, 200, 203, 209, 211, 212, 215, 216
style, 48, 60, 138, 144, 184, 232
    artistic, 138
    cognitive, 48
subjectivity, 47, 50, 188
sublime, 77–79, 95, 138, 163, 164
Suchomel, Franz, 230, 232, 244, 245
Sujo, Glenn, 135, 147, 148, 153, 162, 167, 169
Supreme National Tribunal (*Najwyższy Trybunał Narodowy*), Poland, 105, 111, 123, 126
symbolism, 204
syntax, 204, 224, 226
Szmulewski, David, 9, 71

T
Tagg, John, 92, 100
Tattoo, 59, 138–140, 156, 164, 194
Tauber, Henryk, 111, 115, 116, 126, 127, 132, 161, 216
technology, 76, 195, 197, 198, 227, 230, 232
    of Auschwitz, 199, 227, 230, 233
    of film/video, 79, 183, 191, 198, 199
    and masculinity, 200
Tedeschi, Guliana, 141, 165
teeth, 1, 31, 87, 98, 135, 150, 204
temporality. *See* time
testimony
    oral, 11, 23, 86, 94, 102, 105, 121, 125, 127, 143, 151, 160, 161, 179, 180, 186, 189, 192, 203, 204, 209–211, 225
    reception of, 11, 33, 77, 131, 137, 144, 172, 183, 187, 192, 205
    trial, 3, 14–17, 19, 21, 41, 58, 62, 81, 92, 101, 103–111, 113, 116–128, 130, 133, 151, 154, 156, 160, 221, 224, 237, 246
    video, 14, 16, 18, 19, 66, 125, 143, 144, 151, 160, 171, 172, 179, 180, 182, 183, 187, 189, 191–193, 197–199, 201–203, 207–209, 211, 213, 216, 246
    written, 1, 17, 25, 32, 51, 52, 62, 63, 72, 81, 86, 93, 102, 103, 119, 136, 144, 160, 191, 204, 209, 214, 225, 236, 237, 245
Theresienstadt, Terezín, 64, 238, 244
time
    chronology, 200
    futurity, 74
    past, 6, 7, 12, 94, 178, 192, 203, 220, 221, 236, 238
    present, 108, 182, 192, 203, 206, 221, 222, 237, 238
touch. *See* senses
Tovey, Donald, 179, 209
transcription, 51, 54, 55, 106, 183, 202, 204
translation, 2, 58, 60, 64, 70, 79, 98, 99, 103, 153, 183, 222, 236, 240, 242

transports to Auschwitz, 22, 25, 33, 35, 55, 59, 82, 134, 140, 160, 162, 166, 172, 206, 207, 225, 229–231
trauma, 9, 12, 14, 67, 68, 78, 79, 85, 86, 96, 98, 103, 122, 143–145, 148, 161, 166, 177, 216, 225, 239, 247
Treblinka, 4, 21, 123, 230–232, 237, 238, 244–246
Treblinka trial (Düsseldorf, 1964-65), 237, 246
Trezise, Thomas, 18, 172, 175, 176, 178, 179, 202–205, 207, 208
Trials, 2, 16, 17, 101, 103–106, 108, 111, 118, 122–124, 126, 128, 138, 160
truth, 95, 104, 119–121, 123, 151, 171, 172, 205, 210, 211, 221, 242
  emotional, 119, 172
  historical, 104, 120, 171
  transitional, 104, 121

U
Union Factory, 23, 58, 180, 210
United States Holocaust Memorial Museum (USHMM), 6, 17, 21, 24, 59, 60, 62, 66, 67, 89, 93, 94, 99, 121, 124, 125, 127, 160, 161, 165, 168, 177, 179, 181, 183, 186, 200, 208–214, 216, 242, 244, 246
unrepresentability, 92, 138, 163
uprising. *See* Sonderkommando

V
Venezia, Morris, 185, 193, 195, 196, 203, 204, 209, 212, 215, 216

Venezia, Shlomo, 70, 152, 168, 169, 187, 195, 198, 204, 214–217
Vice, Sue, 237, 245
voice, 5, 18, 34, 36, 44, 47, 64, 104, 141, 174, 189, 198, 221, 222, 226–229, 234, 238, 240–243, 245
voice-over, 219, 220, 222, 224, 226–228, 232, 234, 238, 241
Voss, Peter (*Oberscharführer*), 25, 28, 49, 52–54, 57, 136
Vrba, Rudolf, 21, 230–232, 238, 244, 246

W
Warsaw, 2, 21, 25, 105, 111, 118, 134, 206, 231, 244, 245
Warsaw Ghetto Uprising, 28
wash. *See* ink and wash
Waxman, Zoë, 24, 34, 35, 44, 45, 63, 64, 67, 166
Weiss, Irene, 40, 66, 172, 174, 175, 177, 178, 180, 181, 183, 206–209
Weiss, Peter, 104, 120, 128, 227
Welbel, Leon (Lajzer), 39, 66, 203, 204, 216, 217
Wellers, George, 26, 59
witnessing, 14, 16, 17, 23, 31, 49, 50, 75, 80, 84, 91, 101, 104, 112, 195, 197, 205, 208, 211, 239, 242. *See also* senses; unrepresentability
  observing (*beobakhten*), 50

Y
Yad Vashem, 51, 69, 95, 134, 161, 162, 245
Yale video testimony. *See* Fortunoff Video Archive for Holocaust Testimonies

Yiddish, 22, 32, 50, 58, 60, 64, 119, 120, 204, 237, 239, 242, 245, 246
Young, James, 86, 98, 191, 197, 203, 215, 216

Z

Zemel, Carol, 18, 78, 95, 96, 135, 142, 143, 150, 161, 162, 166, 168, 169
Żywulska, Krystyna, 4, 5, 21, 205, 207

GPSR Compliance

The European Union's (EU) General Product Safety Regulation (GPSR) is a set of rules that requires consumer products to be safe and our obligations to ensure this.

If you have any concerns about our products, you can contact us on

ProductSafety@springernature.com

In case Publisher is established outside the EU, the EU authorized representative is:

Springer Nature Customer Service Center GmbH
Europaplatz 3
69115 Heidelberg, Germany